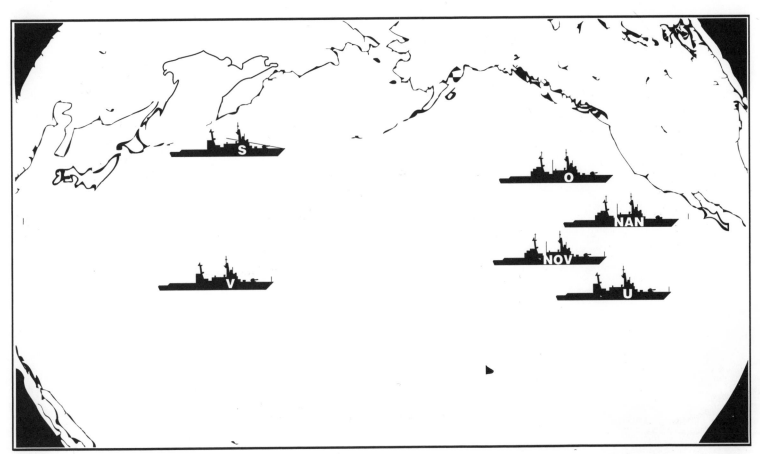

Approximate locations of Ocean Stations
in the Pacific Ocean

U.S. Coast Guard Cutters and Craft

U.S. Coast Guard Cutters and Craft
1946–1990

Robert L. Scheina

Naval Institute Press
Annapolis, Maryland

Library of Congress Cataloging-in-Publication Data

Scheina, Robert L.
   U.S. Coast Guard cutters and craft, 1946–1990 / Robert L. Scheina.
    p.   cm.
  ISBN 0-87021-719-4 :
   1. United States.   Coast Guard—Lists of vessels.   2. United
States.   Coast Guard—History—20th century.   I. Title.
 VA61.S32   1990
 359.9'783'0973—dc20   89-600393
                                               CIP

Printed in the United States of America

9   8   7   6   5   4   3   2   1

Contents

Foreword

One can trace the history of a sea service such as the United States Coast Guard through the ships it has put upon the ocean. For 200 years, Coast Guard missions and its ships have mirrored the nation's concerns in its maritime regions. The Coast Guard's organization and fleet matured during World War II as the nation's own sea power matured. In the half-century since that war, America has demonstrated continued reliance upon its maritime regions: an ocean border that must be protected; a vital repository of agricultural, mineral, and petroleum resources; and a thoroughfare for the cargoes that feed our commerce and industry.

The diversity of these concerns can be seen also in the variety of the Coast Guard ships. The chronology of these ships reflects this diversity as well as the fascinating changes in shipbuilding technology.

The accomplishments of our cutters are monumental. Tens of thousands of search-and-rescue cases, from the most routine to the most harrowing, have tested to the utmost the ships and the professionalism and dedication of their sailors. Furthermore, the Coast Guard's unique ability to contribute to national defense was borne out by the involvement of over 30 major cutters and patrol boats in Vietnam. And in the past decade, the drug-interdiction operations, primarily with medium-endurance cutters and patrol boats, have had tremendous influence on both our operational skill and our tactics.

But there are many other tasks performed by these Coast Guard units that may not immediately come to mind when one thinks of the Coast Guard. This volume recounts stories of our ships and craft setting buoys, fighting fires, suppressing mutinies, disposing of spent mines and torpedoes, building Loran stations, serving as a base for Radio Free Europe, patrolling regattas, breaking ice, and so much more.

As was his earlier book, this one will also be an invaluable resource to historians who research the varied fabric of Coast Guard history. It will also be a source of richly enjoyable stories for the sailors who remember these ships and their daring deeds.

ADMIRAL PAUL A. YOST, USCG
Commandant

Preface

This book is the second in a series devoted to Coast Guard cutters and craft. The first, *U.S. Coast Guard Cutters and Craft of World War II,* was published by the Naval Institute Press in 1982. This volume is an attempt to provide an appreciation of the size of the Coast Guard's fleet and the activities of these cutters since World War II.

The work is organized by cutter types and then classes, which are arranged in reverse chronological order. Key dates, representative characteristics, and histories are provided for each large Coast Guard cutter; a terse review is also given for standard small craft.

The Coast Guard adopted and modified the Navy's hull-numbering system in 1942. Apparently, some Navy ships acquired by the Coast Guard were retained for such a short period of time that they never were assigned a Coast Guard hull number. In these cases, as in my earlier volume, I have cited in brackets a probable designator. This was done to aid those who wish to use this book to calculate the size of the Coast Guard by types.

The histories of the cutters were compiled from numerous sources, including newspapers, welcome-aboard pamphlets, and press releases. The events presented within the histories are representative of the tasks performed by that cutter and, it is hoped, provide information concerning all of the major activities in which the cutter has been engaged. The length of the history is more a reflection on record keeping than on the accomplishments of the cutter. Space and time prohibit listing every rescue and seizure in which a cutter has been involved.

Two individuals bore the weight of producing this book. They are my wife, Linda Lee, and my daughter, Robyn Lynne. Both spent untold hours at the word processor struggling to convert my hieroglyphics into coherent language.

I wish to thank the U.S. Coast Guard for its assistance in the compilation of this book. All photography is courtesy of the U.S. Coast Guard.

Abbreviations

AA	antiair		DESLANT	Destroyers Atlantic Fleet
ABHD	Advanced Base Harbor Defense		DEW	Distant Early Warning
ac	aircraft		dis	displacement
AC&I	Acquisition, Construction, & Improvement		Div	division
AFB	Air Force Base		EA	emergency acquisition
ALASKASEAFRON	Alaska Sea Frontier		EASTSEAFRON	Eastern Sea Frontier
A/N	aids to navigation		ELB	Exposed Location Buoy
ASDEVLANT	Antisubmarine Development Detachment, Atlantic Fleet		EM	emergency manning
			f	future
ASW	antisubmarine warfare		FCMA	Fisheries Conservation Management Act
ATS	Army Transport Service		fl	full load
bn	building number (assigned to cutters)		FV	fishing vessel
BHP	brake horsepower		gal	gallons
BNSI	Bureau of Navigation and Steamboat Inspection		Gov	government
			GULFSEAFRON	Gulf Sea Frontier
bp	between perpendiculars		HAWAIIANSEAFRON	Hawaiian Sea Frontier
BSA	Boy Scouts of America		helo	helicopter
CARIBSEAFRON	Caribbean Sea Frontier		HEW	Department of Health, Education, and Welfare
cal	caliber		IIP	International Ice Patrol
CG	Coast Guard		IOC	initial operational capability
CIC	Combat Information Center		kts	knots
CINC	Commander in Chief		kVa	kilovolt-amperes
CINCLANT	Commander in Chief Atlantic Fleet		lbs	pounds
CINCPAC	Commander in Chief Pacific Fleet		LE	Law Enforcement
CNO	Chief of Naval Operations		LH	lighthouse
comm	commissioned		LNB	Large Navigational Buoy
COTCLANT	Commander Operational Training Command Atlantic Fleet		loa	length overall
			LORAN	long-range aid to navigation
COM4THFLEET	Commander Fourth Fleet		LS	lightship
COM7THFLEET	Commander Seventh Fleet		LSS	lightship station
COM12THFLEET	Commander Twelfth Fleet		MAP	Military Assistance Program
cp	controllable pitch		MARAD	Maritime Administration
CZ	Panama Canal Zone		MATS	Military Air Transportation Service
d	draft		max	maximum
DANFS	Dictionary of American Naval Fighting Ships		mb	molded beam
dc	depth charge		MC	Maritime Commission
decomm	decommissioned		mg	machine gun
Dept I	Department of the Interior		mi	nautical miles

Mk	Mark	SERVPAC	Service Force Pacific Fleet
MLB	motor life boat	SHP	shaft horsepower
MMA	Merchant Marine Academy	SNAME	Society of Naval Architects and Marine Engineers
MV	Merchant Vessel		
N/A	not available	t	tons
NAOTC	Naval Air Operational Training Center	TF	task force
NOAA	National Oceanic and Atmospheric Administration	trans	transferred
		TT	torpedo tubes
NOWESTSEAFRON	Northwest Sea Frontier	TVA	Tennessee Valley Authority
NPS	National Park Service	U	University
NSF	National Science Foundation	unoff	unofficial
oa	overall	USA	United States Army
OPS	Operations	USAAF	United States Army Air Force
OS	Ocean Station	USAF	United States Air Force
PASEAFRON	Panama Sea Frontier	USAT	United States Army Transport
PC	pleasure craft	USCGS	United States Coast & Geodetic Survey
PD	Police Department	USFWS	United States Fish and Wildlife Service
pdr	pounder	USLHS	United States Lighthouse Service
PHILSEAFRON	Philippine Sea Frontier	USN	United States Navy
pos	possibility	USNS	United States Naval Ship (Military Sealift Command)
psi	pounds per square inch		
PSS	Port Security	USPHS	United States Public Health Service
PWA	Public Works Administration	USSB	United States Shipping Board
R & D	research and development	VCNO	Vice Chief of Naval Operations
RCAF	Royal Canadian Air Force	WESTSEAFRON	Western Sea Frontier
RCS	Revenue Cutter Service	wl	waterline
ret	returned	WS	Weather Station
RN	Royal Navy	WSA	War Shipping Administration
SAR	search and rescue	WW I	World War I
SERVLANT	Service Force Atlantic Fleet	WW II	World War II

U.S. Coast Guard Cutters and Craft

High-Endurance Cutters and Their Equivalents

In 1965 the U.S. Coast Guard adopted the term high-endurance cutter to describe its gunboats (WPGs) and seaplane tenders, small (WAVPs) under a single heading. During the following year the designators of these cutters were changed from WPGs and WAVPs to WHECs. Prior to World War II, the large multipurpose cutters were known as cruising cutters. With the exception of icebreakers (WAGB), high-endurance cutters are the largest ships in the Coast Guard. Today, they are primarily used for law enforcement and search and rescue.

Between the end of World War II and 1977, an additional primary duty of these large cutters was to serve on Ocean Station. The purpose of the Ocean Station Program was to provide emergency rescue sites in mid-ocean for ships and aircraft in distress, to report on weather conditions, and to collect oceanographic data. The ebb and flow of the Ocean Station Program directly impacted on the number of large cutters maintained in commission. The program began in 1941, reached its peak during the 1960s, and ended in 1977.

378-FOOT CUTTERS (*HAMILTON* CLASS, ''HERO'' CLASS)

Name	Hull Number	Builder	Keel Laid	Launched	Commissioned	Disposition
Hamilton	WHEC 715 WPG 715	Avondale Shipyards Inc., New Orleans, LA	Jan 65	18 Dec 65	20 Feb 67	Active
Dallas	WHEC 716 WPG 716	Avondale Shipyards Inc., New Orleans, LA	7 Feb 66	1 Oct 66	26 Oct 67	Active
Mellon	WHEC 717 WPG 717	Avondale Shipyards Inc., New Orleans, LA	25 Jul 66	11 Feb 67	22 Dec 67	Active
Chase	WHEC 718 WPG 718	Avondale Shipyards Inc., New Orleans, LA	15 Oct 66	20 May 67	1 Mar 68	Active
Boutwell	WHEC 719 WPG 719	Avondale Shipyards Inc., New Orleans, LA	12 Dec 66	17 Jun 67	24 Jun 68	Active
Sherman	WHEC 720 WPG 720	Avondale Shipyards Inc., New Orleans, LA	13 Feb 67	23 Sep 67	23 Aug 68	Active
Gallatin	WHEC 721 WPG 721	Avondale Shipyards Inc., New Orleans, LA	17 Apr 67	18 Nov 67	20 Dec 68	Active
Morgenthau	WHEC 722	Avondale Shipyards Inc., New Orleans, LA	17 Jul 67	10 Feb 68	14 Feb 69	Active
Rush	WHEC 723	Avondale Shipyards Inc., New Orleans, LA	23 Oct 67	16 Nov 68	3 Jul 69	Active
Munro	WHEC 724	Avondale Shipyards Inc., New Orleans, LA	18 Feb 70	5 Dec 70	27 Sep 71	Active
Jarvis	WHEC 725	Avondale Shipyards Inc., New Orleans, LA	9 Sep 70	24 Apr 71	30 Dec 71	Active
Midgett	WHEC 726	Avondale Shipyards Inc., New Orleans, LA	5 Apr 71	4 Sep 71	30 Mar 72	Active

Cost   See Appropriations table

Hull

Displacement (tons)   3,050 fl (1967); 2,716 standard (1967)

Length   378' oa; 350' wl

Beam   42'8" max

Draft   20' max (1967)

Machinery

Main Engines   2 Fairbanks-Morse diesels or 2 Pratt & Whitney gas turbines

HP   7,000/36,000

Propellers   twin CP

Performance

Max Sustained   29.0 kts, 2,400-mi radius (1967)

Cruising   19.0 kts, 9,600-mi radius (1967)

Economic   11.0 kts, 14,000-mi radius (1967)

Logistics

Fuel Oil (95%)   800 tons

Complement   15 officers, 140 men (1967)

Electronics

Radar   2 SPS-64, 1 SPS-29D (1987); 2 SPS-64, 1 SPS-40B (1990)

Sonar   SQS-38 (1987)

Armament   1 5"/38, 2 20mm/80 (single); 6 Mk 32 ASW TT (triple)—1987

    2 Mk 141 Harpoon antiship missile systems; 1 76mm/62, 1 Mk 15 20mm CIWS gatling gun; 6 Mk 32 ASW TT (triple)—1990

Design

Thirty-six 378-foot cutters were planned; however, only 12 were constructed due to the wind-down of the ocean station program. Ships of the 378-foot class were the largest U.S. warships built with gas-turbine propulsion prior to the navy's *Spruance*-class destroyers. The class has welded steel hulls and aluminum superstructures. Living spaces are air-conditioned, and the cutters were constructed with laboratories for weather and oceanographic research. Although all units were built at the same yard, there is significant variation among them. For example, WHEC 716 through 723 have synchronizing clutches whereas the remaining three cutters have synchro-self-shifting clutches.

All units were modernized from late 1986 through 1990—WHEC 715, 716, 718, and 721 at Bath Iron Works, Bath, ME, and the remainder at Todd Shipyard, Seattle, WA. They received a new armament and a telescoping hangar, as well as extensive defensive systems and electronics modification. These included satellite communication gear, and a Mk 92 mod 1 gunfire-control system.

Boutwell

24 Jun 68–1973 stationed at Boston, MA; 28 Nov–20 Dec 68 served on OS ECHO; 14 Feb–9 Mar 69 served on OS BRAVO; 30 Apr–23 May 69 served on OS CHARLIE; 8–31 Jul 69 served on OS CHARLIE; 26 Sep–19 Oct 69 served on OS ECHO; 11 Oct 69 medevaced crewman from Liberian MV *Saint Nicholas* in mid-Atlantic; 9 Dec 69–1 Jan 70 served on OS BRAVO; 13 Feb 70 rescued two from drifting barge off Jamaica; 19 Aug–11 Sep 70 served on OS BRAVO; 7–30 Nov 70 served on OS DELTA; 26 Jan–18 Feb 71 served on OS BRAVO; 4–28 Apr 71 served on OS BRAVO; 7–30 Jun 71 served on OS ECHO; Feb 72 conducted surveillance of a disabled Soviet nuclear submarine off Newfoundland; 11 Feb–6 Mar 72 served on OS CHARLIE; 24 Jun–18 Jul 72 served on OS BRAVO; 17 Nov–13 Dec 72 served on OS CHARLIE; 1973–Mar 89 stationed at Seattle, WA, and used for LE and SAR; 4–5 Nov 80 rescued 87 survivors and coordinated the rescue of 432 others from burning cruise ship *Prinsendam* in the Gulf of Alaska; 22 Oct 80 removed 18 crewmen from offshore oil platform *Dan Prince* endangered by heavy seas about 650 mi S of Kodiak, AK; 20 Jun 82 seized the sailboat *Orca* 1,500 mi SW of Kodiak, AK, with approx 1.5t of marijuana on board; 6 Jul 82 four crew members were involved in attempting to seize the *Orca*; 25 Jul 83 rescued four from FV *Comet* 20 mi N of Dutch Harbor, AK; 25 Apr 84 helped medevac crewman from FV 120 mi NE of Dutch Harbor, AK; Jan 87

378-FOOT CUTTERS (*HAMILTON* CLASS, "HERO" CLASS)—Appropriations

Name	AC&I Year	Awarded	Scheduled Delivery	Construction Manhours	Costs
Hamilton	1964	16 Jan 64	16 Nov 66	621,312	$13,398,009
Dallas	1965	22 Mar 65	7 Nov 67	522,416	$11,541,573
Mellon	1966	20 Jul 65	6 Jan 68	444,392	$11,122,881
Chase	1966	20 Jul 65	6 Mar 68	434,768	$11,122,881
Boutwell	1966	28 Jun 66	25 Feb 69	469,504	$10,945,166
Sherman	1967	29 Aug 66	14 Jun 69	435,488	$10,921,928
Gallatin	1967	29 Aug 66	13 Aug 69	422,360	$10,926,747
Morgenthau	1967	4 May 67	28 Aug 69	368,584	$11,251,436
Rush	1968	25 Aug 67	22 Dec 69	375,912	$11,207,957
Munro	1968	30 Jun 69	29 Oct 71	520,352	$13,972,530
Jarvis	1969	30 Jun 69	28 Dec 71	468,744	$14,065,811
Midgett	1970	31 Oct 69	28 Mar 72	422,800	$14,069,680

participated in Op Brimfrost 87, an exercise to defend against sabotage; 13 Feb 87 sank burned-out hulk of FV *Fukuyoshi Maru No 85* W of Pribilof Islands by gunfire; Mar 89–1990 underwent modernization at Todd Shipyard, Seattle, WA; 1 Jul 88 seized Panamanian MV *Encounter Bay* after causing it to heave to with small-arms fire—the vessel was carrying 70 t of marijuana.

Chase

1 Mar 68–1990 stationed at Boston, MA, and used for LE and SAR; 28 Aug–20 Sep 68 served on OS ECHO; 3–24 Nov 68 served on OS DELTA; 23 Jan–14 Feb 69 served on OS BRAVO; 18 Apr–11 May 69 served on OS ECHO; 6 Dec 69–28 May 70 assigned to CG Squadron Three, Vietnam; 29 Sep–22 Oct 70 served on OS ECHO; 25 Nov–18 Dec 70 served on OS CHARLIE; 6 Feb–1 Mar 71 served on OS DELTA; 29 Aug–24 Sep 71 served on OS CHARLIE; 7–16 Jan 72 served on OS HOTEL; 22 Jan–11 Feb 72 served on OS CHARLIE; 24 Mar–19 Apr 72 served on OS DELTA; 3–29 Sep 72 served on OS CHARLIE; 24 Apr–18 May 73 served on OS CHARLIE; 2–24 Apr 74 served on OS BRAVO; Aug 80 assisted U.S. containership *American Apollo* 6 mi off SW coast of Haiti; Oct 81 intercepted a sinking 30-ft sailboat carrying 57 illegal Haitian refugees 120 mi NW of Port-au-Prince, Haiti, took them on board, and returned them to Haiti; 12 Nov 81 seized *Fao* carrying 5t of marijuana; 29 Nov 81 seized *Cary* carrying 1.5t of marijuana; 5 Dec 81 seized *Captain Romie* carrying 1 lb of marijuana; 11 Jul 82 helped turn back an 18-ft sailboat with 8 Haitians on board off SE Cuba; 7 Jan 83 seized MV *Hanover* carrying 17t of marijuana; 29 Jul 84 seized FV *Miss Kriss* in Windward Passage carrying 9t of marijuana; 22 Dec 84 seized FV *Galena* in Windward Passage carrying 1.5t of marijuana; 5 Jun 86 seized MV *Juan Robinson* 270 mi off Bermuda carrying 17t of marijuana; Sep 87 intercepted FV *Bethsioa* carrying 72 Haitians and returned them to Haiti; 24 Sep 87 seized *FL-6907-FR* carrying 5t of marijuana; 10 Oct 87 seized 40-foot FV carrying 7.5t of marijuana; 23 Oct 87 seized vessel *New Year* carrying 3t of marijuana; Jul 89–1990 underwent modernization at Bath Iron Works, Bath, ME.

Dallas

26 Oct 67–1990 stationed at New York, NY, and used for LE and SAR; 28 May–20 Jun 68 served on OS DELTA; 13 Jul–5 Aug 68 served on OS DELTA; 19 Sep 68 assisted disabled Dutch tanker *Johannes Frans* 250 mi NE of Bermuda; 20 Sep–13 Oct 68 served on OS ECHO; 13 Dec 68–5 Jan 69 served on OS CHARLIE; 24 Feb–19 Mar 69 served on OS DELTA; 3 Nov 69–19 Jun 70 assigned to CG Squadron Three, Vietnam; 22 Sep–15 Oct 70 served on OS DELTA; 12 Feb–7 Mar 71 served on OS ECHO; 28 Apr–21 May 71 served on OS BRAVO; 11 Nov–10 Dec 71 served on OS CHARLIE; 20 Apr–17 May 72 served on OS ECHO; 17 Nov–14 Dec 72 served on OS DELTA; 1–25 Jul 73 served on OS BRAVO; 28 Sep–15 Oct 73 served on OS HOTEL; 6–26 Nov 73 served on OS CHARLIE; May–Jun 80 on-scene commander of Cuban refugee exodus patrol during which 200,000 plus fled Cuba; 6 Jun 82 seized *Yvette* carrying 5.5t of marijuana; 24 Oct 82 seized *Libra* carrying 3.5t of marijuana; 7–8 Apr 83 towed disabled MV *Grace a Dieu* in Windward Passage to Tortuga I. and assisted grounded sailboat *Leo;* 25 Oct 83 seized *Saint Nicholas* carrying 13t of marijuana; 3 Nov 83 seized *Wammer Jammer* carrying 500 lbs of marijuana; 4 Nov 83 seized *Narwal* carrying 15t of marijuana; 6 Nov 83 seized *Miss Debbie* carrying 11.5t of marijuana; 13 Nov 83

seized *Nistanova* carrying 4t of marijuana; 16 Nov 83 seized *W and V* carrying 5t of marijuana; 23 Nov 83 seized *El Vira III* carrying 2.5t of marijuana; 17 Jun 84 seized MV *Stecarika* and sailboat *Esperance* 150 mi SW of Puerto Rico after finding contraband in a concealed compartment; 23 Feb 85 seized *Star Trek* carrying 15t of marijuana; 28 Jan–7 Feb 86 served as on-scene coordinator for recovery of debris from space shuttle Challenger off Cape Canaveral, FL; Nov 86–Dec 89 underwent modernization at Bath Iron Works, Bath, ME.

Gallatin

20 Dec 68–1990 stationed at New York, NY, and used for LE and SAR; 4 Jan 69 towed disabled FV *Sea Ranger* 200 mi SW of Key West, FL; 21 Feb 69 rescued 11 from Swedish MV *Farida* 210 mi E of Morehead City, NC—*Farida* later dewatered by a tug; 23 Apr–16 May 69 served on OS BRAVO; 15 Jun–8 Jul 69 served on OS CHARLIE; 17 Aug–19 Sep 69 served on OS DELTA; 4–27 Nov 69 served on OS DELTA; 19 Jan–11 Feb 70 served on OS ECHO; 10 Apr–3 May 70 served on OS CHARLIE; 11 Jun–4 Jul 70 served on OS BRAVO; 27 Oct–18 Nov 70 served on OS BRAVO; 20 Mar–12 Apr 71 served on OS CHARLIE; 1–24 Jun 71 served on OS DELTA; 30 Jul–25 Aug 71 served on OS BRAVO; 3–12 Oct 71 served on OS HOTEL; 16 Oct–11 Nov 71 served on OS CHARLIE; 21 Dec 71–16 Jan 72 served on OS DELTA; 6–30 Mar 72 served on OS CHARLIE; 31 May–24 Jun 72 served on OS BRAVO; 30 Jul–24 Aug 72 served on OS ECHO; 3–27 Jan 73 served on OS CHARLIE; 18 Mar–11 Apr 73 served on OS ECHO; 30 Jan–20 Feb 74 served on OS BRAVO; 23 Nov 77 seized *Sea Crust* 230 mi SW of Cape Fear carrying marijuana; 5 Jun 79 seized FV *Charlie M* 130 mi SW of Puerto Rico carrying 17t of

The *Chase* on 26 Aug 87. Like most high-endurance cutters, *Chase* has served in Vietnam, stood watch on ocean station, performed search and rescue, and busted drug smugglers. The 378-foot cutters were the first large cutters designed for the Coast Guard since the 255-foot cutters of the early 1940s.

marijuana; fall 77, when 12 enlisted women and two female officers reported on board, CG became the first U.S. armed service to assign women to duty on an unrestricted basis; 11 Jan 82 rescued 106 Haitians from a leaky 35-foot sailboat, 25 mi W of Haiti; 13 Jan 82 rescued 26 Haitians from a disabled 45-foot motor sailboat; 14 Jan 82 seized *Merilyn* carrying 1 lb of marijuana; 7 Feb 82 seized *Equator* carrying 4t of marijuana; 8 Mar 84 seized FV with marijuana on board 500 mi E of Georgia; 18 Mar 84 seized yacht *Push Push* in Windward Passage carrying .5t of marijuana; 1 Apr 84 seized a PC in the Windward Passage after 1,800 lbs of cocaine were discovered in a hidden compartment; 2 Apr 84 seized *Chinook* carrying 1t of marijuana; 3 Jul 84 seized a 70-foot MV 670 mi NE of Puerto Rico after marijuana was discovered in a hidden compartment; 13 Jan 85 seized FV *Maria Elena* 300 mi N of Puerto Rico with 18t of marijuana on board; 14 Jan 85 seized FV *La Urraca I* 350 mi NW of Puerto Rico with marijuana on board; 7 Feb 85 seized *Luzdary* carrying 6t of marijuana; 19 Feb 85 seized *Sabrina II* carrying 1t of marijuana; 21 Feb 85 seized *Maces Bay* carrying 25t of marijuana; 22 Feb 85 seized *Lisa and Leslie* carrying 7t of marijuana; 10 Nov 85 sank Colombian MV *El Toro* by gunfire after she was intercepted and captured carrying 28t of marijuana 173 mi off Colombia; 9 Sep 87 seized tug *Wamanbay* 400 mi E of Ft. Pierce, FL, carrying 20t of marijuana; 1 Dec 88 boarded FV 130 mi SW of Grand Cayman I. and removed suspected mutineers.

Hamilton

20 Feb 67–1980 stationed at Boston, MA, and used for LE and SAR; 14 Feb–8 Mar 68 served on OS BRAVO; 6 May 68 medevaced seaman from FV *Little Growler*; 20 Jun–13 Jul 68 served on OS DELTA; 5 Jul 68 assisted distressed British MV *Tactician*; 20 Aug–13 Sep 68 served on OS CHARLIE; 16 Dec 68–9 Jan 69 served on OS DELTA; 8–31 Mar 69 served on OS BRAVO; 1 Nov 69–25 May 70 assigned to CG Squadron Three, Vietnam; 8 Oct–3 Nov 71 served on OS BRAVO; 19 Dec 71–14 Jan 72 served on OS BRAVO; 24 Aug–18 Sep 72 served on OS ECHO; 12 Nov–8 Dec 72 served on OS BRAVO; 16 Feb–11 Mar 73 served on OS CHARLIE; 1–25 Jul 73 served on OS CHARLIE; 7–27 Sep 73 served on OS BRAVO; 6–26 Nov 73 served on OS BRAVO; 24 Apr–16 May 74 served on OS BRAVO; 1980–81 stationed at New York, NY, and used for LE and SAR; 1981–90 stationed at Boston, MA, and used for LE and SAR; 6 Oct 81 seized *Dona Victoria* carrying 18.5t of marijuana; 14 Oct 81 seized *Danny* carrying 7.5t of marijuana; 22 Jul 82 seized *Wanda* carrying 2.5t of marijuana; 18 Nov 82 seized *Ramses II* carrying 7.5t of marijuana; 26 Mar 83 fired 18 rounds of 20mm at *Anna I*, disabled her with machine-gun fire, and seized her for carrying contraband; 9 Dec 83 seized *Vanessa* carrying 1 lb of marijuana; 1 Feb 84 seized FV *Rama Cay* 300 mi N of Caicos I. carrying 12t of marijuana; 24 May 84 seized *Janeth* near Crooked I. carrying 9t of marijuana; 27 Nov 84 intercepted FV *Princess* 65 mi N of Punta de la Cruz, Colombia—FV scuttled itself to prevent boarding; Oct 85–Dec 88 underwent modernization at Bath Iron Works, Bath, ME.

Jarvis

30 Dec 71–1988 stationed at San Francisco, CA, and used for LE and SAR; 13 Aug–3 Sep 72 served on OS NOVEMBER; 15 Nov 72 grounded near Iliuliuk Bay causing flooding and loss of power; after losing power and in danger of sinking, towed to safety by FV *Koro Maru No. 3*; 8 Apr–3 May 73 served on OS NOVEMBER; 17 Jun–11 Jul 73 served on OS NOVEMBER; 6–11 Jul 73 towed disabled sailboat *Tou Cas* 650 mi NNE of Hawaii; 15 Sep 73 seized FV *Mitsu Maru No 30* for violating U.S. waters; 9 Oct 75 seized FV *Grant* for fisheries violation; 5 Nov 75 seized Japanese FV *Eikyu Maru 35* 900 mi W of Kodiak, AK, for fisheries violation; 30 Mar 76 seized FV *Eikyu Maru 81* for violating U.S. waters; 1 Aug 76 seized South Korean FV *Dong Wong 707* about 37 mi S of Sitka, AK, for fisheries violation; 12 Nov 83 seized fish transport vessel *Nikko*

The *Hamilton* on 20 Jan 67 during pre-acceptance trials. Her paint scheme was not complete when this photograph was taken. Note that her Navy-supplied ordnance—the 5″ gun and the Mk 32 TTs—are still gray, as well as her stack.

Cutter *Jarvis* launches 24 Apr 71. Only the last few class members launched with their Coast Guard slashes in place.

Maru 120 mi NW of Unimak Pass; 5 Oct 84 seized FV *Haeng Bok 511* for illegally fishing 35 mi SE of Palmyra I.; 1988–90 stationed at Honolulu, HI, and used for LE and SAR; Dec 88 seized FV *Iho Maru No 23* 800 mi NE of Hawaii carrying a large quantity of Thai stick marijuana; after an unsuccessful attempt to scuttle the vessel, the CG sank it because it presented a navigation and pollution hazard; Apr 89 seized Taiwanese FV *Tyi Yong No 1* off Alaska following a three-day chase; May 89 seized Soviet FV *Novoelnya* for poaching.

Mellon

22 Dec 67–1980 stationed at Honolulu, HI, and used for LE and SAR; 18 Jun–11 Jul 68 served on OS CHARLIE; 4–25 Aug 68 served on OS VICTOR; 6–27 Oct 68 served on OS VICTOR; 8–29 Dec 68 served on OS VICTOR; 13 Apr–4 May 69 served on OS VICTOR; 25 May–14 Jun 69 served on OS VICTOR; 27 Jul–17 Aug 69 served on OS VICTOR; 31 Mar–2 Jul 70 assigned to CG Squadron Three, Vietnam; 20 Sep–11 Oct 70 served on OS VICTOR; 22 Nov–13 Dec 70 served on OS VICTOR; 3–24 Jan 71 served on OS VICTOR; 18 Apr–9 May 71 served on OS NOVEMBER; Apr 72 assisted in seizure of Japanese FVs *Kohoyo Maru 31* and *Ryoyo Maru* for fisheries violations; 23 Jul–13 Aug 72 served on OS NOVEMBER; 15 Oct–5 Nov 72 served on OS NOVEMBER; 28 Jan–22 Feb 73 served on OS NOVEMBER; 24 May–17 Jun 73 served on OS NOVEMBER; 29 Jan–21 Feb 74 served on OS NOVEMBER; 4–27 Apr 74 served on OS NOVEMBER; 11–30 Jun 74 served on OS NOVEMBER; 11 Feb 74 medevaced crewman from Norwegian MV *Norbeth* in mid-Pacific; 9 Dec 79 seized *Ryuho Maru 38* for fisheries violation; 26 Oct 80 seized *Ryuho Maru 38* near Alaska for fisheries violation; 1981–90 stationed at Seattle, WA, and used for LE and SAR; Aug 82 assisted MV *Regina Maris* off Hawaii; 14 Feb 84 assisted in rescue of survivors from *Kyowa Maru* 170 mi SW of St. George I., AK; Oct 85–Mar 89 underwent modernization at Todd Shipyard, Seattle, WA.

Midgett

30 Mar 72–1990 stationed at San Francisco, CA, and used for LE and SAR; 22 Feb–18 Mar 73 served on OS NOVEMBER; 19 Mar 74 seized

FV *Ebisu Maru 88* for allegedly violating U.S. waters; 14 Apr 75 seized FV *Kohoku Maru 12* fishing within U.S. waters; 6 Jun 75 seized FV *Jikyu Maru 17* within 3 mi of Aleutian I.; May 79 pursued Soviet FV for possible fisheries violation—escaped into international waters; 6 Feb 80 seized FV *Kaiun Maru* 40 mi N of Gareloi I. for fisheries violation; 22 Feb 80 seized Polish FV *Kolias* 60 mi SW of St. Paul I. for fisheries violation; 8 Jun 80 seized Soviet FV *Prokofyeva* 65 mi SW of Shumagin I. for underlogging mackerel catch; 12 Jun 81 seized FV *Yamasan Maru 85* 180 mi W of St. Matthew I. for fisheries violation; 10 Oct 82 medevaced National Marine Fisheries Service agent from FV *Kyowa Maru 15;* Aug 86 escorted three U.S. crab boats back to waters from which they had been chased by Soviet patrol vessels so the U.S. craft could retrieve 150 crab pots; 17 Aug 86 after a chase of several hours, caught Japanese FV *Hoku Maru No 31* and forced FV to throw back crabs caught in U.S. waters; 4–23 Jun 88 served as on-scene coordinator during successful search for overdue hunters in the Bering Sea; 13 Jun 89 seized FV *Ta Chieh 3* W of Midway I. for fishing violation.

Morgenthau

17 Feb 69–1977 stationed at New York, NY, and used for LE and SAR; 1 Jul 69 escorted distressed MV *Old Forrester* 50 mi from Port Antonio, Jamaica, to that port; 23 Aug–15 Sep 69 served on OS CHARLIE; 19 Sep 69 dewatered and towed Canadian FV *Payzant Sisters* 200 mi SE of Cape Sable until relieved by a Canadian CG cutter; 24 Oct–16 Nov 69 served on OS BRAVO; 12 Jan–4 Feb 70 served on OS DELTA; 29 Mar–21 Apr 70 served on OS ECHO; 30 May–22 Jun 70 served on OS DELTA; 6 Dec 70–31 Jul 71 assigned to CG Squadron Three, Vietnam; 11–12 Apr 71 helped destroy an enemy trawler; 3–29 Nov 71 served on OS BRAVO; 10 Jan–5 Feb 72 served on OS ECHO; 15 Apr–9 May 72 served on OS BRAVO; 30 Oct–23 Nov 72 served on OS ECHO; 29 Mar–24 Apr 73 served on OS DELTA; 25 Jul–16 Aug 73 served on OS CHARLIE; 17 Oct–6 Nov 73 served on OS BRAVO; 16–31 Dec 73 served on OS

The *Morgenthau* making flank speed. President John F. Kennedy believed that the American public needed to be more aware of the services provided by the federal government and identified two agencies that should develop logos—the Coast Guard and the Postal Service. This led to the development of the Coast Guard slash, which was adopted in Apr 67, and the Post Office's eagle.

CHARLIE; 1977–1990 stationed at Alameda, CA, and used for LE and SAR; 1 Mar 77 towed disabled MV *Sabine*; Jan 79 seized *Tsuda Maru* 190 mi NW of St. Matthew I. for fisheries violation; 18 Feb 79 seized Taiwanese FVs *Highly 301* and *Highly 302* in Aleutian I. for fisheries violations; 1 Jul 81 seized Panamanian MV *Kyoto* carrying 24t of marijuana; 26 Feb–7 Mar 83 provided security escort for British royal yacht *Britannia;* 14–15 Mar 83 towed disabled USN oceanographic vessel *De Steiguer* for 250 mi to San Francisco, CA; Nov 84 assisted disabled MV *Ratna Kirti* 200 mi off Cape Mendocino; Nov 86 seized South Korean FV *Shin Yang Ho* after its captain had allegedly attacked a U.S. fisheries observer who was on board; Mar 88 seized FV *Eagle B* carrying 2.5t of marijuana; spring 88 represented CG at 40th anniversary of Japanese Maritime Safety Agency in Tokyo; Sep 89–1990 underwent modernization at Todd Shipyard, Seattle, WA.

Munro

27 Sep 71–1974 stationed at Boston, MA, and used for LE and SAR; 20 Jul–15 Aug 72 served on OS DELTA; 2–28 Oct 72 served on OS DELTA; 2–26 Jan 73 served on OS BRAVO; 17 Jun–11 Jul 73 served on OS BRAVO; 29 Oct–22 Nov 73 served on OS NOVEMBER; 1974–79 stationed at Seattle, WA, and used for LE and SAR; Feb 74 seized Soviet FV *Armaturshchik* near Semidi I. for fisheries violation; 5 Feb 74 seized Soviet FV 220 mi WSW of Kodiak, AK, for fisheries violation; 1979–Dec 86 stationed at San Francisco, CA, and used for LE and SAR; 21 Jun 79 seized Korean FV *Dong Won 13* 70 mi SE of Cordova, AK; 9 Sep 80 seized FV *Shoshin Maru 21* 130 mi SW of Pribilof I. for fisheries violation; Jan 83 escorted damaged tender *Planetree* to Hawaii; 17 Sep 83 rescued USN helicopter crew who were searching for remains of Korean Airlines Flight 007; 8 Sep 84 assisted in medevac from FV *Pelagos* near St. Paul I., AK; 15 Apr 86 seized *Line Island Trader* in the South Pacific carrying 4.5t of marijuana; Dec 86–Nov 89 underwent modernization at Todd Shipyard, Seattle, WA; Nov 89–1990 stationed at San Francisco, CA, and used for LE and SAR.

Rush

3 Jul 69–1990 stationed at Alameda, CA, and used for LE and SAR; 24 Jul 69 helped medevac crewman from Greek tanker *Thios Thanassis* 80 mi E of Great Abaco I.; 19 Dec 69 escorted distressed Greek MV *Dalemos* 25 mi W of Farallon I. to San Francisco, CA; 9 Jan 70 assisted distressed tanker *Connecticut* 100 mi off California; 11 Jan–1 Feb 70 served on OS NOVEMBER; 15 Mar–5 Apr 70 served on OS NOVEMBER; 19 May–7 Jun 70 served on OS NOVEMBER; 28 Oct 70–15 Jul 71 assigned to CG Squadron Three, Vietnam; 21 Nov 70 helped destroy an enemy trawler; 11–12 Apr 71 helped destroy an enemy trawler; 27 Feb–19 Mar 72 served

on OS NOVEMBER; 26 Nov–17 Dec 72 served on OS NOVEMBER; 21 Aug–15 Sep 73 served on OS NOVEMBER; 5–29 Jan 74 served on OS NOVEMBER; 8 Feb 80 seized Taiwanese FV *Golden Dragon* 120 mi SW of St. Paul I. for fisheries violation; 13 Aug 80 seized Japanese FV *Chuyo Maru No. 21* about 250 mi NW of the Pribilof I. for improper logging of catch; 13 Aug 80 seized *Chuyo Maru 21* 170 mi W of St. Matthew I. for fisheries violation; 18 Aug 80 seized Japanese FV *Chuyo Maru No. 22* about 250 mi NW of the Pribilof I. for improper logging of catch; 7 Sep 80 seized Japanese FV *Shinnichi Maru No. 38* near Kiska I. for improper logging of catch; 12 Sep 80 seized *Shoyo Maru* 10 mi NW of Seguam I. for fisheries violation; 17 Sep 80 seized Japanese FV *Shoyo Maru* 10 mi NW of Seguam I.; 11 May 83 seized Japanese FV *Yuryo Maru 31* in the Bering Sea for underlogging catch; 6 May 87 rescued 49 from Korean FV *Tae Woong #63* aground on Uliaga I.; Apr 88 rescued eight from FV *Westward Wind* in the Bering Sea, extinguished fire, and towed to safety; Jul 89–1990 underwent modernization at Todd Shipyard, Seattle, WA.

Sherman

23 Aug 68–1978 stationed at Boston, MA, and used for LE and SAR; 10 Feb 69 stood by disabled MV *Exminister* 200 mi SE of Cape Cod until commercial tugs arrived; 3–24 Mar 69 served on OS ECHO; 23 May–15 Jun 69 served on OS CHARLIE; 24 Jul–16 Aug 69 served on OS BRAVO; 31 Jan–1 Feb 70 rescued remaining crew on distressed Norwegian MV *Gezina Brovig* 270 mi NW of San Juan, PR, and stood by until she sank prior to arrival of salvage tug; 8–31 Oct 69 served on OS CHARLIE; 22 Apr–25 Dec 70 assigned to CG Squadron Three, Vietnam; 21 Nov 70 helped destroy an enemy trawler; 12 Apr–5 May 71 served on OS CHARLIE; 17 Aug–14 Sep 71 served on OS ECHO; 14 Jan–9 Feb 72 served on OS BRAVO; 17 May–10 Jun 72 served on OS ECHO; 24 Mar–15 Apr 72 served on OS BRAVO; 9 Aug–3 Sep 72 served on OS CHARLIE; 17 Oct–12 Nov 72 served on OS BRAVO; 31 Mar–24 Apr 73 served on OS CHARLIE; 7–29 Jun 73 served on OS CHARLIE; 22 Aug–8 Sep 73 served on OS HOTEL; 7–30 Jun 74 served on OS BRAVO; Jun 76 conducted Labrador Current Survey; 15 Oct 76 seized MV *Don Emilio* 500 mi SE of Miami, FL, carrying 35t of marijuana; 1978–79 stationed at Curtis Bay, MD, and used for LE and SAR; 1979–90 stationed at San Francisco, CA, and used for LE and SAR; 16 Mar 80 seized Japanese FV *Kumano Maru 15* in Bering Sea 180 mi NW of St. Paul I. suspected of violating FCM Act; 19 Sep 84 assumed custody of MV *Frieda*, which had strayed into Soviet waters and was released; 5 Oct 85 seized Taiwanese FV *Golden Dragon* off Alaska for violation of the FCM Act; May 86–Jul 89 underwent modernization at Todd Shipyard, Seattle, WA.

NAVY *EDSALL* CLASS

Name	Hull Number	Builder	Keel Laid	Launched	Commissioned	Disposition
Newell	WDE 422 DE 322	Consolidated Steel Co., Orange, TX	5 Apr 43	29 Jun 43	30 Oct 43 (USN) 20 Jul 51 (CG)	*Decomm* 20 Nov 45 (USN) 14 May 54 (CG)
Falgout	WDE 424 DE 324	Consolidated Steel Co., Orange, TX	24 May 43	24 Jul 43	15 Nov 43 (USN) 24 Aug 51 (CG)	*Decomm* 18 Apr 47 (USN) 21 May 54 (CG)
Lowe	WDE 425 DE 325	Consolidated Steel Co., Orange, TX	24 May 43	28 Jul 43	22 Nov 43 (USN) 20 Jul 51 (CG)	*Decomm* 1 May 46 (USN) 1 Jun 54 (CG)
Finch	WDE 428 DE 328	Consolidated Steel Co., Orange, TX	29 Jun 43	28 Aug 43	13 Dec 43 (USN) 24 Aug 51 (CG)	*Decomm* 4 Oct 46 (USN) 23 Apr 54 (CG)
Koiner	WDE 431 DE 331	Consolidated Steel Co., Orange, TX	26 Jul 43	5 Sep 43	27 Dec 43 (USN) 20 Jun 51 (CG)	*Decomm* 4 Oct 46 (USN) 14 May 54 (CG)
Foster	WDE 434 DE 334	Consolidated Steel Co., Orange, TX	31 Aug 43	13 Nov 43	25 Jun 44 (USN) 20 Jun 51 (CG)	*Decomm* 15 Jun 46 (USN) 25 May 54 (CG)
Ramsden	WDE 482 DE 382	Brown Shipbuilding Corp., Houston, TX	26 Mar 43	24 May 43	19 Oct 43 (USN) 28 Mar 52 (CG)	*Decomm* 13 Jun 46 (USN) 10 Apr 54 (CG)
Richey	WDE 485 DE 385	Brown Shipbuilding Corp., Houston, TX	19 Apr 43	30 Jun 43	30 Oct 43 (USN) 28 Mar 52 (CG)	*Decomm* Jun 68 (USN) 14 May 54 (CG)
Vance	WDE 487 DE 387	Brown Shipbuilding Corp., Houston, TX	30 Apr 43	16 Jul 43	1 Nov 43 (USN) 9 May 52 (CG)	*Decomm* 27 Feb 46 (USN) 3 Apr 54 (CG)
Lansing	WDE 488 DE 388	Brown Shipbuilding Corp., Houston, TX	15 May 43	2 Aug 43	10 Nov 43 (USN) 11 Jun 52 (CG)	*Decomm* 25 Apr 46 (USN) 29 Mar 54 (CG)
Durant	WDE 489 DE 389	Brown Shipbuilding Corp., Houston, TX	15 May 43	3 Aug 43	16 Nov 43 (USN) 9 May 52 (CG)	*Decomm* 27 Feb 46 (USN) 10 Apr 54 (CG)
Chambers	WDE 491 DE 391	Brown Shipbuilding Corp., Houston, TX	28 May 43	17 Aug 43	22 Nov 43 (USN) 11 Jun 52 (CG)	*Decomm* 22 Apr 46 (USN) 30 Jul 54 (CG)

Cost $1,539,000 (*Koiner*); $1,539,000 (others)

Hull

Displacement (tons)   1,680 max, 1,200 light (1953)
Length   306' oa; 300' bp
Beam   36'8" max
Draft   10'9" max (1953)

Machinery

Main Engines   4 diesels, direct reversible
BHP   6,250
Propellers   2

Performance

Max Speed   20.4 kts. (1952)
Max Sustained   19.5 kts. 7,100-mi radius (1952)
Economic   12.0 kts. 13,000-mi radius (1952)

Logistics

Fuel Oil (95%)   97,400 gal
Complement   9 officers, 2 warrants, 160 enlisted (1952)

Electronics

Detection Radar   SC-4, SU-1 (*Chambers*)
Sonar   QCT (*Chambers*)
Armament   3 3"/50 (single); 8 40mm/60 (1 quad, 2 twin); 4 20mm/80 (twin), 2 dc tracks; 8 Y-guns; 1 Hedgehog (*Durant*, 1954)

Design

The *Edsall*-class destroyer escort was an outgrowth of a WWII need for an inexpensive destroyer. There was wide variation among the ships of this class, primarily caused by a shortage of power-plant components. During WWII, the CG manned 23 of this class for the USN. (See Scheina, *WWII Cutters*, p. 300.)

The advent of the Korean War created a need for a number of new ocean stations in the Pacific. Although most equipment and supplies for the war effort were transported by sea, most troops were carried to the operational area by air. To help protect these troops, the CG established new ocean-station positions throughout the Pacific along with air detachments strategically placed. The ocean-station ships provided up-to-date weather information, a radio relay, and an emergency crash site should it be needed.

Of the 12 ships taken into the CG, 9 had been manned by the service during WWII. During reactivation, these ships had weather-balloon shelters added and were fitted to carry a self-bailing motor surfboat. The number 100 was added to each hull number in order to eliminate confusion with the WAVPs.

In order to keep each ocean-station occupied, eight to nine ships (mostly WDEs) had to be in constant rotation. One typical tour called for three weeks SAR standby at Midway I., three weeks on OS VICTOR, three weeks on SAR standby at Guam, less than one week on R and R in Japan, three weeks on OS SUGAR, and three weeks on SAR standby at Adak and them home. See *Dictionary of American Naval Fighting Ships* (DANFS), for naval service.

Chambers

11 Jun 52–30 Jul 54 stationed at New Bedford, MA; 5–25 Dec 52 served on OS ECHO; 6–27 Mar 53 served on OS DELTA; 11 Mar 53 assisted tanker *Angy*; 23 May–12 Jun 53 served on OS COCA; 7–29 Aug 53 served on OS ALFA; 12–13 Aug 53 left station due to medical emergency; 2 Sep 53 assisted FV *Eugene H* at 43°20'N, 64°40'W; 29 Sep–17 Oct 53 served on OS ECHO; 11 Oct 53 evacuated medical emergency from MV

Neva West at 36°10′N, 48°00′W and transported to *Cook Inlet* on 12 Oct; 4–25 Dec 53 served on OS DELTA; 9–30 Apr 54 served on OS DELTA.

Durant

9 May 52–10 Apr 54 stationed at Honolulu, HI; 24 Jan–14 Feb 53 served on OS QUEEN; 18–21 Apr 53 served on OS VICTOR; 2–4 Jun 53 searched for 7 men in canoe missing from Ulithi Atoll; 22 Jun–13 Jul 53 served on OS SUGAR; 15 Nov–6 Dec 53 served on OS UNCLE.

Falgout

24 Aug 51–28 Mar 52 stationed at Seattle, WA; 28 Mar 52–21 May 54 stationed at Tacoma, WA; 18 May–8 Jun 52 served on OS QUEEN; 12–13 Jul 52 monitored the International Cruiser Race Regatta, British Columbia; 9–30 Aug 52 served on OS VICTOR; 19 Sep–12 Oct 52 served on OS SUGAR; 4–24 Jan 53 served on OS QUEEN; 29 Mar–19 Apr 53 served on OS NAN; 21 Jun–12 Jul 53 served on OS NAN; 9 Aug 53 monitored the Lake Washington Gold Cup Race; 15 Sep–6 Oct 53 served on OS VICTOR; 15 Nov–6 Dec 53 served on OS SUGAR.

Finch

24 Aug 51–23 Apr 54 stationed at Alameda, CA; 23 Apr–18 May 52 served on OS UNCLE; 21 Jul–9 Aug 52 served on OS VICTOR; 30 Aug–18 Sep 52 served on OS SUGAR, departed due to medical emergency; 23 Nov–14 Dec 52 served on OS QUEEN; 15 Feb–8 Mar 53 served on OS UNCLE; 10–31 May 53 served on OS NAN; 12 Jul 53 searched for transoceanic plane 806 in vicinity of Midway I.; 4–25 Aug 53

served on OS VICTOR; 4–25 Oct 53 served on OS SUGAR; 21 Nov 53 assisted MV *Margo* at 47°47′N, 145°00′W.

Forster

20 Jun 51–25 May 54 stationed at Honolulu, HI; 6–27 Apr 52 served on OS QUEEN; 28 Jun–21 Jul 52 served on OS VICTOR; 9–30 Aug 52 served on OS SUGAR; 16–17 Aug 52 searched for and found MV *Katori Maru* drifting and burning at 39°47′N, 160°55′E—she was not salvageable and sank; 1–23 Nov 52 served on OS UNCLE; 4–25 Jan 53 served on OS UNCLE; 8–29 Mar 53 served on OS UNCLE; 31 Mar–1 Apr 53 diverted to Cape Kawaihoa, Niihau, to provide assistance; 12 May 53 assisted FV *Florence* at 20°55′N, 165°03′W; 14 May 53 assisted MV *Creighton Victory* at 21°49′N, 156°52′W; 31 May–6 Jun 53 served on OS QUEEN; 29 Aug 53 assisted MV *Chuk Maru* near Babuyan Channel; 1–3 Oct 53 assisted MV *Tongshui* aground on Pratas I.; 26 Oct 53 assisted MV *Steel Fabricator* at 13°31′N, 132°02′E.

Koiner

20 Jun 51–14 May 54 stationed at Seattle, WA; 19–20 Dec 51 assisted tanker *Bulkfuel* at 32°00′N, 76°09′W, due to casualty of main engine fuel pump—along with *Blackhaw*, escorted tanker; 16 Mar–7 Apr 52 served on OS NAN; 7–28 Jun 52 served on OS VICTOR; 11 Oct–3 Nov 52 served on OS QUEEN; 24–25 Dec 52 along with *Winona* assisted MV *Maple Cove*; 15 Feb–8 Mar 53 served on OS NAN; 12 May–2 Jun 53 served on OS VICTOR; 13 Jul–3 Aug 53 served on OS SUGAR; 27–29 Jul 53 diverted to Attu I. due to medical emergency; 14–20 Nov 53 assisted MV

Cutter *Lowe* on 3 Jan 52. During WWII she was manned by Coast Guard personnel for the U.S. Navy and during the Korean War was commissioned into the Coast Guard.

Margo, which had lost a propeller at 47°06′N, 145°57′W and was taken under tow by tug *Agnes Foss*; 28 Nov–6 Dec 53 served on OS QUEEN.

Lansing

11 Jun 52–29 Mar 54 stationed at Honolulu, HI; 29 Apr–3 May 53 assisted grounded MV *Hawaii Bear* at Maculabo I.; 30–31 Jul 53 unsuccessfully searched for PBM 5U84; 24 Oct–20 Nov 53 served on OS QUEEN.

Lowe

20 Jul 51–1 Jun 54 stationed at Long Beach, CA; 24–25 Aug 51 assisted MV *Castello Guadalest* at 39°30′N, 58°32′W; 7–27 Apr 52 served on OS NAN; 8–29 Jun 52 served on OS UNCLE; 30 Aug–21 Sep 52 served on OS VICTOR; 12 Oct–1 Nov 52 served on OS SUGAR; 14 Dec 52–4 Jan 53 served on OS NAN; 8–29 Mar 53 served on OS NAN; 23 May 53 medevac transferred from MV *Adelphi Victory* at 27°59′N, 169°05′W and taken to Midway I.; 2–24 Jun 53 served on OS VICTOR; 3–10 Aug 53 served on OS SUGAR—departed for Attu due to medical emergency; 13–24 Aug 53 served on OS SUGAR—departed for Adak due to medical emergency.

Newell

20 Jul 50–14 May 54 stationed at Honolulu, HI; 6–14 Mar 52 unsuccessfully searched for 5 men adrift in a whaleboat off Washington I.; 27 Apr–

18 May 52 served on OS QUEEN—off station for three days due to a medical emergency; 20 Jul–10 Aug 52 served on OS UNCLE; 1–22 Nov 52 served on OS VICTOR; 12 Dec 52–3 Jan 53 served on OS SUGAR; 4–26 Apr 53 served on OS VICTOR; 12 Jul–2 Aug 53 served on OS UNCLE; 7 Aug 53 gave medical assistance to yacht *Jada* at 27°25′N, 157°51′W; 6–8 Oct 53 medevaced patient from MV *Giacomo Piaggio* to Midway I.; 28 Oct–18 Nov 53 served on OS VICTOR.

Richey

1952–54 stationed at Honolulu, HI; 13 Dec 52–4 Jan 53 served on OS UNCLE; 14 Feb–7 Mar 53 served on OS QUEEN; 7–28 May 53 served on OS UNCLE; 25 Aug–15 Sep 53 served on OS VICTOR; 25 Oct–15 Nov 53 served on OS SUGAR and departed for Adak, AK, due to medical emergency.

Ramsden

1952–54 stationed at Honolulu, HI; 23 Nov–13 Dec 52 served on OS UNCLE; 18 Feb–10 Mar 53 served on OS VICTOR; 20 Apr–11 May 53 served on OS SUGAR; 13 Sep–4 Oct 53 served on OS UNCLE; 19–20 Sep 53 stood by USNS *Private Frank J. Petrarca* until relieved by tug.

Vance

9 May 52–3 Apr 53 stationed at Honolulu, HI; 2–23 Aug 53 served on OS QUEEN; 4–24 Oct 53 served on OS QUEEN.

The *Richey* was one of twelve destroyer escorts operated by the Coast Guard during the Korean War. The ships were used primarily for ocean-station duty in the Pacific in order to safeguard troops and supplies being sent by air and sea to Korea. The flags flying from her yard are the cutter's call sign— NHUS.

NAVY *CASCO* CLASS (311-Foot Class)

Name	Hull Number	Builder	Keel Laid	Launched	Commissioned	Disposition
Casco	WHEC 370 WAVP 370 AVP 12	Puget Sound Naval Shipyard, Puget Sound, WA	30 May 40	15 Nov 41	27 Dec 41 (USN) 19 Apr 49 (loaned CG)	*Decomm* 21 Mar 69 *Trans* to USN 21 Mar 69
McCullough (ex-*Wachapreague*)	WHEC 371 WAVP 371 AVP 56 AGP 8	Lake Washington Shipyards, Houghton, WA	1 Feb 43	10 Jul 43	17 May 44 (USN) 25 Nov 46 (CG)	*Decomm & trans* to S. Vietnam 21 Jun 72
Humboldt	WHEC 372 WAVP 372 AVP 21	Boston Naval Shipyard, Boston, MA	6 Sep 40	17 Mar 41	7 Oct 41 (USN) 29 Mar 49 (CG)	*Decomm* 30 Sep 69
Mackinac	WHEC 373 WAVP 373 AVP 13	Puget Sound Naval Shipyard, Puget Sound, WA	29 May 40	15 Nov 41	24 Jan 42 (USN) Apr 49 (CG)	*Decomm* 28 Dec 67 *Trans* to USN 21 Jul 68
Absecon	WHEC 374 WAVP 374 AVP 23	Lake Washington Shipyards, Houghton, WA	23 Jul 41	8 Mar 42	28 Jan 43 (USN) May 49 (CG)	*Decomm & trans* to S. Vietnam 15 Jul 72
Chincoteague	WHEC 375 WAVP 375 AVP 24	Lake Washington Shipyards, Houghton, WA	23 Jul 41	15 Apr 42	15 Apr 43 (USN) 7 Mar 49 (CG)	*Decomm & trans* to S. Vietnam 21 Jun 72
Coos Bay	WHEC 376 WAVP 376 AVP 25	Lake Washington Shipyards, Houghton, WA	15 Aug 41	15 May 42	15 May 43 (USN) 4 May 49 (CG)	*Decomm* 1 Sep 66 *Trans* to USN 2 Dec 67
Rockaway	WHEC 377 WAVP 377 AVP 29	Associated Shipbuilders, Inc., Seattle WA	30 Jun 41	14 Feb 42	6 Jan 43 (USN) 24 Dec 48 (CG)	*Decomm* 29 Jan 72 *Trans* to USN Feb 72
Half Moon	WHEC 378 WAVP 378 AVP 26 AGP 26	Lake Washington Shipyards, Houghton, WA	10 Mar 42	12 Jul 42	15 Jun 43 (USN) 30 Jul 48 (CG)	*Decomm* 15 Jul 69

Cost — N/A

Hull
Displacement (tons) — 2,529 fl (1964); 1,791 light (1964)
Length — 311'7" oa; 299'11" bp
Beam — 41' max
Draft — 13'1" max (1964)

Machinery
Main Engines — 4 electric motors driven by Fairbanks-Morse, direct reversing diesels
BHP — 6,000
Propellers — twin

Performance
Max Sustained — 17.3 kts, 10,138-mi radius (1966)
Economic — 10.0 kts, 20,000-mi radius (1966)

Logistics
Fuel Oil (95%) — 166,430
Complement — 10 officers, 3 warrants, 138 men (1964)

Electronics
Radar — SPS-23, SPS-29A (*Casco*, 1964)
Sonar — SQS-1 (*Casco*, 1964)
Armament — 1 5"/38; 1 mousetrap (1964)

Design

The *Casco*-class ships were built as small seaplane tenders by the USN. They were designed to operate out of small harbors and atolls and had shallow draft. The fact that the class was very seaworthy with good habitability and that its diesel-electric plant gave it good range made this class well suited to ocean-station duty.

A number of changes were made in these ships to better suit them to ocean-station duty. A balloon shelter was added aft; there were spaces devoted to oceanographic equipment and a hydrographic winch was added. See DANFS for naval service.

Absecon

1949–72 stationed at Norfolk, VA; Feb–Mar 50 served on OS HOW; Nov–Dec 51 served on OS BAKER; Sep–Oct 52 served on OS BRAVO; Dec 52–Jan 53 served on OS COCA; Sep 53 served on OS ECHO; Oct 53 served on OS DELTA; Jun–Jul 54 served on OS BRAVO; Sep 54 served on OS DELTA; Feb 55 served on OS DELTA; Mar 55 served on OS ECHO; 5 Mar 55 rendered medical assistance to a cadet on Swedish training ship *Falken* while en route to Bermuda; Oct–Nov 55 served on OS COCA; Jan–Feb 56 served on OS DELTA; Apr 56 served on OS ECHO; Feb–Mar 57 served on OS BRAVO; Sep 57 served on OS DELTA; 21 Sep

Name	Hull Number	Builder	Keel Laid	Launched	Commissioned	Disposition
Unimak	WHEC 379 WTR 379 WHEC 379 WAVP 379 AVP 31	Associated Shipbuilders, Inc., Seattle WA	15 Feb 42	27 May 42	31 Dec 43 (USN) 3 Jan 49 (CG)	*Decomm* 29 Apr 88
Yakutat	WHEC 380 WAVP 380 AVP 32	Associated Shipbuilders, Inc., Seattle WA	1 Apr 42	2 Jul 42	31 May 44 (USN) 23 Nov 48 (CG)	*Decomm & trans* to S. Vietnam 1 Jan 71
Barataria	WHEC 381 WAVP 381 AVP 33	Lake Washington Shipyards, Houghton, WA	19 Apr 43	2 Oct 43	13 Aug 44 (USN) 1 Aug 49 (CG)	*Decomm* 29 Aug 69
Bering Strait	WHEC 382 WAVP 382 AVP 34	Lake Washington Shipyards, Houghton, WA	7 Jun 43	15 Jan 44	19 Jul 44 (USN) 14 Dec 48 (CG)	*Decomm & trans* to S. Vietnam 1 Jan 71
Castle Rock	WHEC 383 WAVP 383 AVP 35	Lake Washington Shipyards, Houghton, WA	12 Jul 43	11 Mar 44	8 Oct 44 (USN) 18 Dec 48 (CG)	*Decomm & trans* to S. Vietnam 21 Dec 71
Cook Inlet	WHEC 384 WAVP 384 AVP 36	Lake Washington Shipyards, Houghton, WA	23 Aug 43	13 May 44	5 Nov 44 (USN) 15 Jan 49 (CG)	*Decomm & trans* to S. Vietnam 21 Dec 71
Dexter (ex-*Biscayne*)	WHEC 385 WAVP 385 APV 11 AGC 18	Puget Sound Naval Shipyard, Puget Sound, WA	27 Oct 39	23 May 41	3 Jul 41 (USN) 20 Sep 46 (CG)	*Decomm* 18 Jan 68 *Trans* to USN 9 Jul 68
Matagorda	WHEC 386 WAVP 386 AVP 22	Boston Naval Shipyard, Boston, MA	6 Sep 40	18 Mar 41	16 Dec 41 (USN) 8 Jun 49 (CG)	*Decomm* 1 Jan 58 *Trans* to USN 30 Oct 68
Gresham (ex-*Willoughby*)	WHEC 387 WAVP 387 AVP 57 AGP 9	Lake Washington Shipyards, Houghton, WA	15 Mar 43	21 Aug 43	18 Jan 44 (USN) 26 Jun 46 (CG)	*Decomm* 1 May 73 *Sold* 25 Oct 73

57 coordinated nine-day search in which 60 MVs of 13 nations participated seeking 87-man crew of German sail-training barque *Pamir* ENE of Bermuda—6 survivors recovered, 1 by *Absecon* and 5 by U.S. MV *Saxon*; Feb 58 served on OS CHARLIE; Jun 58 served on OS CHARLIE; Jun 59 served on OS CHARLIE; 1960 participated in cadet practice cruise to Canada, Europe, and Bermuda; May–Jun 61 served on OS BRAVO; 1962 participated in cadet practice cruise to Canada, Europe, and Bermuda; 7 Mar 62 damaged by heavy seas while proceeding to sea from Norfolk, VA, to assist MVs during a storm; 25 Aug–15 Sep 63 served on OS ECHO; 13 Sep 63 rescued the 3rd engineer of German MV *Freiberg* midway between Bermuda and the Azores after he had fallen overboard and remained in the water for 17 hours; Jul 65 served on OS DELTA; 20–23 Jul 65 stood by disabled MV *Seven Seas* in mid-Atlantic and escorted her to St. John's, Newfoundland; Feb 66 stood by disabled British MV *Parthia* while awaiting commercial tug; 16 Jul–7 Aug 67 served on OS ECHO; 11 Jan–3 Feb 68 served on OS DELTA; 26 Aug–18 Sep 68 served on OS DELTA; 29 Oct–21 Nov 68 served on OS CHARLIE; 16 May–6 Jun 69 served on OS BRAVO; 31 Jul–23 Aug 69 served on OS CHARLIE; 19 Oct–11 Nov 69 served on OS ECHO; 13 Nov 69 medevaced crewman from MV *Morgenstern* in mid-Atlantic; 1–24 Jan 70 served on OS BRAVO; 18 Mar–10 Apr 70 served on OS CHARLIE; 19 May–11 Jun 70 served on OS BRAVO; 22 Jul–14 Aug 70 served on OS ECHO; 10 Oct–2 Nov 70 served on OS CHARLIE; 13 Mar–5 Apr 71 served on OS BRAVO; 24 Sep–16 Oct 71 served on OS CHARLIE.

Barataria

1 Aug 49–Jan 68 stationed at Portland, ME, and used for LE, OS, and SAR; May–Jun 49 served on OS DOG; Oct–Nov 49 served on OS ABLE; Jan 50 served on OS HOW; Mar–Apr 50 served on OS EASY; Feb–Mar 51 served on OS EASY; May–Jun 51 served on OS CHARLIE; Jul–Aug 51 served on OS BAKER; Oct 51 served on OS HOW; Apr 54 served on OS DELTA; Dec 54–Jan 55 served on OS ECHO; Oct 55 served on OS BRAVO; Nov 56 served on OS DELTA; Mar–Apr 57 served on OS BRAVO; Jul–Aug 58 served on OS CHARLIE; Jun 59 served on OS ECHO; Oct–Nov 59 served on OS BRAVO; Dec 59–Jan 60 served on OS CHARLIE; Jul–Aug 60 served on OS ECHO; Sep 62 patrolled America's Cup Race, Newport, RI; Apr 65 served on OS DELTA; 10 Oct–2 Nov 65 served on OS BRAVO; 4 May–25 Dec 67

assigned to CG Squadron Three, Vietnam; 2-23 Mar 69 served on OS
NOVEMBER; 21-27 Mar 69 rescued crew and stood by Peruvian MV
Yavari 960 mi SW of San Francisco, CA—MV sank before a salvage tug
could arrive; Jan 68-Aug 69 stationed at San Francisco, CA, and used for
LE and SAR; 24 Mar 68 sustained engine-room explosion off Unimak I.;
4-25 Aug 68 served on OS NOVEMBER; 15 Sep-6 Oct 68 served on OS
NOVEMBER; 8-29 Dec 68 served on OS NOVEMBER; 4-25 May 69
served on OS NOVEMBER; 6-27 Jul 69 served on OS NOVEMBER.

Bering Strait

14 Dec 48-1954 stationed at Seattle, WA, and used for LE, OS, and SAR;
Oct-Nov 49 served on OS ABLE; Nov-Dec 50 served on OS SUGAR;
Jan 51 served on OS SUGAR; May 51 served on OS NAN; Jul-Aug 51
served on OS NAN; Oct 51 served on OS UNCLE; Dec 51 served on OS
SUGAR; Apr 52 served on OS UNCLE; Jan-Feb 52 served on OS
VICTOR; Jan 53 served on OS SUGAR; 31 May 53 served on OS
QUEEN; Aug 53 served on OS NAN; Nov 53 served on OS NAN; Dec
53-Feb 54 served on OS VICTOR; 1954-1 Jan 71 stationed at San
Francisco, CA, and used for LE, OS, and SAR; Feb 54 served on OS
VICTOR; 13 Feb 60 provided emergency repairs to Japanese training
ship *Toyama Maru* off Palmyra I. after 1 ton of cement patch material had
been air-dropped; 4 May 67-18 Feb 68 assigned to CG Squadron Three,
Vietnam; 14 Jul-4 Aug 68 served on OS VICTOR; 15 Sep-6 Oct 68
served on OS VICTOR; 17 Nov-8 Dec 68 served on OS VICTOR; 9
Feb-2 Mar 69 served on OS VICTOR; 23 Mar-13 Apr 69 served on OS
VICTOR; 6-27 Jul 69 served on OS VICTOR; 7-28 Sep 69 served on
OS VICTOR; 9-30 Nov 69 served on OS VICTOR; 18 Dec 69-11 Jan
70 served on OS VICTOR; 26 Apr-17 May 70 served on OS VICTOR;
17 May-31 Dec 70 assigned to CG Squadron Three, Vietnam; Jan 56
medevaced injured seaman from MV *Madaket*; Dec 64-Jan 65 served on
OS VICTOR and conducted oceanographic experiments; 13 Jan 65
relieved disabled cutter *Matagorda* and stood by disabled Liberian MV
Saint Helena 1,000 mi NW of Midway I. until a commercial tug arrived; 19
Jun-10 Jul 66 served on OS VICTOR and conducted oceanographic
experiments; Feb 70 served on OS VICTOR; 24 Feb-1 Mar 70 fought
fire on Panamanian MV *Grand Ocean* in mid-Pacific.

Casco

19 Apr 49-21 Mar 69 stationed at Boston, MA, and used for LE, OS, and
SAR; 22 Aug 49 rescued the crew of FV *Magellan* and saved the sinking
vessel; 23 Jan 50 towed disabled FV *Wamsutta* from 86 mi N of Nantucket
to Boston, MA; May 50 served on OS DOG; Aug 50 served on OS
EASY; 26 Aug 50 medevaced crewman from Greek MV *Igor* 360 mi NE
of Bermuda; May-Jun 53 served on OS DELTA; Dec 53 served on OS
DELTA; Dec 52 served on OS HOTEL; Dec 53-Jan 54 served on OS
DELTA; Apr-May 54 served on OS DELTA; 24 Nov 54 towed disabled
FV *Sea Ranger*; May 55 served on OS COCA; Aug-Sep 55 served on OS
ECHO; 17 Feb 56 rescued 21 from disabled USN seaplane that ditched
100 mi S of Bermuda; towed seaplane to St. George's Harbor, Bermuda;
Oct-Nov 57 served on OS BRAVO; Jan 58 served on OS CHARLIE;
May 58 served on OS DELTA; Sep 58 patrolled the America's Cup Race;
Oct-Nov 58 served on OS DELTA; 20 Oct 58 medevaced crewman from
MV *Mayo Lykes*; Jan 59 served on OS CHARLIE; Mar 59 served on OS
CHARLIE; Dec 59-Jan 60 served on OS BRAVO; Jul 61 served on OS
ECHO; 29 Jan-16 Feb 63 served on OS ECHO; 28 Mar-19 Apr 63

Cutter *Castle Rock* on 1 May 68. She and most of her sisters saw action in
Vietnam.

served on OS DELTA; 1-19 Aug 63 conducted oceanographic experiments between South America and Africa in cooperation with eastern
universities and international agencies; Jan 64 served on OS BRAVO; 8-
29 Jan 65 served on OS BRAVO; 30 Dec 67-22 Jan 68 served on OS
BRAVO; 26 Feb-20 Mar 68 served on OS DELTA; 27 Mar 68 helped
fight fire on Long Wharf, Boston, MA; 18 Aug-8 Sep 68 served on OS
BRAVO; 11 Oct-13 Nov 68 served on OS DELTA; 28 Jan-20 Feb 69
served on OS CHARLIE.

Castle Rock

18 Dec 48-1967 stationed at Boston, MA, and used for LE, OS, and
SAR; Feb 49 served on OS EASY; Sep-Oct 49 served on OS CHARLIE;
Dec 49 served on OS CHARLIE; May-Jun 50 served on OS HOW; Oct-
Nov 50 served on OS BAKER; 27 Mar-17 Apr 53 served on OS DELTA;
Jun 53 served on OS COCA; Feb-Mar 54 served on OS BRAVO; Feb 55
served on OS BRAVO; May 55 served on OS COCA; Mar 56 towed
disabled Finnish MV *Sunnavik* from 300 mi S of Halifax, Nova Scotia, to
safety; Sep-Oct 58 served on OS DELTA; Feb 59 served on OS BRAVO;
Nov 60 served on OS BRAVO; Mar-Apr 64 served on OS BRAVO; 19
Feb-12 Mar 65 served on OS BRAVO; Aug 65 took part in cadet cruise;
Feb 66 served on OS ECHO; 1967-71 stationed at Portland, ME, and
used for LE, OS, and SAR; 22-23 Feb 67 rescued eight from sinking FV
Maureen and Michael 90 mi SW of Cape Race; Feb-Mar 67 served on OS
DELTA; 27 Nov-19 Dec 67 served on OS ECHO; 31 Mar-23 Apr 68
served on OS BRAVO; 13 Jul-5 Aug 68 served on OS ECHO; 16 Nov-9
Dec 68 served on OS BRAVO; 20 Feb-13 Mar 69 served on OS CHAR-
LIE; 4-27 May 69 served on OS DELTA; 4-27 Dec 69 served on OS
ECHO; 27 Feb-22 Mar 70 served on OS DELTA; 3-26 May 70 served
on OS CHARLIE; 18 Nov-11 Dec 70 served on OS BRAVO; 9 Jul-21
Dec 71 assigned to CG Squadron Three, Vietnam.

Chincoteague

7 Mar 49–21 Jun 72 stationed at Norfolk, VA, and used for LE, OS, and SAR; Oct–Nov 49 served on OS CHARLIE; Feb–Mar 51 served on OS CHARLIE; May 53 served on OS ECHO; Aug 53 served on OS ALFA; Jan–Feb 54 served on OS DELTA; May–Jun 54 served on OS ALFA; Jun–Jul 55 served on OS DELTA; Dec 55 served on OS COCA; Dec 55 pulled MV *Canadian Observer* from danger of going aground off S coast of Newfoundland; Feb–Mar 56 served on OS BRAVO; May–Jun 56 served on OS CHARLIE; Oct 56 served on OS DELTA; 30 Oct 56 rescued 33 crewmen from German MV *Helga Bolten* in North Atlantic by using two inflatable lifeboats during heavy seas and stood by distressed vessels for seven days until towed to Azores by commercial tug; Feb 57 served on OS BRAVO; May–Jun 57 served on OS BRAVO; Jun 58 served on OS CHARLIE; Aug–Sep 58 served on OS BRAVO; Nov 58 served on OS ECHO; Apr–May 59 served on OS ECHO; Jun–Jul 60 served on OS DELTA; Jul–Aug 61 served on OS DELTA; 1–24 Jul 68 served on OS BRAVO; 13 Sep–6 Oct 68 served on OS CHARLIE; 9 Dec 68–1 Jan 69 served on OS BRAVO; 5 Oct 69 towed disabled MV *Kenyon Victory* 30 mi S of San Salvador I. until relieved by a commercial tug; 16 Nov–9 Dec 69 served on OS BRAVO; 31 Jan–23 Feb 70 served on OS CHARLIE; 14 Apr–7 May 70 served on OS DELTA; 18 Jun–11 Jul 70 served on OS CHARLIE; 18 Sep–10 Oct 70 served on OS CHARLIE; 7–30 Dec 70 served on OS ECHO; 22 Apr–15 May 71 served on OS ECHO; 10 Oct–5 Nov 71 served on OS ECHO; 9–18 Nov 71 served on OS HOTEL; 5–29 Feb 72 served on OS HOTEL.

Cook Inlet

15 Jan 49–21 Dec 71 stationed at Portland, ME, and used for LE, OS, and SAR; May–Jun 49 served on OS FOX; Jan 50 served on OS BAKER; Apr–May 50 served on OS BAKER; Jan–Feb 51 served on OS CHARLIE; Feb–Mar 52 served on OS CHARLIE; Oct 52 served on OS COCA; Mar–Apr 53 served on OS HOTEL; 12 Oct 53 received medical patient from *Chambers*; Dec 54 served on OS DELTA; Jul–Aug 56 served on OS DELTA; Oct–Nov 56 served on OS CHARLIE; Mar 57 served on OS ECHO; Jul–Aug 57 served on OS CHARLIE; Oct 57 served on OS ECHO; Aug–Sep 57 served on OS CHARLIE; Jun–Jul 58 served on OS CHARLIE; Jan 59 served on OS BRAVO; Apr–May 59 served on OS DELTA; Apr–May 61 served on OS ECHO; May 65 served on OS ECHO; 27 Jun–14 Jul 65 served on OS BRAVO; Aug 65 took part in cadet cruise; 28 Jan 66 rescued survivors in a swamped PC; 3–8 Feb 66 escorted distressed Liberian MV *Arion* to Bermuda; Dec 67–Jan 68 served on OS ECHO; 8 Jan 68 medevaced crewman from Swedish MV *California*; 18 Apr–5 May 68 served on OS DELTA; 8 Jun–1 Jul 68 served on OS BRAVO; 5–26 Aug 68 served on OS DELTA; 6–29 Oct 68 served on OS CHARLIE; 12 Jan–6 Feb 69 served on OS ECHO; 31 Mar–23 Apr 69 served on OS BRAVO; 19 Jul–11 Aug 69 served on OS ECHO; 19 Sep–12 Oct 69 served on OS DELTA; 4–27 Feb 70 served on OS DELTA; 4–27 Oct 70 served on OS BRAVO; 18 Dec–10 Jan 71 served on OS CHARLIE; 2 Jul–21 Dec 71 assigned to CG Squadron Three, Vietnam.

Coos Bay

4 May 49–1 Sep 66 stationed at Portland, ME, and used for LE, OS, and SAR; Aug 49 served on OS FOX; Dec 49–Jan 50 served on OS EASY; Jul–Aug 50 served on OS BAKER; Feb–Mar 53 served on OS ECHO;

Feb 53 served on OS ECHO; 27 Feb 53 rescued 10-man crew of downed USN patrol aircraft midway between Bermuda and Azores; 11 Mar 53 assisted tanker *Angy*; Aug 53 served on OS HOTEL; Nov 54 served on OS DELTA; Jan 55 served on OS ECHO; 26 Jan 55 rescued six crew of downed USAF transport ac about 1,000 mi E of Bermuda; Mar–Apr 59 served on OS DELTA; Apr–May 58 served on OS ECHO—departed due to medical emergency; Jun–Jul 58 served on OS BRAVO; Mar 59 served on OS DELTA; Aug–Sep 61 served on OS ECHO; 19 Feb 64 rescued survivors from British MV *Ambassador* in N Atlantic; Dec 65 served on OS CHARLIE.

Dexter

20 Sep 46–Dec 52 stationed at Boston, MA, and used for LE, OS, and SAR; Apr 51 served on OS EASY; Feb 52 served on OS HOW; Dec 52 decommissioned and stored at CG Yard, Curtis Bay, MD; 30 Jun 58–18 Jan 68 recommissioned and stationed at Alameda, CA, and used primarily for training reservists; Sep 58 patrolled America's Cup Race, Newport, RI; 18 Jul 59 towed disabled FV *Cloud Nine* and relieved by cutter *Blackhaw*; 5 Feb 65 unsuccessfully searched for F4B ac near San Clemente I.; early Feb 66 towed disabled sloop *Allegro* from 360 mi SSW of San Diego, CA, to Asuncion Bay.

Gresham

26 Jun 46–15 Nov 69 stationed at Alameda, CA, and used for LE, OS, and SAR; Jul–Aug 49 served on OS FOX; Jun–Jul 50 served on OS OBOE; Mar 51 served on OS UNCLE; May–Jul 51 served on OS SUGAR; 25 Oct–19 Nov 51 served on OS NAN; 20 Nov–2 Dec 51 served on OS NAN; Jan–Feb 52 served on OS NAN; Mar–Apr 52 served on OS SUGAR; May 52 served on OS VICTOR; Oct–Nov 52 served on OS UNCLE; Jan–Feb 53 served on OS VICTOR; Mar 53 served on OS SUGAR; Jul–Aug 53 served on OS QUEEN; Oct 53 served on OS NAN; Oct 54 served on OS NAN; Feb–Mar 55 served on OS NAN; Aug 55 served on OS NAN; Dec 55 served on OS NAN; May 56 served on OS NOVEMBER; Feb–Mar 57 served on OS NOVEMBER; Jul–Aug 57 served on OS NOVEMBER; Nov–Dec 57 served on OS NOVEMBER; Apr–May 58 served on OS NOVEMBER; Sep 58 served on OS NOVEMBER; Feb 59 served on OS NOVEMBER; Nov–Dec 59 served on OS NOVEMBER; Apr 60 served on OS NOVEMBER; Sep–Oct 60 served on OS NOVEMBER; Feb 61 served on OS NOVEMBER; Jul 61 served on OS NOVEMBER; 4 May 67–28 Jan 68 assigned to CG Squadron Three, Vietnam; 2–23 Jun 68 served on OS NOVEMBER; 29 Dec 68–19 Jan 69 served on OS NOVEMBER; 7–28 Sep 69 served on OS NOVEMBER; 15 Nov 69 assisted disabled MV *Hawaiian Legislator* in mid-Pacific; 15 Nov 69–Feb 70 placed in storage; 16 Jan–20 Feb 71 served on OS HOTEL; 1–31 Mar 71 served on OS HOTEL; 1–31 Aug 71 served on OS HOTEL; 9 Sep–3 Oct 71 served on OS HOTEL; 12 Oct–9 Nov 71 served on OS HOTEL; 18 Nov–17 Dec 71 served on OS HOTEL; 29 Dec 71–27 Jan 72 served on OS HOTEL; 16 Jan–17 Feb 72 served on OS HOTEL; 26 Feb–31 Mar 72 served on OS HOTEL; 1 Aug–4 Sep 72 served on OS HOTEL; 13 Sep–13 Oct 72 served on OS HOTEL; 22 Oct–21 Nov 72 served on OS HOTEL; 7 Dec 72–11 Jan 73 served on OS HOTEL; 20 Jan–20 Feb 73 served on OS HOTEL; 1 Mar–1 Apr 73 served on OS HOTEL.

Half Moon

30 Jul 48–15 Jul 69 stationed at Staten I. and Governors I., NY, and used for LE, OS, and SAR; Mar 49 served on OS FOX; 24–25 Aug 51 assisted MV *Castello Guadalest* at 39°30′N, 58°32′W; 26 Dec 52–16 Jan 53 served on OS ECHO; Feb–Mar 54 served on OS ECHO; Jul 54 served on OS DELTA; Sep–Oct 54 served on OS ECHO; Dec 54–Jan 55 served on OS COCA; Aug–Sep 56 served on OS BRAVO; Sep 57 served on OS BRAVO; Dec 57–Jan 58 served on OS NOVEMBER; Jan–Feb 58 served on OS BRAVO; Jul–Aug 59 served on OS DELTA; Sep–Oct 59 served on OS ECHO; Jan–Feb 60 served on OS CHARLIE; Mar–Apr 60 served on OS DELTA; May–Jun 60 served on OS DELTA; Aug 60 served on OS BRAVO; Apr 65 served on OS DELTA; 11 Jan 67 seized four U.S. FVs 7 mi NW of Dog Rocks following a shooting in which one was killed and another wounded; 23 Apr–16 May 68 served on OS BRAVO; 4 May–29 Dec 67 assigned to CG Squadron, Vietnam; 20 Jun–13 Jul 68 served on OS ECHO; 11 Jul 68 helped medevac injured crewman from German MV *Brunsdeich*; 24 Oct–16 Nov 68 served on OS BRAVO; 19 Mar–11 Apr 69 served on OS DELTA.

Humboldt

29 Mar 49–Sep 66 stationed at Boston, MA, and used for LE, OS, and SAR; Jan 51 served on OS EASY; Jun 51 served on OS CHARLIE; Aug–Sep 51 served on OS ABLE; Nov–Dec 51 served on OS HOW; Jan–Feb 52 served on OS EASY; Apr–May 52 served on OS DOG; Jul–Aug 52 served on OS BAKER; Sep–Oct 52 served on OS HOTEL; Jun 53 served on OS ECHO; Oct 53 served on OS BRAVO; Jun 54 served on OS DELTA; Nov–Dec 54 served on OS ECHO; Apr–May 55 served on OS BRAVO; Jul 56 served on OS BRAVO; Sep 56 served on OS CHARLIE; Mar–Apr 57 served on OS ECHO; Jun–Jul 57 served on OS CHARLIE; Sep 57 served on OS CHARLIE; Nov–Dec 57 served on OS ECHO; Sep–Oct 58 served on OS DELTA; Dec 58–Jan 59 served on OS ECHO; May 59 served on OS CHARLIE; Jul–Aug 60 served on OS BRAVO; Oct–Nov 60 served on OS CHARLIE; May 61 served on OS CHARLIE; 13 May–2 Jun 65 served on OS BRAVO; Sep 66–30 Sep 69 stationed at Portland, ME, and used for LE, OS, and SAR; 11 Jan–3 Feb 68 served on OS ECHO; 26 May–18 Jun 68 served on OS CHARLIE; 24 Jul–16 Aug 68 served on OS BRAVO; 1–24 Oct 68 served on OS BRAVO; 29 Oct 68 rescued crew from sailboat *Atlantic II* in the Atlantic; 20 Dec 68–18 Jan 69 served on OS ECHO; 31 Mar–7 Apr 69 served on OS CHARLIE; 29 May–19 Jun 69 served on OS DELTA.

Mackinac

1949–67 stationed at New York, NY, and used for LE, OS, and SAR; Sep–Oct 53 served on OS COCA; Nov 53 served on OS DELTA; 13 Nov 53 assisted MV *Empire Nene* at 41°53′N, 43°47′W; Apr 54 served on OS ECHO; Nov–Dec 54 served on OS ECHO; Apr 57 served on OS CHARLIE; Dec 57–Jan 58 served on OS ECHO; Mar–Apr 59 served on OS CHARLIE; Jun–Jul 59 served on OS BRAVO; Sep 60 served on OS ECHO; Nov–Dec 60 served on OS CHARLIE; Apr–May 61 served on OS BRAVO; May 62 served on OS BRAVO.

Matagorda

8 Jun 49–1954 stationed at Boston, MA, and used for LE, OS, and SAR; Jun–Jul 50 served on OS DOG; Jan–Feb 51 served on OS HOW; Jul–Aug 51 served on OS CHARLIE; Dec 51–Jan 52 served on OS BAKER;

Jun 52 served on OS EASY; Nov 52 served on OS COCA; Jan–Feb 53 served on OS BRAVO; Sep 53 served on OS HOTEL; Nov 53 served on OS COCA; 1954–30 Oct 68 stationed at Honolulu, HI, and used for LE, OS, and SAR; Sep–Oct 54 served on OS VICTOR; Mar 55 served on OS VICTOR; Aug–Sep 55 served on OS VICTOR; 26 Jan 56 delivered clothing to orphanage in Japan from Washington Intermediate School, Honolulu, HI; Jul–Aug 56 served on OS VICTOR; Jan 57 served on OS VICTOR; Jun–Jul 57 served on OS VICTOR; Dec 57 served on OS VICTOR; Apr–May 59 served on OS VICTOR; Apr 60 served on OS VICTOR; Aug 60 towed disabled FV *Wild Goose II*; Sep 60 served on OS VICTOR; Mar 61 served on OS VICTOR; Aug 61 served on OS VICTOR; 12–13 Jan 65 stood by disabled Liberian MV *Santa Helena* 1,000 mi NW of Midway I., which sustained hull damage due to heavy seas and was in danger of breaking in two; relieved by cutter *Bering Strait* and proceeded via Midway I. to Hawaii in heavy seas, arriving 21 Jan; mid-Sep 65 escorted disabled Liberian MV *Londias* to Honolulu, HI; 27 Feb 66 transferred 12,000 gal of water to disabled MV *Union Success* and towed her until relieved; Apr 67 served on OS NOVEMBER.

McCullough

26 Nov 46–Jul 66 stationed at Boston, MA, and used for LE, OS, and SAR; May 54 served on OS BRAVO; May–Jun 56 served on OS ECHO; Nov 59 served on OS ECHO; May–Jun 60 served on OS CHARLIE; Dec 60–Jun 61 served on OS BRAVO; early Nov 65 rescued 280 Cuban refugees from small craft in Florida Strait and carried them to Key West, FL; Jul 66–1972 stationed at Wilmington, NC, and used for LE, OS, and SAR; 14 Aug–6 Sep 67 served on OS BRAVO; 14 Oct–5 Nov 67 served on OS ECHO; 8 Sep–1 Oct 68 served on OS BRAVO; 5–23 Nov 68 served on OS ECHO; 9 Jan–1 Feb 69 served on OS DELTA; 7–30 Apr 69 served on OS CHARLIE; 11 Aug–3 Sep 69 served on OS ECHO; 20 Dec 69–12 Jan 70 served on OS DELTA; 11 Mar–3 Apr 70 served on OS BRAVO; 14 May–6 Jun 70 served on OS ECHO; 17 Jun 70 helped fight fire on MV *Tsui Yung* in Wilmington, NC; 3–26 Aug 70 served on OS CHARLIE; 15 Oct–7 Nov 70 served on OS DELTA; 10 Jan–2 Feb 71 served on OS CHARLIE; 28 May–20 Jun 71 served on OS CHARLIE; 4–27 Aug 71 served on OS DELTA; 17–29 Dec 71 served on OS HOTEL.

Rockaway

24 Dec 48–20 Jan 72 stationed at Staten I., NY, and used for LE, OS, and SAR; Sep 50 served on OS BAKER; Nov–Dec 50 served on OS HOW; May 51 served on OS EASY; Oct 51 served on OS BAKER; Nov–Dec 51 served on OS BAKER; Jan 52 served on OS ABLE; Mar–Apr 52 served on OS HOW; May–Jun 52 served on OS CHARLIE; Aug–Sep 52 served on OS CHARLIE; Nov 52 served on OS BRAVO; 17 Oct 53 served on OS ECHO; Feb–Mar 55 served on OS COCA; Dec 55–Jan 56 served on OS BRAVO; Oct 56 served on OS CHARLIE; Jan 57 served on OS ECHO; May–Jun 58 served on OS BRAVO; Sep 58 salvaged a USN seaplane 180 mi from Bermuda; Nov–Dec 58 served on OS CHARLIE; Aug–Sep 60 served on OS BRAVO; Nov–Dec 60 served on OS DELTA; Dec 64 rescued four from MV *Smith Voyager*; Aug 65 took part in cadet cruise; Feb 66 served on OS DELTA; 24 Feb 66 stood by British MV *Parthia* awaiting commercial tug; Nov 67–Jan 68 conducted oceanographic survey off Norfolk, VA; 20 Jan–30 Mar 68 conducted oceanographic survey in eastern tropical Pacific off Mexico; 6–12 May 68 con-

Cutter *Unimak*, 8 Jun 87—the last surviving member of the class. From ocean stations to drug busts, the 311-foot ships were among the most popular large cutters in the Coast Guard. Their reputation as fine sea boats was probably exceeded only by the 327-foot cutters.

ducted oceanographic survey over mid-Atlantic Shelf; 11–18 Jul 68 conducted oceanographic survey over mid-Atlantic Shelf; 14–19 Jan 69 conducted survival craft drift project 150 mi E of Chesapeake Bay; Apr–Aug 69 conducted extensive oceanographic work associated with the Barbados Oceanographic and Meteorological Experiment; 20 Oct–23 Nov 69 conducted oceanographic survey from Nova Scotia to Cape Hatteras; 30 Mar–5 Apr 70 conducted oceanographic survey over mid-Atlantic outer Continental Margin; 19 May–14 Jun 70 conducted oceanographic survey from Nova Scotia to Cape Hatteras; 6–21 Oct 70 conducted oceanographic survey near the Grand Banks; Nov 70 surveyed nerve-gas dump site; 2 Mar–3 Apr 71 conducted fisheries research cruise from Nova Scotia to Cape Hatteras; May 71 conducted Grand Bank research cruise; 15 Jul–18 Sep 71 studied the influence of Mediterranean effluent upon the Atlantic.

Unimak

3 Jan 49–1 Sep 56 stationed at Boston, MA, and used primarily for LE, OS, and SAR; Nov–Dec 49 served on OS EASY; Jan 52 served on OS EASY; Mar 52 served on OS EASY; Feb–Mar 53 served on OS DELTA; May 53 served on OS COCA; Oct–Nov 54 served on OS DELTA; Jun–Jul 55 served on OS COCA; Jun 56 patrolled Newport, RI, to Bermuda race; 1 Sep 56–7 Aug 72 stationed at Cape May, NJ, and used primarily for training reservists, including training cruises to Brazil and Nova Scotia; Aug 65 took part in cadet cruise; 7 Mar 67 rescued six Cuban refugees in Yucatan Channel; 10 Mar 67 rescued survivors from FV *Bunkie III* in Florida waters; 15 Mar 67 rescued 12 Cuban refugees stranded on an island; 29 May 69 towed disabled FV *Sirocco* 35 mi E of Ft. Pierce, FL, to safety; 3 Apr 70 stood by grounded MV *Vassiliki* near Mayaguana I. until commercial tug arrived; 7 Aug 72–31 May 75 stationed at Yorktown, VA, and used to train reservists; 31 May 75–Aug 77 placed out of commission and stored at Curtis Bay, MD; Aug 77–1988 stationed at New Bedford, MA, and used primarily on fishing patrol; 6 Oct 80 seized MV *Janeth* 340 mi SE of Miami, FL, carrying 500 bales of marijuana; 14 Oct 80 seized PC *Rescue* carrying approximately 500 bales of marijuana and PC *Snail* carrying 2 tons of marijuana in Gulf of Mexico; 17 Oct 80 seized MV *Amalaka* SW of Key West, FL, carrying 1,000 bales of marijuana; 19 Oct 80 seized FV *Wright's Pride* SW of Key West, FL, carrying 30t of marijuana; while on OCS training cruise, Mar 81 seized MV *Mayo* carrying

40t of marijuana; 9 Dec 82 towed disabled FV *Sacred Heart* away from David Banks, 45 mi E of Cape Cod in 30-ft seas; 28 Jan–9 Mar 83 deployed on LE patrol to the Caribbean; 27–28 Feb 83 towed dismasted *Wandering Star* to Mathew Town, Great Inagua; 3 Mar 83 towed disabled MV *Yadrina* to Mathew Town, Great Inagua; 30 Nov 84 seized sailboat *Lola* 100 mi N of Barranquilla, Colombia, carrying 1.5t of marijuana; 2 Nov 85 seized tugboat *Zeus 3* and barge 200 mi S of the Dominican Republic carrying 40t of marijuana.

Yakutat

23 Nov 48–1 Jan 71 stationed at New Bedford, MA, and used for LE, OS, and SAR; Apr–May 49 served on OS ABLE; Jun–Jul 49 served on OS HOW; Dec 50 served on OS CHARLIE; Jul–Aug 51 served on OS DOG; Dec 51–Jan 52 served on OS HOW; Feb 52 rescued crew members from tankers *Fort Mercer* and *Pendleton* off Cape Cod after they broke in two and foundered; one gold and five silver Life-Saving Medals were earned by the crew; Jun 52 served on OS DOG; Aug 52 served on OS BAKER; Sep 52 served on OS BRAVO; Nov–Dec 52 served on OS HOTEL; Dec 52 rescued 4 from a downed private ac off St. George's, Bermuda; Mar–Apr 53 served on OS ECHO; Jul 53 served on OS ECHO; Sep 53 served on OS DELTA; 14 Sep 53 performed emergency repairs by constructing a concrete bulkhead and pumping bilges of Spanish MV *Marte*, which had a large hole at waterline, while some 750 mi SE of Argentia, Newfoundland; Jan–Feb 54 served on OS HOTEL; Mar 54 served on OS COCA; May–Jun 54 served on OS ECHO; Mar–Apr 55 served on OS COCA; Jun–Jul 55 served on OS ECHO; fall 1955 assisted Portuguese FV *Jose Alberto*; Sep–Oct 55 served on OS BRAVO; Dec 55 served on OS DELTA; Feb–Mar 56 served on OS ECHO; Feb–Mar 57 served on OS DELTA; Oct–Nov 58 served on OS CHARLIE; Jan–Feb 60 served on OS ECHO; Feb–Mar 64 served on OS BRAVO; 2–23 Apr 65 served on OS BRAVO; 27 Apr–3 May 65 dewatered and shored damaged Liberian MV *Bordabere* 400 mi S of Cape Race, Newfoundland, and escorted her to Halifax, NS; late Nov 65 assisted U.S. MVs *American Pilot* and *Maumee Sun* following their collision W of Cape Cod Canal; 4 May 67–1 Jan 68 assigned to CG Squadron Three, Vietnam; 13 Oct–5 Nov 68 served on OS ECHO; 5–28 Jan 69 served on OS CHARLIE; 28 Feb 69 hit by FV *Seafreeze Atlantic* while docked at New Bedford, MA—minor damage; 24 Mar–18 Apr 69 served on OS ECHO; 6 Jun–1 Jul 69 served on OS BRAVO; 4–27 Aug 69 served on OS DELTA; 12 Oct–4 Nov 69 served on OS DELTA; 17 May–31 Dec 70 assigned to CG Squadron Three, Vietnam.

Crew members of the *Absecon* (374) and the *Yakutat* (380) man the rail on 3 Jun 58. Although at first glance these sisters appear to be identical, a closer examination reveals many differences. Note the heavier deck supports beneath the bridge area of the *Absecon* and the after configuration of each cutter, particularly the armament.

NAVY *TACOMA* CLASS

Name	Hull Number	Builder	Keel Laid	Launched	Commissioned	Disposition
Brownsville	[WPF 10] PF 10	Kaiser Cargo Inc., Richmond, CA	14 Sep 43	14 Nov 43	6 May 44 (USN) 15 Apr 46 (CG)	*Decomm & ret* to the USN 2 Aug 46
Bangor	[WPF 16] PF 16	American Shipbuilding Co., Lorain, OH	20 May 43	6 Nov 43	22 Nov 44 (USN) 15 Apr 46 (CG)	*Decomm & ret* to the USN 16 Aug 46
Orange	[WPF 43] PF 43	Consolidated Steel Corp., Wilmington, CA	7 Jul 43	6 Aug 43	1 Jan 44 (USN) 15 Apr 46 (CG)	*Decomm & ret* to the USN 28 Oct 46
Corpus Christi	[WPF 44] PF 44	Consolidated Steel Corp., Wilmington, CA	17 Jul 43	17 Aug 43	29 Jan 44 (USN) 15 Apr 46 (CG)	*Decomm & ret* to the USN 2 Aug 46
Hutchinson	[WPF 45] PF 45	Consolidated Steel Corp., Wilmington, CA	28 Jul 43	27 Aug 43	3 Feb 44 (USN) 15 Apr 46 (CG)	*Decomm & ret* to the USN 23 Sep 46
Abilene (ex-*Bridgeport*)	[WPF 58] PF 58	Globe Shipbuilding Co., Superior, WI	6 May 43	21 Aug 43	28 Oct 44 (USN) 15 Mar 46 (CG)	*Decomm & ret* to the USN 21 Aug 46
Gladwyne (ex-*Worcester*)	[WPF 62] PF 62	Globe Shipbuilding Co., Superior, WI	14 Oct 43	7 Jan 44	21 Nov 44 (USN) 15 Apr 46 (CG)	*Decomm & ret* to the USN 31 Aug 46
Moberly (ex-*Scranton*)	[WPF 63] PF 63	Globe Shipbuilding Co., Superior, WI	3 Nov 43	26 Jan 44	11 Dec 44 (USN) 15 Apr 46 (CG)	*Decomm & ret* to the USN 12 Aug 46

Cost   N/A

Hull

Displacement (tons)   2,270 fl; 1,246 light (1946)
Length   303'11" oa; 285'6" bp
Beam   37'2" max
Draft   14'7" max (1946)

Machinery

Main Engines   2 triple-expansion reciprocating steam
Main Boilers   2 Babcock and Wilcox
SHP   5,500
Propellers   twin

Performance

Max Speed   19.5 kts (1946)
Max Sustained   17.7 kts, 5,400-mi radius (1946)
Economic   10.5 kts, 9,150-mi radius (1946)

Logistics

Fuel Oil (95%)   213,856 gal
Complement   8 officers, 2 warrants, 127 ratings (1946)

Electronics

Detection Radar   SA-2, SL-1 (1946)
Sonar   QJA (1946)
Armament   2 3"/50 (single), 2 40mm/60 (twin); 9 20mm/80 (single); 1 Mk 10 mousetrap (1946)

Design

The *Tacoma*-class patrol frigates were designed and built for the USN. They were modeled after the British "River" class. The patrol frigates were an attempt to increase the number of ocean escorts by employing maritime construction standards for naval shipbuilding. Although similar in appearance to destroyer escorts, they were decidedly inferior. The patrol frigates were structurally weaker, had poor turning radius, and were poorly ventilated.

During WWII the CG manned 77 of this class for the USN (see Scheina, *WWII Cutters,* pp. 301–3). Most operated on weather patrol. A balloon hangar replaced an aft 3"/50. In early 1946 the CG temporarily needed ships to serve on ocean-station duty in the Pacific to help safeguard returning troops. Eight *Tacoma*-class patrol frigates then being manned by the CG for the USN were transferred from the USN on a loan/charter basis. For a variety of reasons,

including shortages of people and money, all were returned to the USN in a few months. See DANFS for naval service.

Abilene

28 Oct 44–15 Mar 46 crewed by CG for USN; 15 Mar 46 transferred to CG as part of Air Sea Rescue Service.

Bangor

22 Nov 44–15 Apr 46 crewed by CG for USN; 15 Apr 46 transferred to CG, stationed at San Francisco, CA, and served on ocean aircraft station 2 and OS DOG.

Brownsville

6 May 44–2 Aug 46 crewed by CG for USN; 15 Aug 46 transferred to CG, stationed at San Francisco, CA, and served on ocean aircraft station 2 and OS DOG.

Corpus Christi

29 Jan 44–15 Apr 46 crewed by CG for USN; 15 Apr 46 transferred to CG and served on ocean aircraft station 2 and OS DOG.

Gladwyne

21 Nov 44–15 Apr 46 crewed by CG for USN; 15 Apr 46 transferred to CG, stationed at San Francisco, CA, and served on OS 1.

Hutchinson

3 Feb 44–15 Apr 46 crewed by CG for USN; 15 Apr 46 transferred to CG, stationed at San Francisco, CA, and served on OS 1.

Moberly

4 Dec 44–15 Apr 46 crewed by CG for USN; 15 Apr 46 transferred to CG, stationed at Honolulu, HI, and served on OS 2 and OS DOG.

Orange

1 Jan 44–15 Apr 46 crewed by CG for USN; 15 Apr 46 transferred to CG and served on OS 2 and OS DOG.

NAVY *ERIE* CLASS

Name	Hull Number	Builder	Keel Laid	Launched	Commissioned	Disposition
Charleston	PG-51	Charleston Navy Yard, Charleston, SC	27 Oct 34	26 Feb 36	8 Jul 36 (USN) Not applicable (CG)	Negotiations suspended 28 Feb 46

Cost   N/A

Hull
- Displacement (tons)   2,339 trial, 2,000 standard (1936)
- Length   328'6" oa; 308' wl
- Beam   41'3" max
- Draft   11'4" standard (1936)

Machinery
- Main Engines   two steam turbines
- Main Boilers   2
- SHP   6,200
- Propellers   2

Performance
- Max Speed   20 kts
- Cruising   12 kts, 8,000-mi radius (1936)

Logistics
- Fuel Oil (95%)   489t
- Complement   236 officers, 2 warrants, 127 ratings (1946)

Electronics   N/A

Armament   4 6"/47 (single) (1936)

Design

On 5 Jan 46 the Commandant of the Coast Guard wrote to the Chief of Naval Operations stating that the service was desirous of obtaining the *Charleston* if the ship was surplus to Navy needs. The Commandant wrote, "The subject vessel is similar to the *Campbell* type of Coast Guard cutter, which has been found very suitable for performing peacetime functions of the Coast Guard, and if it is obtained it will permit the use of one of the presently operated cutters to be discontinued." On 28 Feb the Commandant again wrote stating that "the personnel situation of the Coast Guard had become exceedingly acute," and the service withdrew the request for the ship.

255-FOOT CUTTERS ("INDIAN TRIBES" CLASS, *OWASCO* CLASS

Name	Hull Number	Builder	Keel Laid	Launched	Commissioned	Disposition
Owasco (ex-*Oneida*)	WHEC 39 WPG 39	Western Pipe & Steel Co., San Pedro, CA	17 Nov 43	18 Jun 44	18 May 45	*Decomm* 27 Jun 73 *Sold* 7 Oct 74
Winnebago	WHEC 40 WPG 40	Western Pipe & Steel Co., San Pedro, CA	1 Dec 43	2 Jul 44	21 Jun 45	*Decomm* 27 Feb 73 *Sold* 7 Oct 74
Chautauqua	WHEC 41 WPG 41	Western Pipe & Steel Co., San Pedro, CA	22 Dec 43	14 May 44	4 Aug 45	*Decomm* 1 Aug 73
Sebago (ex-*Wachusett*)	WHEC 42 WPG 42	Western Pipe & Steel Co., San Pedro, CA	7 Jun 43	28 May 44	20 Sep 45	*Decomm* 29 Feb 72 *Trans* MARAD 14 Apr 72
Iroquois	WHEC 43 WPG 43	Western Pipe & Steel Co., San Pedro, CA	19 Jun 44	22 Oct 44	9 Feb 46	*Decomm* 13 Jan 65 *Sold* 1 Jun 65
Wachusett (ex-*Huron*)	WHEC 44 WPG 44	Western Pipe & Steel Co., San Pedro, CA	3 Jul 44	5 Nov 44	23 Mar 46	*Decomm* 30 Aug 73 *Sold* 18 Nov 74
Escanaba (ex-*Otsego*)	WHEC 64 WPG 64	Western Pipe & Steel Co., San Pedro, CA	25 Oct 44	25 Mar 45	20 Mar 46	*Decomm* 28 Jun 74
Winona	WHEC 65 WPG 65	Western Pipe & Steel Co., San Pedro, CA	8 Nov 44	22 Apr 45	19 Apr 46	*Decomm* 31 May 74
Klamath	WHEC 66 WPG 66	Western Pipe & Steel Co., San Pedro, CA	13 Dec 44	2 Sep 45	19 Jun 46	*Decomm* 1 May 73 *Sold* 18 Nov 74
Minnetonka (ex-*Sunapee*)	WHEC 67 WPG 67	Western Pipe & Steel Co., San Pedro, CA	26 Dec 44	21 Nov 45	11 Jul 46	*Decomm* 31 May 74
Androscoggin	WHEC 68 WPG 68	Western Pipe & Steel Co., San Pedro, CA	30 Dec 44	16 Sep 45	26 Sep 46	*Decomm* 27 Feb 73 *Sold* 7 Oct 74
Mendota	WHEC 69 WPG 69	Coast Guard Yard, Curtis Bay, MD	5 Jul 43	29 Feb 44	2 Jun 45	*Decomm* 1 Nov 73
Pontchartrain (ex-*Okeechobee*)	WHEC 70 WPG 70	Coast Guard Yard, Curtis Bay, MD	5 Jul 43	29 Feb 44	28 Jul 45	*Decomm* 19 Oct 73

Cost	$4,239,702 each (hull & machinery)

Hull

Displacement (tons)	1,978 fl (1966); 1,342 light (1966)
Length	254′ oa; 245′ bp
Beam	43′1″ max
Draft	17′3″ max (1966)

Machinery

Main Engines	1 Westinghouse electric motor driven by a turbine
Main Boilers	2 Foster-Wheeler drum-top fired Express-type, 635 psi, 750°F superheat
SHP	4,000 total (1945)
Propellers	single

Performance

Max Sustained	17.0 kts, 6,157-mi radius (1966)
Economic	10.0 kts, 10,376-mi radius (1966)

Logistics

Fuel Oil (95%)	141,775 gal
Complement	10 officers, 3 warrants, 130 men (1966)

Electronics

Detection Radar	SPS-23, SPS-29, Mk 26, Mk 27 (1966)
Sonar	SQS-1 (1966)
Armament	1 5″/38; Hedgehog; 2 Mk 32 ASW TT (*Winnebago*, 1966—most units without TTs)

Design

"The bow and the stern for each other yearn, and the lack of interval shows. . . ." Myths have long shadowed the design history of the 255-foot class. These cutters were to have been much longer ships, and two theories persist as to why they were shortened. The first is that these cutters were built to replace the ships given to Great Britain under lend lease, and Congress stipulated that the Coast Guard had to build these replacement cutters to the same size and character as those provided to the British. The second is that their length was determined by the maximum length that could pass through the locks of the Welland Canal from the Great Lakes to the St. Lawrence River. The Great Lakes ship-building industry brought pressure to bear on Congress to ensure that it had the potential to bid on the contracts. The first theory seems to be correct, but the second cannot be ruled out.

The Coast Guard had prepared a design for a 316-foot cutter that was to have been an austere 327. This design was cut down into the 255-foot ship. To accomplish this, everything was squeezed down and automated to a degree not before achieved in a turbo-electric-driven ship.

The machinery design of the 255s was compact and innovative, but overly complex. It had pilothouse control, variable-rate (10 to 1) burners, and automatic synchronizing between the turbogenerator and the motor. Westinghouse engineers developed a system of synchronization and a variable-frequency drive for main-propulsion auxiliary equipment, which kept the pumps and other items at about two-thirds the power required for constant-frequency operation. The combined boiler room/engine room was a break with tradition.

The turbo-alternators for ship-service power exhausted at 20 psi gauge pressure instead of into a condenser. This steam was used all over the ship before finally going to a condenser. Space, heating, galley cooking, laundry, freshwater evaporating, fuel, and feed-water heating were all taken from the 20 psi back-pressure line.

The 255-foot class was an ice-going design. Ice operations had been assigned to the Coast Guard early in the war, and almost all new construction was either ice-going or ice-breaking.

The hull was designed with constant flare at the waterline for ice-going. The structure was longitudinally framed with heavy web frames and an ice belt of heavy plating, and it had extra transverse framing above and below the design

waterline. Enormous amounts of weight were removed through the use of electric welding. The 250-foot cutters' weights were used for estimating purposes. Tapered bulkhead stiffeners cut from 12″ I-beams went from the main deck (4′ depth of web) to the bottom (8″ depth of web). As weight was cut out of the hull structure, electronics and ordnance were increased, but at much greater heights. This top weight required ballasting the fuel tanks with seawater to maintain stability both for wind and damaged conditions.

The superstructure of the 255s was originally divided into two islands in order to accommodate an aircraft amidships, but this requirement was dropped before any of the units became operational. Construction of this class received a low priority, and none of the cutters served in the war. Following completion of the preliminary design by the Coast Guard, the work was assigned to George G. Sharp of New York to prepare the contract design.

The number of units—13 of them—had an interesting origin. Three were to have been replacements for overaged cutters—the *Ossipee, Tallapoosa,* and *Unalga;* ten units were to be replacements for the 250-foot class transferred to Great Britain under lend-lease. For economy, all 13 were built to the same design.

Androscoggin

1947–48 stationed at Boston, MA, and used primarily on OS duty in the North Atlantic; 1948–3 Jul 49 stationed at New York, NY, and used primarily on OS duty in the North Atlantic; 31 Oct 49–8 May 50 decommissioned and stored at CG Yard, Curtis Bay, MD; 8 May 50–27 Feb 73 received crew from cutter *Mocoma*, recommissioned, and stationed at Miami Beach, FL—used primarily for LE and SAR; 29–30 May 52 towed a disabled Navy PBM ac from 60 mi SE of Miami, FL, to Miami; Dec 52 served on OS BRAVO; Jan 53 served on OS BRAVO; 1956 served on Campeche Patrol; Apr–May 56 assigned to special duty related to Loran, visiting Ecuador, Jamaica, Colombia, and Panama; Jul 56 served on annual reserve cruise to San Juan, PR, and Port Au Prince, Haiti; 17 Apr–4 Jul 59 shared IIP with cutter *Acushnet*; Jan 60 sailed to Reykjavik, Iceland, on special mission; 1960 served on OS CHARLIE; 1961 escorted Miami to Nassau Race; Nov 61 took part in a special mission involving USAF and Air National Guard related to Berlin crisis; 1962 served as CG schoolship at the Navy's Fleet Sonar School, Key West, FL; late Aug 65 evacuated Cuban refugees from Cay Sal to Key West, FL; Jan 66–Feb served on OS ECHO; 10 Jan 66 rescued crew from sinking MV *Lampsis* and unsuccessfully attempted to save vessel; 3 Feb 66 stood by distressed MV *Aroin* until commercial tug arrived; 19 Feb 66 rescued three Cuban refugees from Anguila Cay and transported them to Miami, FL; 25 May 66 embarked 12 Cuban refugees from Cay Lobos and transported them to Key West, FL; Nov–Dec 66 served on OS ECHO; 4 Dec 67–4 Aug 68 assigned to CG Squadron Three, Vietnam; 1 Mar 68 assisted in destruction of a steel trawler serving as a supply ship in a gun battle at the mouth of the Song Cau R.; May 68 rescued 27 Vietnamese from South China Sea; 24 Nov–16 Dec 68 served on OS DELTA; 6 Feb–3 Mar 69 served on OS ECHO; 3–26 Jun 69 served on OS ECHO; 16 Aug–8 Sep 69 served on OS BRAVO; 11 Nov–4 Dec 69 served on OS ECHO; 1969 assisted Dutch MV *Alida Gothern*; 19 Feb 70 stood by disabled MV *Stellanova* until commercial tug arrived; Mar 70 served on OS ECHO; 3–26 Apr 70 served on OS BRAVO; 29 Apr 70 provided medical assistance to Spanish MV *Coromoto* in mid-Atlantic; 4 May 70 provided medical assistance to USS *Dahlgren* off Bermuda; 6–29 Sep 70 served on OS ECHO; 30 Nov–22 Dec 70 served on OS DELTA; 25 Feb–20 Mar 71 served on OS CHARLIE; 30 Jun–24 Jul 71 served on OS ECHO; 25 Nov–17 Dec 71 served on OS ECHO; 27 Feb–24 Mar 72 served on OS

DELTA; 13 May–2 Jun 72 served on OS DELTA; 18 Jul–7 Aug 72 served on OS BRAVO; 23 Nov–16 Dec 72 served on OS ECHO; 23 Feb–18 Mar 73 served on OS ECHO; 18 May–7 Jun 73 served on OS CHARLIE.

Chautauqua

4 Aug 45–Oct 48 stationed at San Francisco, CA, and used for LE, OS, and SAR; Feb 46 served on OS FOX; Apr 46 served on OS FOX; Aug 46 served on OS FOX; Oct 46 served on OS FOX; Feb 47 served on OS FOX; 19 May 47 searched for reported mine; Jul 47 served on OS FOX; Oct 48–22 Jul 54 stationed at Alameda, CA, and used for LE, OS, and SAR; 11–28 Oct 48 served on OS FOX; 29–30 Oct 48 escorted disabled FV *Reefer King* to Honolulu, HI; 29 Dec 48–23 Jan 49 served on OS ABLE; 18 Apr–8 May 49 served on OS ABLE; 10–31 Jul 49 served on OS FOX; 29 Sep 49–11 Oct 49 served on OS ABLE; 11–14 Oct 49 towed disabled MV *Navigator* until relieved by a commercial tug; 18–24 Oct 49 served on OS ABLE; 17–19 Dec 49 served on OS NAN; 10–13 Mar 50 served on OS OBOE; 15–21 Apr 50 towed disabled tug *Omar* to San Francisco, CA; 1–5 Jun 50 served on OS PETER; Aug 50 served on OS NAN; 19 Nov–1 Dec 50 served on OS PETER; 11 Feb–4 Mar 51 served on OS UNCLE; 24 Apr–1 May 51 served on OS SUGAR; 5–26 May 51 served on OS SUGAR; 16 Jun–7 Jul 51 served on OS SUGAR; 30 Sep–21 Oct 51 served on OS NAN; 2–23 Dec 51 served on OS UNCLE; 3–23 Feb 52 served on OS SUGAR; 15 Mar–5 Apr 52 served on OS VICTOR; 8–29 Jun 52 served on OS NAN; 10–31 Aug 52 served on OS UNCLE; 3–23 Feb 52 served on OS SUGAR; 15 Mar–5 Apr 52 served

on OS VICTOR; 8–29 Jun 52 served on OS NAN; 10–31 Aug 52 served on OS UNCLE; 22 Nov–16 Dec 52 served on OS VICTOR; 26 Jan–16 Feb 53 served on OS SUGAR; 15 May 53 assisted disabled FV *Bering Sea* 20 mi W of Pt. Reyes, CA; 28 May–18 Jun 53 served on OS UNCLE; 23 Aug–13 Sep 53 served on OS UNCLE; 15 Nov–6 Dec 53 served on OS NAN; 27 Feb–20 Mar 54 served on OS VICTOR; 10 Apr–1 May 54 served on OS VICTOR; 22 Jul 54–1973 stationed at Honolulu, HI, and used for LE, OS, and SAR; 4–25 Sep 54 served on OS VICTOR; 9–29 Jan 55 served on OS VICTOR; 18 Feb–12 Mar 55 served on OS VICTOR; 25 Jun–16 Jul 55 served on OS VICTOR; 6–27 Aug 55 served on OS VICTOR; 10–31 Dec 55 served on OS VICTOR; 26 May–16 Jun 56 served on OS VICTOR; 7–28 Jul 56 served on OS VICTOR; 10–22 Nov 56 served on OS VICTOR; 21 Nov 56 medevaced crewman from MV *Evibelle*; 16 Dec 56–13 Jan 57 served on OS VICTOR; 27 Apr–17 May 57 served on OS VICTOR; 7–29 Jun 57 served on OS VICTOR; 12 Oct–1 Nov 57 served on OS VICTOR; 23 Nov–14 Dec 57 served on OS VICTOR; 29 Mar–19 Apr 58 served on OS VICTOR; 8–31 May 58 served on OS VICTOR; 13 Sep–5 Oct 58 served on OS VICTOR; 1–21 Mar 59 served on OS VICTOR; 11–26 Apr 59 served on OS VICTOR; 13 Jul 59 assisted yacht *Cloud Nine* at 23°20′N, 143°00′W; 15–17 Jul 59 patrolled Trans-Pacific Race; 15 Aug–5 Sep 59 served on OS VICTOR; 6 Sep 59 medevaced crewman from MV *Pioneer* at 34°25′N, 162°16′E; 26 Sep–17 Oct 59 served on OS VICTOR; 31 Jan–22 Feb 60 served on OS VICTOR; 13 Mar–1 Apr 60 served on OS VICTOR; 16 Jul–5 Aug 60 served on OS VICTOR; 27 Aug–17 Sep 60 served on OS VICTOR; 1–23 Jan

Cutter *Chautauqua* on 13 Mar 64. As completed, the 255-foot class carried an extremely heavy armament. Much of this was removed shortly after WWII, which lessened topside weight and improved stability. This was particularly important for ocean-station duty, a prime mission of this class. Note that the *Chautauqua* mounts Mk 32 ASW torpedo tubes abeam the after superstructure.

61 served on OS VICTOR; 14 Feb–4 Mar 61 served on OS VICTOR; 17 Jun–9 Jul 61 served on OS VICTOR; 29 Jul–18 Aug 61 served on OS VICTOR; Feb 65 served on OS VICTOR—departed early for Yoko-suka, Japan, due to main motor-bearing casualty; 2–23 Jan 66 served on OS VICTOR; 13 Feb–6 Mar 66 served on OS VICTOR; 20 Jan 67 sustained a fire in CIC while undergoing renovation in a San Francisco yard; Feb 68 served on OS VICTOR; 23 Jun–14 Jul 68 served on OS VICTOR; 25 Aug–15 Sep 68 served on OS VICTOR; 27 Oct–17 Nov 68 served on OS VICTOR; 29 Dec 68–19 Jan 69 served on OS VICTOR; 4–25 May 69 served on OS VICTOR; 15 Jun–6 Jul 69 served on OS VICTOR; 17 Aug–7 Sep 69 served on OS VICTOR; 28 Sep–19 Oct 69 served on OS VICTOR; 11 Jan–1 Feb 70 served on OS VICTOR; 5–26 Apr 70 served on OS VICTOR; 28 Jun–19 Jul 70 served on OS NOVEMBER; 30 Aug–20 Sep 70 served on OS VICTOR; 1–21 Nov 70 served on OS VICTOR; 14 Feb–7 Mar 71 served on OS VICTOR; 9–30 May 71 served on OS NOVEMBER; 11 Jul–1 Aug 71 served on OS NOVEMBER; 24 Oct–14 Nov 71 served on OS NOVEMBER; 5–26 Dec 71 served on OS VICTOR; late Dec 71 was on-scene commander follow-ing the sinking of Danish MV *Heering Kirse* off Midway I.—31 of 36 rescued; 4–30 Jul 72 served on OS ECHO; 14 Dec 72–4 Jan 73 served on OS DELTA; 11–31 Mar 73 served on OS CHARLIE; 27 May–17 Jun 73 served on OS BRAVO.

Escanaba

1946–1954 stationed at Alameda, CA, and used for LE, OS, and SAR; Oct–Nov 49 served on OS FOX; Apr–May 50 served on OS PETER; Oct–Nov 51 served on OS SUGAR; Nov–Dec 51 served on OS VIC-TOR; Feb–Mar 52 served on OS NAN; 29 Jun–20 Jul 52 served on OS UNCLE; Sep 52 served on OS UNCLE; Oct 52 served on OS VICTOR; Nov 52 served on OS SUGAR; 25 Jan–15 Feb 53 served on OS UNCLE; 16 Apr–7 May 53 served on OS UNCLE; Jul 53 served on OS NAN; 6–28 Oct 53 served on OS VICTOR; Apr 54 served on OS NAN; 1954–57 decommissioned and placed in storage; 1957–28 Jun 73 stationed at New Bedford, MA, and used for LE, OS, and SAR; Jan–Feb 57 served on OS BRAVO; Jun 57 served on OS DELTA; Jul–Aug 57 served on OS BRAVO; Dec 57–Jan 58 served on OS BRAVO; Mar 58 served on OS ECHO; Dec 59–Jan 60 served on OS ECHO; Feb–Mar 60 served on OS CHARLIE; Oct 60 served on OS BRAVO; Dec 60–Jan 61 served on OS DELTA; Mar–Apr 61 served on OS ECHO; May–Jun 61 served on OS CHARLIE; 7–23 Aug 65 served on OS BRAVO; late Nov 65 assisted U.S. MVs *American Pilot* and *Maumee Sun* following their collision W of Cape Cod Canal; Jan 66 served on OS ECHO; 10 Jan 66 rescued two survivors from MV *Monte Palomares* that sank in heavy seas with a loss of 31; 5 Feb 67 rescued two Cuban refugees from Elbow Cay; 11 Oct–3 Nov 67 served on OS DELTA; 9 Jan–1 Feb 68 served on OS CHARLIE; 10 Apr–3 May 68 served on OS CHARLIE; 11–31 Jul 68 served on OS CHARLIE; 18 Sep–11 Oct 68 served on OS DELTA; Jan 69 disabled 100 mi E of Virginia Beach, VA, when aft bearing on main motor burned out—20 Jan arrived at Norfolk, VA; 11 Apr–4 May 69 served on OS DELTA; 1–24 Oct 69 served on OS BRAVO; 27 Dec 69–19 Jan 70 served on OS ECHO; 28 Dec 69–2 Jan 70 escorted distressed East German MV *Ange* to Bermuda; 13 Jan 70 stood by Norwegian MV *Chandeleur* in mid-Atlantic until fire damage was repaired; 15 Jan 70 escorted distressed Norwegian MV *Condo* until she could proceed on her own; 6–29 Mar 70 served on OS ECHO; 25 Mar 70 medevaced crewman from Korean MV

Kumsong in mid-Atlantic; 7–30 May 70 served on OS DELTA; 15 Jul–7 Aug 70 served on OS DELTA; 30 Dec 70–22 Jan 71 served on OS ECHO; 9 May–1 Jun 71 served on OS DELTA; 14 Jul–5 Aug 71 served on OS CHARLIE; 20 Sep–14 Oct 71 served on OS DELTA; 29 Nov–19 Dec 71 served on OS BRAVO; 29 Feb–25 Mar 72 served on OS ECHO; 9–31 May 72 served on OS BRAVO; 26 Jun–20 Jul 72 served on OS DELTA; 4–26 Jan 73 served on OS DELTA; 7–27 May 73 served on OS BRAVO.

Iroquois

Aug 46 served on OS 1; 1946–47 stationed at San Francisco, CA; 1948 stationed at Seattle, WA; 1949–1955 stationed at San Francisco, CA; Feb 51 served on OS NAN; Jul–Aug 51 served on OS UNCLE; Oct–Nov 51 served on OS VICTOR; Jan 52 served on OS UNCLE; 8 Jun 52 served on OS QUEEN; Dec 52–Jan 53 served on OS VICTOR; Feb 53 served on OS SUGAR; 25 Jun 53 served on OS QUEEN; Aug 53 served on OS QUEEN; 1955–13 Jan 65 decommissioned and stored.

Klamath

19 Jun 46–1 May 73 stationed at Seattle, WA, and used for LE, OS, and SAR; Jun 49 served on OS FOX; Sep 49 served on OS ABLE; Apr 51 served on OS NAN; Sep 51 served on OS SUGAR; Dec 51 served on OS NAN; Apr 52 served on OS VICTOR; Oct–Nov 52 served on OS NAN; Jan–Feb 53 served on OS NAN; 10 Mar 53 served on OS NAN; 19 Apr 53 served on OS NAN; 4 Aug 53 served on OS VICTOR; 4 Oct 53 served on OS SUGAR; Feb 54 served on OS NAN; Sep 54 served on OS NAN; 1955 conducted Bering Sea Patrol; Jan 56 served on OS NAN; Apr 56 served on OS NAN; Oct–Nov 56 served on OS NOVEMBER; Mar–Apr 57 served on OS NOVEMBER; Aug–Sep 57 served on OS NOVEMBER; May–Jun 58 served on OS NOVEMBER; Oct 58 served on OS NOVEMBER; Mar 59 served on OS NOVEMBER; Aug 59 served on OS NOVEMBER; Dec 59–Jan 60 served on OS NOVEM-BER; Jun–Jul 60 served on OS NOVEMBER; Oct 60 served on OS NOVEMBER; Mar–Apr 61 served on OS NOVEMBER; Jul–Aug 61 served on OS NOVEMBER; 20–24 Mar 66 inspected Russian MV *Oly-utorka*, which had sought haven in U.S. waters following casualty; 25 Mar 66 Japanese FVs *Bansho Maru No 38* and *Tenyo Maru No 3* were discovered in U.S. waters and escorted out; Oct 68 served on OS NOVEMBER; 18 Feb–10 Mar 68 served on OS VICTOR; 31 Mar–21 Apr 68 served on OS VICTOR; 23 Jun–14 Jul 68 served on OS NOVEMBER; 6–27 Oct 68 served on OS NOVEMBER; 17 Nov–8 Dec 68 served on OS NOVEM-BER; 19 Feb–2 Mar 69 served on OS NOVEMBER; 14 May 69–31 Jan 70 assigned to CG Squadron Three, Vietnam; 19 Jul–9 Aug 70 served on OS NOVEMBER; 22 Nov–13 Dec 70 served on OS NOVEMBER; 7–28 Mar 71 served on OS NOVEMBER; 30 May–20 Jun 71 served on OS NOVEMBER; 1–22 Aug 71 served on OS VICTOR; 12 Sep–3 Oct 71 served on OS VICTOR; 26 Dec 71–16 Jan 72 served on OS NOVEM-BER; Feb 72 boarding party helped save badly damaged MV *Tenzan Maru* and escorted her to safety; 9–30 Apr 72 served on OS NOVEMBER; 11 Jun–2 Jul 72 served on OS NOVEMBER; 3–24 Sep 72 served on OS NOVEMBER; 5–26 Nov 72 served on OS NOVEMBER.

Mendota

Apr 46–Jan 47 stationed at Boston, MA, and used for LE, OS, and SAR; 23 May–15 Jun 46 served on OS E; 8–29 Sep 46 served on OS C; 14 Oct–

Life on a North Atlantic ocean station—*Mendota* is roughing it on OS Delta 650 mi SE of Newfoundland on 5 Apr 65.

3 Nov 46 served on OS E; Jan 47–29 Feb 72 stationed at Washington, NC, and used for LE, OS, and SAR; 14 May–23 Jul 47 shared IIP with cutter *Spencer*; 26 Apr–3 Jul 48 shared IIP with cutter *Mocoma*; 30 Oct–19 Nov 48 served on OS ABLE; 8–10 Jan 49 served on OS CHARLIE—departed early due to case of acute appendicitis; 7–27 May 49 served on OS ABLE; 7–29 Jul 49 served on OS HOW; 30 Sep–21 Oct 49 served on OS ABLE; 23 Sep 49–15 Jan 50 served on OS BAKER; 8–27 Mar 50 served on OS EASY; 28–31 Mar 50 towed disabled MV *Edison Mariner* until a commercial tug arrived; 7–28 Jun 50 served on OS HOW; 21–22 Aug 50 towed disabled MV *South Bend Victory* until relieved by a commercial tug; 10 Nov–4 Dec 50 served on OS CHARLIE; 16 Jan–7 Feb 51 served on OS EASY; 10 Apr–2 May 51 served on OS EASY; 29 Jun–21 Jul 51 served on OS CHARLIE; 15 Sep–5 Oct 71 served on OS ABLE; 8–30 Dec 51 served on OS BAKER; 2 Jan 52 medevaced crewman from FV *Silver Bay* at 44°47′N, 56°22′W; 29 Feb–20 Mar 52 served on OS HOW; 2 Mar 52 provided medical aid to MV *Rachel Jackson* at 37°30′N, 66°08′W; 9 Mar 52 recovered buoy and transferred it to tender *Madrona*; 12–13 Mar 52 medevaced crewman from MV *Saxton Star* and transferred him to MV *Queen of Bermuda*; 12 May–1 Jun 52 served on OS DOG; 26 Jul–16 Aug 52 served on OS BAKER; 16 Oct–6 Nov 52 served on OS HOTEL; 17 Jan–8 Feb 53 served on OS COCA; 11 Apr–1 May 53 served on OS ECHO; 20 Jun–11 Jul 53 served on OS DELTA; 25 Aug–3 Sep 53 served on OS HOTEL; 18 Sep 53 medevaced a crewman from MV *Government Camp*; 17 Oct–7 Nov 53 served on OS COCA; 29 Dec 53–18 Jan 54 served on OS HOTEL; 15–17 Mar 54 towed disabled FV *Eagle* to Newfoundland; 23–30 Apr 54 served on OS ECHO; 19 Jun–1 Jul 54 served on OS ALFA; 31 Aug 54 towed disabled tug *Ocean Prince* until relieved; 26 Nov–17 Dec 54 served on OS DELTA; 11–12 Jan 55 escorted disabled MV *Flying Cloud III* to Frying Pan Shoal; 13 Jan 55 assisted disabled FV *Stephen Margo* 15 mi NE of Diamond Shoal; 14 Jan 55

escorted ammunition barge; 4–25 Mar 55 served on OS COCA; 28 May–17 Jun 55 served on OS ECHO; 15–16 Aug 55 rescued 46 crew plus dog from Portuguese FV *Ilhavense Segundo* at 45°N, 41′W; 6–28 Jan 56 served on OS BRAVO; 28 Apr–19 May 56 served on OS ECHO; 11 Sep–1 Oct 56 served on OS BRAVO; 27 Nov–17 Dec 56 served on OS DELTA; 16 Feb–8 Mar 57 served on OS ECHO; 11–12 Mar 57 assisted disabled FV *Stella Maris* 63 mi SW of Louisbourg, Nova Scotia; 30 Apr–21 May 57 served on OS BRAVO; 16 Jul–6 Aug 57 served on OS DELTA; 23 Sep–20 Oct 57 served on OS BRAVO; 7–27 Dec 57 served on OS ECHO; 25 Jan 58 towed disabled USN tug *Sagamore* and destroyer escort *Stewart* to Southport, ME; 22 May 58 rescued pilots from two USAF jets that had collided; 30 Jun–21 Jul 58 served on OS CHARLIE; 19 Aug–9 Sep 58 served on OS DELTA; 6 Jan 59 assisted MV *Hillcrest* at 34°43′N, 62°30′W; 10–28 Mar 59 served on OS CHARLIE; 20 May–8 Jun 59 served on OS ECHO; 4–18 Oct 59 served on OS BRAVO; 2–24 Dec 59 served on OS CHARLIE; 12–28 Jul 60 served on OS ECHO; 1–22 Aug 60 employed on reserve cruise visiting Veracruz, Mexico; 21 Nov–13 Dec 60 served on OS BRAVO; 10–30 Apr 61 served on OS ECHO; 1–24 Jul 61 served on OS DELTA; 15 Nov 62 assisted disabled schooner *Curlew* 90 mi NW of Bermuda; Mar 65 served as on-scene commander following a mid-air collision between two USAF aircraft 200 mi S of Cape Race, Newfoundland—only debris recovered; 9 Jul–1 Aug 67 served on OS CHARLIE; 14 Nov–7 Dec 67 served on OS BRAVO; 12 Apr–5 May 68 served on OS ECHO; 24 Apr 68 took on board 26 survivors from *Irinis Luck*; 28 Feb–3 Nov 69 assigned to CG Squadron Three, Vietnam; 23 Feb–18 Mar 70 served on OS CHARLIE; 4–27 Jul 70 served on OS BRAVO; 11 Dec 70–3 Jan 71 served on OS BRAVO; 20 Feb–1 Mar 71 served on OS HOTEL; 7–30 Mar 71 served on OS ECHO; 15 May–7 Jun 71 served on OS ECHO; 14 Jul–4 Aug 71 served on OS DELTA; 10–31 Dec 71 served on OS CHARLIE; 16 Aug–7 Sep 73 served on OS BRAVO.

Minnetonka

20 Sep 46–7 Mar 51 stationed at San Pedro, CA, and used for LE, OS, and SAR; 6–26 Nov 47 served on OS FOX; 8–25 Mar 48 served on OS FOX; 9–12 Aug 48 served on OS FOX; 27 Oct–1 Nov 48 served on OS FOX; 30 Dec 48–2 Jan 49 served on OS FOX; 24 Mar–20 Apr 49 served on OS FOX; 19 Jun–10 Jul 49 served on OS Fox; 8–29 Jan 50 served on OS NAN; 29 Mar–2 Apr 50 served on OS OBOE; 26 Jun–16 Jul 50 served on OS PETER; 10–30 Dec 50 served on OS SUGAR; 2–3 Jan 51 assisted MV *Keisin Maru* at 38°41′N, 152°00′E; 20 Jan–10 Feb 51 served on OS SUGAR; 23–25 Jan 51 assisted MV *Oregon Mail* at 46°35′N, 166°34′E; 7 Mar 51–31 May 74 stationed at Long Beach, CA, and used for LE, OS, and SAR; 27 May–17 Jun 51 served on OS NAN; 19 Aug–9 Sep 51 served on OS UNCLE; 21 Oct–14 Nov 51 served on OS UNCLE; 22 Dec 51–10 Jan 52 served on OS SUGAR; 2–23 Feb 52 served on OS VICTOR; 18 May–6 Jun 52 served on OS UNCLE; 11–31 Aug 52 served on OS NAN; 12 Oct–2 Nov 52 served on OS NAN; 4–25 Jan 53 served on OS NAN; 29 Mar–16 Apr 53 served on OS UNCLE; 18 Jun–12 Jul 53 served on OS UNCLE; 13 Sep–4 Oct 53 served on OS NAN; 9–26 Dec 53 served on OS VICTOR; 16 Jan–6 Feb 54 served on OS VICTOR; 23 May–14 Jan 54 served on OS NAN; 15 Aug–4 Sep 54 served on OS NAN; 8 Sep 54 assisted FV *American* at 33°08′N, 120°44′W; 30 Jan–20 Feb 55 served on OS NAN; 6–8 May 55 patrolled Ensenada Race; 26 Jun–17 Jul 55 served on OS NAN; 20 Nov–11 Dec 55

served on OS NAN; 15 Apr–6 May 56 served on OS NOVEMBER; 24 Aug 56 towed disabled schooner *Atlantic* to Kodiak, AK; 3–25 Mar 57 served on OS NOVEMBER; 1–22 Sep 57 served on OS NOVEMBER; 2–23 Nov 57 served on OS NOVEMBER; 8 Nov 57 searched for Pan American stratocruiser *Romance of the Skies* between San Francisco, CA, and Honolulu, HI—19 bodies recovered on sixth day of search; 30 Mar–19 Apr 58 served on OS NOVEMBER; 24 Aug–13 Sep 58 served on OS NOVEMBER; 22 Sep–14 Oct 58 served on OS ROMEO; 5–24 May 59 served on OS NOVEMBER; 14 Jun–4 Jul 59 served on OS NOVEMBER; 8 Jul 59 towed disabled FV *Ruth K* to Long Beach, CA; 7–28 Nov 59 served on OS NOVEMBER; 17–18 Dec 59 assisted MV *Guam Pioneer* at 31°23′N, 124°37′W; 6–23 Apr 60 served on OS NOVEMBER; 27 Aug–19 Sep 60 served on OS NOVEMBER; 22 Jan–12 Feb 61 served on OS NOVEMBER; 18 Jun–8 Jul 61 served on OS NOVEMBER; 28–29 Aug 61 towed disabled FV *Alaska Reefer* to Port Towsend, WA; 11–12 Feb 62 assisted FV *Western Fisher*; 10–13 Aug 62 served on reserve cruise; 30 Jul 67 rescued six from FV *Sea Boy* off California; 5 Jan–29 Sep 68 assigned to CG Squadron Three, Vietnam; 1 Mar 68 forced an enemy trawler to abandon its supply mission; 23 Mar–13 Apr 69 served on OS NOVEMBER; 27 Jul–17 Aug 69 served on OS NOVEMBER; 10 Oct–9 Nov 69 served on OS NOVEMBER; 22 Feb–15 Mar 70 served on OS NOVEMBER; 26 Apr–19 May 70 served on OS NOVEMBER; 7–28 Jun 70 served on OS NOVEMBER; 28 Jun–19 Jul 70 served on OS VICTOR; 20 Sep–11 Oct 70 served on OS NOVEMBER; 13 Dec 70–3 Jan 71 served on OS NOVEMBER; 7–28 Mar 71 served on OS VICTOR; 20 Jun–11 Jul 71 served on OS NOVEMBER; 12 SEP–3 Oct 71 served on OS NOVEMBER; 14 Nov–5 Dec 71 served on OS NOVEMBER; 6–27 Feb 72 served on OS NOVEMBER; 19 Mar–9 Apr 72 served on OS NOVEMBER; 21 May–11 Jun 72 served on OS NOVEMBER; 20 Jun 72 one killed and two seriously injured when a hot-water heater exploded while in Long Beach, CA; 2–23 Jul 72 served on OS NOVEMBER; 7–28 Jan 73 served on OS NOVEMBER; 18 Mar–8 Apr 73 served on OS NOVEMBER; 31 Jul–21 Aug 73 served on OS NOVEMBER; 7–29 Oct 73 served on OS NOVEMBER; 14 Dec 73–5 Jan 74 served on OS NOVEMBER; 21 Feb–13 Mar 74 served on OS NOVEMBER; 27 Apr–17 May 74 served on OS NOVEMBER.

Owasco

1946–47 stationed at Staten I., NY, and used for LE, OS, and SAR; 1948–50 stationed at Boston, MA, and used for LE, OS, and SAR; Feb 49 served on OS B; 1951–55 laid up in CG Yard, Curtis Bay, MD; 1956–27 Jun 73 stationed at New London, CT, and used for LE, OS, and SAR;

Cutter *Minnetonka* on 14 Sep 54. She still carries a twin 5-inch gun mount forward.

Oct–Nov 56 served on OS BRAVO; Jun–Jul 59 served on OS DELTA; Oct 61 served on OS DELTA; Jan 62 served on OS BRAVO; 24 Aug 65 grounded on Little Goshen Reef, New London, during cruise for dependents; Mar 67 served on OS BRAVO; 29 Sep–23 Oct 67 served on OS BRAVO; 26 Nov–19 Dec 67 served on OS DELTA; 23 Jul 68–21 Mar 69 assigned to CG Squadron Three, Vietnam; 21 Apr 69 medevaced crew member from Norwegian MV *Norefjell* 300 mi SE of Cape Hatteras; 1–24 Jul 69 served on OS BRAVO; 31 Oct–23 Nov 69 served on OS CHARLIE; 22 Mar–14 Apr 70 served on OS DELTA; 26 May–18 Jun 70 served on OS CHARLIE; 7–30 Aug 70 served on OS DELTA; 22 Oct–14 Nov 70 served on OS ECHO; 22 Dec 70–14 Jan 71 served on OS DELTA; 1–24 Mar 71 served on OS DELTA; 5–28 May 71 served on OS CHARLIE; 6–30 Jul 71 served on OS BRAVO; 3–27 Feb 72 served on OS DELTA; 23 Apr–16 May 72 served on OS CHARLIE; 29 Sep–23 Oct 72 served on OS CHARLIE; 15 Feb–9 Mar 73 served on OS DELTA; 2–23 May 73 served on OS ECHO.

Pontchartrain

1 Apr 46–23 Aug 48 stationed at Boston, MA, and used for LE, OS, and SAR; 20 Oct–10 Nov 46 served on OS C; 17 Oct 47–5 Sep 48 decommissioned and stored at CG Yard, Curtis Bay, MD; 5 Sep 48–12 Nov 49 stationed at Norfolk, VA, and used for LE, OS, and SAR; 6–11 Nov 48 served on OS EASY; 23 Jan–12 Feb 49 served on OS B; 18 Mar–8 Apr 49 served on OS FOX; 17 May–7 Jun 49 served on OS EASY; 17 Jul–6 Aug 49 served on OS DOG; 12 Nov 49–19 Oct 73 stationed at Long Beach, CA, and used for LE, OS, and SAR; 17 Feb–13 Mar 50 served on OS OBOE; 4 May 50 assisted disabled FV *Eta* near Catalina I.; 14 May–5 Jun 50 served on OS PETER; 4–27 Aug 50 served on OS NAN; 6–26 Mar 51 served on OS SUGAR; 13 Apr–5 May 51 served on OS SUGAR; 8–29 Jul 51 served on OS NAN; 21–29 Oct 51 served on OS NAN; 20 Nov–2 Dec 51 served on OS NAN; 23 Dec 51–13 Jan 52 served on OS UNCLE; 23 Feb–16 Mar 52 served on OS SUGAR; 5–25 Apr 52 served on OS SUGAR; 29 Jun–20 Jul 52 served on OS NAN; 22 Sep–12 Oct 52 served on OS NAN; 28 Jan–18 Feb 53 served on OS VICTOR; 30 Mar–20 Apr 53 served on OS SUGAR; 2–23 Jul 53 served on OS UNCLE; 25 Oct–15 Nov 53 served on OS UNCLE; 28 Feb–10 Mar 54 served on OS NAN; 25 Jul–15 Aug 54 served on OS NAN; 17 Oct–7 Nov 54 served on OS NAN; 19 Dec 54–10 Jan 55 served on OS NAN; 15 May–5 Jun 55 served on OS NAN; 20 Aug 55 escorted disabled American MV *John C*; 26–27 Aug 55 assisted disabled FV *Nina Ann*; 18 Sep–8 Oct 55 served on OS NAN; 12 Feb–4 Mar 56 served on OS NOVEMBER; 8–28 Jul 56 served on OS NOVEMBER; 30 Sep–16 Oct 56 served on OS NOVEMBER; while on OS NOVEMBER, on 16 Oct 56 rescued all on Pan American Clipper 943, which ditched 1/2 mi from cutter; 20 Nov 56 assisted LSM 455 aground on San Clemente I.; 21 Dec 56–13 Jan 57 served on OS NOVEMBER; 13 May–9 Jun 57 served on OS NOVEMBER; 26 Aug 57 assisted disabled FV *Modeoday* 2 mi N of North Point Pinos; 22 Sep–13 Oct 57 served on OS NOVEMBER; 22 Nov 57 assisted disabled yacht *Gosling* at 33°59′N, 120°16′W; 17 Feb–8 Mar 58 served on OS NOVEMBER; 25 Feb 58 assisted disabled yacht *Intrepid*; 13 Jul–3 Aug 58 served on OS NOVEMBER; 11–21 Aug 58 served on reserve training cruise; 14 Oct–4 Nov 58 served on OS ROMEO; 7–28 Dec 58 served on OS NOVEMBER; 18 Jan–7 Feb 59 served on OS NOVEMBER; 10 May 59 patrolled Ensenada Bay Race; 10 Jul 59 assisted FV

The *Owasco* refuels from a naval oiler off Vietnam in 1968. Twenty-eight high-endurance Coast Guard cutters served in Vietnamese waters between May 67 and Jan 72.

Carolyn Dee at 33°N, 120°W; 13–14 Jul 59 assisted MV *Mamie*; 27 Sep–17 Oct 59 served on OS NOVEMBER; 17 Jan 60 patrolled Acapulco Yacht Race; 20 Feb–12 Mar 60 served on OS NOVEMBER; 16 Jul–6 Aug 60 served on OS NOVEMBER; 20 Aug–3 Sep 60 served on reserve training cruise; 19 Oct 60 rescued three from ketch *Alpha* at 30°21′N, 117°56′W; 11–31 Dec 60 served on OS NOVEMBER; 22 Jan 61 medevaced patient from USNS *Richfield*; 7–27 May 61 served on OS NOVEMBER; 30 Apr 63 assisted disabled FV *Gaga* 10 mi E of San Nicolas I.; 10–31 Mar 68 served on OS NOVEMBER; 12 May–2 Jun 68 served on OS NOVEMBER; 14 Jul–4 Aug 68 served on OS NOVEMBER; 25 Aug–15 Sep 68 served on OS NOVEMBER; 19 Jan–9 Feb 69 served on OS VICTOR; 2–23 Mar 69 served on OS VICTOR; 25 May–14 Jun 69 served on OS NOVEMBER; 17 Aug–7 Sep 69 served on OS NOVEMBER; 30 Nov–18 Dec 69 served on OS NOVEMBER; 31 Mar–2 Jul 70 assigned to CG Squadron Three, Vietnam; 22 Aug–12 Sep 71 served on OS VICTOR; 3–24 Oct 71 served on OS VICTOR; 8–28 Jun 72 served on OS CHARLIE; 15 Aug–8 Sep 72 served on OS DELTA; 29 Jan–23 Feb 73 served on OS ECHO; 24 Apr–17 May 73 served on OS DELTA; 6–26 Sep 73 served on OS CHARLIE.

Sebago

1 Nov 45–1 Jun 46 stationed at Norfolk, VA, and used for LE, OS, and SAR; 1 Jun 46–15 Aug 47 stationed at Boston, MA, and used for LE, OS, and SAR; 15 Aug 47–31 Oct 49 stationed at Staten I., NY, and used for LE, OS, and SAR; Jan 49 served on OS CHARLIE; 27 Apr 49 rescued four crewmen from MATS C-47 ac that ditched some 380 mi off Newfoundland; Apr–May 49 served on OS DOG; Jun–Jul 49 served on OS CHARLIE; 31 Oct 49–17 Dec 52 decommissioned and stored at CG Yard, Curtis Bay, MD; 17 Dec 52–1 Jul 54 recommissioned and stationed at Boston, MA, and used for LE, OS, and SAR; Jun 53 served on OS

HOTEL; Dec 53 served on OS HOTEL; 1 Jul 54–Jul 64 stationed at Mobile, AL, and used for LE, SAR, and Campeche Patrol; 2 Jan 62 towed disabled MV *Catalina* 310 mi off New Orleans, LA; Jul 64–29 Feb 72 stationed at Pensacola, FL, and used for LE, OS, and SAR; Apr–May 65 served on OS ECHO; late 65 repaired FV *Robbie Dale* near Cayos Arcas; 18 Dec 66 helped fight fire at Frisco Pier, Pensacola, FL; 29 Jun–23 Jul 67 served on OS BRAVO; 30 Aug–23 Sep 67 served on OS ECHO; 28 May–20 Jun 68 served on OS ECHO; 5–28 Aug 68 served on OS ECHO; 2 Mar–16 Nov 69 assigned to CG Squadron Three, Vietnam; 18–19 Dec 69 placed a damage-control party on MV *Jody Re*, brought flooding under control, and stood by until a commercial tug arrived; 20 Dec 69 stood by grounded Danish MV *Helle* 25 mi NE of Cabo Falso until a commercial tug arrived; 11 Feb–6 Mar 70 served on OS ECHO; 26 Apr–19 May 70 served on OS BRAVO; 27 Jul–19 Aug 70 served on OS BRAVO; 14 Jan 71–6 Feb 71 served on OS DELTA; 30 Mar–23 Apr 71 served on OS ECHO; 24 Jun–14 Jul 71 served on OS DELTA; 18 Sep–8 Oct 71 served on OS BRAVO; 1–21 Dec 71 served on OS DELTA.

Wachusett

1946 stationed at Port Angeles, WA, and used for LE, OS, and SAR; 1947–48 stationed at Juneau, AK, and used for LE, Bering Sea Patrol, and SAR; 1949–30 Aug 73 stationed at Seattle, WA, and used for LE, OS, and SAR; Jan–Feb 50 served on OS NAN; Oct 50 served on OS NAN; Feb 51 served on OS SUGAR; Feb–Apr 51 served on OS SUGAR; Jun–Jul 51 served on OS UNCLE; Nov–Dec 51 served on OS UNCLE; Feb–Mar 52 served on OS VICTOR; May–Jun 52 served on OS NAN; Aug–Sep 52 served on OS NAN; 3–23 Nov 52 served on OS QUEEN; Mar 53 served on OS VICTOR; May 53 served on OS SUGAR; Oct 53 served on OS QUEEN; Dec 53 served on OS NAN; May–Jun 54 served on OS NAN; Jan 55 served on OS NAN; Apr–May 55 served on OS NAN; Jul–Aug 55 served on OS NAN; Oct–Nov 55 served on OS NAN; Dec 55 served on OS NOVEMBER; Mar 56 served on OS NOVEMBER; Jul–Aug 56 served on OS NOVEMBER; Dec 56 served on OS NOVEMBER; Apr–May 57 served on OS NOVEMBER; 12 May 57 rescued two crew members from a USAF B-57 when they bailed out between Honolulu, HI, and San Francisco, CA; Jan–Feb 58 served on OS NOVEMBER; 11 Feb 58 assisted tug USS *Yuma* towing USS *Tinian* 10 mi WSW of Cape Flattery; Apr–May 58 served on OS NOVEMBER; Jun–Jul 58 served on OS NOVEMBER; Nov 58 served on OS NOVEMBER; Mar–Apr 59 served on OS NOVEMBER; Sep 59 served on OS NOVEMBER; Nov–Dec 59 served on OS NOVEMBER; Jan–Feb 60 served on OS NOVEMBER; Jul 60 served on OS NOVEMBER; Nov–Dec 60 served on OS NOVEMBER; Apr–May 61 served on OS NOVEMBER; Sep 61 served on OS NOVEMBER; 14 Apr 64 rescued four from FV *Mary Carol* E of Chiniak Bay, AK; 18–22 May 64 stood by disabled Chinese MV *Taihsing* in N Pacific until commercial tug arrived; 19 Aug 64 located barge *Lumberjack* adrift off California; 5 Jun 65 seized Japanese FV *Wakashio Maru* for violation of 1953 International Fishing Convention east of 175°W; 28 Jan–18 Feb 68 served on OS NOVEMBER; 31 Mar–21 Apr 68 served on OS NOVEMBER; 10 Sep 68–1 Jun 69 assigned to CG Squadron Three, Vietnam; 9–30 Nov 69 served on OS NOVEMBER; 1–22 Feb 70 served on OS NOVEMBER; 15 Mar–5 Apr 70 served on OS NOVEMBER; 7–28 Jun 70 served on OS NOVEMBER; 19 Jul–9 Aug 70 served on OS VICTOR; 11 Oct–1 Nov

70 served on OS NOVEMBER; 14 Feb–7 Mar 71 served on OS NOVEMBER; 30 May–20 Jun 71 served on OS VICTOR; 11 Jul–1 Aug 71 served on OS VICTOR; 5–26 Dec 71 served on OS NOVEMBER; 16 Jan–6 Feb 72 served on OS NOVEMBER; 30 Apr–21 May 72 served on OS NOVEMBER; 24 Sep–15 Oct 72 served on OS NOVEMBER; 17 Dec 72–7 Jan 73 served on OS NOVEMBER; 3–24 May 73 served on OS NOVEMBER; 10–31 Jul 73 served on OS NOVEMBER.

Winnebago

1945–Apr 46 stationed at Miami, FL, and used for LE, OS, and SAR; Apr 46–Feb 48 stationed at Boston, MA, and used for LE, OS, and SAR; Feb–Sep 48 laid up in CG Yard, Curtis Bay, MD; Nov 49–Mar 72 stationed at Honolulu, HI, and used for LE, OS, and SAR; Oct 50 served on OS SUGAR; Jan 51–Jul 51 served on OS NAN; Sep–Oct 51 served on OS UNCLE; Jul 52 served on OS SUGAR; Oct 52 served on OS QUEEN; 14 Dec 52–4 Jan 53 served on OS QUEEN; Mar–Apr 53 served on OS QUEEN; Jun 53 served on OS VICTOR; Aug 53 served on OS SUGAR; Dec 53 served on OS VICTOR; Mar–Apr 54 served on OS VICTOR; Sep 54 served on OS VICTOR; Dec 54–Feb 55 served on OS VICTOR; Jul–Aug 55 served on OS VICTOR; Oct 55 served on OS VICTOR; Dec 55 served on OS VICTOR; May–Jul 56 served on OS VICTOR; Oct–Dec 56 served on OS VICTOR; May–Jun 57 served on OS VICTOR; Oct–Nov 57 served on OS VICTOR; Mar–May 58 served on OS VICTOR; Sep–Oct 58 served on OS VICTOR; Feb–Apr 59 served on OS VICTOR; Aug–Sep 59 served on OS VICTOR; Jan–Mar 60 served on OS VICTOR; Jul 60 served on OS VICTOR; Jan–Mar 61 served on OS VICTOR; Jun–Jul 61 served on OS VICTOR; Nov 63 served on OS VICTOR; Nov 63 towed disabled MV *Green Mountain State* 810 mi to Midway I.; Feb–Mar 65 served on OS VICTOR, replacing damaged *Chautauqua*; 27 May 65 medevaced disabled seaman from Japanese FV *Tsuru Maru Nr. 8* 650 mi S of Honolulu, HI; 14 Jul 65 hoisted disabled PC on board 53 mi S of Honolulu, HI; 27 Mar–17 Apr 66 served on OS VICTOR; 8–29 May 66 served on OS VICTOR and provided medical assistance to USS *Navasota*; late May 66 provided medical assistance to Japanese MV *Shoei Maru*; May 67 served on OS VICTOR—medevaced an injured crewman from FV *Shoei Maru* and transferred him to MV *Texas Maru*; 12 May–2 Jun 68 served on OS VICTOR; 20 Sep 68–19 Jul 69 assigned to CG Squadron Three, Vietnam; 19 Oct–9 Nov 69 served on OS VICTOR; 30 Nov–18 Dec 69 served on OS VICTOR; 1–22 Feb 70 served on OS VICTOR; 25 Feb 70 transferred medical team to assist MV *Sylvia Lykes* near Midway I.; 19 May–7 Jun 70 served on OS VICTOR; 9–30 Aug 70 served on OS VICTOR; 11 Oct–1 Nov 70 served on OS VICTOR; 13 Dec 70–3 Jan 71 served on OS VICTOR; 24 Jan–14 Feb 71 served on OS VICTOR; 28 Mar–18 Apr 71 served on OS NOVEMBER; 20 Jun–11 Jul 71 served on OS VICTOR; 3–24 Oct 71 served on OS NOVEMBER; Mar 72–27 Feb 73 stationed at Wilmington, NC, and used for LE, OS, and SAR; 28 Jun–18 Jul 72 served on OS CHARLIE; 4–13 Sep 72 served on OS HOTEL; 18 Sep–8 Oct 72 served on OS ECHO; 16 Dec 72–7 Jan 73 served on OS ECHO; 9–29 Mar 73 served on OS DELTA.

Winona

15 Aug 46–11 Sep 47 stationed at San Pedro, CA, and used for LE, OS, and SAR; 2–22 Oct 46 served on OS DOG; 1–21 Dec 46 served on OS DOG; 30 Jan–19 Feb 47 served on OS DOG; 31 Mar–20 Apr 47 served

on OS ABLE; 30 May–19 Jun 47 served on OS FOX; 11 Sep 47–31 May 74 stationed at Port Angeles, WA, and used for LE, OS, and SAR; 29 Jul–18 Aug 47 served on OS FOX; 16–23 Dec 47 served on OS FOX; 28 Dec 47–6 Jan 48 served on OS FOX; 15 Apr–4 May 48 served on OS FOX; Jul 48 served on OS FOX; 19–22 Sep 48 served on OS ABLE; 26–29 Sep 48 served on OS ABLE; 17 Nov 48 towed disabled MV *Herald of Morning*; 18–21 Nov 48 served on OS FOX; 19–28 Mar 49 served on OS ABLE; 10 Jun 49 assisted FV *Alice B* 2 mi off South Amphitrite Point; 10–31 Jul 49 served on OS ABLE; 30 Sep–21 Oct 49 served on OS FOX; 17–19 Dec 49 served on OS PETER; 13 Feb 50 towed disabled MV *Edgecombe* to Seattle, WA; Apr 50 served on OS NAN; 5–25 Jun 50 served on OS OBOE; 10 Sep–4 Oct 50 served on OS SUGAR; 29 Oct–19 Nov 50 served on OS SUGAR; 22 Jan–11 Feb 51 served on OS NAN; 15 Apr–5 May 51 served on OS NAN; 16 Jun 51 escorted FV *Sea Lark* to Ketchikan, AK; 7–29 Jul 51 served on OS UNCLE; 29 Sep–21 Oct 51 served on OS SUGAR; 10–31 Nov 51 served on OS VICTOR; 2–24 Feb 52 served on OS NAN; 18–19 Mar 52 assisted and towed disabled MV *Darton* until relieved by commercial tug; 27 Apr–18 May 52 served on OS NAN; 20 Jul–11 Aug 52 served on OS NAN; 15 Oct–1 Nov 52 served on OS VICTOR; 22 Nov–12 Dec 52 served on OS SUGAR; 23–25 Dec 52 assisted MV *Maple Cove* at 48°22′N, 134°26′W; 7–29 Mar 53 served on OS QUEEN; 31 May–21 Jun 53 served on OS NAN; 22 Aug–13 Sep 53 served on OS NAN; 18 Nov–9 Dec 53 served on OS VICTOR; 13 Feb 54 assisted FV *Western Fisherman*; 22 Mar–11 Apr 54 served on OS NAN; 4–25 Jul 54 served on OS NAN; 29 Nov–19 Dec 54 served on OS NAN; 20 Dec 54 medevaced crewman from MV *General Pope*; 3–24 Apr 55 served on OS NAN; 7 Aug 55 patrolled Gold Cup Races, Seattle, WA; 28 Aug–18 Sep 55 served on OS NAN; 22 Jan–12 Feb 56 served on OS NAN; Jul–Sep 56 served on Bering Sea Patrol; 11 Nov–2 Dec 56 served on OS NOVEMBER; 7–28 Apr 57 served on OS NOVEMBER; 2–27 Nov 57 served on OS NOVEMBER; 5–26 Jan 58 served on OS NOVEMBER; 6–22 Jun 58 served on OS NOVEMBER; 31 Aug–22 Sep 58 served on OS ROMEO; 25 Oct–16 Nov 58 served on OS NOVEMBER; 22 Mar–14 Apr 59 served on OS NOVEMBER; 16 Aug–6 Sep 59 served on OS NOVEMBER; 10–31 Jan 60 served on OS NOVEMBER; 5–26 Jun 60 served on OS NOVEMBER; 30 Oct–20 Nov 60 served on OS NOVEMBER; 26 Mar–15 Apr 61 served on OS NOVEMBER; 12 Aug–5 Sep 61 served on OS NOVEMBER; 20 Jul–21 Sep 63 conducted Bering Sea Patrol; 25 Jan–17 Oct 68 assigned to CG Squadron Three, Vietnam; 31 Jan 69 stood by MV *Belmona* following a fire 15 mi SW of Cape Flattery until commercial tugs arrived; 13 Apr–4 May 69 served on OS NOVEMBER; 15 Jun–6 Jul 69 served on OS NOVEMBER; 20 Jul 69 assisted following the sinking of a barge loaded with diesel fuel near Admiralty Inlet; 28 Sep–19 Oct 69 served on OS NOVEMBER; 18 Dec 69–11 Jan 70 served on OS NOVEMBER; 22 Feb–15 Mar 70 served on OS VICTOR; 5 Apr–26 May 70 served on OS NOVEMBER; 9–30 Aug 70 served on OS NOVEMBER; 28 Oct 70 provided medical assistance to *Urea Maru* 300 mi off San Francisco, CA; 1–22 Nov 70 served on OS NOVEMBER; 24 Jan–14 Feb 71 served on OS NOVEMBER; 1–22 Aug 71 served on OS NOVEMBER; 14 Nov–5 Dec 71 served on OS VICTOR; 26 Dec 71–16 Jan 72 served on OS VICTOR; 15 Sep–7 Oct 73 served on OS NOVEMBER; 22 Nov–14 Dec 73 served on OS NOVEMBER; 13 Mar–4 Apr 74 served on OS NOVEMBER.

PROJECTED 327-FOOT CLASS

Name	Hull Number	Builder	Keel Laid	Launched	Commissioned	Disposition
—	bn CG-83	—	—	—	—	—
—	bn CG-84	—	—	—	—	—
—	bn CG-85	—	—	—	—	—

Cost	N/A	Electronics	
Hull		Detection Radar	none
Displacement (tons)	N/A	Sonar	N/A
Length	327′ oa; 208′ bp	Armament	4 5″/38 (single); 3 1.5″ (quad) AA; dc tracks; 1 Y-gun
Beam	41′ mb		
Draft	N/A		

Cost   N/A

Hull
Displacement (tons)   N/A
Length   327′ oa; 208′ bp
Beam   41′ mb
Draft   N/A

Machinery
Main Engines   2 double-reduction geared turbines
Main Boilers   2
SHP   N/A
Propellers   twin

Performance
Designed Speed   20 kts (1941)

Aircraft   1 SOC-4

Logistics
Fuel Oil (95%)   N/A
Complement   20 officers, 210 men (1941)

Electronics
Detection Radar   none
Sonar   N/A

Armament   4 5″/38 (single); 3 1.5″ (quad) AA; dc tracks; 1 Y-gun

Design

The projected 327-foot-class cutters were to be replacements for *Ossipee* (1915), *Tallapoosa* (1915), and *Unalga* (1912). In the spring of 1941 the Coast Guard was authorized to build ten 255-foot cutters to replace the 250-foot cutters transferred to Great Britain under lend-lease. The projected 327s were canceled in favor of building 13 255s.

Within the projected 327 design one can clearly see the Coast Guard preparing for war. The aircraft, serviced by a crane, was retained. The armament suite was substantially increased, a sound room (sonar) was added, and minesweeping gear was mounted on the stern.

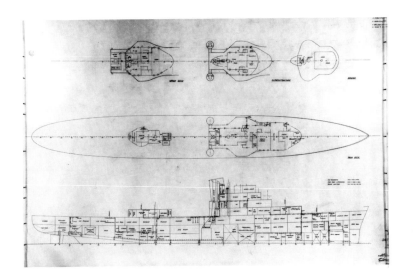
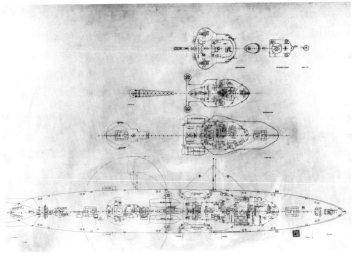
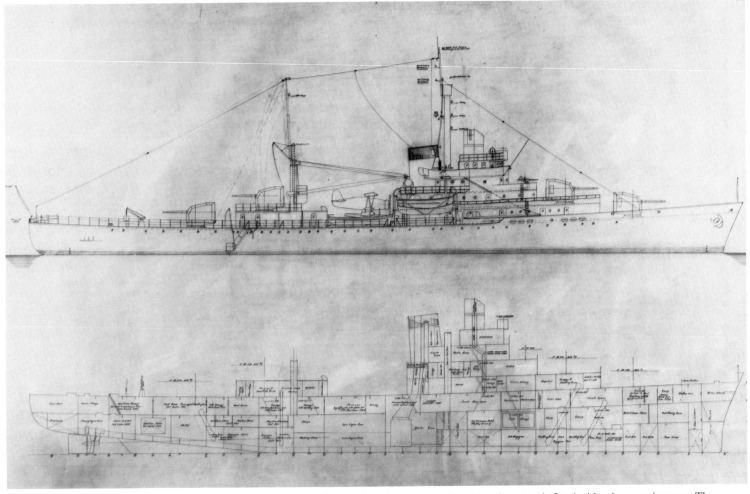

Plans for the projected 327-foot class, dated 17 Mar 41. Note that the aircraft was retained and that the cutter is fitted with minesweeping gear. The armament is similar to the one that *Taney* carried between 1942 and 1944.

327-FOOT CUTTERS ("SECRETARY") CLASS, *CAMPBELL* CLASS, *BIBB* CLASS, *HAMILTON* CLASS

Name	Hull Number	Builder	Keel Laid	Launched	Commissioned	Disposition
Bibb (ex-*George M. Bibb*)	WHEC 31 WPG 31	Charleston Navy Yard, Charleston, SC	15 Aug 35	14 Jan 37	10 Mar 37	*Decomm* 30 Sep 85
Campbell (ex-*George W. Campbell*)	WHEC 32 WPG 32	Philadelphia Navy Yard, Philadelphia, PA	1 May 35	3 Jan 36	16 Jun 36	*Decomm* 1 Apr 82 Sunk as a target 29 Nov 84
Duane (ex-*William J. Duane*)	WHEC 33 WPG 33	Philadelphia Navy Yard, Philadelphia, PA	1 May 35	3 Jun 36	1 Aug 36	*Decomm* 1 Aug 85 Sunk as a reef 27 Nov 87
Ingham (ex-*Sammuel D. Ingham*)	WHEC 35 WPG 35	Philadelphia Navy Yard, Philadelphia, PA	1 May 35	3 Jun 36	17 Sep 36	*Decomm* 27 May 88
Spencer (ex-*John C. Spencer*)	WHEC 36 WPG 36	New York Navy Yard, New York, NY	11 Sep 35	6 Jan 37	1 Mar 37	*Decomm* special status Engineering Training School 23 Jan 74; *decomm* 15 Dec 80; *sold* 8 Oct 81
Taney (ex-*Roger B. Taney*)	WHEC 37 WPG 37	Philadelphia Navy Yard, Philadelphia, PA	1 May 35	3 Jun 36	24 Oct 36	*Decomm* 7 Dec 86 & *trans* to city of Baltimore

Cost	$2,468,460 each
Hull	
Displacement (tons)	2,656 fl (1954), 1,837 light (1965)
Length	327′ oa; 308′ wl
Beam	41′ wl; 41′2″ max
Draft	15′3″ max (1965)
Machinery	
Main Engines	2 Westinghouse double-reduction geared turbines
Main Boilers	2 Babcock & Wilcox sectional express, air-encased, 400 psi, 200°F superheat
SHP	6,200 total
Propellers	twin, 3 blades
Performance	
Max Sustained	19.5 kts, 3,640-mi radius (1965)
Economic	10.5 kts, 9,100-mi radius (1965)
Logistics	
Fuel Oil (95%)	147,000 gal
Complement	10 officers, 3 warrants, 134 men (1965)
Electronics	
Radar	SPS-23, SPS-29, Mk 26 (*Bibb*, 1965; *Taney* 1866)
Sonar	SQS-11 (*Bibb*, 1965; *Taney*, 1966)
Armament	1 5″/38; 1 Hedgehog; 1 Mk 32 TT (*Bibb*, 1965; *Taney*, 1966)

Design

The 327s were designed to meet changing missions of the service as it emerged from the Prohibition era. Because the air-passenger trade was expanding both at home and overseas, the Coast Guard believed that the cutter-based aircraft would be essential for future high-seas search and rescue. Also, during the mid-1930s narcotics smuggling, mostly opium, was on the increase, and long-legged, fairly fast cutters were needed to curtail it. The 327s were an attempt to develop a 20-knot cutter capable of carrying an airplane in a hangar. A preliminary Coast Guard design effort married these desires to the basic qualities of the 250-foot cutters. The resulting design was 316′ x 46′6″ x 16′ on 2,350 tons of displacement—a very broad, deep cutter. The design was a single-screw ship costing $1,500,000—not quite half the cost of the final product. Concurrently, the Navy was developing a 20-knot, 2,000-ton design. After comparison, the Coast Guard selected the Navy design and heavily modified it. The final 327 design was based on the *Erie*-class gunboats; the machinery plant and hull below the waterline were identical. The standardization cut costs of designing and building. In fact, on 23 Jan 46 the Coast Guard requested the USS *Charleston* from the Navy on the basis "of her construction along the lines of the 327-ft. cutters. . . ." This request was withdrawn due to manpower shortage.

Thirty-two preliminary designs based upon the *Erie* class were drawn up before one was finally selected. The healthy sheer forward and the high slope in the deck in the wardroom was known as the "Hunnewell Hump." Commander (Constructor) F. G. Hunnewell, USCG, was head of the Construction and Repair Department at that time.

There is ample evidence that all of the class carried aircraft prior to 1941. In 1941 the CG invited bids for three new cutters. Shaft horsepower was raised to 6,500 but in most respects, these ships were to have been similar to the 327s. Because of wartime demands, the money allocated was used instead to construct the 255s.

All units carried full names until May–June 1937. At that time, names were shortened to surnames only. One sister, the *Alexander Hamilton*, was sunk by *U-132* on 30 Jan 42.

Bibb

1946–47 stationed at Boston, MA, and used for LE, OS, and SAR; 1947–May 69 stationed at New Bedford, MA, and used for LE, OS, and SAR; Oct 47 served on OS CHARLIE; 14 Oct 47 rescued 69 from commercial ac *Bermuda Sky Queen* during a gale in mid-Atlantic; 15 Feb 48 rescued 40 and a dog from Portuguese FV *Gasper* some 300 mi off Newfoundland; May–Jun 49 served on OS ABLE; Aug 49 served on OS DOG; Jun–Jul

Cutter *Bibb* toward the end of her career. In one of the Coast Guard's most dramatic rescues, she saved 69 in mid-Atlantic from the downed commercial aircraft, the Bermuda Sky Queen, during a gale on 14 Oct 47.

50 served on OS HOW; Oct 50 served on OS DOG; Dec 50 served on OS EASY; Mar–Apr 52 served on OS CHARLIE; Nov–Dec 52 served on OS ECHO; Feb 53 served on OS COCA; Jul 53 served on OS DELTA; Mar–Apr 54 served on OS BRAVO; Mar–Apr 56 served on OS BRAVO; Jun 56 served on OS CHARLIE; Aug 56 served on OS DELTA; Dec 56 served on OS DELTA; Aug–Sep 57 served on OS DELTA; May–Jun 58 served on OS ECHO; Jul–Aug 58 served on OS DELTA; Feb–Mar 59 served on OS CHARLIE; Jul 59 served on OS CHARLIE; Apr 60 served on OS CHARLIE; Jun–Jul 60 served on OS ECHO; May 65 served on OS CHARLIE; 24–25 Jan 66 escorted disabled MV *South African Victory* to Boston, MA; Apr 66 served on OS DELTA; 24 Aug–14 Sep 67 served on OS CHARLIE; 4 Jul 68–28 Feb 69 assigned to CG Squadron Three, Vietnam; May 69–Oct 73 stationed at Boston, MA, and used for LE, OS, and SAR; 19 Jun–12 Jul 69 served on OS DELTA; 3–26 Sep 69 served on OS ECHO; 2 Nov 69 towed disabled MV *Caravan* 150 mi SE of Cape Fear to safety; 8–31 Jan 70 served on OS CHARLIE; 14 Aug–6 Sep 70 served on OS ECHO; 2–25 Nov 70 served on OS CHARLIE; 3–26 Jan 71 served on OS BRAVO; 5–29 Aug 71 served on OS CHARLIE; 14 Oct–7 Nov 71 served on OS DELTA; 31 Dec 71–22 Jan 72 served on OS CHARLIE; 10 Jun–4 Jul 72 served on OS ECHO; Sep 72 medevaced crewman from Greek MV *Christia* midway between Bermuda and the Azores; 23 Oct–17 Nov 72 served on OS CHARLIE; 11–20 Jan 73 served on OS HOTEL; 26 Jan–15 Feb 73 served on OS DELTA; 11 Apr–2 May 73 served on OS ECHO; 12 Jun–3 Jul 73 served

on OS ECHO; 27 Sep–17 Oct 73 served on OS BRAVO; Oct 73–30 Sep 85 stationed at New Bedford, MA, and used for LE, OS, and SAR; 26 Nov–16 Dec 73 served on OS BRAVO; 16 May–7 Jun 74 served on OS BRAVO; 5–27 Dec 75 served on OS HOTEL; 17 Jul 82 seized MV *Grimurkamban* 270 mi SE of Cape Cod with 50t of marijuana on board; Jul 82 seized MV *Rio Panuco* with 50t of marijuana on board; Jul–Aug 82 seized FV *Shanti* after crew threw approximately 3t of marijuana overboard; 23 May 83 seized FV 50 mi SE of Cape Cod for fishing violation; 10 Nov 84 seized Turkish *Captain Joe* 100 mi E of Honduras carrying 10t of marijuana.

Campbell

1946–17 Sep 53 stationed at Brooklyn, NY, and used for LE, OS, and SAR; 17 Jun–8 Jul 46 served on OS C; 28 Jul–18 Aug 46 served on OS C; 20 Oct–8 Nov 46 served on OS A; 22 Nov 46 assisted MV *Theodore Parker*; mid-Dec 46 served on OS E; Jan 47 stationed at Stapleton, Staten I., NY, and used primarily for LE, OS, and SAR; 7 Mar 47 assisted MV *Lord Delaware* off New York; 12 Mar 47 assisted MV *Josiah Macy* off New York; Jun–Aug 47 served on cadet practice cruise; 31 Jan–21 Feb 48 served on OS ABLE; Jun–Aug 48 served on cadet practice cruise; 10 Oct–1 Nov 48 served on OS CHARLIE; 4–12 Mar 49 served on OS ABLE; 15–25 Mar 49 served on OS ABLE; Jun–Aug 49 served on cadet practice cruise visiting Europe and Africa; 21 Sep–23 Nov 49 served on OS EASY; 14 Dec 49–4 Jan 50 served on OS EASY; 1–25 Mar 50 served on OS DOG; 4

Jun–2 Aug 51 served on cadet cruise to Europe; 27 Oct–17 Nov 51 served on OS BAKER; 19 Jan–9 Feb 52 served on OS ABLE; 8 Jun–6 Sep 52 served on cadet cruise visiting Europe; 7 Aug 52 assisted tanker *Esso Brussels* at 28°00′N, 45°58′W; 24 Oct–13 Nov 52 served on OS COCA; 1–31 Jan 53 served on OS BRAVO; 26 Jan 53 assisted MV *Dtrangajoekwill* at 58°20′N, 44°05′W; 10–30 Mar 53 served on OS HOTEL; 30 Mar 53 assisted tug *Marion Moran* at 35°19′N, 71°52′W; 13 Jun–3 Jul 53 served on OS ECHO; 17 Sep 53–2 Sep 69 stationed at St. George, Staten I., NY, and used primarily for LE, OS, and SAR; 24 Oct–13 Nov 53 served on OS DELTA; 14–18 Nov 53 stood by disabled MV *Empress Nene* at 42°04′N, 44°46′W until commercial tug arrived; 26 Dec 53 assisted MV *Oklahoma* at 50°40′N, 45°00′W; 1–2 Jan 54 escorted distressed USNS *Nodaway* from 46°40′N, 54°53′W, to Argentia, Newfoundland; 5 Jan 54 medevaced crewman from cutter *Casco* at 45°32′N, 49°06′W; 8 Jan 54 medevaced crewman from MV *Dick Lykes* at 45°07′N, 54°53′W and carried him to Argentia; 20 Feb–12 Mar 54 served on OS COCA; Mar–Apr 54 served on OS BRAVO; 4–24 May 54 served on OS HOTEL; 9–30 Oct 54 served on OS ECHO; 1–22 Jan 55 served on OS COCA; 28 Mar–8 Apr 55 served on OS BRAVO; 27 May 55–3 Sep 55 served on cadet cruise visiting Europe and Bermuda; 12 Nov–2 Dec 55 served on OS COCA; 27 Jan–17 Feb 56 served on OS BRAVO; 9 Jun–11 Aug 56 served on cadet cruise to the Caribbean; 14 Sep 56 medevaced patient from MV *Andrew Jackson* at 40°39′N, 53°34′W; 18 Sep–9 Oct 56 served on OS CHARLIE; 26 Jan–16 Feb 57 served on OS ECHO; 9–30 Apr 57 served on OS BRAVO; 6–26 Aug 57 served on OS DELTA; 26 Oct–15 Nov 57 served on OS ECHO; 6–27 Jan 58 served on OS BRAVO; 30 Aug 58 assisted disabled PC *Golden Eye* to safety; 29 Oct 58 medevaced disabled crewman from MV *Amelie Thyssen*; 4–24 Nov 58 served on OS CHARLIE; 19 Jan–9 Feb 59 served on OS BRAVO; 30 Jan–1 Feb 59 unsuccessfully searched for Danish MV *Hans Hedtoft*, which struck an iceberg near 59°5′N, 43°00′W; 5–26 Apr 59 served on OS DELTA; 20 Jun–10 Jul 59 served on OS CHARLIE; 12 Oct–3 Nov 59 served on OS ECHO; 1–21 Dec 59 served on OS BRAVO; 23 Dec 59 stood by MV *Regina* at 43°33′N, 58°28′W until commercial tug arrived; 29 Apr–21 May 60 served on OS CHARLIE; 10 May 60 transferred two medics to MV *Empress*; 27 May 60 medevaced patient from MV *Avafors*; 18 Jul–8 Aug 60 served on OS BRAVO; 18 Aug 61 assisted MV *Donna Rae* at 44°N, 52′W; Jan 62 served on OS ECHO; Jul 62 served on OS CHAR-LIE; 2 Aug 62 medevaced crewman from MV *Sommersworth* at 39°44′N, 71°35′W; 3–4 Mar 63 medevaced crewman from MV *Amphitrite* at 24°33′N, 53°11′W; Apr 63 served on OS ECHO; 21 Apr 63 rescued crew from sinking MV *Helga Smith* 50 mi SE of Cape Race, Newfoundland; Feb–Mar 67 served on OS ECHO; 14 Dec 67–12 Aug 68 assigned to CG Squadron Three, Vietnam; 1–23 Jan 69 served on OS BRAVO; 11 May–3 Jun 69 served on OS ECHO; 26 Jun–19 Jul 69 served on OS ECHO; 2 Sep 69–Jun 74 stationed at Portland, ME, and used for LE, OS, and SAR; 23 Nov–16 Dec 69 served on OS CHARLIE; 16 Feb–11 Mar 70 served on OS BRAVO; 21 Apr–14 May 70 served on OS ECHO; 18 Feb–13 Mar 71 served on OS BRAVO; 20 Jun–14 Jul 71 served on OS CHARLIE; 25 Aug–18 Sep 71 served on OS BRAVO; 7 Nov–1 Dec 71 served on OS DELTA; 10 Jan–3 Feb 72 served on OS DELTA; 25 Mar–20 Apr 72 served on OS ECHO; 2–26 Jun 72 served on OS DELTA; 7–29 Jan 73 served on OS ECHO; 27 Mar–17 Apr 73 served on OS BRAVO; 10 Jun–4 Jul 73 served on OS DELTA; 16 Oct–6 Nov 73 served on OS

CHARLIE; 18 Dec 73–11 Jan 74 served on OS HOTEL; 20 Feb 74–1 Apr 82 stationed at Port Angeles, WA, and used for LE and SAR; Jan 77 conducted Gulf of Alaska current survey; Sep 77 conducted Gulf of Alaska current survey; Jan 78 conducted Gulf of Alaska survey.

Duane

1939–Aug 72 stationed at Boston, MA, and used for LE, OS, and SAR; 11 May–5 Jun 46 served on OS C; 29 Sep–20 Oct 46 served on OS C; 10 Nov–3 Dec 46 served on OS C; 10–29 Jan 47 served on OS C; 4–27 Apr 47 served on OS ABLE; 10–23 May 47 served on OS C; 2–23 Aug 47 served on OS C; 15–22 Oct 47 served on OS CHARLIE; 26 Oct–8 Nov 47 served on OS ABLE; 17 Jan–6 Feb 48 served on OS CHARLIE; 24 Mar–15 Apr 48 served on OS ABLE; 17 Jul–13 Aug 48 served on OS ABLE; 29 Sep–20 Oct 48 served on OS CHARLIE; 10 Nov–3 Dec 48 served on OS CHARLIE; 10–29 Jan 49 served on OS CHARLIE; 6–27 Apr 49 served on OS ABLE; 10 May–5 Jun 49 served on OS CHARLIE; 17 Jun–9 Jul 49 served on OS ABLE; 2–23 Aug 49 served on OS CHAR-LIE; 15–22 Oct 49 served on OS CHARLIE; 16 Nov–10 Dec 49 served on OS CHARLIE; 1–22 Feb 50 served on OS HOW; 28 Apr–20 May 50 served on OS BAKER; 12 Jul–1 Aug 50 served on OS EASY; 1–22 Oct 50 served on OS DOG; 29 Nov 50 assisted FV *Caracana* at 42°56′N, 66°26′W; 12 Dec 50–4 Jan 51 served on OS HOW; 27 Feb–21 Mar 51 served on OS EASY; 29–30 Apr 51 assisted MV *Jytte Skou* at 30°31′N, 66°17′W; 18 May–8 Jun 51 served on OS CHARLIE; 3–25 Aug 51 served on OS BAKER; 24 Oct–14 Nov 51 served on OS HOW; 9–27 Jan 52 served on OS EASY—cutter placed in quarantine at Bermuda due to medical problems; 29 Mar–19 Apr 52 served on OS DOG; 26 Jun–11 Jul 52 served on OS CHARLIE; 5–26 Sep 52 served on OS BRAVO; 24 Nov–14 Dec 52 served on OS HOTEL; 15 Dec 52 assisted grounded tug; 6–27 Feb 53 served on OS ECHO; 8–30 May 53 served on OS DELTA; 13 Jul–3 Aug 53 served on OS HOTEL; 4–25 Sep 53 served on OS ECHO; 16 Jan–6 Feb 54 served on OS DELTA; 12 Mar–3 Apr 54 served on OS ECHO; 5 May–18 Jun 54 served on OS BRAVO; 14 Aug–4 Sep 54 served on OS DELTA; 9 Sep 54 towed disabled FV *Catherine Amirault*; 30 Oct–19 Nov 54 served on OS ECHO; 17–19 Jan 55 towed disabled MV *Galloway* until relieved by a commercial tug; 20–26 Jan 55 towed disabled MV *Arlesiana* until relieved by a commercial tug; 8–29 Apr 55 served on OS BRAVO; 15 Jul–5 Aug 55 served on OS DELTA; 23 Sep–14 Oct 55 served on OS BRAVO; 18 May–8 Jun 56 served on OS CHARLIE; 23 Jul–14 Aug 56 served on OS DELTA; 1–22 Oct 56 served on OS BRAVO; 21–26 Dec towed disabled MV *Helga Boege* to Bermuda; 19 Apr–11 May 57 served on OS ECHO; 3 May 57 rescued 28 survivors from MV *Bornholm* at 37°09′N, 48°19′W in heavy seas; 9–29 Jul 57 served on OS CHARLIE; 7–10 Sep 57 towed disabled MV *Trondanger* until relieved by a commercial tug; 13 Jan–3 Feb 58 served on OS CHARLIE; 22 Mar–11 Apr 58 served on OS ECHO; 2–22 Jun 58 served on OS BRAVO; 4–25 Aug 58 served on OS BRAVO; 12–20 Oct 58 served on OS DELTA; 14 Dec–4 Jan 59 served on OS CHARLIE; 26 Dec 58 medevaced crewman from MV *World Seafarer* at 54°44′N, 30°40′W; 9 Jan 59 assisted FV *Pauline H* at 41°46′N, 67°20′W; 24 Feb–14 Mar 59 served on OS DELTA; 6–26 Jul 59 served on OS BRAVO; 3 Oct 59 assisted MV *Mormacteal* at 33°55′N, 64°21′W; 4–25 Jan 60 served on OS ECHO; 23–25 Feb 60 assisted grounded MV *Monica Smith*; 18 Mar–8 Apr 60 served on OS CHARLIE; 28 May–19 Jun 60 served on OS DELTA; 19 Sep–9

Oct 60 served on OS BRAVO; 4–25 Dec 60 served on OS DELTA; 10 May–2 Jun 61 served on OS CHARLIE; 30 Jul–22 Aug 61 served on OS BRAVO; 3 Aug 62 medevaced crewman from MV *Elemir*; 24 Mar 63 assisted FV *Felicia and Grace* 35 mi E of Cape Cod; 16–17 Feb 66 escorted fire-damaged U.S. MV *American Importer* from 200 mi E of Saint John's, Newfoundland, to that port; Jun–Jul 67 served on OS ECHO; 4 Dec 67–4 Aug 68 assigned to CG Squadron Three, Vietnam; 21 Nov–13 Dec 68 served on OS CHARLIE; 1–24 Feb 69 served on OS DELTA; 15 Sep–8 Oct 69 served on OS CHARLIE; 7 Oct 69 medevaced crewman from MV *Trade Carrier* in mid-Atlantic; 7 Nov–20 Dec 69 served on OS DELTA; 29 Jun–22 Jul 70 served on OS ECHO; 30 Aug–22 Sep 70 served on OS DELTA; 14 Nov–7 Dec 70 served on OS ECHO; 2–25 Feb 71 served on OS CHARLIE; 16 Apr–9 May 71 served on OS DELTA; May 71 provided support for an at-sea conference between an American ambassador, representatives of the local fishing industries, and the commander of a Soviet Georges Banks fishing fleet; 3 Aug 71 grounded in Hog I. Channel causing modest damage; 31 Aug–9 Sep 71 served on OS HOTEL; 14 Sep–10 Oct 71 served on OS ECHO; 9 Feb–4 Mar 72 served on OS BRAVO; 19 Apr–13 May 72 served on OS DELTA; Aug 1972–1 Aug 85 stationed at Portland, ME, and used for LE, OS, and SAR; 8 Sep–2 Oct 72 served on OS DELTA; 8 Dec 72–2 Jan 73 served on OS BRAVO; 17 May–10 Jun 73 served on OS DELTA; 25 Jul–16 Aug 73 served on OS BRAVO; 26 Nov–16 Dec 73 served on OS CHARLIE; 13 Mar–2 Apr 74 served on OS BRAVO; 31 Jan–17 Feb 74 served on OS HOTEL; 25 Jan–14 Feb 75 served on OS HOTEL; 22 Aug–12 Sep 75 served on OS HOTEL; 24 Oct–14 Nov 75 served on OS HOTEL; 29 Feb–19 Mar 76 served on OS HOTEL; 25 May 78 seized a 55-foot sailboat off Monhegan I. carrying 9t of marijuana; Sep 80 seized FV *Bounty* carrying 20t of marijuana; 7 Nov 82 fired across bow and seized MV *Biscayne Breeze* 400 mi SE of Cape Cod carrying 30t of marijuana; 15

Mar 83 boarded sinking Honduran MV *Civonney* 270 mi E of Cape May, NJ—the crew had abandoned her after setting her on fire and opening sea cocks; the MV was carrying a large quantity of marijuana; 24 Apr 84 towed disabled sailboat *Sandpiper* 400 mi E of Montauk Pt.; Mar 85 helped medevac crewman from Greek MV *Buena Vista* 400 mi off Cape Cod.

Ingham

1946–68 stationed at Norfolk, VA, and primarily used for OS, LE, and SAR; Apr 49 served on OS EASY; Jun 49 served on OS EASY; Aug 49 served on OS CHARLIE; Jan 50 served on OS EASY; Mar–Apr 50 served on OS DOG; 4 Jun–1 Sep 50 served on cadet cruise to Europe; 4–24 Nov 50 served on OS ABLE; 27–28 Nov 50 medevaced patient from MSTS *Henry Gibbons* and transported him to St. John's, Newfoundland; 10–25 Dec 50 served on OS ABLE; 3–24 Feb 51 served on OS CHARLIE; Feb–Mar 53 served on OS HOTEL; May–Jun 53 served on OS DELTA; Nov–Dec 53 served on OS BRAVO; Feb 54 served on OS COLA; Apr–Mar 54 served on OS HOTEL; Jul 55 served on OS ECHO; Mar 56 provided medical assistance to Greek MV *Calli*; Jul–Aug 56 served on OS BRAVO; Dec 56 served on OS CHARLIE; May 57 served on OS ECHO; Feb–Mar 59 served on OS DELTA; May–Jun 59 served on OS DELTA; Sep–Oct 59 served on OS BRAVO; Nov–Dec 59 served on OS CHARLIE; Apr–May 60 served on OS DELTA; Jun–Jul 60 served on OS BRAVO; Jun–Jul 61 served on OS DELTA; 13 Jun–3 Jul 64 served on OS CHARLIE and conducted oceanographic survey—this was the first oceanographic survey undertaken by a 327; 10 May 65 sustained a fire that destroyed the CIC; 27 Feb 67 helped fight fire on MV *Caldas* 50 mi E of Chincoteague, VA; Jul 67 served on cadet cruise; 4 Jul 67 medevaced injured crewman from MV *Lancing* 360 mi NE of Miami, FL; 24 Aug–16 Sep 67 served on OS DELTA; 24 Nov–17 Dec 67 served on OS CHARLIE; 26 Feb–20 Mar 68 served on OS ECHO; 16 Jul 68–3

Cutter *Ingham* in Jun 80 at Key West, FL. She was one of a dozen medium and large cutters employed to escort over 100,000 refugees from Cuba to the United States.

Apr 69 served in CG Squadron Three in Vietnam; 1969–27 May 88 stationed at Portsmouth, VA, and used primarily for LE and SAR; 12 Jul–4 Aug 69 served on OS DELTA; 8 Sep–1 Oct 69 served on OS BRAVO; 16 Dec 69–8 Jan 70 served on OS CHARLIE; 22 Jun–15 Jul 70 served on OS DELTA; 26 Aug–18 Sep 70 served on OS CHARLIE; 22 Jan–12 Feb 71 served on OS ECHO; 13 Jun–6 Jul 71 served on OS BRAVO; 24 Mar–16 Apr 71 served on OS DELTA; 7–16 Jan 71 served on OS HOTEL; 27 Aug–20 Sep 71 served on OS DELTA; 5–25 Nov 71 served on OS ECHO; 30 Mar–23 Apr 72 served on OS CHARLIE; 7–28 Aug 72 served on OS BRAVO; 8–30 Oct 72 served on OS ECHO; 13 Dec 72–3 Jan 73 served on OS CHARLIE; 20 Feb–1 Mar 73 served on OS HOTEL; 7–27 Mar 73 served on OS BRAVO; 23 May–12 Jun 73 served on OS ECHO; 16 Aug–6 Sep 73 served on OS CHARLIE; 9–30 Jan 74 served on OS BRAVO; 9–26 Mar 74 served on OS HOTEL; 6–26 Mar 75 served on OS HOTEL; 3–24 Oct 75 served on OS HOTEL; 16 Jan–6 Feb 76 served on OS HOTEL; Apr–Jun 80 carried out numerous SAR cases during the Cuban exodus; late Apr 80 towed five vessels and took on board 14 survivors from swamped boats as a storm battered refugee boats sailing from Cuba; 1 Apr 82 seized craft *Misfit* carrying 35t of marijuana.

Spencer

10 Feb–24 Jul 46 stationed at New York, NY, and used for LE and SAR; 24 Jul 46–12 Aug 47 stationed at Boston, MA, and used for LE, OS, and SAR; 9 Nov–1 Dec 46 served on OS A; 12 Aug 47–1969 stationed at Brooklyn, NY, and St. George, Staten I., NY, and used for LE, OS, and SAR; 2–23 Feb 47 served on OS A; 8–29 Mar 47 served on OS C; 14 May–23 Jul 47 shared IIP with cutter *Mendota*; 6–16 Jun 47 served on OS ABLE; 13 Sep–4 Oct 47 served on OS C; 20 Dec 47–14 Jan 48 served on OS A; 30 Mar–12 Apr 48 served on OS CHARLIE; 11 Jun–2 Jul 48 served on OS CHARLIE; 29 Aug–2 Sep 48 served on OS C; 17 Nov–10 Dec 48 served on OS ABLE; 12–15 Jan 49 served on OS E—departed due to medical emergency; 15 Mar–5 May 49 served on OS EASY; 15 May–4 Jun 49 served on OS DOG; 25 Jun 49 patrolled Poughkeepsie Regatta; 15 Jul–6 Aug 49 served on OS CHARLIE; 8–29 Oct 49 served on OS CHARLIE; 21 Dec 49–11 Jan 50 served on OS HOW; 20 Mar–4 Apr 50 served on OS ABLE; 28 May–18 Jun 50 served on OS DOG; 8–11 Aug 50 escorted disabled MV *Belfri* to St. John's, Newfoundland; 14 Aug–1 Sep 50 served on OS BAKER; 15 Nov–6 Dec 50 served on OS EASY; 25 Jan–15 Feb 51 served on OS HOW; 27 Jan 51 helped fight fire on MV *Meirdizengoff*; 20 Apr–12 May 51 served on OS BAKER; 30 Jun–21 Jul 51 served on OS DOG; 14 Sep–5 Oct 51 served on OS BAKER; 5–27 Dec 51 served on OS HOW; 19 Dec 51 assisted MV *Atlantic Enterprise*; 8–28 Mar 52 served on OS CHARLIE; 13 May–4 Jun 52 served on OS EASY; 1–28 Aug 52 served on OS CHARLIE; 17 Oct–8 Nov 52 served on OS BRAVO; 9 Nov 52 offered medical assistance to FV *Batavia*; 12–13 Nov 52 towed disabled FV *Brighton* to Portland, ME; 16 Jan–6 Feb 53 served on OS ECHO; 17 Apr–8 May 53 served on OS DELTA; 22 Jun–13 Jul 53 served on OS HOTEL; 30 Oct–20 Nov 53 served on OS BRAVO; 14 Jan 54 medevaced crewman from MV *Vema* off Bermuda; 6–27 Mar 54 served on OS BRAVO; 22 May–12 Jun 54 served on OS DELTA; 24 Sep–16 Oct 54 served on OS DELTA; 6–31 Dec 54 served on OS ECHO; 24 Feb–18 Mar 55 served on OS BRAVO; 24–28 Mar 55 served on OS BRAVO; 27 May–17 Jun 55 served on OS COCA; 30 Jul–20 Aug 55 served on OS ECHO; 31 Dec 55–22 Jan 56 served on OS DELTA; 16 Mar–6 Apr 56

served on OS ECHO; 13–30 Jul 56 served on OS BRAVO; 19 Nov–11 Dec 56 served on OS CHARLIE; 6–26 Feb 57 served on OS BRAVO; 25 Jun–16 Jul 57 served on OS DELTA; 20 Aug–9 Sep 57 served on OS CHARLIE; 5–7 Jan 58 escorted distressed MV *Sydney Breeze* to Bermuda; 4–24 Mar 58 served on OS DELTA; 2–24 May 58 served on OS ECHO; 14–19 Jun 58 patrolled Newport-to-Bermuda Race; 14 Jul–4 Aug 58 served on OS BRAVO; 8 Sep 58 sank derelict Portuguese FV *Anna Maria* at 44°12′N, 50°14′W by gunfire; 9–29 Sep 58 served on OS DELTA; 18 Sep 58 provided medical assistance to USNS *Rose* at 42°21′N, 41°49′W; 29 Nov–19 Dec 58 served on OS ECHO; 18 Apr–8 May 59 served on OS CHARLIE; 14–18 May 59 served on OS DELTA; 28 Jun–19 Jul 59 served on OS DELTA; 9 Nov–1 Dec 59 served on OS BRAVO; 6–26 Feb 60 served on OS CHARLIE; 17 Apr–8 May 60 served on OS DELTA; 22 Aug–12 Sep 60 served on OS ECHO; 4–26 Nov 60 served on OS CHARLIE; 2 May 61 medevaced crewman from MV *American Farmer*; 8–29 May 61 served on OS BRAVO; 25 Jul–15 Aug 61 served on OS ECHO; 30 Nov 62 escorted distressed MV *Erwin Schroeder* until relieved; Jul–Aug 64 served on OS CHARLIE; Jul 65 served on OS DELTA; Feb 66 served on OS BRAVO—sustained shaft casualty; Jan–Feb 67 served on OS ECHO; Feb 67 medevaced crew member from French MV *Fort Fleur d'Epee*; May–Jun 67 served on OS BRAVO; 6 Jun 67 evacuated injured crewman from cutter *Evergreen*; 11 Jul–3 Aug 67 served on OS DELTA; 9 Oct–1 Nov 67 served on OS CHARLIE; 3 Dec 67 escorted distressed Yugoslavian MV *Kotor* to Halifax, Nova Scotia; 24 Feb–18 Mar 68 served on OS CHARLIE; 31 Jul–21 Aug 68 served on OS CHARLIE; 11 Feb–30 Sep 69 assigned to CG Squadron Three, Vietnam; 1969–23 Jan 74 stationed at Governors I., NY, and used for LE, OS, and SAR; 24 Jan–16 Feb 70 served on OS BRAVO; 6–29 Jun 70 served on OS ECHO; 11 Jul–3 Aug 70 served on OS CHARLIE; 11 Sep–4 Oct 70 served on OS BRAVO; 21 May–13 Jun 71 served on OS BRAVO; 24 Jul–17 Aug 71 served on OS ECHO; 17 Dec 71–10 Jan 72 served on OS ECHO; 17–26 Feb 72 served on OS HOTEL; 4–24 Mar 72 served on OS BRAVO; 16 May–8 Jun 72 served on OS CHARLIE; 18 Jul–9 Aug 72 served on OS CHARLIE; 23 Sep–17 Oct 72 served on OS BRAVO; 21 Nov–7 Dec 72 served on OS HOTEL; 27 Jan–16 Feb 73 served on OS CHARLIE; 26 Sep–16 Oct 73 served on OS CHARLIE; 4–28 Nov 73 served on OS HOTEL; 23 Jan 74–15 Dec 80 decommissioned and served in a special status as Engineer Training School.

Taney

Apr 46–Feb 72 stationed at Alameda, CA, and used for LE, OS, and SAR; Jun–Jul 49 served on OS FOX; Jul 49 served on OS ABLE; Sep 50 served on OS FOX; Jun 50 served on OS OBOE; Jan–Feb 51 served on OS UNCLE; Aug–Sep 52 served on OS UNCLE; Nov–Dec 52 served on OS NAN; Apr–May 53 served on OS VICTOR; Jun 53 served on OS SUGAR; 4–25 Oct 53 served on OS UNCLE; Jun–Jul 54 served on OS NAN; Nov 54 served on OS NAN; Jun 55 served on OS NAN; Mar–Apr 56 served on OS NOVEMBER; Jun–Jul 56 served on OS NOVEMBER; Jan–Feb 57 served on OS NOVEMBER; Jun–Jul 57 served on OS NOVEMBER; Oct–Nov 57 served on OS NOVEMBER; Feb–Mar 58 served on OS NOVEMBER; Aug 58 served on OS NOVEMBER; Oct–Nov 58 served on OS ROMEO; Dec 58–Jan 59 served on OS NOVEMBER; May–Jun 59 served on OS NOVEMBER; Oct–Nov 59 served on OS NOVEMBER; Mar–Apr 60 served on OS NOVEMBER; Aug 60

The *Taney* in 1968. Although the Coast Guard slash was approved in Apr 67, it was well over a year before all cutters and units were using the marking. *Taney* was the last cutter to serve on ocean-station duty, departing OS HOTEL on 30 Jul 77.

served on OS NOVEMBER; Jan 61 served on OS NOVEMBER; May-Jun 61 served on OS NOVEMBER; Mar 65 conducted Alaskan Patrol; 29 Mar 65 fought fire and towed disabled FV *Glacier Bear* 15 mi S of Cape Fairweather to safety; 7-28 Jan 68 served on OS NOVEMBER; 18 Feb-10 Mar 68 served on OS NOVEMBER; 21 Apr-12 May 68 served on OS NOVEMBER; 27 Oct-17 Nov 68 served on OS NOVEMBER; 19 Jan-9 Feb 69 served on OS NOVEMBER; 14 May 69-31 Jan 70 assigned to CG Squadron Three, Vietnam; 30 Aug-20 Sep 70 served on OS NOVEMBER; 3-24 Jan 71 served on OS NOVEMBER; 28 Mar-18 Apr 71 served on OS VICTOR; 9-30 May 71 served on OS VICTOR; 22 Aug-12 Sep 71 served on OS NOVEMBER; 24 Oct-14 Nov 71 served on OS NOVEMBER; Feb 72-Sep 76 stationed at Norfolk, VA, and used for LE, OS, and SAR; 13-22 Oct 72 served on OS HOTEL; 28 Oct-17 Nov 72 served on OS DELTA; 26 Jan-15 Feb 73 served on OS BRAVO; 17 Apr-7 May 73 served on OS BRAVO; 1-22 Aug 73 served on OS HOTEL; 8-28 Sep 73 served on OS HOTEL; 15 Oct-4 Nov 73 served on OS HOTEL; 28 Nov-18 Dec 73 served on OS HOTEL; 11-31 Jan 74 served on OS HOTEL; 17 Feb-9 Mar 74 served on OS HOTEL; 26 Mar-15 Apr 74 served on OS HOTEL; 5-25 Jan 75 served on OS HOTEL; 14 Feb-6 Mar 75 served on OS HOTEL; 1-22 Aug 75 served on OS HOTEL; 12 Sep-3 Oct 75 served on OS HOTEL; 14 Nov-5 Dec 75 served on OS HOTEL; 27 Dec 75-16 Jan 76 served on OS HOTEL; 6-29 Feb 76 served on OS HOTEL; 19 Mar-15 Apr 76 served on OS HOTEL—last OS duty by a CG cutter; Sep 76-7 Dec 86 stationed at Portsmouth, VA, and used for LE and SAR; Dec 76 assisted sailboat *Capella* 200 mi off New York; Dec 79 helped seize FV *Eneida* for narcotics violation; 15 Jan 80 seized U.S. MV *Amelia Isle* 425 mi E of Ft. Pierce, FL, carrying 4t of contraband; Nov-Dec 80 seized British MV *William Brice* carrying 12t of contraband and U.S. MV *Party Doll* carrying 10t of contraband; 16 Nov 82 rescued seven from disabled ketch *Klarwasser* off North Carolina; 17 Dec 82 intercepted sailboat *Apre Dien Ni* in Windward Passage carrying 19 migrants—returned them to Port-au-Prince; 30 Sep 84 seized PC *Thriller* in Yucatan Channel carrying 1,000 lbs of marijuana; May 85 assisted disabled FV *Northwind* 300 mi off New York; 4 Oct 85 seized MV *Sea Maid I* towing a barge carrying 160t of marijuana 300 mi off Virginia.

250-FOOT CUTTERS ("LAKE") CLASS

Name	Hull Number	Builder	Keel Laid	Launched	Commissioned	Disposition
Mocoma (ex-HMS *Totland*, ex-*Cayuga*)	WPG 163	United Drydock Inc., Staten I., NY	N/A	7 Oct 31	22 May 32 (CG) 20 Mar 47 (recomm)	*Trans* to G. B. 12 May 41 as *Cayuga; returned* 1946 as *Mocoma; decomm* 8 May 50; *sold* 15 Jul 55
Tampa (ex-*Sebec*, ex-HMS *Banff*, ex-*Saranac*)	WPG 164	General Engineering & Drydock Co., Oakland, CA	N/A	12 Apr 30	2 Oct 30 (CG) 27 May 47 (recomm as *Tampa*)	*Trans* to G. B. 30 Apr 41 as *Saranac; returned* 27 Feb 46 as *Sebec; decomm* 10 Aug 54; *sold* 16 Feb 59
Champlain (ex-HMS *Sennen*, ex-*Champlain*)	WPG 319	Bethelem Shipbuilding Corp., Quincy MA	23 May 28	11 Oct 28	24 Jan 29 (CG) Recomm canceled	*Trans* to G. B. 12 May 41; *returned* 27 Mar 46; *sold* 25 Mar 48
Itasca (ex-HMS *Gorleston*, ex-*Itasca*)	WPG 321	General Engineering & Drydock Co., Oakland, CA	N/A	16 Nov 29	12 Jul 30 (CG) Recomm canceled	*Trans* to G. B. 30 May 41; *returned* 23 Apr 46; *sold* 4 Oct 50

Cost $900,000 each (hull & machinery)

Hull
  Displacement (tons)   2,065 fl (1950), 1,525 light (1950)
  Length   250′ oa; 239′ wl; 236′ bp
  Beam   42′ max
  Draft   16′ max (1950)

Machinery
  Main Engines   1 General Electric motor driven by generator driven by a turbine
  Main Boilers   2 Babcock & Wilcox watertube boilers, 250 psi, 250 degrees
  SHP   3,350
  Propellers   single, 4 blades

Performance
  Max Speed   16 kts (1950)
  Max Sustained   16 kts, 2,815-mi radius (1950)
  Economic   10 kts, 4,635-mi radius (1950)

Logistics
  Fuel Oil (95%)   90,000 gal.
  Complement   10 officers, 2 warrants, 96 enlisted (1950)

Electronics
  Detection Radar   1 SO-4 (*Mocoma*, 1950)
  Sonar   none (*Mocoma*); QGB (*Tampa*, 1954)

Armament   1 3″/50; 2 40mm/60 (single); 4 20mm/80 (twin); Hedgehog—*Tampa* (1954), *Mocoma* without Hedgehog

Design

The 250-foot class was designed by the Coast Guard. Captain Q. B. Newman, USCG, designed its innovative turbine-electric-drive power plant, which developed an amazing 3,000 shp. These were the first to have alternating current, and a synchronous motor for propulsion. The whole ship ran off the main turbine. The auxiliary generators were tied into the main generator electrically, after sufficient speed was attained. At that point, no steam was required to drive the turbines on the auxiliary generators. The propulsion plant achieved remarkable efficiency. This class had a slightly raked steam and a cruiser stern. These features were an attempt to improve sea qualities over the 240-foot class, particularly for service on ice patrol.

Initially this class was made up of ten cutters, all of which were transferred to Great Britain under lend-lease in 1941. Three vessels were lost while in British service, one was not returned, and the remainder turned back to the Coast Guard in 1946. Initially, the Coast Guard planned to renovate the *Champlain, Itasca, Mocoma,* and *Tampa* and return them to service. The remaining two vessels, the *Chelan* and *Tahoe,* were to be stripped of parts for use in the restoration of the other four ships. Due to economic constraints following the war, only the *Mocoma* and *Tampa* were placed in commission.

Mocoma

1947–50 stationed at Miami, FL; 13 Aug 47 towed *Aurora*; 14–22 May 48 served on IIP; 6–22 Jun 48 served on IIP; 23 Dec 48–7 Jan 49 towed *Rockaway* from Orange, TX, to Curtis Bay, MD; 6 Mar 49 assisted FV *Flagship Sinco*; 17–19 Oct 49 towed disabled FV *Leoncita* from 23°12′N, 79°09′W to Miami, FL; 26–28 Oct 49 deployed on training cruise; 13–15 Dec 49 searched for MV *Doros* at 25°41′N, 74°14′W; 9 Jan 50 assisted disabled MV *Annibal* at 42 miles from *St. John's* LS; 27–28 Mar 50 grounded on Star Reef 4 miles south of Fowey Rocks—freed and towed to Miami, FL, by tug *Cable*; 7–11 Apr 50 towed to Curtis Bay, MD, by *Cherokee* and placed out of commission due to damage sustained in grounding; 8 May 50 personnel transferred to *Androscoggin*.

Tampa

1947–54 stationed at Mobile, AL; 8–15 Jan 49 towed *Absecon* from Orange, TX, to Charleston, SC; 9–16 Mar 49 towed *Chincoteague* from Orange, TX, to Charleston, SC; 21–29 Apr 49 towed *Mackinac* from Orange, TX, to Curtis Bay, MD; 20 Jan 50 assisted MV *American Mariner* aground at South Pass, Mississippi R.; 7 Mar 50 searched for FV *Neva E*; 19 Apr–3 May 50 served on IIP; 19 May–4 Jun 50 served on IIP; 8–18 Aug 50 patrolled fishing rodeos at Mobile Bay and Southwest Pass; 9–14

Nov 50 searched for derelict barge; 13–19 Mar 51 towed disabled FVs *Salzinia* and *Teresa Marie* while escorting FV *Jim Milton* from 150 miles off Port Isabel, TX, to port; 20–21 Mar 51 towed disabled FV *Lee Hardiman* to Port Isabel, TX; 8 Apr 51 relieved *Triton* of tow of FVs *Morning Star* and *Buccaneer* at 24°50′N, 96°03′W; 21–23 Apr 51 searched for survivors of tanker *Esso Greensboro*; 29–30 Apr 51 towed disabled *Salvia* from 29°19′N, 92°45′W to Mobile, AL; 21 May 51 searched for overdue FV *San Francisco* off Mobile, AL; 17–22 Jun 51 towed disabled FVs *Morning Star* and *Ponce de Leon* from 20°03′N, 91°21′W to Brazos, TX; 24 Jun 51 searched for overdue MV *Endeavor* in Gulf of Mexico; 24 Jun 51 escorted damaged FVs *Sharon J*, *Crimson Tide*, and *Linda Anita* 200 miles south of Southwest Pass, Mississippi R.; 19–21 Jul 51 towed disabled FV *Captain Carl* from 19°51′N, 93°08′W to Brazos, TX; 7 Aug 51 towed disabled FV *W. E. Fowler* from 26°22′N, 88°55′W to South Pass, Mississippi R.; 2–3 Oct 51 towed disabled MV *Gypsy* from 28°47′N, 87°58′W to South Pass, Mississippi R.; 30 Oct–4 Nov 51 towed disabled FV *Coral* from 25 miles west by south of Campeche Bay to Southwest Pass; 5 Nov 51 assisted grounded FV *Arthur O* on Mobile Bar; 18–20 Nov 51 towed disabled FV *John Francis Taylor* from 23°56′N, 91°05′W to Southwest Pass; 25 Jan 52 on scene of disabled USNS *Mission Carmel* at 28°02′N, 88°46′W; 27 Jan 52 searched

for mine reported at 29°09′N, 86°25′W; 1–3 Mar 52 towed disabled FV *Ora Zorra* from 20°00′N, 93°00′W to Port Isabel, TX; 14–16 May 52 towed disabled FV *Sharon J* from 18°45′N, 92°45′W to Port Isabel, TX; 18–20 May 52 towed disabled FVs *Wasp* and *St. Paul* from 25 miles north of Obregon Light, Bay of Campeche, to Port Isabel, TX; 27–28 Jun 52 assisted disabled FV *St. Cecilla* at 22°29′N, 89°36′W; 1–3 Jul 52 towed disabled FV *Souwester* from 19°50′N, 91°14′W to Port Isabel, TX; 8–9 Jul 52 assisted disabled FV *Barcelona* at 22°45′N, 89°22′W; 8 Aug 52 assisted disabled FV *Francis S* at 24°15′N, 97°35′W; 25–31 Aug 52 unsuccessfully searched for a missing B-17 at approx. 29°10′N, 86°00′W; 19–21 Sep 52 assisted disabled schooner *Gonzalez* off Mobile Bay; 8–22 Nov 52 sent on special mission to Veracruz, Mexico; 9–10 Jul 53 assisted disabled FV *Dennis Jay* at 23°20′N, 87°09′W; 27 Sep 53 surveyed damage from hurricane Florence; 3 Oct 53 assisted disabled FV *Brookhaven* at 26°55′N, 89°13′W; 12–15 Dec 53 secured a barge that was adrift at 28°14′N, 88°35′W; 27–31 Jan 54 assisted disabled FV *Hilda* at 19°00′N, 92°45′W; 2 Apr 54 assisted disabled FV *Taurus* at Port Isabel seabuoy; 11 Apr 54 assisted disabled FV *Fairway* at 24°58′N, 83°24′W; 22–23 May 54 provided medical assistance to FV *Keturah* at 22°20′N, 89°42′W.

The *Tampa*, on 5 Jan 49, is a handsome representative of the pre-WWII Coast Guard. She has a riveted hull, wooden decks, and a natural-draft stack, giving her an unmistakable silhouette. The fleet commander's and commanding officer's cabins had mahogany paneling, and their heads had bathtubs. Oak paneling was used in "officer country."

WHEC-WPG Type Cutters Disposed of Shortly after World War II*

Name	Hull Number	Class	Decomm	Sold/Trans
Tahoe		250-foot	30 Apr 41	27 Oct 47
Chelan		250-foot	2 May 41	23 Oct 47
Unalga	WPG 53	190-foot	10 Oct 45	19 Jul 46
Tallapoosa	WPG 52	165-foot	8 Nov 45	22 Jul 46
Cobb	WPG 181	EA	31 Jan 46	6 Mar 47
Northland	WPG 49	216-foot	27 Mar 46	3 Jan 47
Mayflower	WPG 183	EA	1 Jul 46	8 Jan 47
Modoc	WPG 46	240-foot	1 Feb 47	30 Jun 47
Tampa	WPG 48	240-foot	1 Feb 47	22 Sep 47
Haida	WPG 45	240-foot	13 Feb 47	20 Jan 48
Algonquin	WPG 75	165-foot (A)	18 Apr 47	13 Jul 48
Mojave	WPG 47	240-foot	3 Jul 47	14 Feb 48
Onondaga	WPG 79	165-foot (A)	24 Jul 47	7 Dec 54
Comanche	WPG 76	165-foot (A)	29 Jul 47	10 Nov 48
Mohawk	WPG 78	165-foot (A)	8 Jan 48	1 Nov 48

* See Scheina, *WWII Cutters,* for details.

Medium-Endurance Cutters and Their Equivalents

In 1965 the U.S. Coast Guard adopted the term medium-endurance cutter to describe its two classifications of submarine chasers (WPCs and WSCs) under a single heading. During the following year the designators of these cutters were changed from WPCs to WMECs. From 1942 until 1966, cutters of this size were designated as submarine chasers (WPC and WSC). Prior to World War II, cutters of this type were divided among cruising cutters (today high-endurance cutters), patrol boats, and harbor craft, depending on their size and qualities.

Medium-endurance cutters have ranged significantly in size and qualities. Traditionally, these cutters have been called upon to undertake a wide variety of tasks. In many respects, they are the work horses of the fleet.

270-FOOT CUTTERS (*BEAR* CLASS)

Name	Hull Number	Builder	Keel Laid	Launched	Commissioned	Disposition
Bear	WMEC 901	Tacoma Boatbuilding, Tacoma, WA	23 Aug 79	25 Sep 80	4 Feb 83	Active
Tampa	WMEC 902	Tacoma Boatbuilding, Tacoma, WA	2 Apr 80	19 Mar 81	16 Mar 84	Active
Harriet Lane	WMEC 903	Tacoma Boatbuilding, Tacoma, WA	15 Oct 80	6 Feb 82	20 Sep 84	Active
Northland	WMEC 904	Tacoma Boatbuilding, Tacoma, WA	9 Apr 81	7 May 82	17 Dec 84	Active
Spencer (ex-*Seneca*)	WMEC 905	Robert E. Derecktor, Middletown, RI	26 Jun 82	16 Jun 84	28 Jun 86	Active
Seneca (ex-*Pickering*)	WMEC 906	Robert E. Derecktor, Middletown, RI	16 Sep 82	16 Jun 84	4 May 87	Active
Escanaba	WMEC 907	Robert E. Derecktor, Middletown, RI	1 Apr 83	24 Aug 85	27 Aug 87	Active
Tahoma (ex-*Legare*)	WMEC 908	Robert E. Derecktor, Middletown, RI	28 Jun 83	24 Aug 85	6 Apr 88	Active
Campbell	WMEC 909	Robert E. Derecktor, Middletown, RI	10 Aug 84	30 Aug 86	19 Aug 88	Active
Thetis	WMEC 910	Robert E. Derecktor, Middletown, RI	24 Aug 84	30 Aug 86	30 Jun 89	Active
Forward	WMEC 911	Robert E. Derecktor, Middletown, RI	11 Jul 86	22 Aug 87	1990	Building
Legare	WMEC 912	Robert E. Derecktor, Middletown, RI	11 Jul 86	22 Aug 87	1990	Building
Mohawk	WMEC 913	Robert E. Derecktor, Middletown, RI	26 Jun 87	27 Aug 88	1991	Building

Cost	See Design
Hull	
Displacement (tons)	1,200 light (1987); 1,780 fl (1987)
Length	270' oa
Beam	38' max
Draft	13'6" max (1987)
Machinery	
Main Engines	2 Alco diesels
BHP	7,000
Propellers	twin, CP
Performance	
Max Sustained	19.5 kts, 3,850-mi radius (1987)
Cruising	15.0 kts, 6,370-mi radius (1987)
Economic	12.0 kts, 10,250-mi radius (1987)
Logistics	
Complement	11 officers, 89 men (1987)
Electronics	
Radar	2 SPS-64, 1 Mk 92 FC (1987)
Sonar	provisions for SQR-19A TASS (1987)
Armament	1 76mm/62 Mk 75 and light weapons

Design

The 270-foot cutters were designed for LE and SAR during peacetime and as ASW escorts during war. Although the class carries no ASW sensors or weapons, space and weight have been reserved for them. Ever since the 125-foot cutters were built in the 1920s, the Coast Guard has demanded much mission flexibility from each medium-endurance-cutter design, and as a result none have been terribly comfortable during strong seas.

Initially, Tacoma Boatbuildings Co. had been awarded the contract for WMEC 905 through 913. In Jan 81 the General Accounting Office held that the Coast Guard had erred when it ruled that the lower bidders were "not responsive" because they had filled out bid forms improperly. Tacoma had bid $42 million per cutter; Marine Power and Equipment Co., Seattle, WA, $41 million; and Robert E. Derecktor $37.7 million.

The *Bear* on 1 Mar 83. She is only the second cutter to bear the name.

Bear

4 Feb 83–1990 stationed at Portsmouth, VA, and used for LE and SAR; 6 Apr 83 rescued three from downed Bell Ranger helicopter off Panama; 21 Oct 84 intercepted 96 migrants in a 35-foot sailboat in Windward Passage—returned them to Port-au-Prince; 10 Apr 85 intercepted a 60-ft sailboat carrying 243 Haitians and a 30-ft boat carrying 159 Haitians and took them to Haiti; April 85 seized *Lazy Lady* 100 mi off Haiti carrying a large quantity of marijuana; 8 July 85 seized FV *La Primera* 60 mi SE of Cuba carrying 1t of marijuana; Oct 85 helped fight engine-room fire on Cayman MV *Arron K* 100 mi S of Miami, FL; 20 Oct 85 seized a 37-ft PC about 320 mi S of Miami, FL, carrying 400 lbs of cocaine; late Oct 85 seized a FV off San Salvador, Bahamas, carrying 400 lbs of cocaine; Apr 86 transported 150 stranded Haitian refugees from uninhabited Bahamian island to Port-Au-Prince, Haiti; 30 Apr 86 seized *Rampart* carrying 1t of marijuana; 3 Jun 87 along with cutter *Cape Gull* seized five vessels carrying 88t of marijuana and six kilos of cocaine; 6 Mar 89 responded to hijacked Honduran MV *Madrid* with 36 Haitians on board and delivered Haitians to immigration—discovered a sailboat with 80 Haitians on board while responding to a case and turned them over to immigration as well.

Campbell

19 Aug 88–1990 stationed at New Bedford, MA, and used for LE and SAR.

Escanaba

27 Aug 87–1990 stationed at Boston, MA, and used for LE and SAR; 16 Aug—21 Sep 87 sailed on 5,000-mi Great Lakes cruise and conducted formal commissioning at Escanaba Memorial Park, Grand Haven, MI; 16 Apr–2 May 88 deployed with USN LAMPS I ASW helicopter detachment—a first for the CG; 28 Apr 88 seized FV *Luz Marina* in the Gulf of Mexico carrying 4t of marijuana; 5 Jan 89 towed disabled FV *Orion* to safety in NE gale on Georges Banks; 24 Feb 89 towed disabled FV *Paul and Dominic* to Nantucket Shoals in NE gale with 40–50-knot winds and 30-foot seas.

Forward

1990 stationed at Portsmouth, VA, and used for LE and SAR.

Harriet Lane

20 Sep 84–1990 stationed at Portsmouth, VA, and used for LE and SAR; Dec 86 intercepted FV *St. Bernadette* near Cay Lobos carrying 16 Haitians; July 87 intercepted 201 Haitian migrants and returned them to Haiti; 5 Dec 87 seized FV *Guadalupe* in Yucatan Straits carrying 8t of marijuana; 5 Mar 88 intercepted a sailboat 450 mi SE of Miami, FL, carrying 200 Haitians and returned them to Port-au-Prince; 23 Nov 88 seized PC *Don Rony* 40 mi SW of St. Kitts carrying 5.5t of marijuana.

Legare

1990 stationed at Portsmouth, VA, and used for LE and SAR.

Mohawk

1990 building, to be stationed at Key West, FL, and used for LE and SAR.

The *Harriet Lane* sails past Coast Guard Headquarters in Washington, D.C., towards the Washington Navy Yard where she was commissioned on 20 Sep 84, the first warship to be commissioned in the capital for over one hundred years.

Northland

17 Dec 84–1990 stationed at Norfolk, VA, and used for LE and SAR; 29 Sep 87 intercepted a 25-foot homemade sailboat carrying 53 Haitians and returned them to Haiti; Jan 88 seized MV *Sea Viking* 100 mi SW of Key West, FL, carrying 7t of marijuana.

Seneca

4 May 87–1990 stationed at Boston, MA, and used for LE and SAR; 29 Dec 87 seized PC FL-5383-DW with marijuana residue on board.

Spencer

28 June 86–1990 stationed at Boston, MA, and used for LE and SAR; 26 Jun 87 picked up 500 lbs of floating bales of marijuana.

Tahoma

6 Apr 88–1990 stationed at New Bedford, MA, and used for LE and SAR; Jan 89 towed disabled FV *Orion* over 100 mi in heavy seas; Jan 89 seized MV 250 mi SW of Key West carrying 17t of marijuana.

Tampa

16 Mar 84–1990 stationed at Portsmouth, VA, and used for LE and SAR; Sep 85 helped seize tug *Capstan* 240 mi E of Cape Charles carrying 30t of marijuana; Aug 86 intercepted 249 Haitians in a 45-foot sailboat 10 mi S of Key West, FL, and towed the boat back to Haiti; 5 Jan 87 seized *Shore* carrying 64 lbs of cocaine; 16 Apr 87 seized *Six Kids* carrying 500 lbs of marijuana; 10 May 87 helped seize Venezuelan MV *P.L.-8* 40 mi E of Great Abaco with 3t of marijuana on board; 30 Oct 88 seized PC *Molly Beth* in the Windward Passage carrying 900 lbs of cocaine; Nov 88 rescued 12 Haitians from a 25-foot boat that sank in the Windward Passage; 31 Mar 89 seized vessel *Marina II* carrying 5t of marijuana.

Thetis

1988–90 stationed at New Bedford, MA, and used for LE and SAR.

The *Tampa* commissions on 16 Mar 84. She is the fourth cutter to bear the name. The first was lost with all hands during WWI while escorting merchantmen between Gibraltar and England. The second *Tampa* served between 1921 and 1947. The third was a 250-foot cutter returned by Great Britain following WWII and served in the Gulf of Mexico until 1954.

210-FOOT CUTTERS (*RELIANCE* CLASS)

Name	Hull Number	Builder	Keel Laid	Launched	Commissioned	Disposition
A TYPE						
Reliance	WMEC 615 WTR 615 WPC 615	Todd Shipyard, Houston, TX	28 Aug 62	25 May 63	20 Jun 64	Active
Diligence	WMEC 616 WPC 616	Todd Shipyard, Houston, TX	N/A	20 Jul 63	31 Aug 64	Active
Vigilant	WMEC 617 WPC 617	Todd Shipyard, Houston, TX	N/A	24 Dec 63	1 Oct 64	Active

Name	Hull Number	Builder	Keel Laid	Launched	Commissioned	Disposition
Active	WMEC 618 WPC 618	Christy Corp., Sturgeon Bay, WI	29 Jun 64	31 Jul 65	17 Aug 65	Active
Confidence	WMEC 619 WPC 619	Coast Guard Yard, Curtis Bay, MD	4 Aug 64	8 May 65	19 Feb 66	Active
B TYPE						
Resolute	WMEC 620 WPC 620	Coast Guard Yard, Curtis Bay, MD	17 May 65	30 Apr 66	8 Dec 66	Active
Valiant	WMEC 621 WPC 621	American Ship Building Co., Lorain, OH	28 Feb 66	14 Jan 67	28 Oct 67	Active
Courageous	WMEC 622 WPC 622	American Ship Building Co., Lorain, OH	14 Mar 66	18 Mar 67	19 Apr 68	Active
Steadfast	WMEC 623 WPC 623	American Ship Building Co., Lorain, OH	2 May 66	24 Jun 67	7 Oct 68	Active
Dauntless	WMEC 624 WPC 624	American Ship Building Co., Lorain, OH	15 May 67	21 Oct 67	10 Jun 68	Active
Venturous	WMEC 625 WPC 625	American Ship Building Co., Lorain, OH	22 May 67	11 Nov 67	16 Aug 68	Active
Dependable	WMEC 626 WPC 626	American Ship Building Co., Lorain, OH	17 Jul 67	16 Mar 68	22 Nov 68	Active
Vigorous	WMEC 627 WPC 627	American Ship Building Co., Lorain, OH	10 Nov 67	4 May 68	23 Apr 69	Active
Durable	WMEC 628 WPC 628	Coast Guard Yard, Curtis Bay, MD	1 Jul 66	29 Apr 67	8 Dec 68	Active
Decisive	WMEC 629 WPC 629	Coast Guard Yard, Curtis Bay, MD	12 May 67	14 Dec 67	23 Aug 68	Active
Alert	WMEC 630 WPC 630	Coast Guard Yard, Curtis Bay, MD	5 Jan 68	19 Oct 68	28 Jul 69	Active

Cost   See Appropriations table

Hull

Displacement (tons)	759 light (1987); 930 fl (1987)
Length	210′6″ oa
Beam	34′ max
Draft	10′6″ max (1987)

Machinery

Main Engines	2 Alco diesels
BHP	5,000
Propellers	twin CP

Performance

Max Sustained	18.0 kts, 2,700-mi radius (1987)
Cruising	14.0 kts, 6,100-mi radius (1987)

Logistics

Complement	8 officers, 54 men (1987)

Electronics

Detection Radar	2 SPS-64

Armament   1 3-in/50 and light weapons

Design

The design of the 210-foot cutters emphasizes SAR; its high bridge has 360-degree visibility. The cutters are capable of towing a 10,000-ton-vessel. Like most modern warships, these cutters have welded steel hulls and aluminum superstructures.

WMEC 615 through 619 were initially fitted with a CODAG propulsion plant, with two 1,500-hp Cooper-Bessemer diesels and two Solar Saturn gas turbines. These five cutters were reengined when they underwent major renovations at the Coast Guard Yard, Curtis Bay, MD, between 1986 and 1990. The remaining units were renovated by Colonna Shipyard, Norfolk, VA, during the same period.

During the renovation, the cutters received stacks (reducing the size of the helo pad), enlarged superstructures, and increased fire-fighting capabilities.

The *Active* leaves the Coast Guard Yard, Curtis Bay, MD, following a major renovation in 1985. Note the stack that has been added. Previously, the engine exhaust was vented through the stern. The old method increased the helicopter landing pad area but significantly decreased interior space.

210-FOOT CUTTERS (*RELIANCE* CLASS)—Appropriations

Name	AC&I Year	Awarded	Scheduled Delivery	Construction Manhours	Costs
Reliance	1962	30 Aug 61	19 Apr 63	N/A	$4,920,804
Diligence	1962	30 Aug 61	18 Jun 63	N/A	$4,920,804
Vigilant	1963	21 Sep 62	N/A	N/A	$2,317,178
Active	1964	12 Nov 63	12 Aug 65	N/A	$2,215,580
Confidence	1964	13 Nov 63	6 Jan 66	286,289	$3,820,647
Resolute	1965	4 Sep 64	4 Aug 66	284,941	$3,621,651
Valiant	1965	15 Jun 65	7 Apr 67	353,808	$3,089,429
Courageous	1965	15 Jun 65	6 Jun 67	348,080	$3,089,429
Steadfast	1965	15 Jun 65	5 Aug 67	376,544	$3,089,429
Dauntless	1965	15 Jun 65	4 Oct 67	283,040	$3,089,429
Venturous	1965	15 Jun 65	3 Dec 67	247,344	$3,089.429
Dependable	1966	22 Jul 65	1 Feb 68	229,808	$3,089,429
Vigorous	1966	22 Jul 65	1 Apr 68	227,176	$3,089,429
Durable	1966	9 Aug 65	9 Nov 67	297,433	$3,793,333
Decisive	1966	15 Dec 65	15 Jun 68	297,433	$3,793,333
Alert	1966	15 Dec 65	15 Mar 69	297,433	$3,793,333

Active

17 Aug 65–Oct 84 stationed at New Castle, NH, and used primarily for LE and fisheries patrol; June 74 towed FV *Miss Maxine* to Gloucester, MA; Jul 74 towed FVs *Thomas D, Porpoise, Captain Albino, Apollo* to safe waters; Aug 74 towed disabled FV *Ruth and Lorraine* for 155 mi; 20–21 Aug 74 salvaged ditched CG HH3F helicopter in Cape Cod Bay; Sep 74 patrolled America's Cup Race; Oct 74 towed disabled FV *Irene and Hilda* to Nantucket and escorted distressed FV *North Atlantic* to Provincetown; Nov 74 towed disabled FV *St. Nicholas* to Gloucester, MA, towed disabled FV *Mother and Grace* to Gloucester, MA, and towed disabled FV *Palombo I* to Nantucket, MA; Jan 75 assisted the distressed coastal tanker *Barma* 60 mi S of Cape Sable; Mar 75 towed disabled *Eugene H* to No Mans Land; 18 Mar 75 towed disabled FV *Teresa R* to Provincetown, MA; Jun 75 towed disabled FV *Cape May* from 150 mi offshore to Provincetown, MA; Jul 75 towed disabled FV *Atlantic Challenge* 145 mi off Cape Cod, FV *Four Brothers* from 95 mi E of Nantucket I., and FV *Florence B* to safe waters; Feb 76 towed disabled FV *Notre Dame* to Nantucket I.; 3 Mar 76 dewatered Danish MV *Svanur* and escorted her to Portland, ME; 15 Mar 76 towed disabled FV *Diane and Lisa* to Martha's Vineyard I., MA; 24 Mar 76 towed disabled FV *Gary and Aaron* to Nantucket I.; 31 May 76 towed disabled lobster boat *Julie Ann* 60 mi SE of Nantucket following a fire; Nov 81 towed the disabled FV *Kegan David Drew* from 100 mi E of Portland, ME, to that port; 10 Jul 82 seized Spanish stern trawler *Mirador del Fito* 100 mi E of New Jersey for violation of the Fisheries Conservation Act;

Oct 84–15 Feb 87 underwent major overhaul at CG Yard, Curtis Bay, MD; Feb 84–1990 stationed at Port Angeles, WA, and used primarily for LE and fisheries patrol.

Alert

28 Jun 69–1990 stationed at Cape May, NJ, and used primarily for LE and SAR; 19 May 68 medevaced crewman from FV *Mark Reshetnicov* 20 mi W of Pt. Loma; 24 Dec 69 towed disabled sailboat *Pilgrim* to Cape May, NJ; 13 Apr 70 medevaced crewman from Polish MV *Morskie Oko* off Cape May; 1978 seized FV *Lady Ellen* in the Mona Passage carrying marijuana; 1980 aided refugees during Cuban exodus; Oct–Nov 80 rescued five from sinking sailboat *Miriah*; Oct–Nov 80 seized FV *Judith Lee Rose* with contraband; 25 Feb 80 helped seize MV *Jell II* 50 mi SE of Cape Fear carrying 1t of marijuana; Oct–Nov 80 seized MV *Diana Cecelia* with contraband; 26 Feb 81 seized FV *Lazy Lass* carrying 20t of contraband; 15 Mar 81 seized FV *Sea Shell* carrying 30t of contraband; 12 Nov 81 rescued lone crew member of PC *Halcyon* in 40-ft seas 300 mi NE of Cape Fear; May 82 assisted by FBI, captured 24 mutineers, rescued 12 hostages, and seized the tanker *Ypapanti* on behalf of Liberia following a mutiny of six weeks' seige; 4 Nov 82 towed disabled sailboat *Chicken George* to safety; 9 Nov 82 entered Cuban waters with permission and rescued four from PC *Cheshire*; 31 Jan 83 seized *Gold Coast* carrying 10t of marijuana; 9 Feb 84 rescued five on a raft 40 mi N of Great Inagua I.; 14 Feb 84 seized *Jupiter II* in Windward Passage carrying 12.5t of marijuana; 18 Feb 84 seized

Mont Joli in the Windward Passage carrying 14.5t of marijuana; 25 Feb 84 seized *Diana Lina* carrying 1 lb of marijuana near Navassa I.; 25 Feb 84 seized *Irola B III* carrying 10t marijuana; 25 Feb 84 stood by disabled MV *Christo K* until aided by commercial tug; 9 Mar 84 seized FV *Miss Joan* 350 mi E of Puerto Rico carring 15t of marijuana; 26 Feb 84 seized *Elena* carrying 1 lb of marijuana near Navassa I.; 27 Feb 84 seized *Elizabeth* carrying 11t of marijuana near Navassa I.; 12 Jun 84 seized PC *Peggy Jean* near Cape Fear, NC, carrying marijuana residue; 16 Sep 84 intercepted 140 Haitians on board a 35-foot sailboat in the Windward Passage and returned them to Haiti; 6 Jun 85 seized *Kuluska* carrying 12.5t of marijuana; 31 Aug 85 seized *Skylark I* 520 mi SE of New York with 24t of marijuana on board; 25 Aug 87 seized *Henri* carrying 10t of marijuana; Sep 87 evacuated 235 Haitians from a small island 30 mi W of Great Exuma and transported them to Haiti; 30 Nov 87 intercepted nine Haitian refugees in a sailboat 600 mi SE of Miami, FL, and returned them to Haiti; Dec 87 intercepted 50 Haitian refugees on the 52-foot *Rose Melin* and delivered them to immigration; 15 Dec 87 assisted following collision between MVs *Explorer* and *Qarouh* 700 mi off Palm Beach, FL.

Confidence

19 Apr 66–1979 stationed at Seattle, WA, and used for LE and SAR; 18–21 May 67 fought fire on abandoned tug *Pacific Titan*—took tug and barge in tow 4 mi S of Murder Point, Attu I., and towed them to Adak; 17 Jul 67 seized Japanese FV *Tenyo Maru 3* for fishing within territorial waters off Alaska; 8 Nov 67 towed disabled FV *Kiska* from Little Tonki Bay; early Jan 68 stood by disabled MV *Nichiwa Maru* 850 mi SW of Kodiak, AK, until commercial tug arrived; 1 Mar 68 rescued three from a PC adrift 6 mi E of Cape Creville; 25 Mar 68 escorted distressed cutter *Barataria* to Kodiak, AK; 12 Nov 68 medevaced a seaman from MV *Seroglazna* to Kodiak, AK; 27 Aug 69 seized Japanese FV *Matsuei Maru No 72* for fishing under the 12-mi contiguous zone; 20 Nov 69 assisted in medevac and escorted disabled MV *Atlantic Engineer* to Homer, AK; 27–30 Mar 70 dewatered and towed FV *Stardust* from Adak I. to Kodiak, AK; 6–7 Jul 70 provided medical assistance to MV *Pacemerchant* 420 mi S of Kodiak, AK; Feb 71 seized a Soviet trawler for fisheries violation; 24 Feb 78 seized FV *Sachi Maru 22* for fisheries violation; 8 Aug 75 seized South Korean FV *Kum Kang San* near Sanak I. for fisheries violation; 3 Sep 76 seized Panamanian FV *Kwany Myong 21* 55 mi NW of Sitka, AK, for violation of U.S. waters; 1 Sep 77 seized Taiwanese FV *Highly 301* 87 mi WNW of Cape Sarichef for violation of U.S. waters; 1980–83 stationed at Kodiak, AK, and used for LE and SAR; 11 Mar 80 seized Soviet FV *Zelenograd* 100 mi SW of Kodiak, AK, for fisheries violation; 1983–Oct 86 stationed at Port Angeles, WA, and used for LE and SAR; 20 Dec 83 seized Taiwanese FVs *Highly 301* and *Highly 302* for underlogging catch; 23 Jul 84 seized sailboat *Haja* 150 mi SE of Baja, CA, carrying 30 lbs of marijuana on board; 19 Jan 86 helped seize MV *Eagle 1* in Straits of Juan de Fuca carrying 447 lbs of cocaine in a secret compartment; Oct 86–Jun 88 underwent major renovation; Jun 88–1990 stationed at Cape Canaveral, FL, and used for LE and SAR; 8 Mar 89 rescued over 200 Haitians from two sailboats 30 mi N of Haiti and delivered them to immigration.

Courageous

19 Apr 68–1971 stationed at New York, NY, and used for LE and SAR; 10 Sep 68 towed disabled sailboat *Ibex* 20 mi N of Bimini to Miami, FL; 6

Oct 68 medevaced a boy with bends from FV *M. M. Winter* off Florida; 21 Apr 69 boarded German MV *Helga Witt* following a request by CO concerning armed men on board—escorted her to San Juan, PR; 29–30 Apr 69 assumed duty of on-scene commander following fire on British tanker *Mobile Apex*—took blazing tanker in tow and took her out of St. Croix, Virgin I.; 7 Aug 69 stood by MV *Pionyr* following grounding until arrival of commercial tug; 30 Apr 70 assisted in medevac from sailboat 320 mi N of San Juan, PR; 12 Oct 70 helped in medevac and towed FV *Janice Elaine* to Miami, FL; 1 Aug 71 seized yacht *White Cloud* near Cuba and arrested two for aiding draft evaders; 1972–82 stationed at Cape Canaveral, FL, and used for LE and SAR; 21 Dec 77 seized vessel *Isla de Aruba* carrying contraband; 18 Mar 82 seized Cayman I. *Damocles* carrying 28t of marijuana; 1983–Mar 87 stationed at Key West, FL, and used for LE and SAR; 25 Jan 84 seized a work boat with 20t of marijuana on board; 17 Mar 84 seized a 110-ft work boat with marijuana on board NW of Providence Channel; 20 Mar 84 seized FV *Griffon* 75 mi E of Great Abaco I. carrying 30 lbs of marijuana; 27 Mar 84 seized FV with 5t of marijuana on board near Rum Cay; 18 Aug 84 seized *Mayo* near Rum Cay carrying 5t of marijuana; 6 May 84 seized MV *Canta Dora* 14 mi N of New Providence I. carrying 10t of marijuana; 25 Jun 84 seized MV *Henry I* 100 mi N of Yucatan Channel carrying 8.5t of marijuana; 18 Aug 84 seized *Miriam C* 65 mi NE of Nassau carrying 15t of marijuana; 24 Aug 84 rescued ten from MV *Rio Teta,* which was scuttled 30 mi W of Samana Cay to avoid a search; 14 Jan 85 seized FV *Black Stallion* 330 mi NW of Puerto Rico carrying 10t of marijuana; Mar 87–Jan 90 underwent major overhaul; 1990 stationed at Panama City, FL, and used for LE and SAR.

Dauntless

10 Jun 68–90 stationed at Miami Beach, FL, and used for LE and SAR; 16 Jun 69 towed disabled tug *Victoria* 15 mi off Cuba to safety; 18 Jun 69 rescued eight Cuban refugees without water from 19-foot sailboat 120 mi SSE of Miami, FL; 20 Oct 69 stood by grounded Liberian tanker *Oriental Challenger* until a commercial tug arrived; 14 Dec 69 towed disabled FV *Tortugas* 15 mi off Cuba until power restored; 14 Jan 70 rescued crew from grounded Panamanian MV *Commercial Dispatch* then sighted flares and rescued 19 from Panamanian *Western Venture* grounded on Samana Cay, which had been sent by the owners to assist the *Commercial Dispatch*; 17 Feb 70 evacuated 33 Cuban refugees from Cay Lobos; 2 Jul 70 towed Cuban FV *Santa Maria* 150 mi W of Key West to that port; 26 Jul 70 assisted in medevac of crewman from Dutch MV *Artemis* 240 mi SE of Miami, FL; 14 Aug 70 towed disabled FV *Ponce One* to Jacksonville, FL; 3–5 Oct 70 rescued two groups of Cuban refugees and transported them to Key West; 30 Dec 77 helped seize vessel *Donna Petra* carrying contraband; 17 Apr 78 seized FV *San Rafael* 200 mi E of Ft. Pierce, FL, carrying contraband; Jun 78 seized FV *Fiavesa III* carrying 10t of marijuana; Jan 80 seized *Ali Manolo* off Cay Sal Bank carrying 4t of marijuana; Jan 80 seized *El Loco* off Cay Sal Bank carrying 7t of marijuana; Mar 80 seized *Judy K* near Dry Tortugas carrying 150 lbs of marijuana; 23 Apr–13 May 80 towed 25 vessels, saved eight, and carried out 55 SAR cases during Cuban exodus; 10 Jul 80 seized *Blue Fire* for conspiracy to import illegal aliens; 23 Aug 80 seized *Margie T* off Eleuthera I. carrying 4.5t of marijuana; 8 Oct 80 seized *Santa Maria* off Andros I. carrying 20t of marijuana; Nov 80 seized *Cavu* off Ft. Lauderdale, FL, carrying automatic

weapons; Nov 80 seized *Silent Harmony* in Windward Passage carrying 1.5t of marijuana; Feb 81 seized *Captain Kris* in Yucatan Channel carrying 25t of marijuana; Feb 81 seized *Pleyades* off Florida Keys carrying 8t of marijuana; Mar 81 seized *Pilot II* near Cay Verde carrying 13t of marijuana; Mar 81 seized *Lucky Strike* near Grand Turk I. carrying 12t of marijuana; May 81 seized *Blue Seas* in Yucatan Channel carrying 18t of marijuana; May 81 seized *Grand Lake* off Eleuthera I. carrying 21t of marijuana; Jul 81 seized *Ceja II* off Berry I. carrying 10t of marijuana; 13 Jan 83 seized MV carrying 25t of marijuana; 16 Feb 84 fired 102 rounds of 50 cal at *Captain Black* and found 20t of marijuana; 18 Feb 84 seized *Nite Hawk II* in Yucatan Channel carrying 300 lbs of marijuana; 6 Mar 84 arrested crew of FV *Sue C* who scuttled their ship in the Yucatan Channel—bales of marijuana floated to the surface; 7 Apr 84 seized FV *Reindeer* in the Yucatan Channel with 20t of marijuana on board; 20 Apr 84 seized FV *Rosemary* in the Yucatan Channel carrying 15t of marijuana; 4 Jun 84 seized FV *Natalie Nicole* in Yucatan Channel carrying 2.5t of marijuana and 17 gal of hashish oil; 18 Jun 84 seized FV *Camray* in the Yucatan Channel with marijuana on board; 19 Jun 84 fired 50 rounds of 50 cal and seized FV *Camray* in Yucatan Channel carrying 17t of marijuana; 2 Aug 84 seized *Dona Cecelia* 60 mi SE of Freeport, Bahamas, carrying 20t of marijuana; 11 Jun 85 seized PC *Sam's Song* 10 mi W of Great Isaac Lighthouse carrying 500 lbs of marijuana; 1 Nov 85 intercepted and captured the shrimp boat *Argus* 150 mi off Key West with 20t of marijuana on board; 26 Jan 86 rescued 67 Haitians from a disabled sailboat 21 mi off Miami, FL, in 60-mph winds and 20-ft seas; Jan–Feb 86 recovered debris from space shuttle Challenger off Cape Canaveral, FL; 3 Jul 87 intercepted 140 Haitians on a sailboat 6 mi from Nassau and turned them over to immigration; 31 Aug 87 assisted following a bomb threat against cruise ship *Scandinavian Star*; 5 Jan 88 seized vessel *Marilyn B* carrying 2.5t of marijuana; 9 Jan 88 intercepted a boat in Windward Passage carrying 259 Haitians who were returned to Port-au-Prince; 18 Jan 88 recovered floating bales of marijuana weighing 120 lbs; 23 Jan 88 recovered floating bales of marijuana weighing 780 lbs; 8 Jan 89 rescued 193 Haitians from a 35-foot sailboat and delivered them to immigration; 7 Mar 89 rescued 38 Haitians from a sailboat 17 mi E of Ft. Lauderdale, FL, and delivered them to immigration.

Decisive

23 Aug 68–1982 stationed at New Castle, NH, and used for LE and SAR; 27 Aug 68 dewatered and escorted FV *Linda L* to port; 21 Oct 69 fought fire on PC *Royal Stranger II* at York R. entrance; 22 Oct 69 dewatered and towed disabled PC *Nancy Lee* 10 mi NW of Cape Henry to safety; 18 Dec 69 medevaced crewman from East German FV *Bertolt Brecht* 19 mi E of Cape Ann; 1 Feb 70 escorted distressed FV *Bjartland* 60 mi NE of Cape Cod to safety; 8 Jul 70 rescued nine from Norwegian FV *Skallabjorn* 26 mi E of Portsmouth, NH; Oct 74 seized Japanese FV *Taiyo Maru* off Monhegan I. for territorial violation; 1982–90 stationed at St. Petersburg, FL, and used for LE and SAR; 4 Mar 82 fired 423 rounds of .50 cal mg at Colombian *Cone* and discovered 20t of marijuana on board; 8 Oct 83 intercepted 30-ft sailboat with 69 Haitians on board and returned them to Port-au-Prince, Haiti; 15 Oct 83 seized *No Vessel* carrying 70 lbs of marijuana; 7 Feb 84 seized MV *Vera* in Yucatan Channel carrying 15t of marijuana; 4 Aug 84 helped seize FVs *Captain James L* and *Grand's Anse II*

in the Yucatan Channel with 30t of marijuana on board; 18 July 85 fired 41 rounds of 50 cal at Colombian *El Toro*—one crewman suffered shrapnel wounds; 15 Feb 87 rescued crew from MV *Pat Lytal* in life rafts and recovered two large van-type containers containing marijuana; 25 Jan 88 recovered 240 lbs of floating marijuana; 11 Feb 88 seized MV *Sabrina* carrying 28t of marijuana.

Dependable

22 Nov 68–Aug 89 stationed at Panama City, FL, to be used for LE and SAR. 6 Mar 69 dewatered and towed FVs *Alert* and *Lemperia* to Dry Tortugas; 19 Oct 69 towed disabled FV *Charles Singleton* 80 mi W of Dry Tortugas to safety; Feb–Mar 70 assisted following a fire at oil wells off entrance to Mississippi River Gulf-Outlet Channel; 4 Feb 70 relighted running lights on anchored barges off Florida that had been released by tug due to steering problems; 9 Mar 70 rescued operator from 25-foot sailboat 120 mi SW of Panama City, FL; 29 Jun 70 towed disabled FV *Captain Tick* 60 mi to Panama City, FL; Dec 70 helped fight fire on oil-rig platform in Bay Marchand off Louisiana; 18 Jan 74 battled fire for four days in upper Mississippi River at site of collision of 657-ft bulk carrier *Baune* and the 551-ft tanker *Key Trader*; 4 Oct 76 seized FV *Rio Charges* in Yucatan Channel carrying 10t of marijuana; 21 May 78 seized PC *Island Queen* in Yucatan Channel with 9t of marijuana; 17 June 78 seized FV *Cracker Jack* in Yucatan Channel with 20t of marijuana; 17 Jun 78 seized FV *Sundance* 50 mi S of Key West with 5t of marijuana; 26 June 78 seized MV *Laurence* 20 mi W of Dry Tortugas with 25t of marijuana; 29 Jul 78 seized FV *Los Dos Amigos* 12 mi W of St. Petersburg with 20t of marijuana; 4 Aug 78 seized FV *Ajax* 12 mi E of Miami with 20t of marijuana; 7 Aug 78 seized FV *Rio Chico* 70m SE of Miami with 20t of marijuana; 7 Aug 78 on-scene commander during seizure of MV *Heidi* carrying 120t of marijuana; 13 Oct 78 seized FV *Rio Miosa* 250 mi SW of St. Petersburg with 20t of marijuana; 25 Nov 78 seized PC *Summerwind* 255 mi SW of St. Petersburg with 600 lbs of marijuana; 14 Jan 79 seized FV *Santa Barbara* in Yucatan Channel with 25t of marijuana; 14 Mar 79 seized FV *Miss Phyllis* 150 mi SW of Key West with 30t of marijuana; 25 Nov 79 seized PC *Danielle* 300 mi S of Panama City with 3t of marijuana; 30 Nov 79 seized FV *Sea Horse* with 25t of marijuana; 15 Mar 80 seized PC *Mystar* 100 mi W of Naples, FL, with 5t of marijuana; 28 May 80 seized FV *Sanson* in Yucatan Channel with 10t of marijuana after firing warning shots across vessel's bow with .50 caliber; Apr 80 involved in 32 SAR cases as the first major cutter on scene during Cuban refugee exodus; 22 Apr 80 seized PC *Slow Poke* with 1t of marijuana; 24 Dec 80 seized FV *Ocean Lady* with 10t of marijuana; 10 Dec 80 seized FV *Four Roses* with 26t of marijuana; 13 Feb 81 seized tug *Don Pacho* 200 mi S of New Orleans with 50t of marijuana; 1 Apr 81 seized FV *Broadfire* with 8t of marijuana; 10 Jul 81 seized FV *Jolly Roger* in Yucatan Channel with 26t of marijuana; 15 Jul 81 seized FV *Connie Amos* in Yucatan Channel with 13t of marijuana; 23 Aug 81 seized FV *Sea King* in the Yucatan Channel carrying 9t of marijuana, marking the seizure of one million pounds of marijuana; 31 Aug 81 seized FV *Patsy Ann* with 20t of marijuana; 4 Jan 82 seized FV *Misterioso* carrying 16t of marijuana 55 mi SW of Tampa, marking the first seizure to occur under the U.S.-U.K. agreement for all U.S. boardings of British vessels on the high seas to prevent illegal importation of marijuana; 13 Feb 82 seized FV *Don Pacho* in Gulf of Mexico with 40t of marijuana; 30 Mar 82 seized FV *Lurie Renee* in Gulf of Mexico with 16t of marijuana; 8 Apr 82 seized FV

Kris in Gulf of Mexico with 10t of marijuana; 2 Oct 82 seized FV *Adam* with 14.5t of marijuana; 24 Nov 82 seized FV *My Brother & Me* with 12t of marijuana; 15 Jul 84 seized 50-ft lobster boat *Terry Lee* in Yucatan Channel with 12t of marijuana; 24 Sep 84 seized MV *Jenny Connor* in Yucatan Channel with 15.5t of marijuana; 28 Dec 84 seized shrimper *Susan Ann* in Yucatan Channel with 8.5t of marijuana; 12 Mar 85 seized MV *Tempora* in northern Gulf for the presence of marijuana residue; 30 Sep 85 seized lobster boat *Cloud* 340 mi S of Mobile, AL, with 4.5t of marijuana; 2 Oct 85 seized FV *Gramma J.* 340 mi S of Mobile, AL, with 7t of marijuana; 12 Dec 85 seized FV *Chief C* in Yucatan Channel with 9t of marijuana; 22 Feb 86 seized Honduran MV *Karia* 30 mi W of Dry Tortugas; 21 May 86 seized PC *Gator* in Yucatan Channel with 600 lbs of marijuana; 12 Oct 86 seized FV *Melissa* 280 mi SW of Miami, FL, carrying 10t of marijuana; Feb 87 rescued six from a raft after sinking of *Pat Lytal* 60 mi W of Jamaica and recovered 35t of marijuana; 15 Mar 87 seized FV *Lady Hamilton III* in Yucatan Channel with 22t of marijuana; 2 Jun 87 successfully completed 7000th helicopter landing, establishing *Dependable* as the leader in Coast Guard Ship Helo operations; 10 Aug 87 seized PC *Iron Mistress* in Yucatan Channel with 417 lbs of marijuana; 20 Sep 87 seized PC *Panacea* below Yucatan Channel with 600 lbs of marijuana; 23 Sep 87 seized FV *La Nina* below Yucatan Channel with 5t of marijuana; Apr 89–1990 underwent major overhaul.

Diligence

31 Aug 64–1985 stationed at Key West, FL, and used for LE and SAR; 11 Sep 65 assisted in tow of disabled FV *Carousel* W of Tampa, FL; late Sept 65 took on board 21 Cuban refugees who had been rescued by Honduran MV *Choloma* and took them to Key West, FL; mid-Dec 65 towed Cuban refugee sailboat with 11 on board from 140 mi SE of Miami, FL, to Key West; 24–26 Jan 67 towed barge and escorted tug *Viking Prince* to Key West, FL, after tug lost partial power; 10 April 67 towed boat carrying three Cuban refugees from 60 mi SSE of Key West, FL, to that port; 28 Jun 67 embarked 28 Cuban refugees from three small boats and transported them to Key West, FL; 29 Nov 68 rescued four from FV *Macedonia* 35 mi SSE of Sombrero Key; 15 Mar 69 dewatered and towed disabled PC *Apollo 8* 50 mi SW of Key West, FL, to that port; 18 Aug 69 towed disabled Danish MV *Mercantine* off Florida until relieved by a commercial tug; Apr 78 seized MV *Heriberto* carrying 25t of marijuana; 31 Oct 80 seized FV *Lady Mona* SW of Key West, FL, carrying 20t of marijuana; 5 Mar 82 fired on, stopped, and seized a Colombian MV in the Windward Passage—20t of marijuana were on board; 26 Oct 83 seized FV *Ona* carrying 20t of marijuana; 9 Mar 84 helped fight fire on board cruise ship *Scandinavian Sea* at Port Canaveral, FL; 20 May 84 seized MV *Bismarck* 230 mi E of Miami, FL, carrying 30t of marijuana; 2 Jun 84 seized ferry *Mystic Isle* in the Bahamas with 5t of marijuana in a concealed compartment; 22 Sep 84 rescued crew of PC *Iggy III* 60 mi N of Great Inagua I. after they had scuttled their craft with marijuana on board; 1985–90 stationed at Cape Canaveral, FL, and used for LE and SAR; Dec 85 rescued 72 Haitians from a sinking 40-foot sailboat N of Andros I. and delivered them to immigration; Dec 86 intercepted a 35-foot sailboat carrying 124 migrants 30 mi N of Cuba and returned them to Haiti.

Durable

8 Dec 68–1969 stationed at Galveston, TX, and used for LE and SAR; 1969–Oct 86 stationed at Brownsville, TX, and used for LE and SAR;

The *Diligence* undergoes trials on 23 Aug 64. A unique feature of this class is the 360-degree visibility from the bridge. SAR qualities were emphasized when this class was designed.

Jun 69 assisted grounded FV *Dahlia* 125 mi S of Galveston, TX; Feb–Mar 70 monitored situation following fire on oil rig off Mississippi R. entrance; 25 Sep 82 seized 2 U.S. FVs off the Yucatan Peninsula carrying 13t of marijuana; 13 May 83 seized *Afco VI* carrying 14.5t of marijuana; 5 Feb 84 seized a 70-foot vessel in the Yucatan Channel—vessel tried to prevent boarding by ramming cutter—marijuana discovered; 27 Mar 84 seized an FV with 15t of marijuana on board in the Yucatan Channel; Oct 86–Oct 88 underwent major overhaul; Oct 88–1990 stationed at St. Petersburg, FL, and used for LE and SAR.

Reliance

20 June 64–1975 stationed at Corpus Christi, TX, and used for LE and SAR; Mar–Apr 65 served on Campeche Patrol; 29 May 65 evacuated ill seaman from Veracruz, Mexico, to Corpus Christi, TX; Jan–Feb 67 served on Campeche Patrol; 12 Feb 67 towed disabled FV *Esto Queen* from 140 mi SE of Port Isabel to that port; 12 Mar 68 escorted distressed FV *Southern Crest* to Port Aransas, TX; Dec 68 served on Campeche Patrol; 5 Feb 69 towed disabled FV *La Crevette VII* 360 mi S of Panama City, FL, to Port Isabel, TX; Mar 70 monitored situation following fire on oil rig off Mississippi R. entrance; May–Jun 70 assisted following explosion and fire on oil rig off Galveston, TX; 1976–82 stationed at Yorktown, VA, and used for reserve training; 15 Jul 76 towed disabled sailboat to Montauk, NY; 8 Feb 80 assisted sailboat *Rapier*, which was taking on water off

Bermuda; 20 Oct 80 seized Spanish FV *Isla Alegranza* for violation of Fisheries Conservation and Management Act of 1976 70 mi SE of Cape May, NJ; 1982–Apr 87 stationed at Port Canaveral, FL, and used for LE and SAR; 23 Jul 84 seized sailboat *Jasmine* in Yucatan Channel carrying 400 lbs of marijuana; 30 Nov 84 fought fire and towed *Seaward Explorer*, which had been under tow by Cuban gunboat; Sep 85 intercepted boats carrying over 200 Haitians and delivered them to immigration; 16 Jan 86 helped fight fire on cruise ship *Oceanic* at Port Canaveral, FL; 4 Nov 86 seized *Rella* carrying 5t of marijuana; Apr 87–Jan 89 underwent major renovation at CG Yard, Curtis Bay, MD; Jan 89–1990 stationed at New Castle, NH, and used for LE and SAR.

Resolute

8 Dec 66–1976 stationed at San Francisco, CA, and used for LE and SAR; 9–12 Apr 67 picked up raft and debris from Canadian FV *Sea Ranger* 45 mi N of Unalaska I., AK—no survivors; 19 Aug 67 towed disabled FV *Yvette* from 10 mi NW of Farallon I. to Drake's Bay; 10 Jan 68 collided with cutter *Avoyel* 100 mi S of San Francisco, CA, during underway replenishment—slightly damaged; 16–19 May 68 towed disabled tug *Neptune* 10 mi N of Unimak I. to Dutch Harbor, AK; 27 Jun 68 towed disabled yacht *Hyding* 34 mi W of Cape Mendocino; 3 Mar 69 towed disabled FV *Rebel* 100 mi SW of San Francisco, CA, to that port;

1976–79 stationed at Alameda, CA, and used for LE and SAR; 1979–90 stationed at Astoria, OR, and used for LE and SAR; 18 Apr 80 towed disabled FV *Driftwood* to Yaquina Bay; 20 Jun 80 assisted tug *Miriam M. Defelice* near Alsea Bay; 24 Jun 80 assisted sailboat *Sea Wink* 50 mi off Oregon; 6 Sep 80 medevaced crewman from FV *Centurion*; 17 Oct 80 towed disabled FV *Clara II* 30 mi to Coos Bay; 9 Jan 81 towed disabled MV *Concord* and prevented her from grounding near Columbia River Bar; 15 Jun 81 assisted disabled sailboat *Breezie* off Oregon; 7–13 Aug 81 towed NOAA data buoy from San Diego, CA, to Astoria, OR; Dec 88 towed disabled Navy research vessel *Pacific Escort* to safety.

Steadfast

7 Oct 68–1990 stationed at St. Petersburg, FL, and used for LE and SAR; 1 Mar 70 monitored situation following seizure of U.S. FV *Jocelyn C* by Cuban Navy for territorial violation; 25 Nov 70 towed disabled FV *Anna Marie* until relieved by a commercial tug; 13 Jan 77 seized FV *Truent VI* off Jacksonville, FL, carrying 3.5t of marijuana; 25 Dec 77 seized vessel *Thanet* carrying contraband; 27 Dec 77 helped seize vessels *Miss Connie* and *Ecopesca IV* off Great Bahama Bank carrying 35t of marijuana; Apr 78 seized MV *Lemar III* carrying 15t of marijuana; Jan 79 seized MV *Mini I* carrying 50t of marijuana; 20 Oct 80 seized MV *Little Bugger* SW of Key West, FL, carrying 17t of marijuana; 24 Oct 80 seized a PC SW of Key

Cutter *Reliance* on 20 Jun 64 undergoing drills with an HH-52 helicopter. Initially home-ported at Corpus Christi, TX, she was the first cutter fitted with a helicopter landing pad to operate in the Gulf of Mexico.

West, FL, carrying 50 bales of marijuana; 21 Jun 81 fired 75 rounds of .50 cal mg at *Snowflake*; 4 Nov 81 screened Soviet trawlers from area where space shuttle Columbia's booster fell into the ocean; 18 Jul 83 intercepted a 25-ft Haitian sailboat in the Windward Passage with 21 on board—returned people to Port-au-Prince, Haiti; 1 Jan 84 seized an FV under tow by an MV after discovering marijuana on board; 9 Mar 84 helped fight fire on cruise ship *Scandinavian Sea* at Port Canaveral, FL; 26 Mar 84 helped seize FV *Claudina* E of the Bahamas with marijuana on board; 26 May 85 seized FV *Jorge Louis* 120 mi N of Turks and Caicos Islands carrying 6t of marijuana; 7 Jun 85 seized *Argana II* in Yucatan Channel carrying 30t of marijuana; 29 Aug 85, following a trail of marijuana bales located tug *Atlantic King* and discovered a secret compartment containing 200 bales of marijuana; 4 Sep 85 intercepted a 40-ft sailboat carrying 125 Haitians; Jan 86 intercepted three unseaworthy craft carrying Haitians—a 45-ft sailboat carrying 84 60 mi W of Haiti, and another 45-ft sailboat carrying 104 20 mi W of Haiti—all were returned to Haiti; 30 Apr 86 seized *Six Kids* carrying 1 lb of marijuana; Oct 86 seized FV *Shangri-La* carrying 5t of marijuana—crew scuttled FV; 2 Jun 87 seized *Nomadic Star* carrying 260 lbs of marijuana; 4 Aug 87 rescued 339 Haitians from a leaking shrimp boat and transported them to Port-au-Prince, Haiti; 6 Aug 87 seized *El Condor* carrying .5t of marijuana; 3 Aug 87 intercepted 339 Haitians on the 65-ft MV *Green Waters* in the Bahamas and returned them to Haiti; 13 Aug 87 intercepted sailboat *Patience* carrying 42 Haitians and returned them to Haiti.

Cutter *Vigilant*, 5 Jun 87. Although she has spent her entire career stationed at New Bedford, MA, *Vigilant* and many other cutters take their turn in the Caribbean searching for drug smugglers.

Valiant

28 Oct 67–1990 stationed at Galveston, TX, and used for LE and SAR; 14 Jul 69 stood by disabled tanker *Texaco Nevada* 275 mi S of New Orleans, LA, until a commercial tug arrived; 22 Oct 69 helped dewater and escorted leaking Panamanian MV *Lamolinera* 250 mi SE of Galveston, TX, to Southwest Pass, Mississippi R.; 26 Jun 80 seized FV *Alex Luz* off Mexico carrying marijuana; 21 Mar 84 assisted in rescue of 15 from Panamanian MV *Panky* 150 mi SW of Tampa, FL; 8 Jun 84 seized FV *Baru* off Yucatan Peninsula carrying 4.5t of marijuana; 16 Jun 84 seized sailboat *Pride* 135 mi SW of Key West, FL, carrying 1.5t of marijuana; 13 Aug 84 seized MV *Laura Rosa* 30 mi NE of Nassau carrying 7t of marijuana in a hidden compartment; 15 Aug 84 seized MV *Ensa Quemada* in Yucatan Channel carrying 12t of marijuana; 26 Sep 84 seized PC *Sea Gull* 170 mi SW of Jamaica carrying 7.5t of marijuana; 2 Aug 84 seized FV *El Pulpo* SE of the Yucatan Channel with 8 tons of marijuana on board; 26 Sep 84 seized a PC 170 mi SW of Jamaica with 7t of marijuana on board; 7 Oct 84 seized FV *Julie Ann* 75 mi NE of Alacran Reef with 3.5t of marijuana on board; 20 Jul 85 seized FV *Juan XXIII* 125 mi SE of Cozumel, Mexico, carrying 22t of marijuana; 24 Jul 85 detained and turned over to Mexican authorities FV *Caloa* 35 mi N of Yucatan Peninsula carrying 7t of marijuana; 31 Jul 85 seized 6t of marijuana from MV *Langstrand,* which scuttled herself in the Yucatan Channel; 27 Jan 88 rammed by Haitian MV *Dieu Qui Donne* E of the Bahamas—*Valiant* sustained no damage, but the MV sank.

Venturous

16 Aug 68–1970 stationed at San Diego, CA, and used for LE and SAR; 13 Nov 69 recovered abandoned sailboat *Jazz Limited* anchored off Mexico; 22–23 Dec 69 towed disabled FV *Crusader* to San Diego, CA; 1970–79 stationed at San Pedro, CA, and used for LE and SAR; 9 Jan 70 helped tow disabled tanker *Connecticut* 100 mi off California; 26 Feb 70 towed disabled FV *Myrtle L* to safety; 20 Jul 70 towed disabled PC *Moon Spinner* from Cape Cross to Pelican, AK; 1979–90 stationed at Terminal I., CA, and used for LE and SAR; 24 Jul 82 maintained surveillance of Soviet intelligence trawler *Sarychev* off Strait of Juan de Fuca.

Vigilant

1 Oct 64–Dec 88 stationed at New Bedford, MA, and used for LE and SAR; mid-Jul 65 served as on-scene coordinator during unsuccessful search for ditched USAF C-121 85 mi E of Nantucket; 10 Jan 66 medevaced injured American fisherman from Russian FV *Zelenoborsk* and assumed tow of disabled FV *Venture I* from Russian FV and towed to Nantucket Lightship; 19 Jan 66 watched two damaged Russian FVs that sought shelter in Provincetown, MA; 4 Jan 67 escorted disabled Liberian MV *Failaika* to Portland, ME; 19 Apr 67 received 12 Cuban refugees from HMS *Zest* and transported them to Miami; 10 Sep 67 medevaced crew member from FV *Chilmark Voyager* 130 mi ESE of Nantucket; 13 Jul 69 took on board disabled 26-foot PC 130 mi N of Bermuda; Jun 70 assisted sailboats participating in the Newport, RI, to Bermuda Race that were hit by a storm; 2 Jul 70 seized West German FV *Conrad* for fishing inside Contiguous Zone; 23 Nov 70 returned defecting Lithuanian seaman Simas Kudirka to Soviet FV *Sovietskaya Litva* near Martha's Vineyard, MA; Jul 78 seized MV *Sir Echo* 280 mi SE of Wilmington, NC, carrying a large amount of marijuana; Apr 80 assisted MV *Charleston* due to contaminated fuel; Sep 80 seized U.S. MV *The Hydra* in Mona Passage carrying 31t of marijuana; Sep 80 assisted in

medevac of crewman from *Charlotte Lykes* to San Juan, PR; Jul 81 seized U.S. sailboat *Quest* and FV *Viviana* carrying 30t of marijuana; Jul 81 assisted disabled sailboat *Amphitrite*; 10 Dec 83 seized FV *Mario E* carrying 16.5t of marijuana; 13 Dec 83 seized PC *Natacha* near Great Isaac I. for narcotics violation; 27 Feb 84 seized MV *Elizabeth* in Windward Passage carrying 15t of marijuana in a hidden compartment; 1 Jul 84 assisted sailboat *Charity* 30 mi E of Andros I.; 4 Aug 84 escorted damaged MV *Wellwood* to Miami, FL; 13 Aug 84 seized the Panamian tug *Laura Rosa* 20 mi SW of Great Abaco I. after 10t of marijuana was discovered in a false fuel tank; 28 Jan 85 seized Cayman *Emanuel II* carrying 659 lbs of cocaine; 18 Apr 86 seized the U.S. FV *Stella del Mare* 130 mi off Cape Cod for using nets with mesh smaller than regulation size—first seizure for net violation; May 87 seized MV *Dick II* in the Caribbean with 15t of marijuana on board; Oct 88–90 underwent major overhaul. Jun 90 stationed at Cape Canaveral, FL, and used for LE and SAR.

Vigorous

23 Apr 69–Oct 1989 stationed at New London, CT, and used for LE and SAR; 8 Aug 69 medevaced patient from USNS *Lynch* to New London,

CT; 3 Feb 70 towed disabled FV *Barnacle Bill* 40 mi S of Long Island to safety; 17 Aug 75 seized Cuban FV *Playa de Varadera* for fisheries violation 50 mi E of Nantucket I.; 21–23 Mar 80 shadowed and seized suspected drug runner *Jose Gregorio* off NY, finding 30t of marijuana; 25 Apr 80 picked up crew from downed CG HH52 helicopter 190 mi SE of Cape Hatteras, NC, after being given their location by a CG C-130 patrol plane; 29 Apr 82 seized *Diamante* carrying 7.5t of marijuana; 11 Oct 82 rescued three men from capsized trimaran *Gonzo* off Cape Cod in 40-ft seas; 22 Oct 83 seized Italian FV *Maria Michela* 100 mi E of New Jersey for underlogging catch; 2 Nov 83 seized *Hetty* carrying 15t of hashish 90 mi E of Cape May, NJ; 1 May 84 seized FV *Marie Julie* in Windward Passage with marijuana residue on board; 1 Jul 84 repaired a sinking 36-foot sailboat; 2 Jun 85 intercepted MV *Lady Sea* 18 mi S of Great Inagua, Bahamas, carrying illegal immigrants; 9 Dec 86 helped fight fire and towed FV *Old Colony* from 60 mi SE of Montauk Point to safety; 4 Jul 86 rescued four from a Zodiac 200 mi S of Puerto Rico; 6 Mar 88 intercepted a 40-ft boat carrying 154 Haitians and returned them to Haiti; Oct 89–1990 underwent major overhaul.

230-FOOT CUTTER

Name	Hull Number	Builder	Keel Laid	Launched	Commissioned	Disposition
Storis (ex-*Eskimo*)	WMEC 38 WAGB 38 WAG 38 WAGL 38	Toledo Shipbuilding Co., Toledo, OH	14 Jul 41	4 Apr 42	30 Sep 42	Active

Cost	$2,072,889 (hull & machinery)
Hull	
Displacement (tons)	1,715 fl (1945)
Length	230' oa
Beam	43'2" mb
Draft	15' max (1945)
Machinery	
Main Engines	1 electric motor driven by generators driven by 3 Cooper-Bessemer-type GN-8 8-cyl diesels
BHP	1,800
Propellers	single
Performance	
Max Sustained	12.5 kts, 11,300-mi radius (1945)
Cruising	10.0 kts, 15,500-mi radius (1945)
Logistics	
Fuel Oil (95%)	108,430 gal
Complement	17 officers, 131 men (1945)
Deck Gear	
Boom Capacity	20 tons
Hoist Power	Electricity
Electronics	
Detection Radar	Bk (1943); SL (1945)
Sonar	QCL-2 (1945)
Armament	2 3"/50 (single); 4 20mm/80 (single); 2 dc tracks; 4 Y-guns; 2 mousetraps

Design

The *Storis* was designed by the U.S. Coast Guard, with detail drawings by Toledo Shipbuilding Company, to be a supply ship for the Greenland area with a degree of icebreaking capability. Contract was let 26 Jan 41. Her design closely parallels the smaller 180-foot tenders of 1942–44. She was to be named the *Eskimo*. However, during her construction the State Department, concerned that the natives of Greenland might find the name offensive, requested that another name be selected. The *Storis* was the first tender fitted with a double top-lift boom.

Storis

1942–47 stationed at Boston, MA, and used for wartime duties; 1 Dec 47–15 Sep 48 stationed at Curtis Bay, MD, and used to support military preparedness; 15 Sep 48–Dec 57 stationed at Juneau, AK, and used for LE and SAR; 16 Dec 54 rescued survivors from CG plane crash, Haines harbor, AK; summer 55 deployed with USN for Artic Ops; 17 Jan 56 fought fire at cold-storage plant, Juneau, AK; summer 56 deployed with USN for Artic Ops; Jul–Dec 57 beginning in Seattle, WA, circumnavigated North America via NW Passage accompanied by cutters *Bramble* and *Spar*; Dec 57–1990 stationed at Kodiak, AK, and used for LE and SAR; summer 58 assisted in resupply of DEW Line stations; 7 Apr 59 medevaced seaman from Soviet MV *Piscavaya Industriya* in Akun Bay, Aleutian I.; Jan–Feb 65 unsuccessfully searched for three Russian trawlers reported to be in vicinity of St. Paul I., St. George I., and Unimak Pass; Mar 65 intercepted Russian FV *Pavel Chebotnyagin* crabbing for king crab in a restricted fishing area off Alaska and escorted her to sea; 18 May 65 transferred recovered seaman to Russian FV *Dozorny* at Seward, AK; 22–23 Jun 65 discovered Russian factory ship *Konstantin Sukhanov* and picker boats hauling tangle nets 15 mi S of Unimak I., AK, and informed her of the King Crab Agreement while she was departing; Apr 66 discovered and warned Russian FV fishing in U.S. territorial waters off Bluff Point; 13 Nov 66 took on board survivors of FV *Emerald C* from FV *Endeavor*; 2 Mar 67 seized Russian FV *Srtm 8-413* for fishing within 3-mi limit 300 mi SW of Kodiak, AK; 22 Mar 67 diverted to scene by CG ac and seized Russian FV *Srtm 8-457* for fishing within 12-mi contiguous zone 210 mi SE of Kodiak, AK; 26 Dec 67 medevaced crewman from FV *Koshin Maru No 2* 180 mi S of Kodiak, AK; 30 Jul 68 refloated and towed disabled FV *Rebecca* from Humpback Bay to Dutch Harbor, AK; 15 May 69 medevaced crewman from Russian MV *Topol*; 7 Jun 69 seized Japanese FVs *Zento Maru No 6* and *FS 2-2150* in Norton Sound for fishing inside 12-mi zone; 7 Sep 69 holed by ice while assisting beset tug *Active* and barge near Point Barrow, AK; 15 Jul 70 towed Canadian FV *Kaare* from 150 mi SW of Kodiak until relieved by commercial tug; 18 Aug 70 seized FV *Kaki Maru No 18* off Middleton I. for violation of the 12-mi contiguous zone; 17 Jan 72 seized Soviet factory ship *Lamut* and FV *Kolyvan* for illegally fishing near St. Matthew I.; Apr 72 assisted in seizure of Japanese FVs *Kohoyo Maru 31* and *Ryoyo Maru* for fisheries violations; Jun 79 seized FV *Kaiyo Maru 53* for fisheries violation; 27 Mar 83 seized *Shinei Maru 21* 165 mi NW of Midway I. for fisheries violation; 30 Mar 83 seized fishing tender *Hiyo Maru 7* and FV *Tomi Maru No 83* 165 mi off St. Matthews I. for improperly logging fishing activity; 16 Sep 87 seized FV *Rebecca Irene* for fishing violation 30 mi S of Akutan I.

Cutter *Storis* on 2 Sep 86. She was designed during the early days of WWII to service remote stations in Greenland. Since that time she has performed a wide variety of tasks including a transit of the Northwest Passage across the top of North America. In 1986 her well, or buoy, deck was shortened in order to gain interior space. Note the Coast Guard shield adorning the poop deck.

NAVY *DIVER* CLASS

Name	Hull Number	Builder	Keel Laid	Launched	Commissioned	Disposition
Escape	WMEC 6 ARS 6	Basalt Rock Co., Napa, CA	24 Aug 42	22 Nov 42	20 Nov 43 (USN) 5 Jan 80 (CG)	Active
Acushnet (ex-*Shackle*)	WMEC 167 WAGO 167 WAT 167 ARS 9	Basalt Rock Co., Napa, CA	26 Oct 42	1 Apr 43	5 Feb 44 (USN) 23 Aug 46 (CG)	Active
Yocona (ex-*Seize*)	WMEC 168 WAT 168 ARS 26	Basalt Rock Co., Napa, CA	28 Sep 43	8 Apr 44	3 Nov 44 (USN) 28 Jun 46 (CG)	Active

Cost N/A

Hull
  Displacement (tons)   1,756 fl (1964); 1,246 light (1964)
  Length   213'6" oa; 207' bp
  Beam   40'8" max
  Draft   13'11" max (1964)
Machinery
  Main Engines   2 diesels
  BHP   3,030
  Propellers   twin

Performance
  Max Sustained   14.4 kts, 10,000-mi radius (1964)
  Economic   10.3 kts, 13,700-mi radius (1964)
Logistics
  Fuel Oil (95%)   95,960 gal
  Complement   7 officers, 1 warrant, 68 men (1964)
Electronics
  Detection Radar   OS-8E (*Acushnet*—1964)
  Sonar   none—1964
Armament   2 20mm/80 (*Acushnet*—1964)
Design
  The *Diver*-class ships were designed as salvage ships for USN.

Acushnet

1947 towed cutter *Yamacraw* from West Coast to Charleston, SC; Sep 47–1968 stationed at Portland, ME; Sep 47 fought fire in Bar Harbor, ME; Apr 50 served on IIP; 3–19 May 50 served on IIP; Jun 50 served on IIP; 4 Oct 50 along with cutters *Cowslip* and *Snohomish* freed MV *Berwindvale* aground in Kennebec R.; 5 Mar–10 Aug 57 shared IIP with cutter *Evergreen*; 17 Apr–4 Jul 59 shared IIP with cutter *Androscoggin*; Nov 59 salvage gear removed and SAR gear added; Mar 60 salvaged cutter *General Greene* that had been driven 100 yards onto Springhill Beach, Cape Cod, during a violent gale; Apr 61 assisted sinking MV *Marine Merchant* 40 mi SE of Portland, ME; 16 Dec 61 towed disabled FV *Felicia and Grace* from 170 mi E of Sable I. for 600 mi during a gale; 26 Dec 61 rescued 10 from dredge *Cartagena* 200 mi off Cape Cod during a severe storm with 75 mph winds and 30-foot seas; Nov 62 towed disabled FV *Wawenock* E of Sable I. into Portland during a gale, a distance of 690 mi; May 63 salvaged crashed CG helicopter 600 yards off Duxbury Beach, MA; 9 Jan 66 medevaced fisherman from FV *Rush* 120 mi SE of Nantucket—transferred him to a hospital by a CG HH52 helicopter; 24–25 Jan 66 escorted disabled MV *South African Victory* to Boston, MA; 22 Feb 66 escorted FV *Anita C. Rose* from 30 mi SE of Nantucket LS to New Bedford, MA; 1 Dec 66 assisted in medevac from FV *Judy and Linda Four*; 8 Dec 66 towed disabled FV *Michele* and passed her to Canadian CG; 30 Apr 67 towed disabled FV *Plymouth* from 90 mi E of Cape Cod to Boston, MA; 30 Oct 67 rescued Cuban refugee from distresed 17-foot PC 50 mi SE of Key West, FL; 15 Feb 68 escorted distressed FV *Johnnie and Nick* 47 mi SE of Cape Cod to Gloucester, MA; 30 Jun 68 towed disabled sailboat *Coila* to Portland, ME; 1968–mid-71 stationed at Gulfport, MS; 8 Jul 68–1978 designated WAGO and used in support of the National Data Buoy Project of NOAA; Jul 68–Jun 71 made 11 extended cruises mooring and servicing oceanographic research buoys in the North Pacific; 12 Oct 70 assisted in medevac from MV *Lisboa*; mid-1971–90 stationed at Gulfport, MS, location of NASA test facility; 11 Aug–7 Sep 75 conducted SAR research off Gulf of Mexico shelf area; mid-1978 designated WMEC; 1 Mar 84 seized

Cutter *Yocona* circa 1985. Since the late nineteenth century the Coast Guard and its forefather, the Revenue Cutter Service, have stationed powerful tugs in the Pacific Northwest to assist large vessels in distress. *Yocona* and other cutters stationed in this region have also been very busy with fisheries protection.

tugboat *Todo Mio* in Gulf of Mexico carrying 26t of marijuana; 5 Apr 84 seized FV *Hermlou* in Yucatan Channel carrying 8t of marijuana; 8 Apr 84 seized FV *Lady Lynn* in Yucatan Channel carrying 18t of marijuana; 12 Sep 84 seized FV *Queen Anne* 120 mi S of Jamaica carrying 4t of marijuana; 21 Oct 84 seized MV *Mosquitia* in the Yucatan Channel carrying 13t of marijuana; 23 Oct 84 seized a workboat in the Yucatan Channel with 6t of marijuana on board; 1 Nov 84 guided Mexican authorities to MV *Yaimara* carrying 15t of marijuana; 5 Nov 84 guided Mexican authorities to MV *Asterix* carrying 20t of marijuana; 8 Nov 84 seized MV *Aurora I* 100 mi N of Yucatan Channel carrying 18t of marijuana; 8 Nov 84 seized MV in the Yucatan Channel with 500 bales of marijuana on board; 23 Dec 87 seized PC *Blind Melon* N of Cuba with 18 bales of marijuana on board.

Escape

1980–90 stationed at Charleston, SC, and used for LE and SAR; 2 Dec 82 seized *My Lord* carrying 5t of marijuana; Sep 83 seized a Panamanian shrimp boat 1,575 mi E of Miami, FL, carrying 13t of marijuana—forced to train fire hose on pilothouse after shrimper refused to heave to; 8 Jan 84 seized a FV off Mysteriosa Bank 300 mi SE of the Yucatan Channel with 10t of marijuana on board; 27 Feb 84 seized yacht *Blue Light* off the Bahamas carrying 3t of marijuana; 1 Mar 84 seized FV *Blue Boy* E of Great Inagua I. carrying 4t of marijuana; 1 May 84 seized sailboat *Cangceiro* 35 mi N of Haiti carrying 4t of marijuana; 7–8 May 86 seized FV *Cape Blanco* 1,000 mi off East Coast during heavy weather carrying 20t of marijuana; 6 Dec 88 seized MV *Mr. Ted* 100 mi off Miami, FL, carrying 7t of marijuana.

Yocona

1946–53 stationed at Eureka, CA, and used for LE and SAR; 1954–83 stationed at Astoria, OR, and used for LE and SAR; 11 Nov 55 maneuvered alongside sinking FV *Ocean Pride*, and crew of 13 jumped on board

The *Acushnet* on 13 Jan 61 as an oceangoing tug (WAT). WATs had black hulls until 1958. Previously *Acushnet* had a boom on her foremast and had a protective hull streak.

in heavy seas 50 mi off Cape Lookout, OR; 25 Sep 59 rescued 10 survivors from a downed USN P5M seaplane off Oregon after they had been located by a CG aircraft; 26 Jan 65 escorted listing U.S. MV *Elaine* from 180 mi W of Astoria, OR, to Tongue Point, OR; 13 Sep 69 repaired engine on disabled FV *Karre* 300 mi SE of Kodiak I.; 6 Jun 70 seized South Korean FVs *Tae Yang 203* and *Tae Yang 205* for territorial waters violation off Alaska; 1984–90 stationed at Kodiak, AK, and used for LE and SAR; 19 Jan 87 towed disabled FV *Seattle Star* to Unalaska Bay; 26 Jan 87 provided medical assistance to FV *Pacific Enterprise*; 27 Jan 87 assisted MV *Tempest* off Cape Pankoff; 7 Feb 87 fought fire on FV *Amatuli* 45 mi E of St. George I.; 8 Feb 87 assisted FV *Fukuyoshi Maru No 85*; 20 Aug 87 seized FV *Constitution* in Peterson Bay for using illegal gear.

NAVY *CHEROKEE/NAVAJO* CLASS

Name	Hull Number	Builder	Keel Laid	Launched	Commissioned	Disposition
Ute	WMEC 76 T-ATF 76	United Engineering Co., Alameda, CA	27 Feb 42	24 Jun 42	13 Dec 42 (USN) 30 Sep 80 (CG)	*Decomm* May 88
Lipan	WMEC 85 T-ATF 85	United Engineering Co., Alameda, CA	30 May 42	17 Sep 42	29 Apr 43 (USN) 30 Sep 80 (CG)	*Decomm* 31 Mar 88
Avoyel	WMEC 150 WAT 150 ATF 150	Charleston Shipbuilding & Dry Dock Co., Charleston, SC	25 Mar 44	9 Aug 44	8 Jan 45 (USN) 3 Oct 56 (CG)	*Decomm* 1969
Chilula	WMEC 153 WAT 153 ATF 153	Charleston Shipbuilding & Dry Dock Co., Charleston, SC	13 Jul 44	1 Dec 44	5 Apr 45 (USN) 3 Oct 56 (CG)	Active
Cherokee	WMEC 165 WAT 165 ATF 66	Bethlehem Shipbuilding Corp., Staten I., NY	23 Dec 38	10 Nov 39	26 Apr 40 (USN) 29 Jun 46 (CG)	Active
Tamaroa (ex-*Zuni*)	WMEC 166 WAT 166 ATF 95	Commercial Iron Works, Portland, OR	8 Mar 43	31 Jul 43	9 Oct 43 (USN) 29 Jun 46 (CG)	Active

Cost   N/A
Hull
  Displacement (tons)   1,641 fl (1966); 1,536 light (1966)
  Length   205′3″ oa; 195′ bp
  Beam   38′7″ max
  Draft   16′10″ max (1966)
Machinery
  Main Engines   4 electric motors driven by 4 Allis Chalmers generators driven by 4 General Motors diesel engines
  BHP   3,000
  Propellers   single
Performance
  Max Sustained   16.5 kts, 4,055-mi radius (1966)
  Economic   10.1 kts, 13,097-mi radius (1966)
Logistics
  Fuel Oil (95%)   97,581 gal
  Complement   7 officers, 1 warrant, 68 men (1961)
Electronics
  Detection Radar   SPN-25 (1961)
  Sonar   none
Armament   1 3″/50
Design
  The *Cherokee* class was designed as a fleet ocean tug.

Avoyel

3 Oct 56–1957 stationed at Eureka, CA; 1957–69 stationed at Fields Landing, CA; Mid-Aug 65 rescued survivor from FV *Kay-D* 15 mi NW of Humboldt Bay following a collision between the FV and tug *Sea Robin*; 27–29 Dec 65 relieved *Cape Carter* of tow and towed tug *Sea Wolf* to Humboldt Bay; early Aug 67 seized Russian FV *Srtm 8-457* for fishing in U.S. waters in the Aleutian I.; 10 Jan 68 collided with cutter *Resolute* 100 mi S of San Francisco, CA, during underway replenishment—*Resolute* slightly damaged.

Cherokee

1946–90 stationed at Norfolk, VA, and used for LE and SAR; 27 Feb 47 escorted storm-battered MV *President Garfield* from 75 mi S of Diamond Shoal into Hampton Roads; 25 Dec 49 rescued crew from Argentine tanker that broke in half and towed her aft section to port; 14 May 51 assisted following collision between MV *Thomas Tracey* and naval vessel; 6 May–1 Jun 52 relieved *Kaw* of tow of *Tahoma* at 43°48′N, 64°47′W, and continued to Curtis Bay, MD; 28 Feb 54 freed grounded Panamanian MV *Rio Mar* off Cape Henry; Jan 55 assisted MV *Steelore* 275 mi off Cape Henry; Jan 56 towed MV *Hellespont* 176 mi E of False Cape; Feb 56 towed British MV *Irene M* to Virginia Capes; 19 Mar 56 fought fire on MV *Ciudad de Quito* loaded with nitrates in the James R.; Mar 56 assisted stranded Greek MV *Navarchos Kounduriotis* off Newport News, VA; summer 56 towed cutters *Avoyel* and *Chilula* from Orange, TX, to Curtis Bay,

MD; 5 Feb 57 assisted Italian MV *Emanuele V. Parodi* following explosion; 26 Apr 65 assisted in search for debris from Navy aircraft off Virginia Capes; 6 Oct 65 removed depth charge, which was caught in a net, from Canadian FV *Lady Anna* and disposed of it in deep water off Cape Henry, VA; 29 Jan 67 assisted following a collision between MVs *Bodoro* and *Beaver State* on Potomac R.; 1 Feb 67 towed disabled tug *Lambert's Point* to Norfolk, VA; 27–28 Feb 67 helped fight fire on MV *Caldas* and towed her to anchorage in lower Delaware R.; 4 Dec 67 assisted after the barge *Mohawk* hit the Chesapeake Bay Bridge; 27 Apr 68 towed disabled FV *Ok Service Five* 132 mi ESE of Cape Henry to Little Creek, VA; 13 Jul 68 took on board disabled 21-foot PC in the Florida Straits; 14 Nov 68 towed disabled sailboat *Windless* 90 mi E of Cape Hatteras to Oregon Inlet; Feb 69 maintained surveillance over 12 foreign FVs that sought a haven off the Chesapeake during a storm; 20 Apr 69 towed FV *Captain Johnny* 25 mi ESE of Chesapeake Light Tower to safety; 11 Dec 69 towed disabled FV *Bobby and Jack* to Chesapeake Bay; 4 Jul 70 helped fight fire in oil storage tank, Sewells Point, VA; 10 Jul 70 helped fight fire on MV *Atlantic Saga* in York Spit Channel; 2 Dec 76 seized MV *Valborg* 40 mi NE of Norfolk, VA, carrying 3t marijuana; 2 Nov 78 seized MV *Friendship IV* off Cape Hatteras for smuggling; 22 May 79 fought fire on FV *Linda Lee* for six hours; 16 Jan 80 escorted disabled FV *Decco 13* to Cape Charles; 18 Mar 80 rescued four from FV *Decco 5* following its sinking SE of New Jersey; 3 Apr 84 seized MV *Somape II* 390 mi E of Norfolk, VA, after marijuana was

discovered on board; 18 Nov 84 seized tug *Arikok* 30 mi N of Grand Bahama Bank with 15t of marijuana on board; 27 Nov 84 intercepted a boat carrying 105 Haitians and returned them to Haiti; 12 Oct 87 rammed by MV *Camaronero II* attempting to avoid being boarded in the Yucatan Channel—23t of marijuana found on MV; 21 Feb 89 seized FV *Sea Power* 85 mi E of Cape Cod for allegedly using illegal nets.

Chilula

3 Oct 56–1975 stationed at Morehead City, NC, and used for LE and SAR; 24 Jul 67 rescued four from FV *Dorothy Bee* off Cape Lookout; 28 Sep 67 assisted grounded MV *Wolverine State* 10 mi W of Cuba; 25 Feb 68 escorted distressed Liberian tanker *Potomac* 130 mi SE of Cape Hatteras to Wilmington, NC; 5 Dec 68 towed abandoned yacht *Good Hope* 70 mi E of Cape Fear to Morehead City, NC; 7 Dec 68 picked up seven bodies after FV *Fenwick Island* sank; 20 May 69 towed FV *Glen Echo* to Morehead City, NC; 30 Dec 69 towed disabled tanker *N. W. Cokey* 90 mi SE of Cape Fear until relieved by a commercial tug; 20–28 Jan 70 towed and fought fire which kept reigniting on *Thordis Presthus* off North Carolina; 2 May 70 towed disabled USS *Mississinewa* 100 mi SE of Cape Hatteras until relieved by USS *Hoist*; 4 Jul 70 party from cutter helped fight fire in downtown Morehead City, NC; 28 Oct 70 towed disabled FV *Sheela L* from 15 mi SE of Cape Lookout to safety; 30 Oct 70 towed disabled tug *Linda* to Georgetown, SC; 6 Nov 70 rescued five from MV *Caribbean Mist*

The *Chilula* on 4 Dec 64 practices SAR ops with a Coast Guard HH-52 helicopter from Air Station Elizabeth City, NC.

150 mi off Cape Fear; 12 Aug 84 seized FV *Max* in Windward Passage carrying 3t of marijuana; 18 May 85 seized FV *Tripolina* for fishing inside a closed area; 1975–90 stationed at Atlantic Beach, NC, and used for LE and SAR; July 85 seized FV 30 mi SE of Cuba carrying marijuana; Nov 86 rescued eight from PC *Skivvy Waver* 240 mi E of Delaware R. during a heavy storm.

Lipan

1980–88 stationed at Key West, FL, and used for LE and SAR; 28 Jun 83 seized *Alex* carrying 50t of marijuana; 21 Dec 83 seized FV *Julie Jean* carrying 8t of marijuana; 22 Dec 83 seized MV *Global Charter* carrying 16t of marijuana; 23 Dec 83 seized FV *Patty Too* carrying 12t of marijuana; 23 Dec 83 seized FV *Victor Y. Jorge* carrying 2t of marijuana; 31 Jan 84 seized FV in Yucatan Channel after firing two volleys of warning shots—20t of marijuana on board; 24 May 84 seized MV *Rosangel* in Providence Channel carrying 5t of marijuana; 3 Jun 84 seized *Mrs White* carrying 17t of marijuana in the Bahamas; 7 Jun 84 seized PC *Blue Jacket* in Providence Channel carrying 470 lbs of marijuana; 20 Jul 84 sank burned-out hulk of *Captain Morgan* 50 mi S of Grand Turk I.; 16 Jul 84 removed 36 Haitians from a sailboat for their return to Haiti; 13 Aug 84 seized the Panamanian tug *Nora I* with 8t of marijuana in a secret compartment; 25 Sep 84 seized yacht *Sin Bad* in the Yucatan Channel with 10t of marijuana on board.

Tamaroa

1946–85 stationed at New York, NY, and used for LE and SAR; 5 Jan 52 towed disabled FV *Gudyontiff*; Mar 63 sank in her docks—raised and repaired; 2 Jan 67 towed disabled yacht *Petrel* to Montauk Point; 30 Apr

67 towed disabled FV *Deepwater* from 180 mi E of New York City to New Bedford, MA; 2 Jul 67 towed disabled FV *Foam* from 100 mi SE of Cape Cod to New Bedford, MA; 22 Jul 76 seized Italian FV *Amoruso Quarto* 80 mi ESE of Tom's R. for fisheries violation; 28 Jul 76 seized Japanese FV *Ookumi Maru* 77 mi SE of Cape May, NJ; 7 May–28 Jun 79 towed garbage and sludge out of NY to sea for dumping during strike; 25 Sep 80 seized Panamanian MV *Roondiep* carrying 20t of marijuana approx 400 mi E of New York City after firing .50 cal warning shots across bow; 13 Jan 82 seized Cayman I. *Jim Hawkins* carrying 7t of marijuana; 24 Feb 84 seized FV *Apollo III* 30 mi NE of Cape Cod with 16t of marijuana on board; 1985–90 stationed at New Castle, NH, and used for LE and SAR; Aug 85 rescued survivor off a sailboat 65 mi off Cape May, NJ; Jun 87 collected hydrographic and driftbuoy data of the Grand Banks using a mobile laboratory as part of IIP; 31 Aug 87 boarded cruise ship *Scandinavian Star* and helped search for a bomb following a threat.

Cutter *Tamaroa*, photographed in May 49, and the other members of this class serving in the Coast Guard had black hulls while classified as WATs. *Tamaroa* and her sisters are powerful enough to tow the largest oceangoing ships.

Ute

1980–88 stationed at Key West, FL, and used for LE and SAR; 11 Jul 82 helped turn back an 18-foot sailboat with eight Haitians on board off SE Cuba; 10 Jun 83 rescued four from FV *Don Pepe II* in Yucatan Channel; 26 Jun 83 fired 15 rounds of .50 cal at *Miss Shirley*; 22 Dec 83 seized Cayman *Neptune* carrying 42.5t of marijuana; 6 Feb 84 intercepted sailboat *Saint Augustin* in the Windward Passage carrying 57 illegal migrants—returned to Haiti; 4 Aug 84 helped seize *Grand's Anse II* in the Yucatan Channel with 30t of marijuana on board; 12 Aug 84 seized MV *San Andrea* 30 mi SW of Freeport carrying 7.5t of marijuana; 15 Sep 84 seized MV *Garcia Masiques* 200 mi SW of Jamaica carrying 10t of marijuana; 30 Sep 84 seized *Yemaya* 140 mi W of Jamaica carrying 1.5t of marijuana; 12 Nov 84 seized MV *Bierum* 100 mi E of Belize carrying 10t of marijuana; 3 Jan 85 seized sailboat *Maranatha* in Yucatan Channel carrying 175 lbs of marijuana; 9 Mar 85 seized Cayman *Chata One* carrying 19t of marijuana.

Cutter *Lipan* moored at Key West, FL, late in her career. While serving in the Coast Guard, she seized several hundred tons of marijuana. As illustrated by the *Cherokee*-class members serving in the Coast Guard, sometimes the Service retains the names and numbers given by the Navy and other times not.

NAVY *SOTOYOMO* CLASS

Name	Hull Number	Builder	Keel Laid	Launched	Commissioned	Disposition
Modoc (ex-*Bagaduce*)	WMEC 194 ATA 194 ATR 121	Levingston Shipbuilding Co., Orange, TX	7 Nov 44	4 Dec 44	15 Feb 45 (USN) 15 Apr 59 (CG)	*Decomm* 1980
Comanche (ex-*Wampanoag*)	WMEC 202 ATA 202 ATR 129	Gulfport Boiler & Welding Works, Port Arthur, TX	24 Aug 44	10 Oct 44	8 Dec 44 (USN) 25 Feb 59 (CG)	*Decomm* 1979

Cost   N/A

Hull
  Displacement (tons)   754 fl (1969); 521 light (1969)
  Length   143' oa; 125'8" bp
  Beam   33'10"
  Draft   13'3" max (1964)
Machinery
  Main Engines   2 electric motors driven by 2 generators driven by 2 General Motors diesels
  BHP   1,500
  Propellers   single
Performance
  Max Sustained   12.0 kts, 7,300-mi radius (1969)
  Economic   8.5 kts, 12,000-mi radius (1969)
Logistics
  Fuel Oil (95%)   49,796 gal
  Complement   4 officers, 1 warrant, 42 men (1969)
Electronics
  Detection Radar   SPS-23 (1969)
  Sonar   none
Armament   1 20mm/80
Design
  The *Sotoyomo* class was designed by the USN as auxiliary ocean tugs.

Comanche

1959–60 stationed at Morro Bay, CA, and used for LE and SAR; 1961 stationed at Sausalito, CA, and used for LE and SAR; 1962–67 stationed at San Francisco, CA, and used for LE and SAR; 4 Aug 65 stood by disabled U.S. FV *Mark Christopher* near Half Moon Bay, CA, awaiting a tug; 26 Sep 66 helped fight fire on barge in San Francisco harbor; 1967–69 stationed at Corpus Christi, TX, and used for LE and SAR; 7 Jan 68 towed disabled FV *Mermaid* from 70 mi SE of Port Aransas, TX, to that port; 9 Oct 68 rescued three from MV *Elsie* 15 mi SSE of Port Isabel, TX; 1970–79 stationed at Eureka, CA, and used for LE and SAR.

Modoc

1959–69 stationed at Coos Bay, OR, and used for LE and SAR; 20 Sep 67 escorted disabled Danish MV *Marieskou* following a collision with *Chitose Maru* 4 mi N of Cape Flattery; 17 Mar 68 assisted USS *Chowanoc* recover tow of DE 373 25 mi W of Coos Bay; 30 Apr 68 assisted following collision between Japanese MV *Suwaharu* and Liberian MV *Mandoil II* off Oregon; 1 Aug 68 rescued lone survivor from FV *Rodoma*; 1970–76 stationed at Seattle, WA, and used for LE and SAR; 15 May 75 seized Polish FV *Kalmar* 10 mi off Monterey, CA, for violating U.S. waters; 1977–80 stationed at Coos Bay, OR, and used for LE and SAR.

The *Modoc* on 7 Mar 70. Although she is wearing a Coast Guard slash, it has not yet been painted on her whale boat.

NAVY PCE(R) 848 CLASS

Name	Hull Number	Builder	Keel Laid	Launched	Commissioned	Disposition
Jackson	WPC 120 PCE(R) 858	Pullman Standard Car Manufacturing Co., Chicago, IL	3 Jan 44	13 May 44	16 May 45 (USN) 28 Feb 46 (CG)	*Decomm* 24 Jul 47 *Sold* 23 Dec 47
Bedloe	WPC 121 PCE(R) 860	Pullman Standard Car Manufacturing Co., Chicago, IL	25 Jan 44	30 Jan 45	31 Mar 45 (USN) 18 Sep 46 (CG)	*Decomm* 17 Jul 47 *Sold* 23 Dec 47

Cost	$1,778,737
Hull	
Displacement (tons)	870 fl (1944)
Length	184′6″
Beam	34′
Draft	9′6″ max
Machinery	
Main Engines	General Motors Mod 12-278A diesel
BHP	2,000
Propellers	1
Performance	
Max Sustained	14.5 kts, 2,200-mi radius (1944)
Economic	9 kts (1944)
Logistics	
Complement	4 officers, 1 warrant, 54 enlisted (1944)
Electronics	
Detection Radar	SF-1 (1944)
Armament	1 3″/50; 2 20mm (1946)

The cutter *Jackson* on 12 Apr 46. Although commissioned in the Coast Guard at the time this photograph was taken, the *Jackson* still wears her Navy hull number. The *Jackson* and *Bedloe* were named for two 125-foot cutters lost during a hurricane off Cape Hatteras on 14 Sep 44.

Design

These Patrol Rescue Escorts (PCE(R)) were constructed of steel. Due to a shortage of personnel these ships were not retained.

Bedloe

1 Jan 47–17 Jul 47 stationed at Curtis Bay, MD.

Jackson

18 Aug 46–2 Jul 47 stationed at Curtis Bay, MD.

165-FOOT (B) CUTTERS

Name	Hull Number	Builder	Keel Laid	Launched	Commissioned	Disposition
Ariadne	WMEC 101 WPC 101	Lake Union Dry Dock & Machine Works, Seattle, WA	15 Nov 33 (contracted)	23 Mar 34	9 Oct 34	*Decomm* 23 Dec 68 *Sold* 26 Sep 69
Aurora	WMEC 103 WPC 103	Bath Iron Works, Bath, ME	21 Jan 31 (contracted)	28 Nov 31	21 Dec 31	*Decomm* 17 Jan 68 *Sold* 16 Dec 68
Dione	WPC 107	Manitowoc Shipbuilding Corp., Manitowoc, WI	10 Nov 33 (contracted)	30 Jun 34	5 Oct 34	*Decomm* 8 Feb 63 *Sold* 24 Feb 64
Nemesis	WPC 111	Marietta Manufacturing Co., Point Pleasant, WV	17 Nov 33 (contracted)	7 Jul 34	10 Oct 34	*Decomm* 20 Oct 64 *Sold* 9 Feb 66
Nike	WPC 112	Marietta Manufacturing Co., Point Pleasant, WV	17 Nov 33 (contracted)	7 Nov 34	24 Oct 34	*Decomm* 5 Nov 64 *Sold* 9 May 66
Pandora	WPC 113	Manitowoc Shipbuilding Corp., Manitowoc, WI	10 Nov 33 (contracted)	30 Jun 34	1 Nov 34	*Decomm* 1 May 59 *Sold* 4 Nov 59

Name	Hull Number	Builder	Keel Laid	Launched	Commissioned	Disposition
Perseus	WPC 114	Bath Iron Works, Bath, ME	21 Jan 31 (contracted)	11 Apr 32	27 Apr 32	*Decomm* 26 Jun 59 *Sold* 4 Nov 59
Triton	WMEC 116 WPC 116	Marietta Manufacturing Co., Point Pleasant, WV	17 Apr 34	7 Jul 34	20 Nov 34	*Decomm* 12 Jan 67 *Sold* 16 Jan 69

Cost $258,000 each

Hull
  Displacement (tons)   370 fl (1962); 305 light (1962)
  Length   165′ oa; 160′ bp
  Beam   25′3″ max
  Draft   9′3″ max (1962)

Machinery
  Main Engines   2 Winton diesels
  BHP   1,340
  Propellers   twin, 3 blades

Performance
  Max Sustained   12.9 kts, 1,600-mi radius (1962)
  Economic   10.0 kts, 3,110-mi radius (1962)

Logistics
  Fuel Oil (95%)   7,770 gal
  Complement   4 officers, 1 warrant, 50 men (1962)

Electronics
  Detection Radar   SPS-23 (1962)
  Sonar   QCU (1962)

Armament   1 3″/50 (1962)

Design

The 165-foot (B) cutters were a follow-on to the 125-foot cutters, both classes being designed to enforce prohibition. The decommissioning dates cited are those when the cutters were first removed from service, even though their removal was considered temporary at the time.

The following 165-foot (B) cutters were laid up and disposed of shortly after WWII: *Argo, Atalanta, Calypso, Cyane, Daphne, Electra, Galatea, Hermes, Icarus,* and *Thetis.*

Ariadne

1 Nov 45–Apr 46 stationed at Miami, FL; 2 Apr 46 took over tow of PC *New Era* from *Air Falcon*; May 46–Aug 49 placed in caretaker status at Key West, FL, and later St. Petersburg, FL; 11 Aug 49 recommissioned at Curtis Bay, MD, and stationed at Key West, FL; 27 Mar 50 attempted to assist *Mocoma* grounded on Star Reef; 18 Oct 64–23 Dec 68 stationed at St. Petersburg, FL, and employed on Cuban patrols; 25 Feb 65 escorted burning German MV *Schanenberg* to explosive anchorage at Tampa, FL; 26 Jun 65 escorted burning Irish MV *Irish Poplar* to explosive anchorage at Tampa, FL; late Aug 65 evacuated 39 Cuban refugees from Cay Sal in the Bahamas and delivered them to Key West, FL; Oct 65 rescued 36

Cutter *Ariadne,* on 12 Nov 66. She was the last of the 165-foot B-class cutters to be decommissioned. *Ariadne* spent her entire post-WWII career in Florida waters and is understandably fitted with sun awnings abeam the stack and aft over the poop deck.

Cuban refugees from Cay Sal and transported them to Key West, FL; 12 Feb 66 rescued 14 Cuban refugees from Anguilla Cays and transported them to Key West, FL; 17 Feb 67 rescued Cuban refugees from Cay Sal and transported them to Key West, FL; 11 Dec 67 towed disabled PC *Ginger II* 30 mi NNW of St. Petersburg, FL, to that port; 1 Jul 68 towed Cuban refugee boat 125 mi S of Miami, FL, to Key West.

Aurora

1 Feb–1 Sep 46 stationed at Jacksonville, FL; 1 Sep 46–23 Jul 47 stationed at Mayport, FL, and placed "in commission in reserve"; 23 Jul 47–Apr 59 stationed at Savannah, GA; 15 Oct 56 positioned next to sinking shrimp trawler *Miss Beulah* during heavy seas to allow two-man crew to jump to safety while 10 mi off Georgia; Apr 59–17 Jan 68 stationed at San Juan, PR; 6–10 Jun 65 unsuccessfully searched for missing AF aircraft off FL; 14 Feb 66 assisted in rescue of 18 from Liberian MV *Pensacola* 40 mi S of Isla Saona.

Dione

1946 stationed at Norfolk, VA, and used for LE and SAR; 1947–51 placed out of service due to a shortage of personnel; 1952–63 stationed at Freeport, TX, and used for LE and SAR; 2–5 Jan 57 towed disabled cutter *Iris* to New Orleans, LA.

Nemesis

4 Nov 34–20 Oct 64 stationed at St. Petersburg, FL, and used for LE and SAR.

The *Perseus* on 12 Jun 53. Her mousetrap ASW rocket launchers on the forecastle are in a raised position. Note the gravity-release liferaft amidships. A Coast Guard WWII study showed that those who chose a liferaft over a lifeboat were more likely to safely abandon ship but less likely to survive than those who successfully did get away in a lifeboat.

The cutter *Triton,* Nov 58. The 165-foot B class was designed to shadow "mother ships" during Prohibition. The "mother ships" would lie outside the 12-mile limit and transfer their illegal cargoes to small, fast craft that would attempt to run the Coast Guard blockade. Extensive plans for this class appear in Scheina, *WWII Cutters.*

Nike

1941–64 stationed at Gulfport, MS, and used for LE and SAR; 17 Aug 63 escorted NASA missile barge *Promise.*

Pandora

1946–47 stationed at Miami, FL, and used for LE and SAR; 1948–59 stationed at San Juan, PR, and used for LE and SAR.

Perseus

21 Mar 34–59 stationed at San Diego, CA, and used for LE and SAR; 20 Oct 50 patrolled Governors Cup Race at San Diego; 12–26 Jan 53 patrolled Acapulco Yacht Race; 3–15 Jun 53 undertook reserve training cruise to Los Angeles, CA; 11 Nov 53 medevaced crewman from FV *Idaho* in Ballenas Bay; Jan 54 patrolled Acapulco Yacht Race; May 54 patrolled Ensenada Yacht Race.

Triton

1945–67 stationed at Corpus Christi, TX, and used for LE and SAR; 8 Apr 51 towed disabled FV *Morning Star*; 10 May 65 assisted grounded FV *Compass Rose* in the Gulf of Mexico.

125-FOOT CUTTERS ("BUCK & A QUARTER" CLASS)

Name	Hull Number	Builder	Keel Laid	Launched	Commissioned	Disposition
Active	WSC 125	American Brown Boveri Electric Corp., Camden, NJ	N/A	30 Nov 26	13 Jan 27	*Decomm* 2 Apr 62 *Sold* 6 Sep 63
Agassiz	WMEC 126 WSC 126	American Brown Boveri Electric Corp., Camden, NJ	31 Jul 26	30 Nov 26	20 Jan 27	*Decomm* 13 Oct 69 *Trans* to MMA, 16 Oct 69
Alert	WMEC 127 WSC 127	American Brown Boveri Electric Corp., Camden, NJ	27 May 26 (contracted)	30 Nov 26	27 Jan 27	*Decomm* 10 Jan 69 *Sold* 6 Oct 69
Bonham	WSC 129	American Brown Boveri Electric Corp., Camden, NJ	N/A	30 Nov 26	29 Jan 27	*Decomm* 20 Apr 59 *Sold* 30 Dec 59
Boutwell	WSC 130	American Brown Boveri Electric Corp., Camden, NJ	N/A	27 Jan 27	21 Feb 27	*Decomm* 7 May 63 *Sold* 16 May 64
Cahoone	WMEC 131 WSC 131	American Brown Boveri Electric Corp., Camden, NJ	N/A	27 Jan 27	21 Feb 27	*Decomm* 11 Mar 68 *Sold* 12 Dec 68
Cartigan	WMEC 132 WSC 132	American Brown Boveri Electric Corp., Camden, NJ	N/A	27 Jan 27	3 Mar 27	*Decomm* 12 Oct 68
Colfax (ex-*Montgomery*)	WSC 133	American Brown Boveri Electric Corp., Camden, NJ	27 May 26 (contracted)	22 Mar 27	7 Apr 27	*Decomm* 9 Nov 54 *Sold* 5 Jan 56
Diligence	WSC 135	American Brown Boveri Electric Corp., Camden, NJ	N/A	27 Jan 27	22 Feb 27	*Decomm* 30 Sep 61 *Sold* 30 Jan 69
Ewing	WMEC 137 WSC 137	American Brown Boveri Electric Corp., Camden, NJ	N/A	15 Mar 27	26 Mar 27	*Decomm* 23 Jun 67 *Sold* 23 Jan 69
Frederick Lee	WSC 139	American Brown Boveri Electric Corp., Camden, NJ	N/A	15 Mar 27	4 Apr 27	*Decomm* 15 Dec 64 *Sold* 19 May 66
General Greene	WMEC 140 WSC 140	American Brown Boveri Electric Corp., Camden, NJ	N/A	14 Feb 27	7 Apr 27	*Decomm* and *trans* to Newburyport, MA, as a museum 15 Nov 68
Kimball	WMEC 143 WSC 143	American Brown Boveri Electric Corp., Camden, NJ	N/A	25 Apr 27	7 May 27	*Decomm* 31 Dec 68 *Sold* 24 Feb 70
Legare	WMEC 144 WSC 144	American Brown Boveri Electric Corp., Camden, NJ	N/A	14 Feb 27	17 Mar 27	*Decomm* 5 Mar 68 *Sold* 29 Nov 68
Marion	WSC 145	American Brown Boveri Electric Corp., Camden, NJ	N/A	15 Mar 27	6 Apr 27	*Decomm* 15 Feb 62 *Sold* 8 Mar 63
McLane	WMEC 146 WSC 146	American Brown Boveri Electric Corp., Camden, NJ	N/A	22 Mar 27	8 Apr 27	*Decomm* 31 Dec 68 *Sold* 14 Nov 69
Morris	WMEC 147 WSC 147	American Brown Boveri Electric Corp., Camden, NJ	N/A	4 Apr 27	19 Apr 27	*Decomm* 7 Aug 70 *trans* to BSA 5 Nov 71
Travis	WSC 153	American Brown Boveri Electric Corp., Camden, NJ	N/A	18 Apr 27	29 Apr 27	*Decomm* 5 Jun 62 *Sold* 15 Nov 62

Name	Hull Number	Builder	Keel Laid	Launched	Commissioned	Disposition
Vigilant	WSC 154	American Brown Boveri Electric Corp., Camden, NJ	N/A	25 Apr 27	3 May 27	*Decomm* 9 Nov 54 *Sold* 3 Jan 56
Yeaton	WMEC 156 WSC 156	American Brown Boveri Electric Corp., Camden, NJ	N/A	2 May 27	10 May 27	*Decomm* 18 Jul 69 *Sold* 16 Jul 70
Cuyahoga	WIX 157 WMEC 157 WSC 157	American Brown Boveri Electric Corp., Camden, NJ	N/A	27 Jan 27	3 Mar 27; *recomm* 17 May 41	*Decomm* and *trans* to Navy 27 May 33; lost in collision 20 Oct 78

Cost $63,173 each

Hull
  Displacement (tons)   289 fl (1960); 236 light (1960)
  Length   125′ oa; 120′ wl
  Beam   24′ max
  Draft   9′ max (1960)

Machinery
  Main Engines   2 General Motors diesels
  BHP   800
  Propellers   twin, 3 blades

Performance
  Max Sustained   12.0 kts, 2,500-mi radius (1960)
  Economic   9.5 kts, 3,300-mi radius (1960)

Logistics
  Fuel Oil (95%)   6,800 gal
  Complement   2 officers, 1 warrant, 25 men (1960)

Electronics
  Detection Radar   SPS-23 (1960)
  Sonar   none (1960)

Armament   1 40mm/60 (1960)

Design

To combat smuggling during prohibition, the CG developed offshore patrol vessels for an outer ring and inshore patrol craft for an inner one. The 125-foot cutters were the first class to be designed for the outer patrol. They were designed to trail "mother ships" to intercept the illegal liquor when it was transferred to small, fast craft. They were reengined during the 1930s and 1940s. In mid-1941, in order to meet the need for more vessels equipped to service aids to navigation, the CG temporarily converted the following 125s for use as buoy tenders: the *Active, Colfax, Crawford, Ewing, Harriet Lane, Legare, McLane, Vigilant, Diligence,* and *Woodbury.* However, wartime needs soon caused these units to be reconverted to patrol craft. The following 125-foot cutters were disposed of shortly after World War II: *Crawford, Dix, Faunce, Harriet Lane, Nemaha, Pulaski, Reliance, Rush, Tiger,* and *Woodbury.*

Active

1946 stationed in Boston, MA—inactive due to a shortage of personnel; 1947–50 laid up at Cleveland, OH; 1951–60 stationed at Monterey, CA, and used for A/N and LE; 1961–62 stationed at Alameda, CA, and used for A/N and LE.

Agassiz

Jun 45–Oct 56 stationed at Morehead City, NC; Jan 56 assisted disabled *Manitou* 275 mi SE of Cape Henry; Jan 56 assisted disabled MV *Marvin*

McIntyre 40 mi E of Cape Fear; Oct 56–13 Oct 69 stationed at Cape May, NJ; 18 Oct 61 assisted yawl *Septic Nerve,* which had grounded in Little Egg Inlet, NJ; 1967 assisted disabled Canadian FV *Clara and Linda* 160 mi E of NY during a storm; 1 Mar 68 escorted distressed FV *Bright Star* 25 mi SE of Cape May to safety.

Alert

1941–21 Jun 49 stationed at Alameda, CA, and used primarily for LE and SAR; 21 Jun 49–20 Feb 59 stationed at Morro Bay, CA, and used primarily for LE and SAR; 20 Feb 59–10 Jan 69 stationed at San Diego, CA, and used primarily for LE and SAR; Jan 66 assisted FVs *Alpha Rock* and *Viking* 70 mi S of Punta Baja; Aug 67 fought fire on FV *Mondego* 2 mi off Pt. Loma, CA.

Bonham

1946–59 stationed at Coos Bay, OR, and used for LE and SAR.

Cutter *Active* on 23 Aug 60. Ten 125s, including the *Active,* were fitted to service small buoys. This accounts for her black hull and boom forward. She mounts a 20mm gun abaft the stack.

Boutwell

1941–51 stationed at Panama City, FL, and used for LE and SAR; 1952–53 stationed at Port Isabel, TX, and used for LE and SAR; 1954–63 stationed at Brownsville, TX, and used for LE and SAR; 3 Oct 61 assisted drilling barge *Mr. Louis* damaged in a storm off Port Isabel, TX.

Cahoone

1946–54 stationed at Mt. Edgecumbe, AK, and used for LE and SAR; 1955–68 stationed at Galveston, TX, and used for LE and SAR; Jan–Feb 68 served on Campeche Patrol.

Cartigan

1946–47 in storage at Cleveland, OH, due to a shortage of personnel; 15 Aug 47–11 Jul 50 stationed at New York, NY, and used for LE and SAR; 1950–53 stationed at Galveston, TX, and used for LE and SAR; 1953–68 stationed at Panama City, FL, and used for LE and SAR; 20 Jan 55 rescued survivors from tug *Berth R* in Gulf of Mexico; Jul 66 served on Campeche Patrol; 5 May 68 towed disabled PC *Hornblower* 50 mi SE of Panama City, FL to that port; 11 Jul 68 assisted in rescue of survivors from 19-foot PC near Panacea, FL.

Colfax

1 Jul 45–1 Feb 48 stationed at Cape May, NJ; 21 May 46 assisted PC *Buccaneer*; 26 Jul 46 assisted MV *G. M. Cohan*; 1948–51 stored at Cape May, NJ; 8 Jun 51 towed to CG Yard by *Sassafras*; 18 Sep 51 towed to Cape May, NJ, by *Firebush*; 1951–54 stationed at Cape May, NJ.

Cuyahoga

1946–47 stationed at Norfolk, VA, and used for LE and SAR; 1948–58 stationed at Curtis Bay, MD, and used for LE and SAR; 1959–78 stationed at Yorktown, VA, and used for training; 2 May 68 towed disabled PC to Little Creek, VA; 20 Oct 78 sank following collision with Argentine MV *Santa Cruz II* near the mouth of the Potomac R.—11 CG men perished and 18 were rescued by the MV.

Diligence

2 Sep 41–30 Sep 61 stationed at San Pedro, CA, and used for LE, A/N, and SAR.

Ewing

Aug 46–Aug 47 stationed at Seward, AK, and used for LE and SAR; 1947–48 laid up inactive due to shortage of personnel; 22 Jun 49–Sep 60 stationed at Alameda, CA, and used for LE and SAR; Sep 60–Jun 67 stationed at Monterey, CA, and used for LE and SAR; 22 Aug 65 escorted damaged PC *Mariposa* from 15 mi W of Cape San Martin to port.

Frederick Lee

1 May 42–3 Oct 46 stationed at Boston, MA, and used for LE and SAR; 3 Oct 46–15 Jul 51 stationed at Chicago, IL, and used for LE and SAR; 15 Jul 51–7 Jan 63 stationed at New Bedford, MA, and used for LE and SAR; 7 Jan 63–15 Dec 64 stationed at Freeport, TX, and used for LE and SAR.

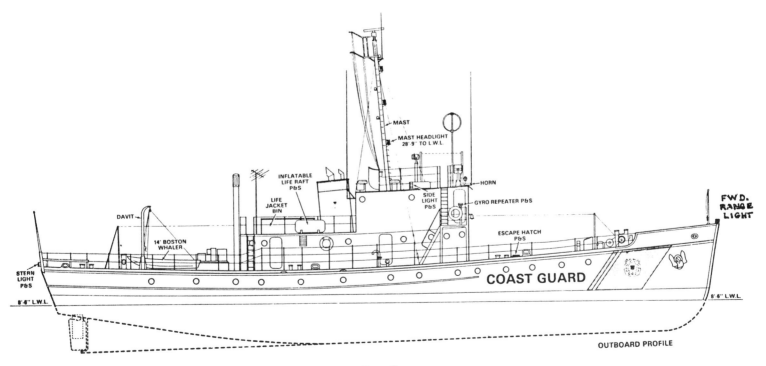

Figure 2

The outboard profile of the cutter *Cuyahoga* extracted from her *Casualty Review Report*.

This overhead view of the *Ewing* provides an excellent view of the topside layout. Note the towing bitt on the poop deck, a common feature on practically all Coast Guard cutters.

General Greene

1946–47 stationed at Woods Hole, MA, and used for LE and SAR; 1947–68 stationed at Gloucester, MA, and used for LE and SAR; 7 Mar 60 grounded at East Sandwich, MA, during a storm; 6 Dec 67 fought fire on FV *Agda W* 10 mi S of Nantucket.

Kimball

25 Oct 46–18 Aug 47 stationed at Two Harbors, MN, and used for LE and SAR; 18 Aug 47–11 Jul 50 placed in storage at Cleveland, OH, due to a shortage of personnel; 15 Mar 50–18 Jun 58 stationed at Ketchikan, AK, and used for LE and SAR, including halibut patrol; 1958 stationed at Venice, LA, and used for LE and SAR; 1959–Dec 68 stationed at Brownsville, TX, and used for LE and SAR; May 65 served on Campeche Patrol; 8 Dec 66 escorted disabled FV *Penny Michale* to Port Isabel, TX.

Lagare

1945–46 stationed at Gloucester, MA, and used for LE and SAR; 1947–Dec 64 stationed at New Bedford, MA, and used for LE and SAR; 2 Mar 47 towed disabled FV *Lucy & Evelyn* off Nantucket I. and passed tow to cutter *Algonquin*; 15 May 47 towed disabled FV *Saint Victoria* 200 mi to safety; Dec 64–12 Mar 68 stationed at Freeport, TX, and used for LE and SAR; 30 Jul 67 towed disabled PC *Marie Corneille* from 360 mi SE to Corpus Christi, TX; 14 Jan 68 towed disabled 15-foot PC from 60 mi S of Freeport, TX, to that port.

Marion

1946–15 Feb 62 stationed at Norfolk, VA, and used for LE and SAR; Jun 55 towed *Siboney* 300 mi E of Norfolk, VA.

McLane

1945–46 stationed at Sitka, AK, and used for LE and SAR; 1947–62 stationed at Aberdeen, WA, and used for LE and SAR; 1962–68 stationed at Brownsville, TX, and used for LE and SAR; 4 Mar 66 towed disabled FV *Margie* to Port Isabel, TX; 27 Mar 66 with permission entered Mexican waters and assisted FV *Nugent*; 27 Nov 66 towed disabled FV *Debbie* to Port Isabel, TX; 9 Apr 67 escorted disabled FV *Bahia Honda* to Port Isabel; Dec 67 served on Campeche Patrol.

Morris

1942–47 stationed at San Diego, CA, and used for wartime duties plus LE and SAR; 17 Jan 47–2 May 49 placed in storage at Kennydale, WA, due to a shortage of personnel; 13 May 49–7 Aug 70 stationed at San Pedro, CA, and used for LE and SAR; 25 Mar 68 assisted following collision between MVs *Atlantic Trader* and *Steel Designer* 2 mi off Point Fermin, CA.

Travis

1945–47 stationed at Cockspur I., GA, and used for LE and SAR; 1948–54 stationed at Charleston, SC, and used for LE and SAR.

Vigilant

15 Jul 34–1 Feb 48 stationed at Ft. Pierce, FL; May 46 towed cutter *Air Parakeet* to CG Yard, Curtis Bay, MD; May 46 towed *Scoter* to CG Yard, Curtis Bay, MD; Jul 47 towed cutters *Aurora* and *Pandora* to CG Base, Cape May, NJ; May 48 towed by tender *Gentian* to CG Yard, Curtis Bay, MD, and then to CG Base, Cape May, NJ, and placed in storage.

Yeaton

1945–69 stationed at New London, CT, and used for LE and SAR.

Cutter *Yeaton* on 28 Jun 66. The lack of freeboard in this class is revealed by the exaggerated bow wake in these moderate seas.

WMEC/WSC TYPE CUTTERS DISPOSED OF SHORTLY AFTER WORLD WAR II*

Name	Hull Number	Class	Decomm	Sold/Trans
Blaze	WPC 336	Navy SC 1	25 Sep 44	8 Mar 46
Bowstring	WPC 365	Navy SC 1	22 Dec 44	6 Jan 45
Boone	WPC 335	Navy SC 1	6 Jun 45	8 Mar 46
Belleville	WPC 372	Navy SC 1	30 Jun 45	2 May 46
Harriet Lane	WSC 141	125-Foot	29 Apr 46	16 Jun 48
Electra	WPC 187	165-Foot B	23 May 46	N/A
Icarus	WPC 110	165-Foot B	21 Oct 46	1 Jul 48
Daphne	WPC 106	165-Foot B	29 Nov 46	7 Dec 54
Pulaski	WSC 149	125-Foot	4 Dec 46	14 Jul 48
Woodbury	WSC 155	125-Foot	11 Dec 46	6 Jul 48
Thetis	WPC 115	165-Foot B	1 Jul 47	1 Jul 48
Calypso	WPC 104	165-Foot B	18 Jul 47	2 Nov 55
Nemaha	WSC 148	125-Foot	21 Jul 47	14 Jun 48
Reliance	WSC 150	125-Foot	8 Aug 47	16 Jun 48
Crawford	WSC 134	125-Foot	15 Aug 47	28 Nov 55
Rush	WSC 151	125-Foot	21 Aug 47	16 Jun 48
Cyane	WSC 105	165-Foot B	15 Sep 47	7 Dec 54
Tiger	WSC 152	125-Foot	21 Nov 47	14 Jun 48
Dix	WSC 136	125-Foot	13 Jan 48	16 Jun 48
Faunce	WSC 138	125-Foot	13 Jan 48	16 Jun 48
Galatea	WPC 108	165-Foot B	15 Mar 48	1 Jul 48
Argo	WPC 100	165-Foot B	30 Oct 48	2 Nov 55
Hermes	WPC 109	165-Foot B	2 Nov 48	16 May 58
Atalanta	WPC 102	165-Foot B	1 Aug 50	7 Dec 54

* See Scheina, *WWII Cutters,* for details.

Patrol Boats

The Coast Guard has used the patrol boat designation since the early 1950s. Prior to that time, the term patrol boat was used but not the designator WPB. The patrol boat was introduced into the service for the first time in large numbers during the 1920s to help enforce Prohibition.

120-FOOT PATROL BOAT CLASS ("HERITAGE CLASS")

Name	Hull Number	Builder	Keel Laid	Launched	Commissioned	Disposition

1 prototype and 34 production units projected, the prototype to be in service by 1991.

Cost	N/A	Performance	
Hull		Max Sustained	30.0 kts, 720-mi radius (1988)
Displacement (tons)	140 light (1988); 160 fl (1988)	Cruising	12.0 kts, 1,520-mi radius (1988)
Length	120′ oa	Logistics	
Beam	22′6″ max	Complement	2 officers, 14 men (1988)
Draft	8′4″ max (1988)	Electronics	
Machinery		Detection Radar	1 SPS-64 (V)
Main Engines	2 diesels	Armament	1 20mm/60 and machine guns
BHP	N/A	Design	
Propellers	twin		

Design

These craft are being designed to replace the aging 82-foot patrol-boat class. The new class will have a "deep-vee" hull form. The prototype is being built at the Coast Guard Yard, Curtis Bay, MD. It is scheduled for delivery in late 1991. Series production could begin as early as mid-1994.

110-FOOT PATROL BOAT CLASS ("ISLAND" CLASS)

Name	Hull Number	Builder	Keel Laid	Launched	Commissioned	Disposition
A TYPE						
Farallon	WPB 1301	Bollinger Machine Shop & Shipyard, Lockport, LA	26 Dec 84	27 Aug 85	15 Nov 85	Active
Manitou	WPB 1302	Bollinger Machine Shop & Shipyard, Lockport, LA	7 Jan 85	9 Oct 85	24 Jan 86	Active
Matagorda	WPB 1303	Bollinger Machine Shop & Shipyard, Lockport, LA	1 Mar 85	18 Nov 85	24 Apr 86	Active
Maui	WPB 1304	Bollinger Machine Shop & Shipyard, Lockport, LA	8 Apr 85	11 Jan 86	22 Mar 86	Active
Monhegan	WPB 1305	Bollinger Machine Shop & Shipyard, Lockport, LA	2 Jun 85	15 Feb 86	16 Jun 86	Active
Nunivak	WPB 1306	Bollinger Machine Shop & Shipyard, Lockport, LA	5 Aug 85	14 Mar 86	2 May 86	Active
Ocracoke	WPB 1307	Bollinger Machine Shop & Shipyard, Lockport, LA	20 Sep 85	3 Apr 86	4 Aug 86	Active
Vashon	WPB 1308	Bollinger Machine Shop & Shipyard, Lockport, LA	14 Oct 85	10 May 86	15 Aug 86	Active
Aquidneck	WPB 1309	Bollinger Machine Shop & Shipyard, Lockport, LA	18 Nov 85	13 Jun 86	25 Jul 86	Active
Mustang	WPB 1310	Bollinger Machine Shop & Shipyard, Lockport, LA	23 Dec 85	11 Jul 86	3 Dec 86	Active
Naushon	WPB 1311	Bollinger Machine Shop & Shipyard, Lockport, LA	13 Jan 86	22 Aug 86	5 Dec 86	Active
Sanibel	WPB 1312	Bollinger Machine Shop & Shipyard, Lockport, LA	10 Feb 86	3 Oct 86	28 May 87	Active
Edisto	WPB 1313	Bollinger Machine Shop & Shipyard, Lockport, LA	10 Mar 86	21 Nov 86	7 Jan 87	Active
Sapelo	WPB 1314	Bollinger Machine Shop & Shipyard, Lockport, LA	7 Apr 86	8 Jan 87	14 May 87	Active
Matinicus	WPB 1302	Bollinger Machine Shop & Shipyard, Lockport, LA	5 May 86	26 Feb 87	19 Jun 87	Active
Nantucket	WPB 1316	Bollinger Machine Shop & Shipyard, Lockport, LA	5 Jun 86	17 Apr 87	10 Aug 87	Active

Name	Hull Number	Builder	Keel Laid	Launched	Commissioned	Disposition
B TYPE						
Attu	WPB 1317	Bollinger Machine Shop & Shipyard, Lockport, LA	12 Apr 87	4 Dec 87	9 May 88	Active
Baranof	WPB 1318	Bollinger Machine Shop & Shipyard, Lockport, LA	18 May 87	15 Jan 88	20 May 88	Active
Chandeleur	WPB 1319	Bollinger Machine Shop & Shipyard, Lockport, LA	22 Jun 87	19 Feb 88	8 Jun 88	Active
Chincoteague	WPB 1320	Bollinger Machine Shop & Shipyard, Lockport, LA	27 Jul 87	25 Mar 88	8 Aug 88	Active
Cushing	WPB 1321	Bollinger Machine Shop & Shipyard, Lockport, LA	1 Sep 87	29 Apr 88	8 Aug 88	Active
Cuttyhunk	WPB 1322	Bollinger Machine Shop & Shipyard, Lockport, LA	6 Oct 87	3 Jun 88	15 Oct 88	Active
Drummond	WPB 1323	Bollinger Machine Shop & Shipyard, Lockport, LA	11 Nov 87	8 Jul 88	19 Oct 88	Active
Key Largo (ex-*Largo*)	WPB 1324	Bollinger Machine Shop & Shipyard, Lockport, LA	14 Dec 87	12 Aug 88	24 Dec 88	Active
Metompkin	WPB 1325	Bollinger Machine Shop & Shipyard, Lockport, LA	19 Jan 87	16 Sep 88	12 Jan 89	Active
Monomoy	WPB 1326	Bollinger Machine Shop & Shipyard, Lockport, LA	24 Feb 88	21 Oct 88	16 Dec 88	Active
Orcas	WPB 1327	Bollinger Machine Shop & Shipyard, Lockport, LA	30 Mar 88	25 Nov 88	20 Jan 89	Active
Padre	WPB 1328	Bollinger Machine Shop & Shipyard, Lockport, LA	5 May 88	6 Jan 89	24 Feb 89	Active
Sitkinak	WPB 1329	Bollinger Machine Shop & Shipyard, Lockport, LA	10 Jun 88	10 Feb 89	31 Mar 89	Active
Tybee	WPB 1330	Bollinger Machine Shop & Shipyard, Lockport, LA	16 Jul 88	17 Mar 89	9 May 89	Active
Washington	WPB 1331	Bollinger Machine Shop & Shipyard, Lockport, LA	5 Aug 88	21 Apr 89	9 Jun 89	Active
Wrangell	WPB 1332	Bollinger Machine Shop & Shipyard, Lockport, LA	10 Sep 88	26 May 89	24 Jul 89	Active
Adak	WPB 1333	Bollinger Machine Shop & Shipyard, Lockport, LA	16 Oct 88	30 Jun 89	18 Aug 89	Active
Liberty	WPB 1334	Bollinger Machine Shop & Shipyard, Lockport, LA	21 Nov 88	4 Aug 89	22 Sep 89	Active
Anacapa	WPB 1335	Bollinger Machine Shop & Shipyard, Lockport, LA	22 Dec 88	8 Sep 89	27 Oct 89	Active
Kiska	WPB 1336	Bollinger Machine Shop & Shipyard, Lockport, LA	2 Feb 89	1989	1 Dec 89	Active
Assateague	WPB 1337	Bollinger Machine Shop & Shipyard, Lockport, LA	10 Mar 89	1989	1990	Building

Cost — approx $7,000,000 per unit—does not include program costs

Hull
- Displacement (tons) — 117 light (1986); 165 fl (1986)
- Length — 110' oa
- Beam — 21' max
- Draft — 7'4" max (1986)

Machinery
- Main Engines — 2 Alco-Paxman Valenta diesels
- BHP — 5,760
- Propellers — twin

Performance
- Max Speed — 26 kts, plus (1986)
- Cruising — est. 15 kts, 1,850-mi radius (1986)

Logistics
- Fuel Oil (95%) — N/A
- Complement — 2 officers, 14 men (1986)

Electronics
- Detection Radar — SPS-64(V)

Armament — 1 20mm/80, machine guns

Design

The hull of the Island class is based on a design by Vosper-Thornycroft of England. The interior, deck arrangement, and superstructure were designed by Bollinger to Coast Guard specifications. The Island class has a round-bilge planning hull equipped with an active fin-stabilization system. The hull was constructed in an inverted position to achieve better hull fairness. The steel hull and aluminum superstructure are joined by the Detacouple bonding technique. The class is designed with a five-day endurance. These craft have a 3-ton payload margin.

Fourteen boats were ordered by the Coast Guard in FY 84. Two additional craft were purchased as replacements for 110-foot WYTMs used for patrol missions. The Navy purchased 16 more boats for the Coast Guard under the FY-86 DOD Coastal Defense Augmentation appropriation. The Coast Guard acquired five additional craft under the Anti-Drug Abuse Act of 1986. Twenty-two of the 110-foot patrol boats are replacements for the 95-foot boats.

Changes in the B Type include structural plating reinforcement and an improved water purification system, improved habitability, and improved mooring fittings.

Adak

1989–90 stationed at Sandy Hook, NJ, and used for LE and SAR.

Anacapa

1990 stationed at Petersburg, AK, and used for LE and SAR.

Aquidneck

1986–90 stationed at Portsmouth, VA, and used for LE and SAR; 15 May 88 seized PC VA-5923-V at 36°50'N 75°51'W carrying marijuana; 18 May 88 seized PC *Beachcomber* at 34°04'N 76°06'W with marijuana residue on board.

Assateague

1989–90 stationed at Honolulu, HI, and used for LE and SAR.

Attu

1988–90 stationed at San Juan, PR, and used for LE and SAR; 29 Aug 88 seized FV *Grace Caroline* at 17°41'N 67°17'W carrying 3.5t of marijuana; 13 Sep 88 seized MV *Agapi* 12 mi off Vieques I. carrying 3.5t of marijuana; 21 Sep 88 seized sailboat *Windsong* after finding marijuana residue on board; 25 Sep 88 rescued 62 persons from a 26-foot boat in the Mona

Passage and delivered them to immigration; 12 Jan 89 rescued crew of ditched CG HH-65A helicopter between Puerto Rico and the Dominican Republic.

Baranof

1988–90 stationed at Miami, FL, and used for LE and SAR; 1 Jun 88 seized yacht *Jomara* 300 mi E of Miami, FL, carrying 400 lbs of marijuana.

Chandeleur

1988–90 stationed at Miami Beach, FL, and used for LE and SAR; Aug 88 assisted four Cuban refugees who were fleeing from Cuba in a 15-foot boat.

Chincoteague

1988–90 stationed at Mobile, AL, and used for LE and SAR.

Cushing

1988–90 stationed at Mobile, AL, and used for LE and SAR.

Cuttyhunk

1988–90 stationed at Port Angeles, WA, and used for LE and SAR.

Drummond

1988–90 stationed at Port Canaveral, FL, and used for LE and SAR.

Edisto

1987–90 stationed at Crescent City, CA, and used for LE and SAR; 15 Dec 88 seized MV *Eros* off northern California carrying 7t of marijuana.

Farallon

1985–90 stationed at Miami Beach, FL, and used for LE and SAR; 31 Mar 86 assisted sinking PC between Freeport and Lake Worth; 1 Jun 86 seized FV *Abra Ca Dabra* at 25°55′N 79°52′W carrying 7t of marijuana; 25 Jun 86 seized PC FL-6817-AN at 25°27′N 79°52′W carrying 7t of

marijuana; 20 Jul 86 seized PC *La Mouette* at 25°48′N 79°28′W carrying cocaine residue; 30 Jul 86 helped fight fire on cruise ship *Emerald Sea* off the Bahamas; 2 Aug 86 recovered 60 lbs of floating marijuana; 16 Sep 86 recovered .5t of floating marijuana; 5 Mar 87 seized MV *Mar-Ze* at 19°49′N 74°1′W carrying 3.5t of marijuana; 14 Apr 87 seized sailboat *Quest* at 18°54′N 73°48′W carrying 14t of marijuana; 17 Apr 87 seized MV *Dios Coros* at 23°59′N 75°44′W carrying 11t of marijuana; 22 Apr 87 seized MV *Linda Patricia* at 23°53′N 74°44′W carrying 16.5t of marijuana; May 87 seized sailboat *Jacqueline* off Cuba carrying 450 lbs of marijuana—sank while under tow; 18 Sep 87 seized PC *Genesis II* at 25°46′N 79°37′W carrying 400 lbs of marijuana.

Kiska

1990 stationed at Hilo, HI, and used for LE and SAR.

Key Largo

1988–90 stationed at Tybee, GA, and used for LE and SAR.

Liberty

1989–90 stationed at Auke Bay, AK, and used for LE and SAR.

Manitou

1986–90 stationed at Miami Beach, FL, and used for LE and SAR; 5 May 86 seized PC FL-2936-AN at 25°38′N 79°59′W carrying marijuana residue—seized vessel proved to be old CG cutter *Crawford;* 12 May 86 seized MV *Sun Bird* 150 mi NE of Miami, FL, carrying 24t of marijuana; 18 May 86 seized MV *Mayan Trader* at 25°46′N 80°03′W carrying 16t of marijuana; 24 Nov 86 seized PC *Alternative* in the Windward Passage carrying 26 lbs of marijuana and 3 gallons of hashish oil; 22 Feb 87 recovered 30 lbs of floating marijuana; 11 May 87 seized PC *Cathouse* at 19°31′N 86°05′W carrying 480 lbs of marijuana; 19 Jul 87 seized MV *Black and White* at 23°44′N 75°13′W carrying 8t of marijuana 4 Nov 88 rescued 50 Haitians from a 30-foot sailboat 450 mi SE of Miami, FL, and returned them to Haiti.

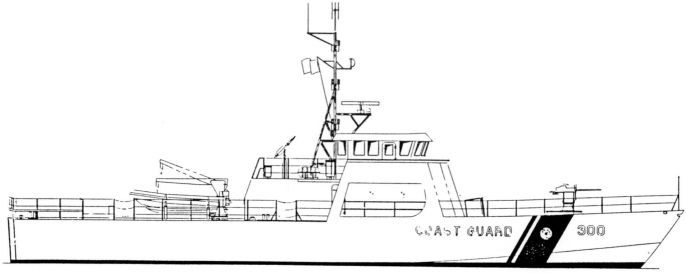

Drawing of a 110-foot patrol boat.

Cutter *Farallon* during 1987. She wears six marijuana leafs on the starboard side of her bridge, demonstrating that the cutter is already a veteran.

Matagorda
1986–90 stationed at Miami Beach, FL, and used for LE and SAR; 29 Jun 86 seized PC *Marquitin* at 25°49′N 79°56′W carrying 796 lbs of marijuana; 2 Jul 86 seized PCV FL-2336-SH at 25°45′N 79°33′W carrying 60 lbs of marijuana; 21 Jul 86 seized PC *Leslie Lee* at 25°51′N 79°32′W carrying 60 lbs of marijuana; 25 Aug 86 seized PC FL-7872-EA at 25°35′N 79°03′W carrying 1t of marijuana; 20 Sep 86 seized PC FL-0016-DW at 25°43′N 79°26′W carrying 350 lbs of marijuana; 20 Oct 86 seized PC *North* at 18°55′N 77°42′W carrying 1t of marijuana; 28 Oct 86 seized FV *Bahamas Runner* at 18°00′N 74°27′W carrying 6.5t of marijuana; 26 Jan 87 seized FV *Jackie Pan* at 23°19′N 77°41′W carrying 2t of marijuana; 22 Mar 87 seized FV *Wet Dreams* 120 mi SE of Miami, FL, carrying 1.5t of marijuana; 7 Jul 87 seized PC *Thunderbird* off Exuma carrying 1,418 lbs of cocaine; 5 Sep 87 recovered 50 lbs of floating marijuana; 16 Nov 88 rescued 86 Haitians from a 26-foot boat 60 mi S of Miami, FL, and returned them to Haiti.

Matinicus
1987–90 stationed at Cape May, NJ, and used for LE and SAR.

Maui
1986–90 stationed at Miami Beach, FL, and used for LE and SAR; 12 Jul 86 seized PC FL-5357-EY at 25°44′N 79°49′W carrying 120 lbs of marijuana; 30 Jul 86 helped fight fire on cruise ship *Emerald Sea* off the Bahamas; 2 Sep 86 seized PC *Jackie O* at 25°59′N 79°31′W carrying 211 lbs of marijuana.

Metompkin
1989–90 stationed at Charleston, SC, and used for LE and SAR; Jan 89 rescued three from a raft dropped by a CG aircraft to sinking FV *Retriever* 140 mi off Savannah, GA.

Monhegan
1986–90 stationed at Puerto Rico and used for LE and SAR; 19 Apr 87 seized PC *Rainbow I* at 22°30′N 74°40′W carrying 920 lbs of marijuana; 1 Nov 87 seized vessel *Stella;* 3 Dec 88 rescued 21 Dominicans from 25-foot boat capsized off Dominican Republic—more than 30 drowned.

Monomoy
1988–90 stationed at Woods Hole, MA, and used for LE and SAR.

Mustang
1986–90 stationed at Seward, AK, and used for LE and SAR.

Nantucket
1987–90 stationed at Miami, FL, and used for LE and SAR.

Naushon
1986–90 stationed at Ketchikan, AK, and used for LE and SAR.

Nunivak
1986–90 stationed at Puerto Rico and used for LE and SAR; 31 Oct 87 seized FV *Por Fin* in the West Indies carrying 2t of marijuana; 4 Sep 88 seized MV *Sheme* at 18°14′N 64°35′W carrying 1,287 lbs of cocaine after firing warning shots.

Ocracoke
1987–90 stationed at Roosevelt Roads, PR, and used for LE and SAR; 28 Oct 86 seized FV *Spartacus* at 14°21′N 69°45′W carrying 10t of marijuana; 24 Nov 86 seized the MV *Judy Ann* 25 mi N of Hispaniola with 13t of marijuana on board; 8 May 87 seized *La Toto* NW of St. Croix with 2t of cocaine on board—one of the largest seizures of that narcotic; 22 Jan 88 seized FV *Omaira* at 17°27′N 63°22′W carrying 1t of marijuana; 16 Dec 88 assisted following collision between MV *Wishing Star* and MV *Nedloyd Van Noort* 10 mi NE of Cabo San Juan.

Orcas
1989–90 stationed at Coos Bay, OR, and used for LE and SAR.

Padre
1989–90 stationed at Key West, FL, and used for LE and SAR.

Sanibel
1986–90 stationed at Woods Hole, MA, and used for LE and SAR.

Sapelo
1987–90 stationed at Eureka, CA, and used for LE and SAR.

Cutter *Matinicus* during Jul 88.

Sitkinak

1989–90 stationed at Key West, FL, and used for LE and SAR.

Tybee

1989–90 stationed at San Diego, CA, and sued for LE and SAR.

Vashon

1986–90 stationed at Puerto Rice and used for LE and SAR; 29 Sep 86 seized FV *Patsy* at 15°34'N 65°51'W carrying 18t of marijuana; 29 Oct 86 seized PC *Kato Sobom* at 17°09'N 67°17'W carrying 775 lbs of marijuana;

11 Apr 87 seized PC *Dea Bheatach* at 17°59'N 68°05'W carrying 1.5t of marijuana; 27 Oct 87 seized PC *Bright Eagle* at 18°30'N 67°30'W carrying 50 lbs of marijuana; 16 Feb 88 seized PC *Carpe Diem* at 17°30'N 67°00'W carrying 1,400 lbs of marijuana.

Washington

1989–90 stationed at Honolulu, HI, and used for LE and SAR.

Wrangell

1989–90 stationed at Portsmouth, NH, and used for LE and SAR.

110-FOOT SURFACE-EFFECT SHIP CLASS

Name	Hull Number	Builder	Keel Laid	Launched	Commissioned	Disposition
Sea Hawk	WSES 2	Bell Halter Inc., New Orleans, LA	N/A	N/A	17 Nov 82	Active
Shearwater	WSES 3	Bell Halter Inc., New Orleans, LA	N/A	N/A	17 Nov 82	Active
Petrel	WSES 4	Bell Halter Inc., New Orleans, LA	N/A	N/A	8 Jul 83	Active

Cost	N/A
Hull	
Displacement (tons)	105 fl (1987)
Length	109'1" oa
Beam	39' max
Draft	8'3" (at rest, 1987); 5'6" on cushion (1987)
Machinery	
Main Engines	2 General Motors diesels
Lift Engines	2 Detroit 350-hp diesels
BHP	1,800 hp
Propellers	twin
Performance	
Max Speed	in excess of 30 kts (1987)
Cruising	25 kts, 1,100-mi radius (1987)
Logistics	
Complement	2 officers, 1 warrant, 14 men (1987)
Electronics	
Radar	navigation
Armament	small arms (1987)

Design

The surface-effect ships are rigid sidewall hovercraft. They are constructed of an aluminum alloy. The lift engines power fans that create a pressurized air cushion under the cutter; this lifts the craft, thus reducing drag and draft. The solid sidewalls pierce the water, creating a catamaran hull, and the air cushion is sealed by flexible rubberized skirts at the bow and stern.

Sea Hawk

1982–90 stationed at Key West, FL, and used for LE and SAR; 26 Jan 84 seized two vessels with 400 bales of marijuana on board in the Bahamas; 2 Feb 84 intercepted a 45-ft sailboat N of Cay Sal Bank with 143 Haitians on board—transferred them to cutter *Hamilton* for return to Haiti; 15 Feb 84 seized PC *Michelle* off Bahamas carrying 10t of marijuana; 8 Mar 84 seized two FVs S of Williams I. after observing them transfer bales of marijuana; 13 Oct 84 seized FV 40 mi E of Andros I. with marijuana on board; 13 Oct 84 seized FV *Nice* 75 mi SE of Miami, FL, carrying 5t of

marijuana; 15 Oct 84 intercepted 10 Haitians on a 20-foot PC and delivered them to immigration; 4 Dec 84 intercepted sailboat 190 mi SE of Miami, FL, carrying 265 Haitians; 14 Jan 85 seized PC *El Cid* 150 mi SE of Key West, FL, carrying marijuana residue; 9 Mar 85 seized FV 100 mi SW of Miami, FL, carrying marijuana and cocaine in a secret compartment; 7 Apr 86 collided with abandoned PC *Profiteer* 75 mi NW of Dry Tortugas while trying to disable the PC by entangling its propeller— *Profiteer*, carrying 8t of marijuana, sank; 22 Jul 87 intercepted over 100 Haitians on *Deu Minnocen* 20 mi SE of Miami and turned them over to immigration; 31 Aug 87 assisted following a bomb threat against cruise ship *Scandinavian Star*; 1 Sep 87 seized Haitian MV *Lucelia* 25 mi NE of Dog Rocks carrying 869 bricks of cocaine.

Shearwater

1982–90 stationed at Key West, FL, and used for LE and SAR; 14 Feb 84 intercepted 20-foot sailboat 20 mi E of Boca Raton with 30 Haitians on

Cutter *Sea Hawk* in Oct 84. She and her sisters have made numerous drug seizures from their base in southern Florida.

board—transferred them to cutter *Alert* for return to Haiti; 25 Feb 84 rescued crew from PC *Owl and Pussycat* near Andros I.—crew had scuttled craft to avoid inspection; 9 Mar 84 seized two PC attempting to transport illegal immigrants into the country; 20 Mar 84 seized PC near Great Bahama Bank carrying 5t of marijuana; 30 Mar 84 seized PC *Ide* near Bahama Banks carrying 10t of marijuana; 11 Apr 84 seized FV *Teruca* near Orange Cay carrying 1t of marijuana in the Straits of Florida; 4 Jun 84 seized FV *V & S* near Cay Sal Bank carrying 3.5t of marijuana; 11 Jun 84 seized two outboards in the Bahamas after an ac attempted to drop them drugs; 12 Jun 84 seized two PC off Andros I. carrying marijuana residue, with 400 pounds floating nearby; 14 Jun 84 seized a 40-foot lobster boat, *Mabelu,* NE of Cay Sal Bank with marijuana on board; 2 Jul 84 seized a 41-foot FV in Old Bahama Channel with marijuana on board; 12 Nov 84 seized a PC 10 mi W of Bimini, Bahamas, with 1t of marijuana on board; 24 Dec 84 seized FV *Barracuda* in Key West, FL, carrying 1t of marijuana in a hidden compartment; 5 Mar 86 helped fight fire on burning tug *Navigator* 18 mi SW of Key West, FL; 8 Oct 86 seized *Jouer* carrying 214 lbs of marijuana; 16 May 87 seized sailing vessel *Algernon* 200 mi SW of Key West, FL, carrying 100 bales of marijuana in a secret compartment; 5 Jul 89 seized merchant vessel *Barlovento* 200 mi SW of Key West, carrying 38,566 lbs of cocaine concealed in a cargo of cement.

Petrel

1983–90 stationed at Key West, FL, and used for LE and SAR; 14 Jan 84 seized PC carrying 6t of marijuana; 14 Jan 84 seized FV *Moses* carrying 1t of marijuana; 17 Jan 84 seized a FV near Cay Sal Bank with marijuana on board; 31 Mar 84 seized PC *Bay Trawler* S of NW Providence Channel after 1.5t of marijuana was discovered in a concealed compartment; 6 Apr 84 seized three craft near Orange Cay after marijuana was discovered; 3 Jun 84 seized abandoned FV *Ocean Queen* off Cay Sal Bank carrying 6t of marijuana; 24 Jun 84 seized a 39-foot FV, *Old Horse,* on Great Bahama Bank with 1t of marijuana on board; 9 Sep 84 intercepted 100 Haitians on board a 40-foot sailboat in Old Bahama Channel and transferred them to immigration; 7 Jan 85 seized PC FL-3783-DL 10 mi SE of Miami, FL, carrying marijuana residue; 13 Mar 85 seized MV in Yucatan Channel carrying 15t of marijuana; 2 Sep 86 seized a 55-foot lobster boat 110 mi SW of Dry Tortugas carrying 10t of marijuana—the boat unsuccessfully tried to ram the cutter; 14 Oct 86 seized FV *Rainbow Chaser* 280 mi SW of Miami, FL, carrying 1.5t of marijuana; 13 Feb 88 seized FV *Malaijar* after it had ejected 12 canisters containing 650 lbs of cocaine; 9 Dec 88 seized Honduran MV *Caroline* after forcing her to stop with small-arms fire.

110-FOOT SURFACE-EFFECT SHIP

Name	Hull Number	Builder	Keel Laid	Launched	Commissioned	Disposition
Dorado	WSES 1	Bell Halter Inc., New Orleans, LA	N/A	N/A	18 Jun 81	*Decomm & trans* to USN Sep 82

Cost	N/A
Hull	
Displacement (tons)	162 fl; 134 light (1981)
Length	110′ oa; 97′ wl
Beam	39′ mb
Draft	7′10″ (at rest, 1981); 4′6″ (on cushion, 1981)
Machinery	
Main Engines	2 General Motors diesels
Lift Engines	2 Detroit diesels
BHP	3,600
Propellers	twin
Performance	
Max Speed	33 kts (1981)
Max Sustained	26 kts, 575-mi radius (1981)
Logistics	
Fuel Oil (95%)	7,000 gal
Complement	14 (1981)
Electronics	
Detection Radar	navigation type
Armament	small arms

Design

The cutter *Dorado* was acquired to evaluate the SES concept and its possible application to CG missions. The cutter was borrowed from the USN.

Dorado

18 Jun 81–Sep 82 stationed at New Orleans, LA, and used for test and evaluation.

Cutter *Dorado,* one of a number of high-performance craft that the Coast Guard has borrowed from the Navy over the years for test and evaluation.

PATROL GUNBOAT (HYDROFOIL)

Name	Hull Number	Builder	Keel Laid	Launched	Commissioned	Disposition
Flagstaff	WPBH 1 PGH 1	Grumman Aircraft Engineering Corp., Stuart, FL	N/A	9 Jan 68	14 Sep 68 in service (USN) 2 Mar 77 (CG)	*Decomm* 30 Sep 78

Cost   N/A

Hull
  Displacement (tons)   70 (fl)
  Length   82′ oa; 73′ bp
  Beam   21′6″
  Draft   4′4″ foils retracted; 18″ foils extended (1977)

Machinery
  Engines   Rolls Royce Tyne gas turbine (foilborne)
                       2 General Motors diesels (hullborne)
  Propellers   single

Performance
  Design Speed,   45 plus kts
    Foilborne
  Design Speed,   8 kts
    Hullborne

Logistics
  Complement   1 officer, 12 men (1977)

Electronics
  Radar   navigation type

Armament   small arms

Design
  The hydrofoil *Flagstaff* was developed by the Navy principally as a test platform. In 1974 the *Flagstaff* was borrowed from the Navy for two months and evaluated off the Southern California coast. During 1977–78 the CG tested the craft in New England waters.

Flagstaff
2 Mar 77–30 Sep 78 stationed at Woods Hole, MA, and used for test and development.

Cutter *Flagstaff* on 1 Oct 76 while being tested by the Coast Guard.

82-FOOT PATROL BOAT CLASS

Name	Hull Number	Builder	Keel Laid	Launched	Commissioned	Disposition
Point Caution	WPB 82301	Coast Guard Yard, Curtis Bay, MD	1 Jun 59	N/A	5 Oct 60	*Decomm & trans* 29 Apr 70 to S. Vietnam as *Nguyen An*
Point Hope	WPB 82302	Coast Guard Yard, Curtis Bay, MD	N/A	N/A	5 Oct 60	Active
Point Young	WPB 82303	Coast Guard Yard, Curtis Bay, MD	N/A	N/A	26 Oct 60	*Decomm & trans* 16 Mar 70 to S. Vietnam as *HQ 714*
Point League	WPB 82304	Coast Guard Yard, Curtis Bay, MD	N/A	N/A	9 Nov 60	*Decomm & trans* 16 May 69 to S. Vietnam as *Le Phuoc Duc*
Point Partridge	WPB 82305	Coast Guard Yard, Curtis Bay, MD	N/A	N/A	23 Nov 60	*Decomm & trans* 27 Mar 70 to S. Vietnam as *Bui Viet Thanh*

Name	Hull Number	Builder	Keel Laid	Launched	Commissioned	Disposition
Point Jefferson	WPB 82306	Coast Guard Yard, Curtis Bay, MD	N/A	N/A	7 Dec 60	*Decomm & trans* 21 Feb 70 to S. Vietnam as *HQ 712*
Point Glover	WPB 82307	Coast Guard Yard, Curtis Bay, MD	N/A	N/A	7 Dec 60	*Decomm & trans* 14 Feb 70 to S. Vietnam as *Dao Van Danh*
Point White	WPB 82308	Coast Guard Yard, Curtis Bay, MD	11 Feb 60	N/A	18 Feb 61	*Decomm & trans* 12 Jan 70 to S. Vietnam as *HQ 708*
Point Arden	WPB 82309	Coast Guard Yard, Curtis Bay, MD	N/A	N/A	1 Feb 61	*Decomm & trans* 14 Feb 70 to S. Vietnam as *Pham Ngoc Chau*
Point Garnet	WPB 82310	Coast Guard Yard, Curtis Bay, MD	30 Jun 60	N/A	15 Mar 61	*Decomm & trans* 16 May 69 to S. Vietnam as *Le Van Nga*
Point Verde	WPB 82311	Coast Guard Yard, Curtis Bay, MD	29 Jun 60	N/A	15 Mar 61	Active
Point Swift	WPB 82312	Coast Guard Yard, Curtis Bay, MD	3 Aug 60	7 Sep 60	22 Mar 61	Active
Point Slocum	WPB 82313	Coast Guard Yard, Curtis Bay, MD	2 May 60	N/A	12 Apr 61	*Decomm & trans* 11 Dec 69 to S. Vietnam as *HQ 706*
Point Thatcher	WPB 82314	Coast Guard Yard, Curtis Bay, MD	11 Jul 60	24 Mar 61	13 Sep 61	Active
Point Clear	WPB 82315	Coast Guard Yard, Curtis Bay, MD	15 Aug 60	N/A	26 Apr 61	*Decomm & trans* 15 Sep 69 to S. Vietnam as *Haynh Van Duc*
Point Mast	WPB 82316	Coast Guard Yard, Curtis Bay, MD	26 May 60	N/A	10 May 61	*Decomm & trans* 15 Jun 70 to S. Vietnam as *Ho Dang La*
Point Comfort	WPB 82317	Coast Guard Yard, Curtis Bay, MD	1 Jul 60	16 Nov 60	24 May 61	*Decomm & trans* 17 Nov 69 to S. Vietnam as *Dao Thuc*
Point Herron	WPB 82318	Coast Guard Yard, Curtis Bay, MD	10 Aug 60	N/A	14 Jun 61	Active
Point Orient	WPB 82319	Coast Guard Yard, Curtis Bay, MD	11 Jul 60	N/A	28 Jun 61	*Decomm & trans* 14 Jul 70 to S. Vietnam as *Ngu Yen Kim Hung*
Point Kennedy	WPB 82320	Coast Guard Yard, Curtis Bay, MD	14 Sep 60	21 Mar 61	19 Jul 61	*Decomm & trans* 16 Mar 70 to S. Vietnam as *HQ 713*
Point Lomas	WPB 82321	Coast Guard Yard, Curtis Bay, MD	Dec 60	N/A	9 Aug 61	*Decomm & trans* 26 May 70 to S. Vietnam as *HQ 718*
Point Hudson	WPB 82322	Coast Guard Yard, Curtis Bay, MD	N/A	N/A	30 Aug 61	*Decomm & trans* 11 Dec 69 to S. Vietnam as *HQ 707*
Point Grace	WPB 82323	Coast Guard Yard, Curtis Bay, MD	N/A	N/A	27 Sep 61	*Decomm & trans* 15 Jun 70 to S. Vietnam as *Dam Thoai*
Point Grey	WPB 82324	Coast Guard Yard, Curtis Bay, MD	17 Nov 60	N/A	11 Oct 61	*Decomm & trans* 14 Jul 70 to S. Vietnam as *Nuy Bo*
Point Dume	WPB 82325	Coast Guard Yard, Curtis Bay, MD	N/A	N/A	1 Nov 61	*Decomm & trans* 14 Feb 70 to S. Vietnam as *Truong Truyen*
Point Cypress	WPB 82326	Coast Guard Yard, Curtis Bay, MD	N/A	N/A	22 Nov 61	*Decomm & trans* 11 Nov 69 to S. Vietnam as *Ho Duy*
Point Banks	WPB 82327	Coast Guard Yard, Curtis Bay, MD	14 Feb 61	N/A	13 Dec 61	*Decomm & trans* 26 May 70 to S. Vietnam as *HQ 719*
Point Gammon	WPB 82328	Coast Guard Yard, Curtis Bay, MD	14 Mar 61	24 Aug 61	31 Jan 62	*Decomm & trans* 11 Nov 69 to S. Vietnam as *Ngu Yen Dao*
Point Welcome	WPB 82329	Coast Guard Yard, Curtis Bay, MD	1 Mar 61	N/A	14 Feb 62	*Decomm & trans* 29 Apr 70 to S. Vietnam as *Ngu Yen Han*
Point Ellis	WPB 82330	Coast Guard Yard, Curtis Bay, MD	27 Apr 61	N/A	28 Feb 62	*Decomm & trans* 9 Dec 69 to S. Vietnam as *HQ 705*

Name	Hull Number	Builder	Keel Laid	Launched	Commissioned	Disposition
Point Marone	WPB 82331	Coast Guard Yard, Curtis Bay, MD	15 May 60	N/A	14 Mar 62	*Decomm* & *trans* 15 Aug 70 to S. Vietnam as *HQ 724*
Point Roberts	WPB 82332	Coast Guard Yard, Curtis Bay, MD	N/A	N/A	6 Jun 62	Active
Point Highland	WPB 82333	Coast Guard Yard, Curtis Bay, MD	N/A	N/A	27 Jun 62	Active
Point Ledge	WPB 82334	Coast Guard Yard, Curtis Bay, MD	N/A	N/A	18 Jul 62	Active
Point Countess	WPB 82335	Coast Guard Yard, Curtis Bay, MD	10 Oct 61	N/A	8 Aug 62	Active
Point Glass	WPB 82336	Coast Guard Yard, Curtis Bay, MD	N/A	N/A	29 Aug 62	Active
Point Divide	WPB 82337	Coast Guard Yard, Curtis Bay, MD	4 Dec 61	N/A	19 Sep 62	Active
Point Bridge	WPB 82338	Coast Guard Yard, Curtis Bay, MD	5 Feb 62	N/A	10 Oct 62	Active
Point Chico	WPB 82339	Coast Guard Yard, Curtis Bay, MD	N/A	N/A	29 Oct 62	Active
Point Batan	WPB 82340	Coast Guard Yard, Curtis Bay, MD	N/A	N/A	21 Nov 62	Active
Point Lookout	WPB 82341	Coast Guard Yard, Curtis Bay, MD	5 Mar 62	N/A	12 Dec 62	Active
Point Baker	WPB 82342	Coast Guard Yard, Curtis Bay, MD	9 May 63	N/A	30 Oct 63	Active
Point Wells	WPB 82343	Coast Guard Yard, Curtis Bay, MD	20 May 63	N/A	20 Nov 63	Active
Point Estero	WPB 82344	Coast Guard Yard, Curtis Bay, MD	20 Jun 63	N/A	11 Dec 63	Active
Point Judith	WPB 82345	J.M. Martinac Shipbuilding Corp., Tacoma, WA	17 May 65	16 Mar 66	26 Jul 66	Active
Point Arena	WPB 82346	J.M. Martinac Shipbuilding Corp., Tacoma, WA	24 May 65	24 Mar 66	26 Aug 66	Active
Point Bonita	WPB 82347	J.M. Martinac Shipbuilding Corp., Tacoma, WA	17 Sep 65	11 May 66	12 Sep 66	Active
Point Barrow	WPB 82348	J.M. Martinac Shipbuilding Corp., Tacoma, WA	11 Oct 65	10 May 66	4 Oct 66	Active
Point Spencer	WPB 82349	J.M. Martinac Shipbuilding Corp., Tacoma, WA	20 Oct 65	13 Jun 66	25 Oct 66	Active
Point Franklin	WPB 82350	J.M. Martinac Shipbuilding Corp., Tacoma, WA	14 Sep 65	15 Jun 66	14 Nov 66	Active
Point Bennett	WPB 82351	J.M. Martinac Shipbuilding Corp., Tacoma, WA	2 Feb 66	18 Jul 66	19 Dec 66	Active
Point Sal	WPB 82352	J.M. Martinac Shipbuilding Corp., Tacoma, WA	3 Feb 66	1 Aug 66	5 Dec 66	Active
Point Monroe	WPB 82353	J.M. Martinac Shipbuilding Corp., Tacoma, WA	7 Feb 66	2 Aug 66	27 Dec 66	Active
Point Evans	WPB 82354	J.M. Martinac Shipbuilding Corp., Tacoma, WA	6 Apr 66	5 Sep 66	10 Jan 67	Active
Point Hannon	WPB 82355	J.M. Martinac Shipbuilding Corp., Tacoma, WA	10 May 66	N/A	23 Jan 67	Active
Point Francis	WPB 82356	J.M. Martinac Shipbuilding Corp., Tacoma, WA	24 May 66	N/A	3 Feb 67	Active
Point Huron	WPB 82357	J.M. Martinac Shipbuilding Corp., Tacoma, WA	25 May 66	N/A	17 Feb 67	Active
Point Stuart	WPB 82358	J.M. Martinac Shipbuilding Corp., Tacoma, WA	N/A	N/A	17 Mar 67	Active

Name	Hull Number	Builder	Keel Laid	Launched	Commissioned	Disposition
Point Steele (ex-*Point Buchon*)	WPB 82359	J.M. Martinac Shipbuilding Corp., Tacoma, WA	8 Aug 66	N/A	26 Apr 67	Active
Point Winslow	WPB 82360	J.M. Martinac Shipbuilding Corp., Tacoma, WA	N/A	N/A	3 Mar 67	Active
Point Charles	WPB 82361	J.M. Martinac Shipbuilding Corp., Tacoma, WA	5 Dec 65	N/A	15 May 67	Active
Point Brown	WPB 82362	J.M. Martinac Shipbuilding Corp., Tacoma, WA	8 Aug 66	N/A	30 Mar 67	Active
Point Nowell	WPB 82363	J.M. Martinac Shipbuilding Corp., Tacoma, WA	6 Oct 66	3 May 67	13 Jun 67	Active
Point Whitehorn	WPB 82364	J.M. Martinac Shipbuilding Corp., Tacoma, WA	5 Dec 66	17 May 67	13 Jul 67	Active
Point Turner (ex-*Point Houghton*)	WPB 82365	J.M. Martinac Shipbuilding Corp., Tacoma, WA	29 Aug 66	N/A	14 Apr 67	Active
Point Lobos	WPB 82366	J.M. Martinac Shipbuilding Corp., Tacoma, WA	N/A	N/A	29 May 67	Active
Point Knoll	WPB 82367	J.M. Martinac Shipbuilding Corp., Tacoma, WA	27 Oct 66	4 May 67	27 Jun 67	Active
Point Warde	WPB 82368	J.M. Martinac Shipbuilding Corp., Tacoma, WA	5 Jan 67	7 Jun 67	14 Aug 67	Active
Point Heyer	WPB 82369	J.M. Martinac Shipbuilding Corp., Tacoma, WA	5 Dec 66	24 May 67	3 Aug 67	Active
Point Richmond	WPB 82370	J.M. Martinac Shipbuilding Corp., Tacoma, WA	31 Jan 67	14 Jun 67	25 Aug 67	Active
Point Barnes	WPB 82371	Coast Guard Yard, Curtis Bay, MD	27 Jan 69	24 Jul 69	21 Apr 70	Active
Point Brower	WPB 82372	Coast Guard Yard, Curtis Bay, MD	17 Feb 69	25 Jul 69	21 Apr 70	Active
Point Camden	WPB 82373	Coast Guard Yard, Curtis Bay, MD	10 Mar 69	6 Oct 69	4 May 70	Active
Point Carrew	WPB 82374	Coast Guard Yard, Curtis Bay, MD	31 Mar 69	6 Oct 69	18 May 70	Active
Point Doran	WPB 82375	Coast Guard Yard, Curtis Bay, MD	21 Apr 69	17 Nov 69	1 Jun 70	Active
Point Harris	WPB 82376	Coast Guard Yard, Curtis Bay, MD	12 May 69	17 Nov 69	22 Jun 70	Active
Point Hobart	WPB 82377	Coast Guard Yard, Curtis Bay, MD	2 Jun 69	5 Jan 70	13 Jul 70	Active
Point Jackson	WPB 82378	Coast Guard Yard, Curtis Bay, MD	23 Jun 69	5 Jan 70	3 Aug 70	Active
Point Martin	WPB 82379	Coast Guard Yard, Curtis Bay, MD	14 Jul 69	16 Feb 70	20 Aug 70	Active

Cost   N/A

Hull
  Displacement (tons)   69 fl; 60 light (1960)
  Length   82′10″ oa; 78′ bp
  Beam   17′7″ max
  Draft   5′11″ max (1960)

Machinery
  Main Engines   2 Cummins diesels—see Design
  BHP   1,200 or 1,600
  Propellers   twin

Performance
  Max Speed   16.8 kts (1,200 hp, 1960)
                        22.9 kts (1,600 hp, 1963)
  Max Sustained   14.5 kts, 577-mi radius (1,200 hp, 1960); 18.0 kts, 542-mi radius (1,600 hp, 1963)
  Economic   10.7 kts, 1,271-mi radius (1,200 hp, 1960); 9.4 kts, 1,500-mi radius (1,600 hp, 1963)

Logistics
  Fuel Oil (95%)   1,840 gal
  Complement   8 men (1960); 2 officers, 8 men (1965)

Electronics
  Radar   SPN-11 or CR-103 (1960)
  Armament   1 20mm (1960) 4.50 cal mg, 1 81mm rocket
                        launcher (Vietnam service)

Design

The 82-foot patrol boats have mild steel hulls and aluminum superstructures. Longitudinally framed construction was used to save weight.

These boats were completed with a variety of power plants. 82301 through 82313, 82315 through 82317, and 82319 through 82331 were powered by two Cummins 600-hp diesels. Boats 82318 and 82332 through 82378 received two 800-hp diesels by the same manufacturer. The 82314 was fitted with two 1,000-hp gas turbines and controllable-pitch propellers. The purpose of this installation was to permit the service to evaluate the propulsion equipment. All units were eventually fitted with the 800-hp diesels. Remaining units will be re-engined beginning in mid-1990 with Caterpillar diesels.

WPB 82301 through 82344 were commissioned without names; at that time the Coast Guard did not name patrol craft shorter than 100 feet. In January 1964 they were assigned names.

Point Arden

1961–65 stationed at Point Pleasant, NJ, and used for LE and SAR; Jul 65–Feb 70 assigned to CG Squadron One, Division 12, Vietnam.

Point Arena

1966–90 stationed at Norfolk, VA, and used for LE and SAR; 18 Jul 68 helped extract a bomb fouled in *Sea Rover*'s nets 42 mi SE of Chesapeake Bay; 26 Jun 69 medevaced crewman from tug *Lead Horse* 243 mi SE of Cape Hatteras; 20 Sep 69 dewatered and escorted FV *Anthony Anne* out of the Chesapeake to Norfolk, VA; 8 Apr 70 medevaced crewman from MV *Irish Cedar* off the Chesapeake; 9 Apr 70 medevaced crew member from MV *Frubel Oceania* off the Chesapeake; 25 Jun 70 towed disabled 18-foot PC to Lynnhaven Inlet.

Point Baker

1963–66 stationed at Port Isabel, TX, and used for LE and SAR; 27 Dec 66 towed disabled FV *Sherry Ann* to Port Aransas, TX; 1967–90 stationed at Port Aransas, TX, and used for LE and SAR; 15 Jun 67 towed FV *Old Man* from 50 mi ESE of Freeport, TX, to Aransas Pass, TX, following medevac by CG ac of its master; 10 Dec 67 towed disabled FV *Baroness* 90 mi ENE of Port Aransas, TX, to that point; 8 Sep 68 towed disabled FV *Gulf Star* to Port Aransas, TX.

Point Banks

1961–65 stationed at Woods Hole, MA, and used for LE and SAR; Mar–Apr 65 escorted USS *Atka*, which was taking on water off New Bedford, MA; Jul 65–May 70 assigned to CG Squadron One, Division 11, Vietnam.

Point Barnes

1970–75 stationed at Miami Beach, FL, and used for LE and SAR; 1976–90 stationed at Ft. Pierce, FL, and used for LE and SAR; Sep 82 seized an Honduran MV off Palm Beach, FL, carrying 30t of marijuana; 27 Mar 84 helped seize FV E of Bahamas with marijuana on board; 16 Aug 84 sustained an engine-room fire; 7 Apr 85 seized PC *Shelly* N of Andros I. carrying 77 lbs of cocaine; 18 Jun 86 seized an FV 6 mi W of Bimini carrying traces of cocaine—the FV fired on the cutter during pursuit; 30 Mar 87 intercepted 60-foot *Marie Flore* carrying 141 Haitians; 10 May 87

helped seize Venezuelan MV *P. L.-8* 40 mi E of Great Abaco with 3t of marijuana on board.

Point Barrow

1966–70 stationed at San Francisco, CA, and used for LE and SAR; Sep 67 medevaced patient from Norwegian MV *Gausdal* near San Francisco Lightship; 3 Jun 70 helped fight fire on Alcatraz I.; 23 Apr 80 towed disabled PC *Solaris* 10 mi S of Farallon I. to San Francisco, CA, after it had been located by a CG aircraft; 1981–90 stationed at Monterey, CA, and used for LE and SAR; 21 Mar 83 assisted, following the collapse of an 85-foot jack-up drill rig 5 mi SW of Pt. Conception, CA.

Point Batan

1962–65 stationed at Fort Hancock, NJ, and used for LE and SAR; mid-Oct 65 towed disabled CG-44322, which had grounded during a rescue, to Point Pleasant, NJ; 1966–84 stationed at Point Pleasant, NJ, and used for LE and SAR; 25 Oct 80 damaged by a massive wave in Manasquan Inlet, NJ, during a storm and forced to abort a search and rescue mission; 1985–90 stationed at Cape May, NJ, and used for LE and SAR.

Point Bennett

1967–90 stationed at Port Townsend, WA, and used for LE and SAR; Jul–Aug 69 conducted safety patrols during salvage of a barge sunk near Admiralty Inlet; 17 May 84 fought fire and towed disabled FV *Tonia Rae* 7 mi W of Port Angeles, WA; 14 Apr 86 rescued 275 from grounded ferry *Hyak* near Anacortes, WA.

Point Bonita

1966–71 stationed at Nantucket, MA, and used for LE and SAR; 28 Apr 68 medevaced crewman from MV *Selfoss* off Nantucket; 5 Jun 68 escorted distressed MV *Siasconsett*, which had grounded off Hyannis, MA; 3 Sep 68 medevaced crewman from FV *Jane and Ursala* 67 mi E of Nantucket; 4 Oct 69 rescued one from a disabled 14-foot PC 27 mi ESE of Nantucket;

Cutter *Point Bonita*, 15 Oct 87. Note the tow bitt mounted on the poop deck.

1972–88 stationed at Woods Hole, MA, and used for LE and SAR; 2 Oct 82 helped rescue two from PC *Adjustment* and towed PC to safety; 22 May 83 seized FV *Linda* 40 mi SE of Cape Cod for fisheries violation; 1988–90 stationed at South Portland, ME, and used for LE and SAR.

Point Bridge

1962–64 stationed at San Pedro, CA, and used for LE and SAR; 1965–78 stationed at Venice, CA, and used for LE and SAR; Jan 66 towed distressed sailboat *Eros* in heavy seas—*Eros* sank and crew was rescued; 26–27 Jul 68 assisted in pollution clean-up in Ballona Creek, CA; 23 Jun 69 fought fire on FV *The Lady* off Paradise Cove, CA; 4 Oct 69 fought fire on PC *Hi-C* 10 mi N of Santa Barbara I.; 1979–90 stationed at Marina Del Rey, CA, and used for LE and SAR; Mar 83 stood by capsized drilling rig 5 mi off Point Conception to warn shipping.

Point Brower

1970–89 stationed at San Diego, CA, and used for LE and SAR; 13 Jul 70 disabled 11 mi SE of Long Beach, CA, due to damage sustained in a roll-towed to San Pedro, CA, by cutter *Point Judith*; 25 Jul 70 towed disabled 19-foot PC to San Diego, CA; 28 Nov 70 towed disabled PC *Broken* to San Diego, CA; fall 89–1990 stationed at San Francisco, CA, and used for LE and SAR.

Point Brown

30 Mar 67–1980 stationed at Norfolk, VA, and used for LE and SAR; 7 Jan 68 escorted distressed FV *Avalon* to Hampton Roads, VA; 14 Mar 69 provided escort following collision between FV *Endeavor* and MV *African Neptune* off VA; 5 Mar 70 towed disabled FV *Our Lady of Fatima* 60 mi E of Cape Henry to Hampton, VA; 21 Apr 70 towed disabled FV *Sea Queen* to Hampton, VA; 4 Jul 70 helped fight fire in oil-storage tank, Sewells Point, VA; 7 Oct 70 medevaced crewman from Argentine MV *Rio Dulce* off Cape Henry; 22 Nov 70 towed disabled PC *Nita Bee* to Little Creek, VA; 7 Jan 79 towed disabled FV *Faith* to Hampton, VA; 23 Feb 79 assisted FVs *Triton 7* and *Margery Snow* that were aground on Little Cobb I.; 1980–late 88 stationed at Oregon Inlet, NC, and used for LE and SAR; 23 Jul 80 towed disabled naval skiff; 24 Apr 84 seized PC *Sport Fishing* NW of the Windward Passage with 2.5t of marijuana on board; late 88–1990 stationed at Morehead City, NC, and used for LE and SAR.

Point Camden

1970–90 stationed at San Pedro, CA, and used for LE and SAR; 18 Oct 70 towed disabled 23-foot PC to San Pedro, CA.

Point Carrew

1970–84 stationed at San Pedro, CA, and used for LE and SAR; 1985–90 stationed at Oxnard, CA, and used for LE and SAR; 25 May 87 towed disabled sailboat to Ventura, CA—rescued five from a sinking PC 5 mi off Point Mugu during a storm.

Point Caution

1960–65 stationed at Galveston, TX, and used for LE and SAR; Jul 65–Apr 70 assigned to CG Squadron One, Division 12, Vietnam.

Point Charles

1967–88 stationed at Cape Canaveral, FL, and used for LE and SAR; 13 Mar 68 towed disabled FV *Scalawag* 80 mi WSW of Key West to safe water; 1988–90 stationed at West Palm Beach, FL, and used for LE and SAR.

Point Chico

1963–65 stationed at Sausalito, CA, and used for LE and SAR; 14 Jun 65 escorted damaged FV *Salmon Queen* 18 mi SW of Point Bonita, CA, to Sausalito, CA; 1966–74 stationed at Benicia, CA, and used for LE and SAR; 26 Sep 66 helped fight fire on barge in San Francisco harbor; 1974–4 Aug 80 stationed at Yerba Buena I., CA; 7 Apr 80 towed disabled 633-foot tanker *Austin* into the wind 35 mi NW of Morro Bay buying time for engineers working on damaged wiring as tanker drifted toward the Piedras Blancas; 4 Aug 80–1990 stationed at Bodega Bay, CA; 9 Sep 83 towed disabled PC *Sabra* into San Francisco, CA; 16 Sep 83 towed disabled FV *Huyne Long* from off Farallon I. to San Francisco, CA; 8 Nov 83 rescued two divers off Mendocino Bay.

Point Clear

1961–65 stationed at San Pedro, CA, and used for LE and SAR; Jul 65–Sep 69 assigned to CG Squadron One, Division 11, Vietnam.

Point Comfort

1961–65 stationed at Benicia, CA, and used for LE and SAR; Jul 65–Nov 69 assigned to CG Squadron One, Division 11, Vietnam.

Point Countess

1962–65 stationed at Bellingham, WA, and used for LE and SAR; 1966–67 stationed at Everett, WA, and used for LE and SAR; 1968–88 stationed at Port Angeles, WA, and used for LE and SAR; 8 Jul 68 towed disabled PC to Everett, WA; 1 Oct 68 towed disabled FV *Beatrice* 30 mi W of Port Angeles, WA, to that port; 21 Feb 69 towed disabled PC *Betty J II* from 25 mi W of Port Angeles, WA, to that port; 18 Jan 86 helped seize MV *Eagle 1* entering Strait of Juan de Fuca carrying 447 lbs of cocaine; 1988–90 stationed at Nokomis Beach, FL, and used for LE and SAR; late 1988 seized PC *Premolo* in the Yucatan Channel carrying 800 lbs of cocaine in a concealed compartment.

Point Cypress

1961–65 stationed at Boston, MA, and used for LE and SAR; Feb 66–Aug 70 assigned to CG Squadron One, Division 13, Vietnam; 10 May 66 helped destroy an enemy trawler.

Point Divide

1962–65 stationed at Newport Beach, CA, and used for LE and SAR; 1966–90 stationed at Corona del Mar, CA, and used for LE and SAR; 10 May 69 dewatered and towed PC *At Last* to Newport, CA; 29 Jan 70 rescued passenger, righted and towed a 14-foot sailboat to Newport, CA; 16 Jul 70 towed dead whale to sea from Salt Creek Beach; 29 May 85 seized FV *Ocean Joy* 15 mi SW of San Clemente I. with 10t of marijuana on board—the crew of the FV attempted to scuttle her.

Point Doran

1962–90 stationed at Everett, WA, and used for LE and SAR.

Point Dume

1961–65 stationed at Fire I., NY, and used for LE and SAR; Feb 65 assisted in search for bodies and debris from Eastern DC-7 crash off Long I.; Jul 65–Feb 70 assigned to CG Squadron One, Division 12, Vietnam.

Point Ellis

1962–65 stationed at Port Townsend, WA, and used for LE and SAR; Jul 65–Dec 69 assigned to CG Squadron One, Division 12, Vietnam; 14 Mar 67 destroyed an enemy trawler.

Point Estero

1964–90 stationed at Gulfport, MS, and used for LE and SAR; 21 Jun 69 rescued one from 16-foot PC 20 mi S of Gulfport, MS; 11 Apr 89 dispatched to MV *Julia* after master found 65 lbs of cocaine on board.

Point Evans

1967–90 stationed at Long Beach, CA, and used for LE and SAR; 21 Feb 70 helped fight pier fire at Rincon, CA; 2 Aug 73 fought fire on FV *Heimark* 5 mi off Los Angeles, CA.

Point Francis

1967–76 stationed at Fort Hancock, NJ, and used for LE and SAR; 1977–90 stationed at Highlands, NJ, and used for LE and SAR; 4 May 68 assisted following a collision between dredges *Essoyons* and *Tsui Yung* off New York; Mar 78 seized a Liberian ship carrying 40,000 pounds of hashish off Sandy Hook, NJ; May 79 seized MV *Olang* off New Jersey with 41,000 pounds of hashish on board; 10 Oct 80 fired 55 rounds of .50 cal mg into U.S. lobster boat *Thomas E* 150 mi E of Key West, FL, after she doused her lights, refused to heave-to, and ran for Bahamian waters—approx 13t of marijuana found on board.

Point Franklin

1967–90 stationed at Cape May, NJ, and used for LE and SAR; 26 Nov 67 medevaced wounded crewman from MV *Timaru Star* 45 mi SSW of Delaware LS; 1 Mar 68 escorted distressed FV *Bright Star* 25 mi SE of Cape May to safe waters; 17 Aug 68 assisted distressed MV *Green Lake* 25 mi SE of Ocean City, MD; 25 Aug 69 assisted and escorted distressed 19-foot PC off Ocean City, MD; 12 Dec 69 towed disabled sailboat *Dora* to Ocean City, MD; 26 Nov 70 towed disabled FV *Sharron Ann* following a collision with MV *Concordia Sun* off Cape May, NJ; 15 Dec 86 fought fire on tug *Kathryne McAllister* 5 mi E of Avalon, NJ; Sep 85 helped seize tug *Capstan* 240 mi E of Cape Charles carrying 30t of marijuana.

Point Gammon

1962 stationed at Fort Bragg, CA, and used for LE and SAR; 1963–65 stationed at Alameda, CA, and used for LE and SAR; 20 Apr 65 towed disabled PC *Amigo del Mar* after dewatering into Port Richmond, CA; Jul 65–Nov 69 assigned to CG Squadron One, Division 12, Vietnam; 1 Jan 67 destroyed an enemy trawler.

Point Garnet

1961–65 stationed at Norfolk, VA, and used for LE and SAR; Jul 65–May 69 assigned to CG Squadron One, Division 11, Vietnam.

Point Glass

1962–70 stationed at Tacoma, WA, and used for LE and SAR; 1971–89 stationed at Gig Harbor, WA, and used for LE and SAR; 26 May 65 damaged when rammed by Canadian tug *Marpole* while moored at Tacoma, WA; 1989–90 stationed at Fort Lauderdale, FL, and used for LE and SAR.

Point Glover

1961–65 stationed at Fort Hancock, NJ, and used for LE and SAR; 6 May 62 towed disabled PC near Sandy Hook, NJ; Jul 65–Feb 70 assigned to CG Squadron One, Division 11, Vietnam.

Point Grace

1961–65 stationed at Crisfield, MD, and used for LE and SAR; Feb 66–Jun 70 assigned to CG Squadron One, Division 13, Vietnam; 29 Feb–1 Mar 68 helped destroy an enemy trawler.

Point Grey

1961–65 stationed at Norfolk, VA, and used for LE and SAR; Jul 65–Jul 70 assigned to CG Squadron One, Division 11, Vietnam; 10 May 66 helped destroy an enemy trawler; 29 Feb–1 Mar 68 helped destroy an enemy trawler.

Point Hannon

1967–90 stationed at West Jonesport, ME, and used for LE and SAR; 12 Jul 67 while towing FV *Stanley Butler*, tow was hit by FV *Hope II* in Great Round Shoals Channel—cutter commenced tandem tow until relieved by cutter *Cape Horn*; 22 Oct 67 helped fight fire on Indian MV *Vishva Mangal* near Searsport, ME; 15 Jan 84 rescued a man clinging to a buoy 12 mi off Rockland, ME.

Point Harris

1962–77 stationed at Bodega Bay, CA, and used for LE and SAR; 1978–80 stationed at San Francisco, CA, and used for LE and SAR; 1981–89 stationed at Honolulu, HI, and used for LE and SAR.

Point Herron

1961–64 stationed at Lewes, DE, and used for LE and SAR; 1965 stationed at Cape May, NJ, and used for LE and SAR; 1966–81 stationed at Bay Shore, NY, and used for LE and SAR; 1982–90 stationed at Babylon, NY, and used for LE and SAR.

Point Heyer

1967–87 stationed at San Francisco, CA, and used for LE and SAR; 25 Sep 69 fought fire at Pier 14, San Francisco, CA; 25 Jan 70 towed PC *Sink*

Point Heyer on 16 Aug 78. This cutter has served her entire career at San Francisco, CA.

Army to San Francisco, CA; 8 Jul 70 towed sailboat *Frol* 40 mi from Morro Bay to safety; Jan 1987–90 stationed at Morro Bay, CA, and used for LE and SAR.

Point Highland

1962–65 stationed at Norfolk, VA, and used for LE and SAR; 16 Jun 65 stood by Norwegian MV *Blue Master* and USS *Hartley* following a collision off Cape Henry; 1966–80 stationed at Crisfield, MD, and used for LE and SAR; 29 Jan 67 assisted following a collision between MVs *Bodoro* and *Beaver State* on Potomac R.; 22 Feb 67 towed disabled tug *Hay-de* and barge following a collision with MV *Hellenic Halcyon* 10 mi N of Smith Point; 21 Jan 70 located and towed barge containing 1,200t of sulfuric acid 4 mi NW of Tangier I. until relieved by a commercial tug; 23 Mar 70 recovered a Navy LCM that had been abandoned in the Chesapeake Bay; 17 Jul 87 towed disabled FV *Betty J* to Chincoteague, VA; 1981–90 stationed at Chincoteague, VA, and used for LE and SAR.

Point Hobart

1970–90 stationed at Oceanside, CA, and used for LE and SAR.

Point Hope

5 Oct 60–1990 stationed at Port Arthur, Sabine Pass, TX, and used for LE and SAR; 26 Feb 68 towed disabled FV *Hope* 60 mi SSE of Sabine, TX, to that port; 6 Oct 68 towed disabled FV *Miss Cubit* 30 mi S of Galveston, TX, to that port; 11 Mar 69 fought fire and towed disabled tug *Gulf Master* 18 mi SW of Sabine, TX, to that port; 30 Sep 71 helped fight fire on gas drilling rig in Gulf of Mexico; 17 Oct 84 rescued seven from jack-up barge that had capsized in the Gulf of Mexico; May 87 transported endangered loggerhead turtles to deep water.

Point Hudson

1961–65 stationed at Panama City, FL, and used for LE and SAR; Feb 66–Dec 70 assigned to CG Squadron One, Division 13, Vietnam; 20 Jun 66 helped capture an enemy trawler; 29 Feb–1 Mar 68 helped destroy an enemy trawler.

Point Huron

1967–90 stationed at Norfolk, VA, and used for LE and SAR; 4 Dec 67 assisted after the barge *Mohawk* hit the Chesapeake Bay Bridge; 15 Jun 69 refloated grounded PC *Miss Cindy* in Great Machipongo Inlet; 9 Aug 69 medevaced crewman from MV *Ciudad de Barquisimet* 185 mi E of Cape Henry; 3 Feb 70 medevaced a crewman from Polish FV *Kanaryjka* to Norfolk, VA; 5 Jul 70 medevaced crewmen from MV *Clelia Campanella* 2 mi off Cape Henry; 8 Jul 70 towed yacht *Enterprise* to Hampton Roads; 26 Jul 70 medevaced crewman from MV *Gulf Knight* off Cape Henry; 11 Apr 87 escorted FV *John Wills*, which had caught a torpedo in it nets, to a disposal area.

Point Jackson

1970–90 stationed at Woods Hold, MA, and used for LE and SAR; 22 Jun 83 seized *Ocean Overture* carrying 2.5t of marijuana; 5 Aug 87 towed disabled FV *Daarnoc* to Nantucket.

Point Jefferson

1960–65 stationed at Nantucket, MA, and used for LE and SAR; 18 Aug 63 towed MV *Yankee* with 149 on board to Provincetown, MA; 18 Oct 64–

29 Jan 65 served on Cuban patrol; Feb 66–Feb 70 assigned to CG Squadron One, Division 13, Vietnam.

Point Judith

1966–72 stationed at San Pedro, CA, and used for LE and SAR; 8 Mar 70 fought fire and rescued operator of FV *Mikki Sue* off Long Beach, CA; 13 Jul 70 towed disabled cutter *Point Brower* to San Pedro, CA; 1973–90 stationed at Santa Barbara, CA, and used for A/N and SAR; 15 Jun 83 helped U.S. Customs Service seize Greenpeace vessel *Pacific Peacemaker*, which was attempting to disrupt a test of the MX missile off Vandenberg AFB; 22 Nov 84 seized yacht *Mir* 5.5 mi N of Santa Rosa I. with 7t of marijuana on board; 21 Sep 87 assisted following a collision between MVs *Pacharoness* and *Atlantic Wing* 15 mi SW of Point Conception.

Point Kennedy

1961–65 stationed at San Juan, PR, and used for LE and SAR; 15 Jul 65 assisted in rescue of four and recovery of six bodies from ditched aircraft near St. Thomas airport; Feb 66–Feb 70 assigned to CG Squadron One, Division 13, Vietnam.

Point Knoll

1967–81 stationed at New London, CT, and used for LE and SAR; late Nov 69 monitored oil spill from Liberian tanker *Hilda* at New Haven, CT, and near Block I.; 1982–86 stationed at Port Isabel, TX, and used for LE and SAR; 28 Feb 86 towed disabled FV *Marnana* to Port Isabel, TX; 1986–90 stationed at New London, CT, and used for LE and SAR.

Point League

1961–65 stationed at Morgan City, LA, and used for LE and SAR; Feb 66–May 69 assigned to CG Squadron One, Division 13, Vietnam; 20 Jun 66 helped capture enemy trawler.

Point Ledge

1962–90 stationed at Fort Bragg, CA, and used for LE and SAR; 31 May 65 rescued crew from FV *Christine* as it sank 20 mi NW of Fort Bragg, CA; 5 Sep 66 helped rescue four from PC *Aquilo* and unsuccessfully fought fire 3 mi off Fort Bragg, CA; 7 Mar 68 rescued pilot from downed USAF F-101 off Eureka, CA.

Point Lobos

1967–90 stationed at Panama City, FL, and used for LE and SAR; 18 Jan 69 escorted distressed tug *Brenton* to Mobile, AL; 13 Feb 69 escorted distressed yacht *Southwind* 45 mi SE of Apalachicola, FL, to Carrabelle, FL; 8 Sep 69 towed disabled FV *Sea Star* 55 mi S of Apalachicola, FL, to Panama City, FL, 21 Feb 70 towed disabled FV *Chief* 36 mi S of Pensacola, FL, to that port.

Point Lomas

1961–65 stationed at Port Aransas, TX, and used for LE and SAR; Jul 65–70 May assigned to CG Squadron One, Division 12, Vietnam.

Point Lookout

1962–64 stationed at Pascagoula, MS, and used for LE and SAR; 1965–90 stationed at Morgan City, LA, and used for LE and SAR; 1 Mar 65 towed disabled yacht *Circe* 120 mi ESE of Key West, FL, and passed tow to cutter *Cape Knox*; Mar 66 towed disabled FV *Rex* from 40 mi SW of

A formation of 82-foot patrol craft arrives in South Vietnamese waters during Jul 65. Note that cutter *Point Lomas* in the foreground does not bear the words Coast Guard on her hull. These cutters were all part of Division 11.

Morgan City, LA, to that port; 15 Jun 66 escorted Norwegian MV *Saga Sky* to Southwest Pass after she had struck a submerged object; 24 Sep 67 towed disabled FV *Christopher* 45 mi SE of Sabine, TX, to Morgan City, AL; 17 Apr 68 assisted following the collision 6 mi W of Morgan City, LA, between tugs, one of which was towing a barge carrying a highly explosive substance; 23 May 68 served as on-scene commander following a spill of 50 barrels of asphalt near New Orleans, LA; 19 Jun 66 helped fight fire on barges in Intercoastal Waterway 10 mi S of Abbeville, LA; 10 Aug 69 assisted in rescue of a man off an oil rig in the Gulf of Mexico; 21 Oct 69 assisted Corps of Engineers in warning offshore rigs and barges in Morgan City, LA, area of approach of hurricane Laurie.

Point Marone

1962–65 stationed at San Pedro, CA, and used for LE and SAR; Jul 65–Aug 70 assigned to CG Squadron One, Division 11, Vietnam; 29 Feb–1 Mar 68 helped destroy an enemy trawler.

Point Martin

1970–73 stationed at Norfolk, VA, and used for LE and SAR; 16 Oct 70 towed USN 50-foot utility boat to Cape Charles after it had broken its towline; 1974–83 stationed at Wrightsville Beach, NC, and used for LE and SAR; 29 Jan 79 towed disabled FV from 20 mi SSE of Cape Hatteras to safety; 25 Feb 80 helped seize MV *Jell II* 50 mi SE of Cape Fear carrying 1t of marijuana; 1983–90 stationed at Atlantic Beach, NC, and used for LE and SAR.

Point Mast

1961–65 stationed at Long Beach, CA, and used for LE and SAR; Jul 65–Jun 70 assigned to CG Squadron One, Division 11, Vietnam.

Point Monroe

1967–68 stationed at Galveston, TX, and used for LE and SAR; 1969–90 stationed at Freeport, TX, and used for LE and SAR; 26 Jul 67 escorted

disabled MV *State Star* to Galveston, TX; 29 Jan 68 towed FV *Bryan Paul* 30 mi NE of Freeport, TX, to Galveston, TX; 11 Feb 68 rescued three from FV *Julie* 90 mi SE of Galveston, TX; 28 Oct 68 towed disabled FV *Lyco 4* 21 mi S of Freeport, TX, to that port; 30 Oct 68 dewatered and towed disabled FV *Traveler* 13 mi SW of Freeport, TX, to that port; 23 Jan 69 escorted distressed FV *Sassy Gal* 120 mi SE of Freeport, TX, to that port; 18 Mar 70 towed disabled FV *Little Paul* 75 mi S of Port Aransas, TX, to safety; May–Jun 70 assisted following explosion and fire on oil rig 10 mi off Galveston, TX.

Point Nowell

1967–90 stationed at Port Isabel, TX, and used for LE and SAR; 4 Sep 67 towed distressed FV *Guppy* from 30 mi S of Port Isabel, TX, to that port; 25 May 68 towed disabled FV *Girtie L* 58 mi S of Port Aransas, TX, to Port Isabel, TX; 25 Feb 70 towed disabled MV *Sally* 120 mi SE of Corpus Christi, TX, to safety.

Point Orient

1961–65 stationed at Ft. Pierce, FL, and used for LE and SAR; Jul 65–May 70 assigned to CG Squadron One, Division 12, Vietnam; 15 Jul 67 captured an enemy trawler; 15 Jan 65 towed disabled PC *Fury* 50 mi E of Daytona Beach, FL, to Ft. Pierce, FL.

Point Partridge

1960–65 stationed at Beals and West Jonesport, ME, and used for LE and SAR; Feb 66–Mar 70 assigned to CG Squadron One, Division 13, Vietnam.

Point Richmond

1967–90 stationed at Anacortes, WA, and used for LE and SAR; 5 Jul 68 helped salvage 18-foot PC off Anacortes, WA; 15 Feb 69 rescued three from grounded FV *Ester* at Eliza I.; 18 Jul 70 dewatered and towed disabled yacht *Scout* to Anacortes, WA.

Point Roberts

1962–90 stationed at Mayport, FL, and used for LE and SAR; 26 Feb 65 towed disabled FV *Cherry Lee* 25 mi SE of St. Augustine, FL, to Mayport, FL, during rough weather; 15 May 66 rescued a skin diver off Jacksonville, FL; 12 May 68 rescued three from FV *Kingfisher* 5 mi E of St. Johns R. mouth; 21 Jul 68 medevaced injured seamen from tanker *Transhudson*; 12 Jan 69 escorted distressed FV *Eagle* 25 mi NW of Key West, FL, to that port; 4 Aug 70 medevaced crewman from Japanese Navy training ship *Katori* off Jacksonville, FL; 28 Nov 82 helped seize MV *Lago Izabel* and FV *Gigi* 120 mi E of Georgia carrying 25t of marijuana—fired 50 rounds of 50-cal mg at *Lago Izabel*; Jan–Feb 86 recovered debris from space shuttle Challenger off Cape Canaveral, FL; Aug 88 escorted Honduran MV *Unicorn Express* into Mayport, FL, where over 1,000 lbs of cocaine were found in a secret compartment.

Point Sal

1967–90 stationed at Grand Isle, LA, and used for LE and SAR; 16 Nov 67 escorted distressed FV *Robert Frank* 45 mi SW of Grand Isle, LA, to Belle Pass; 10 Dec 67 stood by grounded MV *Arkansas* 60 mi ESE of New Orleans, LA; 25 Dec 67 assisted in fighting fire on MV *Gulf Supreme* at Ostrica, LA; 28 Dec 67 helped fight fire on tug *Todd Rick* 20 mi W of Southwest Pass; 11 Feb 68 towed disabled FV *Noah's Ark* 30 mi SSE of

Grand Isle, LA, to that port; 3 Apr 68 helped disperse oil slick by applying a chemical dispersant off Grand Isle, LA; 20 Apr 68 escorted distressed FV *Wilma Ann* 15 mi SE of Grand Isle to that port; 21–22 Aug 68 assisted following a fire on oil rig *Little Bob* 25 mi E of Grand Isle, LA; 14 Jul 69 stood by disabled tanker *Texaco Nevada* 275 mi S of New Orleans, LA, until a commercial tug arrived; 20 Aug 85 seized *Macvic* carrying 25t of marijuana.

Point Slocum

1961–65 stationed at St. Thomas, VI, and used for LE and SAR; Feb 66–Dec 69 assigned to CG Squadron One, Division 13, Vietnam; 20 Jun 66 helped capture enemy trawler.

Point Spencer

1967–May 85 stationed at New Orleans, LA, and used for LE and SAR; 25 Dec 67 assisted in fighting fire on MV *Gulf Supreme* at Ostrica, LA; 2 Jan 68 helped salvage Beechcraft ac from Lake Pontchartrain; 14 Jan 68 towed disabled tug *La Crevette 7* to Gulfport, MS; 31 Mar 68 assisted Dutch MV *Woltersom* 160 mi SW of New Orleans, LA, following a fire; 4 Dec 68 towed disabled cutter *Loganberry* to New Orleans, LA; 7–8 Dec 68 searched for survivors from cutter *White Alder*; 31 Jan 69 assisted disabled barge 5 mi S of St. Marks, FL; Feb–Apr 70 assisted following a fire at oil wells off entrance to Mississippi R. Gulf Outlet Channel; 20 Nov 80 fired 40 rounds of .50 cal mg into a fleeing U.S. MV *Polaris* off Grand Isle, LA,—approx 75t of marijuana were on board; 11 Dec 80 seized a grounded 110-ft MV on a sandbar in the Mississippi R. Gulf Outlet east of New Orleans—80t of marijuana were on board; May 85–1990 stationed at Galveston, TX, and used for LE and SAR; 29 Jan 87 fought fire on board FV *T-Kip III* 80 mi SE of Galveston, TX.

Point Steele

1967–69 stationed at Rockaway, NY, and used for LE and SAR; 25 Aug 69 towed disabled yacht *Cirrus* to Sodus Bay, NY; 1970–80 stationed at Oswego, NY, and used for LE and SAR; 1969–73 escorted Communist-bloc MVs through the St. Lawrence Seaway from Massena, NY, to the Welland Canal; 1981 stationed at Key West, FL, and used for LE and SAR; 1982–90 stationed at Ft. Myers Beach, FL, and used for LE and SAR; 5 Jan 84 fought fire on FV *Skyware* 30 mi off Cape Romano, FL; 19 Mar 84 seized FV *El Principe del Golfo* 100 mi W of Ft. Myers Beach, FL, carrying 10t of marijuana; 10 Nov 84 seized FV *Adriana Belle* 30 mi S of Ft. Myers Beach, FL, with 5t of marijuana on board; 3 Dec 84 seized and destroyed due to health hazard workboat *New Jerusalem* 8 mi SE of Miami, FL, carrying 49 illegal migrants and 200 lbs of marijuana; 28 Aug 85 seized FV *Crusader* carrying 10t of marijuana; Sep 85 intercepted 100 Haitian migrants on board a sailboat 50 mi S of Nassau and delivered them to immigration; 14 Oct 85 seized shrimp boat *Black and White* 34 mi SW of Sanibel I. carrying 27.5t of marijuana; 31 Mar 87 sustained hull damage in heavy seas and was towed to St. Petersburg, FL, by cutter *Point Swift*; 5 May 87 seized FV *My Girls* 30 mi W of Cape Romano, FL, with 25t of marijuana on board.

Point Stuart

1967–90 stationed at San Diego, CA, and used for LE and SAR; 25 Mar 68 assisted following collision between MVs *Atlantic Trader* and *Steel Designer* 2 mi off Point Fermin, CA; 18 Jun 70 towed disabled sloop *Tioga*

to San Diego, CA; 13 Jul 70 towed disabled 30-foot PC to San Diego, CA; 2 Nov 70 towed disabled PC from 1 mi off Coronado I. to safety.

Point Swift

22 Mar 61–1968 stationed at St. Petersburg, FL, and used for LE and SAR; 26 Jun 65 provided firefighting material to burning Irish MV *Irish Poplar* in Tampa Bay; 11 Sep 65 assisted in tow of disabled FV *Carousel* W of Tampa, FL; 19 Nov 67 escorted distressed FV *Mistress* to Clearwater Pass; 7 Jan 68 escorted distressed Liberian MV *Pochteca* to Tampa Bay; 21 Sep 68 rescued three from PC *Blue Star* 30 mi S of Anclote Key, FL; 12 Nov 68 rescued two and salvaged equipment from FV *Mystery II* 40 mi W of St. Petersburg, FL; 1969–90 stationed at Clearwater Beach, FL, and used for LE and SAR; 4 Feb 70 stood by anchored barges that had been released by tug due to steering problems; 31 Mar 87 towed disabled cutter *Point Steel* 80 mi W of St. Petersburg to that port.

Point Thatcher

1961–63 stationed at Miami Beach, FL, and used for LE and SAR; 1964–65 stationed at Norfolk, VA, and used for LE and SAR; 16 Jun 65 stood by Norwegian MV *Blue Master* and USS *Hartley* following a collision off Cape Henry; 24 Jul 65 escorted FV *Explorer* with casualties on board to Little Creek, VA; 1966–71 stationed at Miami Beach, FL, and used for LE and SAR; 19 Feb 66 transported 16 Cuban refugees from Gun Cay, Bahamas, to Miami, FL; 4 Oct 66 grounded, holed, and abandoned off Miami Beach, FL, while going to rescue of grounded MV *Transporter*, which freed herself—9 Oct refloated and towed to Miami, FL; 28 Mar 67 embarked seven Cuban stowaways from MV *Amfialia* and delivered them to Key West, FL; 31 May 70 refueled and escorted distressed 18-foot PC to Miami, FL; 1972–84 stationed at Sarasota, FL, and used for LE and SAR; 28 Dec 77 seized vessel *Marania* carrying contraband; 1985–90 stationed at Nokomis, FL, and used for LE and SAR; 7 May 85 rescued three from raft in Gulf; 2–3 Mar 87 towed disabled FV *St. Andrew Bay* 70 mi S of Panama City, FL, to that port; 4–6 Mar 87 towed the disabled FV *Beach King* 225 mi S of Mobile, AL, to St. Petersburg, FL, during a storm; 7–8 Mar 87 towed disabled FV *Miss Ann* and PC *Grenada II* to Ft. Myers, FL, in 18-foot seas.

Point Turner

1967–90 stationed at Newport, RI, and used for LE and SAR; 18 Jul 68 towed disabled PC *Hell-o* 7 mi E of Boston LS to Gloucester, MA; 10 May 70 transported explosive ordnance team to FV *Moby Dick*, which had recovered a live 500-lb bomb–defused and carried to Quonset Point by the cutter.

Point Verde

1961–68 stationed at Venice, LA, and used for LE and SAR; Sep 65 assisted in cleanup operations in the Gulf of Mexico following hurricane Betsy; mid-Nov 65 escorted raised barge carrying chlorine to a chemical plant; 15 Jun 66 escorted Norwegian MV *Sage Sky* to Southwest Pass after she had struck a submerged object; 26 Feb 67 removed two seamen from MV *Ashley Lykes* near Southwest Pass following a knife fight; 2 Apr 67 escorted disabled FV *Lovie D.* to South Pass; 30 Oct 67 medevaced passenger from MV *Bhaskara Jayanti* 380 mi SE of New Orleans; 25 Dec 67 assisted in fighting fire on MV *Gulf Supreme* at Ostrica, LA; 30 Oct 68 towed disabled 19-foot PC near Mobile Point to Dauphin I.; 13 Jan 69 sustained a fire while in dry dock at New Orleans, LA; 1969–79 stationed at Dauphin I., LA, and used for LE and SAR; 1980–90 stationed at Pensacola, FL, and used for LE and SAR.

Point Warde

1967–Jul 87 stationed at San Juan, PR, and used for LE and SAR; 5 Mar 68 assisted following grounding of tanker *Ocean Eagle* off Puerto Rico; 11 Apr 68 helped fight fire on MV *Pizarro* at San Juan, PR; 11–12 Oct 69 stood by grounded British MV *Hawthorne Enterprise* until relieved by salvage tug; 20 Feb 70 helped fight fire on Spanish MV *La Mancha* off San Juan, PR; 9 Aug 70 towed disabled FV *Western 10* 10 mi NW of Cabo Engano until relieved by commercial tug; 6–10 Oct 70 evacuated refugees during flooding in Puerto Rico; 27 Mar 84 intercepted 27-foot FV in the Mona Passage with 30 illegal immigrants on board—taken to Mayaguez, PR; 1 Sep 84 intercepted 4 sailboats and transported 52 to immigration officials; 30 Sep 84 seized FV *Three Brothers* 30 mi SW of Puerto Rico with 14t of marijuana on board; 27 Jul 84 towed disabled FV *Keika Michille* to Puerto Rico; Aug 87–1990 stationed at Wrightsville Beach, NC, and used for LE and SAR.

Point Wells

1963–90 stationed at Montauk, NY, and used for LE and SAR; 4 Jul 67 towed disabled sloop *Waterloo* from 120 mi S of Montauk Point to NY; 17 Sep 68 towed disabled FV 35 mi SE of Montauk Point to Greenport, NY; 4 Aug 69 towed disabled PC *Peggy II* 30 mi SW of Montauk Point to safety; 9 Dec 86 helped fight fire on FV *Old Colony* off Montauk Point.

Point Welcome

1962–65 stationed at Everett, WA, and used for LE and SAR; Jul 65–Apr 70 assigned to CG Squadron One, Division 12, Vietnam; 29 Feb–1 Mar 68 helped destroy an enemy trawler.

Point White

1961–65 stationed at New London, CT, and used for LE and SAR; Feb 66–Jan 70 assigned to CG Squadron One, Division 13, Vietnam.

Point Whitehorn

1967–90 stationed at St. Thomas, Virgin I., and used for LE and SAR; 4 Mar 68 assisted following grounding of tanker *Ocean Eagle* off Puerto Rico; 11 Apr 68 helped fight fire on MV *Pizarro* at San Juan, PR; 29–30 Apr 69 helped fight fire on British tanker *Mobile Apex* near St. Croix, Virgin I.; 6 Jan 70 assisted in escorting disabled tanker *Antonatos*; 20 Feb 70 helped fight fire on Spanish MV *La Mancha* off San Juan, PR; 23 Nov 70 helped fight fire in Krum Bay, Virgin I.; 29 Mar 82, assisted by a CG helicopter, seized a shrimp boat carrying 10t of marijuana after a six-hour chase; 16 Aug 83 assisted MV *Westbridge* 26 mi SW of St. Thomas; 24 May 84 rescued two from Cessna ac in San Juan harbor; 6 Aug 84 assisted in rescue of survivors from a PC off Cooper I., British Virgin Islands; 17 Aug 84 seized sailboat *Arawak* 60 mi E of St. Thomas carrying 2t of marijuana; 23 Oct 84 seized FV *Carolina One* 150 mi S of Puerto Rico with marijuana on board; 11 Dec 84 seized Panamanian MV *Silver Star II* 180 mi E of St. Martin with 10t of marijuana in a secret compartment; 16 Dec 84 towed disabled MV *Kim-G* 30 mi SE of St. Thomas to safety.

Point Winslow

1967–80 stationed at San Francisco, CA, and used for LE and SAR; 19 Aug 67 assisted FV *Yvette* 10 mi NW of Farallon I.; 21 Jul 69 fought fire at fuel docks in Richmond, CA; 1981–87 stationed at Eureka, CA, and used for LE and SAR; Jan 87–1990 stationed at Morro Bay, CA, and used for LE and SAR; Aug 88 helped seize FV *Prygos* N of Santa Cruz, CA, carrying 2t of marijuana.

Point Young

1960–stationed at Grand Isle, LA, and used for LE and SAR; Jul 65–Mar 70 assigned to CG Squadron One, Division 11, Vietnam.

Point Young on 13 Nov 65 wears a new coat of gray paint for service in Vietnam. The cutter mounts an over-under .50 cal. mg-81mm mortar on her forecastle. The mount for this weapon was developed by the Coast Guard.

95-FOOT PATROL BOAT CLASS

Name	Hull Number	Builder	Launched	Commissioned	Disposition
A TYPE					
Cape Small	WPB 95300	Coast Guard Yard, Curtis Bay, MD	19 Mar 53	17 Jul 53	*Decomm* 13 Apr 87 *Trans* Marshall Is., 10 Dec 87
Cape Coral	WPB 95301	Coast Guard Yard, Curtis Bay, MD	N/A	21 Sep 53	*Decomm* 6 Jun 83
Cape Higgon	WPB 95302	Coast Guard Yard, Curtis Bay, MD	N/A	14 Oct 53	*Decomm* Jan 90

Name	Hull Number	Builder	Launched	Commissioned	Disposition
Cape Upright	WPB 95303	Coast Guard Yard, Curtis Bay, MD	N/A	2 Jul 53	*Decomm* 6 Jan 89
Cape Gull	WPB 95304	Coast Guard Yard, Curtis Bay, MD	26 Feb 53	8 Jun 53	*Decomm* 15 May 88
Cape Hatteras	WPB 95305	Coast Guard Yard, Curtis Bay, MD	N/A	28 Jul 53	Active
Cape George	WPB 95306	Coast Guard Yard, Curtis Bay, MD	N/A	10 Aug 53	*Decomm* 3 Sep 89
Cape Current	WPB 95307	Coast Guard Yard, Curtis Bay, MD	N/A	24 Aug 53	*Decomm* 1 May 89
Cape Strait	WPB 95308	Coast Guard Yard, Curtis Bay, MD	N/A	10 Sep 53	*Decomm* 21 Jan 83
Cape Carter	WPB 95309	Coast Guard Yard, Curtis Bay, MD	N/A	7 Dec 53	*Decomm* Jan 90
Cape Wash	WPB 95310	Coast Guard Yard, Curtis Bay, MD	N/A	15 Dec 53	*Decomm* 1 Jun 87
Cape Hedge	WPB 95311	Coast Guard Yard, Curtis Bay, MD	4 Aug 53	21 Dec 53	*Decomm* 7 Jan 87
B TYPE					
Cape Knox	WPB 95312	Coast Guard Yard, Curtis Bay, MD	N/A	13 Jun 55	*Decomm* 10 Feb 89
Cape Morgan	WPB 95313	Coast Guard Yard, Curtis Bay, MD	N/A	5 Jul 55	*Decomm* 20 Oct 89
Cape Fairweather	WPB 95314	Coast Guard Yard, Curtis Bay, MD	N/A	18 Jul 55	*Decomm* 3 Apr 85
La Crete a Pierrot	WPB 95315	Coast Guard Yard, Curtis Bay, MD	N/A	1 Aug 55	*Trans* to Haiti 27 Feb 56
Cape Fox	WPB 95316	Coast Guard Yard, Curtis Bay, MD	N/A	22 Aug 55	*Decomm* 30 Jun 89
Cape Jellison	WPB 95317	Coast Guard Yard, Curtis Bay, MD	N/A	7 Sep 55	*Decomm* 12 Dec 86
Cape Newagen	WPB 95318	Coast Guard Yard, Curtis Bay, MD	26 Feb 55	26 Sep 55	*Decomm* Sep 82
Cape Romain	WPB 95319	Coast Guard Yard, Curtis Bay, MD	N/A	11 Oct 55	*Decomm* 11 Aug 89
Cape Starr	WPB 95320	Coast Guard Yard, Curtis Bay, MD	N/A	15 Aug 56	*Decomm* 16 Jan 87
C TYPE					
Cape Cross	WPB 95321	Coast Guard Yard, Curtis Bay, MD	N/A	20 Aug 58	*Decomm* 2 Mar 90
Cape Horn	WPB 95322	Coast Guard Yard, Curtis Bay, MD	N/A	3 Sep 58	*Decomm* Jan 90
Cape Darby	WPB 95323	Coast Guard Yard, Curtis Bay, MD	N/A	3 Oct 58	*Decomm* 11 Sep 68 *Trans* to S. Korea 24 Mar 69 as *PB 11*
Cape Shoalwater	WPB 95324	Coast Guard Yard, Curtis Bay, MD	N/A	17 Oct 58	*Decomm* 9 Dec 88
Cape Florida	WPB 95325	Coast Guard Yard, Curtis Bay, MD	N/A	28 Oct 58	*Decomm* 18 Sep 68 *Trans* to S. Korea 13 Nov 68 as *PB 7*
Cape Corwin	WPB 95326	Coast Guard Yard, Curtis Bay, MD	N/A	14 Nov 58	*Decomm* 6 Apr 90
Cape Porpoise	WPB 95327	Coast Guard Yard, Curtis Bay, MD	N/A	21 Nov 58	*Decomm* 24 Sep 68 *Trans* to S. Korea 13 Nov 68 as *PB 8*
Cape Henlopen	WPB 95328	Coast Guard Yard, Curtis Bay, MD	N/A	5 Dec 58	*Decomm* 28 Sep 89
Cape Kiwanda	WPB 95329	Coast Guard Yard, Curtis Bay, MD	N/A	28 Apr 59	*Decomm* 18 Sep 68 *Trans* to S. Korea 24 Mar 69 as *PB 12*
Cape Falcon	WPB 95330	Coast Guard Yard, Curtis Bay, MD	N/A	12 May 59	*Decomm* 15 Aug 68 *Trans* to S. Korea 13 Nov 68 as *PB 9*
Cape Trinity	WPB 95331	Coast Guard Yard, Curtis Bay, MD	N/A	26 May 59	*Decomm* 16 Aug 68 *Trans* to S. Korea 13 Nov 68 as *PB 10*
Cape York	WPB 95332	Coast Guard Yard, Curtis Bay, MD	N/A	9 Jun 59	*Decomm* 26 May 89
Cape Rosier	WPB 95333	Coast Guard Yard, Curtis Bay, MD	N/A	23 Jun 59	*Trans* to S. Korea 24 Sep 68 as *PB 3*
Cape Sable	WPB 95334	Coast Guard Yard, Curtis Bay, MD	N/A	7 Jul 59	*Decomm* 16 Aug 68 *Trans* to S. Korea 24 Sep 68 as *PB 5*
Cape Providence	WPB 95335	Coast Guard Yard, Curtis Bay, MD	N/A	21 Jul 59	*Decomm* 30 Aug 68 *Trans* to S. Korea 24 Sep 68 as *PB 6*

Cost	N/A
Hull	
Displacement (tons)	102 fl (A); 105 fl (B); 98 fl (C)
Length	95' oa; 90' wl
Beam	20' max
Draft	6'4" (A); 6'5" (B); 6'2" (C) as completed
Machinery	
Main Engines	4 Cummins VT-600 diesels (A, B, & C); 2 Detroit 16V149 diesels (renovated)
BHP	2,200 (A, B, & C); 2,470 diesels (renovated)
Propellers	twin
Performance	
Max Speed	20 kts (A & B); 22 kts (C); 24 kts (renovated) as completed
Cruising	12 kts, 1,418-mi radius (A–1961)
	12 kts, 1,700-mi radius (B–1961)
	12 kts, 1,780-mi radius (C–1961)
Logistics	
Fuel Oil (95%)	3,114 gal
Complement	15 (1961)
Electronics	
Radar	SPS-64 (1987)
Sonar	retractable type, A & B, as completed; none C
Armament	2 mousetrap, 2 dc racks, 2 20mm (twin), 2 .50-cal mg—A as completed; 2 mousetrap, 2 dc racks, 1 40mm, 2 .50-cal mg—B as completed; 2 .50-cal mg—C as completed; 2 12.7mm mg 2 40 mm Mk 64 grenade launchers (1987)

Design

The 95-foot or Cape class was an outgrowth of a need for shallow-draft ASW craft brought on by the increasing tensions during the years immediately following World War II.

During the period of construction, three distinctive sub-classes evolved as the Coast Guard's mission emphasis shifted from ASW to SAR. The A Type 95-footer was outfitted primarily for ASW. The B Type differed by mounting a 40 mm vice 20 mm gun and being fitted with scramble nets, a towing bit, and a large searchlight—all important SAR tools. The C-type units were constructed without the heavy armament, and for economy some of the SAR equipment was also deleted. However, the Coast Guard added these SAR items to both the As and Cs during various refits. A renovation program began in the mid-1970s but was ended, due to increasing expenses and a shortage of funds, after 16 boats had been overhauled.

The 95-footers were designed by the Coast Guard, and their hulls and superstructure were made of steel. These cutters remained unnamed until Jan 64.

Cape Carter

1953–60 stationed at Alameda, CA, and used for LE and SAR; 1961–82 stationed at Crescent City, CA, and used for LE and SAR; 26–27 Dec 65 took disabled tug *Sea Wolf* and barge under tow 18 mi NNW of Crescent City, CA, in 10-foot seas, tow line parted and one man was injured—she was relieved by cutter *Avoyel* and two commercial tugs; 19 Jul 65 assisted U.S. FV *Chief* and Colombian *Ciudad de Manizales* following their collision—*Chief* sank and *Cape Carter* was subsequently damaged in collision with *Ciudad de Manizales* 9 mi SSW of Blunts Reef; 2 May 69 rescued two from FV *Flyer* 3 mi NW of Crescent City, CA; 1983 underwent major renovation; 1984–90 stationed at Auke Bay, AK, and used for LE and SAR.

Cape Coral

1954–83 stationed at Juneau, AK, and used for LE and SAR; 6 Apr 65 accidently grounded off Keen I., Wrangell Narrows, AK; 12 Jun 65 rescued two from PC wrecked on Seduction Point, AK; 17 Jan 66 rescued survivors from a PC and transported them to Haines, AK; 13 Jul 67 towed and intentionally grounded disabled powered barge *Columbia* near Gastineau Channel, Juneau, AK; 28 Aug 67 medevaced a crew member from Japanese FV *Takachiho Maru* 250 mi SW of Ketchikan, AK; 12 Jun 68 medevaced seaman from FV *Fuji Maru* off Sitka, AK; 9–11 Sep 68 salvaged FV *Valerie M* aground off Sullivan I.

Cape Corwin

1958–81 stationed at Honolulu, HI, and used for LE and SAR; 22 Jun 64 towed yacht *Vida Mia* 12 mi SE of Diamond Head, HI; 12 Jan 65 medevaced injured seaman from barge *Western Offshore No. 3*; 12 Jun 65 towed PC *Sea Sharp* to Honolulu, HI, following injury to operator; Jan 66 medevaced a seaman from commercial tug *Hudson* 280 mi SW of Honolulu, HI; 4 Dec 67 rescued three from MV *Jeannie Marie*; 21 Sep 68 rescued one from a rubber raft off Kaena Point; 2 Nov 70 towed disabled 23-foot PC from 37 mi off Diamond Head to safety; 1982 underwent major renovation; 1983–90 stationed at Maui, HI, and used for LE and SAR; Aug 85 helped disabled FV *Manta* 195 mi S of Hawaii; Feb 89 helped recover debris from United Airlines Flight 811.

Cape Cross

1959–68 stationed at New Castle, NH, and used for LE and SAR; mid-Jul 65 assisted in unsuccessful search for ditched USAF C-121 85 mi E of Nantucket; 28 May 67 medevaced a crewman from FV *Phillip J*; 11 Jun 67 escorted two Polish MVs from U.S. waters; 26 Sep 67 escorted lost FV 45 mi ESE of Boston, MA, to that port; 2 May 68 escorted distressed FV *Stella Maris* 110 mi E of Nantucket to Newport, RI; 1969–90 stationed at Gloucester, MA, and used for LE and SAR; 10 Jan 77 rescued two from FV *Chester A. Poling* off Cape Ann, MA; 1982 underwent major renovation; 1983–15 Apr 87 stationed at Crescent City, CA, and used for LE and SAR; 15 Apr 87–1990 stationed at Hilo, HI, and used for LE and SAR.

Cape Current

1953–60 stationed at Norfolk, VA, and used for LE and SAR; Jan 56 escorted damaged MV *Gulfwater* into Hampton Roads; 1961–66 stationed at Ocracoke, NC, and used for LE and SAR; 1967–68 stationed at Little Creek, VA, and used for LE and SAR; 29 Jan 67 assisted following a collision between MVs *Bodoro* and *Braver State* on Potomac R.; 1969–77 stationed at Savannah, GA, and used for LE and SAR; 1978 underwent major renovations; 1979–82 stationed at Dania, FL, and used for LE and SAR; 26 Sep 80 seized FV *Santa Martha* carrying 20t of marijuana; 1983–89 stationed in the Miami, FL, area and used for LE and SAR; 2 Jul 84 helped seize a 28-foot PC 60 mi SE of Miami, FL; 15 Jul 84 intercepted seven Haitians in a 21-foot sailboat 15 mi E of Ft. Lauderdale, FL; Jan 86 seized FV 230 mi E of Miami, FL, carrying 4t of marijuana; 5 Oct 86 seized vessels *All Together* and *Spellbinder* 4 mi W of Bimini carrying 750 lbs of cocaine; 23 Jun 84 seized PC FL-6466-AY near Miami, FL, carrying 60 lbs of marijuana; 30 Jul 84 seized a FV 50 mi SE of Orange Cay, Bahamas, with 1t of marijuana on board; 4 Aug 84 seized PC FL-6388-PL 30 mi S of Miami, FL, carrying marijuana residue; 7 Oct 84 seized abandoned FV *Miss Pat* 15 mi N of Grand Bahama I. carrying 10t of marijuana; 24 Jul 85 seized seaplane N3122P 44 mi SE of Miami, FL, carrying a large amount of cash; 27 May 87 intercepted 55-foot vessel *Jesula* 55 mi E of Miami, FL, carrying 157 Haitians—transferred custody to cutter *Chase*; Jun 87 intercepted MV *Miracle's Express* with illegal aliens on board—returned to their country; Jul 87 intercepted MV *Ella Marie* S of Freeport carrying 201 Haitians who were picked up by the cutter *Harriet Lane*; 12 Oct 87 rescued crew of Venezulan MV *Alma Llanera* off Florida in 15-foot seas during Hurricane Floyd.

Cape Darby

1958–63 stationed at Provincetown, MA, and used for LE and SAR; 1964–68 stationed at Key West, FL, and used for LE and SAR; 22 Aug 65 towed disabled FV *Miss Queenie* 230 mi W of Key West, FL, to that port; mid-Sep 65 towed and took on board 50 Cuban refugees from two boats and carried them to Dry Tortugas, FL; 27 Jan 66 escorted refugee boat carrying four Cubans to Key West, FL; 5 Jan 67 towed disabled small craft carrying four Cuban refugees to Key West, FL; 13 Apr 67 escorted MV *Gran Lempira*, which had rescued 29 Cuban refugees, to Key West, FL; late Aug 67 picked up six Cuban refugees from a raft 60 mi S of Key West, FL; 23 Oct 67 escorted disabled FV *Sea Spray* 50 mi SW of Dry Tortugas to Miami, FL; 23 Jan 68 embarked four Cuban refugees from FV *Stella Mystery*; 28 May 68 rescued nine Cuban refugees from a raft 80 mi SE of Key West, FL.

Cape Fairweather

1955–85 stationed at New London, CT, and used for LE and SAR; 24 Aug 65 removed dependents from cutter *Owasco* grounded on Little Goshen Reef; 26 Aug 69 helped fight fire in New London, CT; Feb 70 supported salvage operation of a commercial ac .5 mi S of Seaside Point,

CT; 15 Oct 70 escorted leaking barge to New Haven, CT; 9 Aug 82 seized PC *Fiesta* carrying 6t of marijuana.

Cape Falcon

1959–68 stationed at Chincoteague, VA, and used for LE and SAR.

Cape Florida

1958–63 stationed at Port Isabel, TX, and used for LE and SAR; 1964–68 stationed at Anacortes, WA, and used for LE and SAR; 5 Jan 65 towed disabled Canadian Widgeon amphibian 4 mi WSW of Patos Light near British Columbia for 5 mi to rendezvous with Canadian vessel; 29 May 66 transported doctor to injured girl on Saddlebag I., WA; 30 Aug 66 fought fire on FV *Gretchen Cay* SE of Lopez I.; 28 Oct 67 freed grounded Japanese MV *Kirishima Maru* from shoal W of Sitka, AK.

Cape Fox

1955–64 stationed at New London, CT, and used for LE and SAR; 1965–79 stationed at Riviera, FL, and used for LE and SAR; 12 Feb 66 rescued five crew members from the Panamanian MV *Padre Island* aground 45 mi E of Miami, FL; 12 Jan 69 towed disabled yacht 30 mi NE of Miami, FL, to West Palm Beach; 8 Mar 69 rescued tug of houseboat *Stand Pat*—line parted in heavy seas and boat sank—two on board rescued by FV; 25 Dec 77 seized *Iris Marie* off Miami, FL, carrying 4t of marijuana; 26 Dec 77 seized *Miss Connie* and *Ecopesca IV* off Great Bahama Bank carrying 35t of marijuana; 30 Dec 77 helped seize vessel *Dona Petra* carrying contraband; 27 Mar 78 seized *Lyniv IV* off Stuart, FL, carrying 80t of marijuana; 8 Jun 78 seized PC off Little Bahama Bank carrying 28t of marijuana; 28 Jul 78 seized PC off Little Bahama Bank carrying 200 lbs of marijuana; 4 Aug 78 seized *My Lady* off Miami, FL, carrying 2t of marijuana; 29 Aug 78 seized *Mabell* off Great Bahama Bank carrying 20t of marijuana; 17

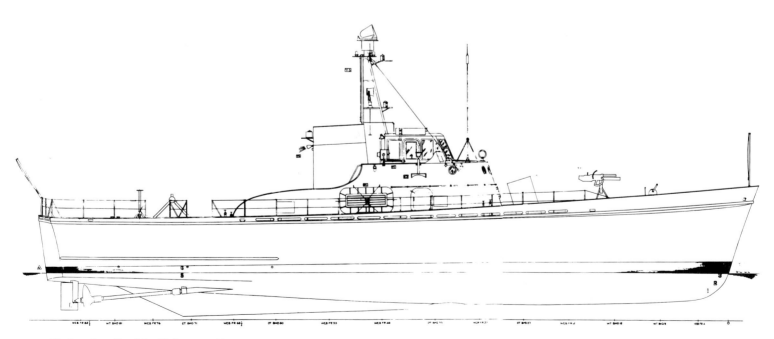

Outboard profile of the 95-foot patrol boat.

Nov 78 seized MV *Faruk* off Little Bahama Bank carrying 37t of marijuana; 1980 underwent major renovation; 1982-89 stationed at Key West, FL, and used for LE and SAR; Dec 83-Feb 84 conducted surveillance from St. Georges, Grenada; 21 Mar 84 assisted in rescue of 15 from Panamanian MV *Panky* 150 mi SW of Tampa, FL; 6 Apr 84 removed stowaway from MV *Gargoyle*; 3 Aug 84 seized FV inside protected waters 25 mi N of Key West, FL, for operating illegally; 15 Dec 84 seized FV *Captain David* 3 mi off Lode Key, FL, carrying marijuana residue; 25 May 85 seized FVs *Angelita*, carrying 10t of marijuana, and *Ocean Lady*, also carrying 10t of marijuana, off Keys; 5 Mar 86 helped fight fire on tug *Navigator* 18 mi SW of Key West, FL; 6-7 Apr 86 chased abandoned PC *Profiteer* 75 mi NW of Dry Tortugas carrying 8t of marijuana, which sank after colliding with the cutter *Sea Hawk*.

Cape George

1953-62 stationed at Ft. Hancock, NJ, and used for LE and SAR; 1962-63 stationed at Fairhaven, MA, and used for LE and SAR; 1962 assisted following collision between MVs *Fernview* and *Dynafuel* near Cape Cod Canal; 1964 temporarily stationed in Miami, FL, following Cuban missile crisis; 1964-79 stationed at New Bedford, MA, and used for LE and SAR; 23 Jan 65 assisted FV *Kim*; Mar 65 escorted damaged Russian mothership *Slavnlj* while she remained in U.S. waters to effect repairs off Cape Cod; Oct 67 recovered floating dry dock near New Bedford breakwater; 29 May 68 towed disabled sailboat *Betty D II*, which had grounded near Cape Cod Canal; 1980 stationed at Woods Hole, MA, and used for LE and SAR; 1981 underwent major renovation; 1982-89 stationed at Guam and used for LE and SAR; 30 Dec 86 rescued a swimmer off Guam.

Cape Gull

1953-65 stationed at New York, NY, and used for LE and SAR; 1966-69 stationed at Ft. Hancock, NJ, and used for LE and SAR; 8 Sep 66 helped fight fire at petroleum facility, Perth Amboy, NJ; 17 Feb 70 freed grounded barge at Port Monmouth, NJ; 1970-74 stationed at Atlantic City, NJ, and used for LE and SAR; 1974-76 held for transfer to Lebanon under MAP; 1977-78 underwent major renovation at CG Yard, Curtis Bay, MD; 25 Nov 78 seized MV *China Doll* 65 mi E of Miami, FL, carrying 6t of marijuana; 1979 stationed at Miami, FL, and used for LE and SAR; 18 Feb 79 rescued nine from MV *Bimini* that sank 70 mi NE of Miami, FL; 9-10 Jun 79 seized FV *Tarpon* 75 mi SE of Miami, FL, carrying 6t of marijuana; 9-10 Jun 79 detained Bahamian FV *Mrs. Eureka* until Bahamian authorities arrived; 3 Jul 79 seized PC *Bahia Mar 17* 70 mi SE of Miami, FL, carrying 2.5t of marijuana; 26 Sep 79 rescued two from ditched private ac in Straits of Florida; 2 Oct 79 seized FV *Captain John Bolden* 50 mi SE of Miami, FL, carrying 3t of marijuana and three million quaalude tablets; 4-5 Oct 79 helped rescue 146 Haitians from a 40-ft sailboat 120 mi S of Miami, FL; 4 Nov 79 rescued four Haitians from a sinking boat 20 mi E of Miami, FL, in heavy seas; 25 Nov 79 seized FV *Star II* 75 mi SE of Miami, FL, with 8t of marijuana on board; 8 Dec 79 seized MV *Carman* 90 mi SE of Miami, FL, carrying 12t of marijuana; 24 Dec 79 seized FV *Mr. White* 60 mi SE of Miami, FL, carrying 3t of marijuana and methaqualone powder; 9 Mar 80 seized PC *Sweet Mama* 70 mi ESE of Miami, FL, carrying 1.5t of marijuana; 31 Jan 82 seized *Tiburon* carrying 10t of marijuana; Dec 83-Feb 84 conducted surveillance from St. Georges, Grenada; 27 Mar 84 assisted in rescue of three 35 mi W

of Grenada; 24 Aug 85 rescued three from PC *Jane's* 25 mi E of Miami, FL; Jan 86 towed disabled PC *Defiance* to safety; 30 Jul 86 helped fight fire on cruise ship *Emerald Sea* off the Bahamas; 3 Jun 87 along with cutter *Bear* seized five vessels carrying 88t of marijuana and six kilos of cocaine; 26 Feb 88 seized a MV carrying 550 lbs of cocaine hidden under yams.

Cape Hatteras

1953-73 stationed in the Long Beach-San Pedro-Santa Barbara, CA, area; 25 Mar 68 assisted following collision between MVs *Atlantic Trader* and *Steel Designer* 2 mi off Point Fermin, CA; 16 Jul 68, at request of Los Angeles PD, crew boarded ketch *Resolute* after repeated orders to heave to and shots across the bow were ignored near Treasure I.; 12 Jul 68 escorted distressed research vessel *Pacific Seal* to Port Hueneme, CA; 20 Feb 70 helped fight pier fire at Rincon, CA; 22 Apr 70 towed disabled PC *Mazal Tub* to Santa Barbara, CA; 1974-76 held for transfer to Ceylon under MAP; Nov 80 underwent major renovation at CG Yard, Curtis Bay, MD; 1981-82 stationed at Seattle, WA, and used for LE and SAR; 1982-90 stationed at Petersburg, AK, and used for LE and SAR; 10 May 83 seized Canadian FV *Cassiar* for fishing in a closed area; Jun 83 seized Canadian FV *Cassiar 67* in Dixon Entrance for illegally fishing; 15 Jun 83 seized Canadian FV *Salmon King* near Cordova Bay for illegally fishing; 22 Jul 83 seized Canadian FV *Happy Queen* for fishing in U.S. waters without a permit; 5 Jul 84 seized Canadian FV *Viewpoint* in Nicholas Bay, AK, for fishing violation; 7 Jul 84 seized FV *Evie-A* in Nicholas Bay for fishing violation.

Cape Hedge

1955-63 stationed at Alameda, CA, and used for LE and SAR; 1964-67 stationed at Bodega Bay, CA, and used for LE and SAR; 30 Mar 65 assisted by a CG helicopter, rescued survivors from a PC that had wrecked on Bodega Rock near San Francisco, CA; 10 Jul 65 took over tow of abandoned PC *Geni* and towed to Bodega Bay, CA; 22 Aug 65 found survivors of PC *Willow the Wisp* on rocks off Bluff Pt., Tiburon, and dewatered PC; early Oct 65 escorted Japanese MV *Louisiana Maru* and U.S. tug *Las Plumas* to port following a collision off Yerba Buena I.; 5

Cape Higgon on 15 Jun 59. Note the heavy armament on this A-type 95-foot cutter. A pair of mousetrap ASW rocket launchers are mounted on the forecastle, behind the stack is a twin 20mm cannon, and depth charges are mounted abaft the gun.

Sep 66 helped rescue four from PC *Aquilo* and unsuccessfully fought fire 3 mi off Fort Bragg, CA; 1968–87 stationed at Morro Bay, CA, and used for LE and SAR; 29 Oct–3 Nov 76 seized FV *Dong Phat* near San Simeon Bay carrying a large quantity of drugs; 17 May 83 collided with FV *Cape Mala* near Morro Bay; 18 May 83 helped transfer oil from leaking barge 30 mi W of Lopez, CA; 19 Jul 83 boarded disabled FV *Maggio-O* at 35°27′N, 121°W—brought flooding under control and towed her to Morro Bay, CA.

Cape Henlopen

1959–Dec 66 stationed at Port Townsend, WA, and used for LE and SAR; Dec 66–68 stationed at Port Angeles, WA, and used for LE and SAR; 29 Oct 67 escorted distressed Russian MV *Altajaskie Gory* while in U.S. waters off Washington; 20 Nov 67 escorted distressed Russian FV *Ogonj* and other Russian vessels while in U.S. seas off Washington; 1969–81 stationed at Petersburg, AK, and used for LE and SAR; 4–5 Oct 79 assisted FVs and PC *Black Bear, Diane, Heidi,* and *Will Do Too* in Stephens Passage following a storm; 1 May 80 repaired and refloated MV *Biorkau*; 1980–82 underwent major renovation; 1983–89 stationed at Woods Hole, MA, and used for LE and SAR; 28 Jul 85 assisted in the rescue of 118 from passenger vessel *Pilgrim Bell* off Cuttyhunk I.

Cape Higgon

14 Oct 53–64 stationed in the Long Beach–Los Angeles, CA, area and used for LE and SAR; 1964–70 stationed at Newport Beach, CA, and used for LE and SAR; 16 Jun 68 assisted following collision between MV *Copper State* and USNS *Cossatot* 60 mi W of Long Beach, CA; 3 Jan 70 rescued three from PC *Tailwind* 4 mi off Abalone Point; 1970–72 stationed at Corona Del Mar, CA, and used for LE and SAR; 1974–76 held for transfer to Ceylon under MAP; 1979–81 modernized at CG Yard, Baltimore, MD; 1981–90 stationed at Gloucester, MA, and used for LE and SAR.

Cape Horn

1958–66 stationed at Provincetown, MA, and used for LE and SAR; Aug 62 fought fire on FV *Norseman*; Apr–Jul 65 temporarily assigned to Miami, FL, to assist in Cuban exodus; 1 Sep 65 escorted Cuban MV *Bahia Santiago de Cuba* from Cape Cod to international waters following unauthorized entry; 26 Feb 66 escorted FV *Anita C. Rose* from 30 mi SE of Nantucket LS to New Bedford, MA; 1966–82 stationed at Woods Hole, MA, and used for LE and SAR; 12 Jul 67 found FV *Hope II* near New Bedford, MA; 7 Sep 67 towed disabled FV *Blue Fin* from 170 mi E of Cape Cod to Nantucket; 28 Jan 68 towed disabled FV *Silver Bay* 60 mi S of Nantucket to New Bedford, MA; 1 Feb 68 escorted distressed FV *Leroy* 83 mi SSE of Newport, RI, to that port; 2 May 68 escorted distressed FV *Stella Maris* 110 mi E of Nantucket to Newport, RI; 7 Feb 80 rescued six from FV *Hattie Rose* off Provincetown during a gale; 1983 underwent major renovation; 1984–89 stationed at Fort Tilden, NY, and used for LE and SAR.

Cape Jellison

1956–73 stationed at San Diego, CA, and used for LE and SAR; 24 Jun 69 helped rescue five from grounded PC on North Coronado I.; 19 Jul 69 rescued those on PC *El Gusto* N of North Coronado I.; 3 Oct 69, after a chase boarded a craft off San Diego, CA, carrying marijuana and other

contraband; 5 Oct 69 recovered 200 lbs of marijuana that had been intentionally dropped off 20 mi S of San Diego, CA; 8 Jul 70 refloated sailboat *Siestar* aground near La Mision, Mexico; 16 Jul 70 towed disabled 18-foot PC to San Diego, CA; 19 Jul 70 towed disabled PC *Cleff* from Rosarita Beach to San Diego, CA; 9 Aug 70 dewatered PC *Dowager Jones* off Shelter I.; 1973–18 Nov 86 stationed at Seward, AK, and used for LE and SAR; 7 Dec 82 towed FV *Kathy Joanne* from Pilot Rock to Seward, AK, during a storm.

Cape Kiwanda

1959–68 stationed at Cape May, NJ, and used for LE and SAR; 17 Jun 65 medevaced injured seaman from MV *Stella Nova* off Cape May, NJ; 27 Feb 67 helped fight fire on MV *Caldas* and rescued five 50 mi E of Chincoteague, VA; 25 Aug 68 medevaced seaman from Polish MV *Gryf Pomorski* off Five Fathom Bank.

Cape Knox

1956–64 stationed at Norfolk, VA, and used for LE and SAR; 1965–77 stationed at Miami Beach, FL, and used for LE and SAR; 1 Mar 65 assumed tow of disabled yacht *Circle* from cutter *Point Lookout* and towed her to Miami Beach, FL; Nov 65 transported Cuban refugees to Florida; 12 Feb 66 rescued 24 survivors from the Panamanian MV *Padre Island* aground 45 mi E of Miami, FL; 29 Mar 66 escorted Cuban PC *Marite* with four refugees on board into international waters—crew had been forced to bring them to U.S.; 24 Mar 68 towed PC *Vedette* 15 mi SE of Ft. Lauderdale, FL, to Miami, FL; 1 Apr 69 took on board eight Cuban refugees 45 mi SW of Key West, FL, who had forced the two-man crew of a sailboat to sail to the U.S.; 3 Jan 70 towed disabled PC *Goodtime* to Freeport, FL; 10 Sep 72 helped seized MV *Mont Boron* off Florida, suspected of drug smuggling; 5 Jan 78 seized FV *Lady B* carrying 18t of marijuana; 7 Feb 78 seized FV *Unwinder* carrying 8t of marijuana; 7 Feb 78 seized FV *Sea Nymph* carrying 8t of marijuana; 7 Feb 78 seized FV *Hawarden Bridge* after discovering marijuana residue; Aug 78 assisted in seizure of MV *Heidi* carrying 120t of marijuana; 1978–79 underwent major renovation; 1980–89 stationed at Charleston, SC, and used for LE and SAR; 24 Nov 83 seized *Maxima* carrying 1.5t of marijuana; 17–18 Mar 84 seized two boats following a night collision in Savannah, GA, after drugs were found; 16 Jan 86 helped fight fire on cruise ship *Oceanic* at Port Canaveral, FL; Sep 86 served as on-scene commander during a search for survivors from two Marine F-4s off Georgia.

Cape Morgan

1955–79 stationed at Charleston, SC, and used for LE and SAR; 1–2 May 66 stood by grounded Liberian MV *Vara* on Long Reef until she refloated; 1 Jun 67 embarked four Cuban refugees at Dry Tortugas and transported them to Key West, FL; 4 Jun 67 embarked six Cuban refugees from FV *Lupy* and delivered them to Key West, FL; 12 Dec 67 escorted distressed schooner *Citrisita* to Georgetown, SC; 28 Jun 69 towed disabled PC *Mon-How II* 30 mi SE of Charleston, SC, to that port; 16 Mar 70 medevaced crewman from U.S. MV *Mobilgas* off Charleston, SC; 2 Oct 70 towed disabled PC *Miss Carriage* to Charleston, SC; 20 Nov 70 escorted disabled sailboat *Westmoreland* to Charleston, SC; 1980 underwent major renovation; 1981–89 stationed at South Portland, ME, and used for LE and SAR; 29 Apr 84 helped rescue crew of FV 35 mi E of Portsmouth, NH; 10 Jul 84 helped fight fire on a 42-foot lobster boat 2 mi

Cape Morgan on 31 May 87. This B-type 95-footer has undergone numerous modifications during her long career.

off Salem, MA; 14 Nov 84 helped seize a MV with 7t of marijuana on board.

Cape Newagen

1956–68 stationed at Point Loma, CA, and used for LE and SAR; 19 May 66 rescued seven from a Navy P2V ac that had ditched 6 mi S of San Diego, CA; 1969–82 stationed at Maui, HI, and used for LE and SAR; 23 Sep 69 dewatered and towed disabled tug 6 mi WSW of Mahukona LH, HI.

Cape Porpoise

1959–60 stationed at Sausalito, CA, and used for LE and SAR; 1961–68 stationed at Morro Bay, CA, and used for LE and SAR; late Jan 66

rescued four survivors from PC *Seawolf* and unsuccessfully tried to tow the craft 19 mi W of Morro Bay; 16 Jun 66 recovered six bodies from private ac off Point Sal.

Cape Providence

1959–64 stationed at Nawiliwili, HI, and used for LE and SAR; 1965–68 stationed at Pago Pago, Samoa, and used for LE and SAR; 18 Mar 59 towed disabled small craft *Sea Gull* 25 mi SE of Nawiliwili, HI; 28 Nov 66 rescued 13 survivors from FV *Main Sun No. 2* off Pago Pago—four others were rescued by FV *Chie Hong* and two were lost.

Cape Romain

1955–62 stationed at Point Loma, CA, and used for LE and SAR; 1963–86 stationed at Ketchikan, AK, and used for LE and SAR; 7 Jul 68 helped fight fire at Ketchikan; 23 Aug 68 medevaced a crewman from MV *Taisei Maru No. 24* 7 mi W of Sitka, AK; 13 Dec 68 medevaced two from Wrangell, AK, to Ketchikan; 17 Feb 69 refloated FV *Martha R* aground near Chichagof I.; Dec 75 rescued stranded crew from tug *Hornet*; May 76 rescued crew from FV *Foxy Tu* in Moira Sound; Jan 79 rescued crew from tug *Fearless* near Dull Head; 10 Aug 83 plugged leak on Canadian FV *Sandra Mae II* off Tracey Bay; 23 Jul 84 seized FV *Mystic Dawn* off Ketchikan, AK, for violating U.S. conservation laws; 1986–90 stationed at San Francisco, CA, and used for LE and SAR; 16 Jun 87 seized ketch *Myth of Ecurie* 130 mi W of Point Sur carrying 3.5t of marijuana; May 88 seized tug *Intrepid Venture* and barge carrying 20t of marijuana and 33t of hashish; Aug 88 helped seize FV *Prygos* N of Santa Cruz, CA, carrying 2t of marijuana.

Cape Rosier

1959–68 stationed at Kahului, HI, and used for LE and SAR; late Jun 68 towed disabled sailboat *Sharolyn* 750 mi SE of Honolulu, HI, to that port.

Cape Porpoise on 22 Apr 60, shortly after commissioning. This elevated view shows the austere outfitting the C-type received when built.

Cape Sable

1959-68 stationed at Santa Barbara, CA, and used for LE and SAR.

Cape Shoalwater

1958-62 stationed at Mayport, FL, and used for LE and SAR; 1963-78 stationed at Ft. Lauderdale, FL, and used for LE and SAR; 9 Aug 65 towed Panamanian MV *Seven Seas* from 32 mi SE of Sombrero Key following mutiny on board the MV in which three were murdered; 18 Aug 65 escorted Cuban refugee boat from 12 mi SW of Bimini to Port Everglades, FL, carrying six persons; 5 May 66 towed a sailboat carrying nine refugees from 40 mi SE of Miami, FL, to that port; 25 May 66 rescued five Cuban refugees from a drifting boat and carried them to Port Everglades, FL; 18 Jun 69 towed disabled houseboat *Sin Bad V* to Lake Worth Inlet; 19 Aug 70 towed disabled 18-foot PC to Miami, FL; 23 May 74 refloated sailboat *Lorisel II* aground 1 mi SE of North Rock, Bahamas; 1978 underwent major renovation; Feb 78 seized MV *Piter* carrying contraband; 16 Apr 78 seized MV *Moctezuma* 70 mi NE of Ft. Pierce, FL, carrying marijuana; 1980-88 stationed at Riviera Beach, FL, and used for LE and SAR; 20 Aug 80 seized FV *Our Bobby* 7 mi E of Miami, FL, carrying 2t of marijuana; 29 Jan 81 fired 50 rounds of .50 cal mg at U.S. FL-6883-SH that refused to stop; Dec 83-Feb 84 conducted surveillance from St. George's, Grenada; 11 Apr 84 seized FV *Miss Arlene* in the Straits of Florida carrying 5t marijuana; 15 Apr 84 seized PC FL-8056-EM near Miami, FL, carrying 1.5t of marijuana; 3 Oct 84 seized FV *Pasica* 30 mi S of Bimini I. carrying 1,000 pounds of marijuana in a hidden compartment; 7 Nov 84 seized FV *Dady Express* 10 mi E of Miami, FL, carrying 67 cases of rum and 80 gallons of grain alcohol in false fuel tanks; 2 Dec 84 seized two PC SE of Miami, FL, carrying 200 lbs of marijuana; 5 Dec 84 seized PC *Betty II* 30 mi SE of West Palm Beach, FL, carrying 1t of marijuana; 7 Dec 84 seized PC FL-4312-DL 100 mi SE of Miami, FL, carrying illegal Cuban migrants; 8 Dec 84 seized PC *Miss Asley* E of West Palm Beach carrying 3.5 lbs of cocaine; 12 Dec 84 seized three PC off Miami, FL, carrying almost 1t of marijuana and nine lbs of cocaine; 19 Dec 84 seized PC FL-4389-EM 5 mi off Miami, FL, carrying 1,000 lbs of marijuana; 6 Jan 85 seized PC off Florida carrying 35 kilos of cocaine and a second PC with 2t of marijuana; 17 Jan 85 seized fastboat 30 mi NE of Fort Lauderdale, FL, carrying 800 lbs of marijuana; 28 Jan 85 rescued 72 from sailboat *La Pinta*; 30 Jul 85 seized a 20-foot PC 30 mi W of Palm Beach, FL, carrying 400 lbs of marijuana; 5 Mar 86 helped fight fire on tug *Navigator* 18 mi SW of Key West, FL; 12 Oct 87 stood by abandoned MV *Alma Llanera* off Florida until a commercial tug arrived.

Cape Small

1953-87 stationed at Hilo, HI, and used for LE and SAR; mid-Dec 68 rescued pilot from ditched Piper Cherokee ac 9 mi NNW of the island of Hawaii; Oct 83 towed disabled FV *Wings* 300 mi to Hawaii.

Cape Starr

1957-61 stationed at New London, CT, and used for LE and SAR; 10 Apr 61 assisted after a collision between MVs *South African Pioneer* and *Powhatan* at 38°33′N 74°10′W; 1962-69 stationed at Atlantic City, NJ, and used for LE and SAR; 1969-74 stationed at Cape May, NJ, and used for LE and SAR; 8 Apr 69 medevaced crewman from Polish MV *Senjo* off New Jersey; 4 Mar 70 medevaced crewman from Polish FV *Goplo* off

Cape Henlopen; 5 Mar 70 medevaced crewman from Polish FV *Morskie Oko* off Cape May; 1974-87 stationed at Atlantic City, NJ, and used for LE and SAR.

Cape Strait

1953-83 stationed at Fort Tilden, NY, and used for LE and SAR; 1963 deployed to Florida during Cuban missile crisis; Nov 64 assisted in rescue of survivors from Norwegian MV *Folt Dagali*; 2 May 67 escorted disabled FV *Marjorie Dorothy* to Brooklyn, NY; 11 Aug 70 towed disabled FV *Great Eastern* 20 mi E of Seaside Park, NY, to Fire I.; Mar 80 shadowed suspected drug runner *Jose Gregorio* and passed surveillance to cutter *Vigorous* 50 mi S of Montauk Point; early summer 80 deployed to Florida waters during Cuban exodus; 17 Aug 80 assisted in fighting fire on board FV *Tiny Tim* off Rockaway, NY.

Cape Trinity

1959-68 stationed at Savannah, GA, and used for LE and SAR; 12 Nov 67 rescued three from 15-foot *Best Bet* 70 mi SE of Charleston, SC; 4 Feb 68 embarked five Cuban refugees from a raft and transported them to Key West, FL.

Cape Upright

1953-60 stationed at Norfolk, VA, and used for LE and SAR; 1961-69 stationed at Southport, NC, and used for LE and SAR; 29 Apr 69 medevaced crewman from FV *Thalia*; 28 Jul 69 towed disabled schooner *Chauve Souris* 19 mi W of Frying Pan Light Tower to Southport, NC; 24 Dec 69 towed disabled FV *Dream One* 45 mi E of Wrightsville Beach, NC, to Masonboro Inlet; 31 Jul 70 towed disabled sailboat *Pandora* 35 mi SE of Cape Fear to Wrightsville Beach, NC; 1970-73 stationed at Wrightsville Beach, NC, and used for LE and SAR; 1974-76 held for transfer to Lebanon under MAP; 1976-77 underwent major renovation at CG Yard, Curtis Bay, Baltimore, MD; 1978-89 stationed at Savannah, GA, and used for LE and SAR; 10 Sep 82 helped seize MV *Mont Boron*, which was suspected of drug smuggling off Florida; 28 Nov 82 seized Cayman I. *Lago Izabel* carrying 30t of marijuana after stopping with gunfire; 18 Nov 86 seized a speedboat in the Straits of Florida with marijuana on board; 21 Nov 86 seized MV *Don Yeyo* 120 mi E of Miami, FL, carrying 12t of marijuana.

Cape Wash

1954-64 stationed at Alameda, CA, and used for LE and SAR; 30 May 60 sustained engine-room fire in Oakland, CA; 25 Oct 60 towed wreckage of *Leaky Teaky* to Yerba Buena I.; 26-27 Oct 61 assisted MVs *Hoegh Cape* and *Waitemata* following a collision 13 mi W of Bodega Bay; 19 Nov 62 assisted grounded FV *Pelican* at Half Moon Bay; 1964-67 stationed at San Francisco, CA, and used for LE and SAR; 1968-81 stationed at Monterey, CA, and used for LE and SAR; 7 Apr 80, along with CG and commercial vessels, assisted disabled tanker *Austin* off Morro Bay; 1982-87 stationed at Morro Bay, CA, and used for LE and SAR; 22 Feb 83 assisted in rescue of students from capsized charter boat *San Mateo* outside Morro Bay; 18 May 83 helped transfer oil from a leaking barge 30 mi W of Lopez, CA.

Cape York

1959-63 stationed at Pascagoula, MS, and used for LE and SAR; 1964-65 stationed at Brownsville, TX, and used for LE and SAR; 1966-67 stationed at Pensacola, FL, and used for LE and SAR; late Jul 66 captured PC *Venus*, which had been stolen, and towed her NW to Venice, LA; 18 Dec 66 helped fight fire at Frisco Pier, Pensacola, FL; 1968–89 stationed at Key West, FL, and used for LE and SAR; 14 Jul 70 towed disabled 60-foot Cuban FV until relieved by Cuban Navy; 1 Nov 70 rescued 30 Cuban refugees from a disabled craft 140 mi NW of Havana, Cuba; 1981 underwent major renovation; 26 Jan 84 seized FV *Fiabesa IV* W of Anguilla Cay in the Bahamas carrying several hundred bales of marijuana; 29 Jan 84 seized FV *Sharon-N-Darren* 120 mi SE of Key West after a residue was found; 29 Aug 84 seized FV *Square One* 30 mi N of Dry Tortugas carrying marijuana residue; 5 Oct 85 helped fight engine-room fires on Cayman MV *Arron K.* 100 mi S of Miami, FL; 28 Mar 87 rescued 17 from Cuban FV *Sigma VI* near Cay Sal Bank; 1 Jan 88 boarded MV *Boxer* 50 mi SE of Key West, FL, in heavy seas and subdued crewman who had killed the captain; Feb 88 seized Panamanain MV *Mercado Maru* carrying 1,850 lbs of cocaine.

NAVY SC 497 CLASS

Name	Hull Number	Builder	Keel Laid	Launched	Commissioned	Disposition
Air Brant (ex-SC 499)	WAVR 412	Fisher Boat Works, Detroit, MI	24 Feb 41	24 Mar 41	18 Mar 42 (USN) 20 Aug 45 (CG)	*Sold* 20 Jan 48
Air Cardinal (ex-SC 511)	WAVR 413	American Cruiser Co., Detroit, MI	1 Aug 41	1 Apr 42	29 Jun 42 (USN) 18 Aug 45 (CG)	*Decomm* 20 Jan 47 *Sold* 27 Jan 48
Air Condor (ex-SC 512)	WAVR 414	American Cruiser Co., Detroit, MI	12 Aug 41	26 Mar 42	10 Jul 42 (USN) 24 Oct 45 (CG)	*Decomm* 17 Dec 46 *Sold* 17 Jan 48
Air Cormorant (ex-SC 536)	WAVR 415	Peterson Boat Works, Sturgeon Bay, WI	29 Apr 41	5 Mar 42	23 Apr 42 (USN) 19 Feb 46 (CG)	*Decomm* 1 Apr 47 *Sold* 9 Feb 48
Air Crow (ex-SC 539)	WAVR 416	Peterson Boat Works, Sturgeon Bay, WI	17 May 41	7 Apr 42	30 May 42 (USN) 4 Dec 45 (CG)	*Decomm* 29 Dec 47 *Sold* 21 Jan 48
Air Curlew (ex-SC 540)	WAVR 417	Robinson Marine Construction Co., Benton Harbor, MI	27 Jul 41	6 Apr 42	22 Apr 42 (USN) 18 Aug 45 (CG)	*Decomm* 20 Jan 47 *Sold* 9 Feb 48
Air Drake (ex-SC 541)	WAVR 418	Robinson Marine Construction Co., Benton Harbor, MI	1 Aug 41	11 Mar 42	6 May 42 (USN) 31 Oct 45 (CG)	*Decomm* 15 May 47 *Sold* 2 Feb 48
Air Eider (ex-SC 635)	WAVR 419	Mathis Yacht Building Co., Camden, NJ	6 Jun 42	12 Oct 42	23 Oct 42 (USN) 19 Oct 45 (CG)	*Decomm* 20 Jan 47 *Sold* 30 Sep 47
Air Egret (ex-SC 642)	WAVR 420	Peterson Boat Works, Sturgeon Bay, WI	28 Oct 41	30 May 42	4 Aug 42 (USN) 24 Jan 46 (CG)	*Decomm* 20 Jan 47 *Sold* 11 Mar 48
Air Falcon (ex-SC 653)	WAVR 421	Julius Peterson, Nyack, NY	15 Dec 41	18 Apr 42	8 Jul 42 (USN) 30 Oct 45 (CG)	*Decomm* 18 Apr 47 *Sold* 20 Jan 48
Air Finch (ex-SC 656)	WAVR 422	Snow Shipyards Inc., Rockland, ME	6 Dec 41	2 May 42	11 Aug 42 (USN) 17 Jan 46 (CG)	*Decomm* 2 Apr 47 *Sold* 23 Jan 48
Air Gannet (ex-SC 659)	WAVR 423	American Cruiser Co., Detroit, MI	16 Dec 41	29 Jun 42	7 Oct 42 (USN) 19 Oct 45 (CG)	*Decomm* 20 Jan 47 *Sold* 26 Sep 47
Air Goose (ex-SC 662)	WAVR 424	Fisher Boat Works, Detroit, MI	4 Nov 41	11 Apr 42	10 Jun 42 (USN) 11 Oct 45 (CG)	*Decomm* 18 Apr 47 *Sold* 11 Mar 48
Air Grayleg (ex-SC 665)	WAVR 425	Dachel-Carter Shipbuilding Corp., Benton Harbor, MI	25 Nov 41	12 May 42	10 Aug 42 (USN)	*Sold* 21 Jul 50 (USN)
Air Grebe (ex-SC 670)	WAVR 426	Inland Waterways Inc., Duluth, MN	17 Nov 41	6 Jul 42	2 Sep 42 (USN) 19 Mar 46 (CG)	*Decomm* 2 Apr 47 *Sold* 19 Jan 48
Air Hawk (ex-SC 682)	WAVR 428	American Cruiser Co., Detroit, MI	8 Apr 42	18 Sep 42	9 Nov 42 (USN) 11 Nov 45 (CG)	*Decomm* 4 Apr 47 *Sold* 28 Jan 48
Air Heron (ex-SC 684)	WAVR 429	American Cruiser Co., Detroit, MI	6 Jul 42	21 Nov 42	12 Jan 43 (USN) 12 Jan 46 (CG)	*Decomm* 17 Dec 46 *Sold* 19 Jan 48
Air Ibis (ex-SC 710)	WAVR 430	Dooley's Basin & Drydock Co., Fort Lauderdale, FL	11 Mar 42	7 Sep 42	7 Nov 42 (USN) 23 Aug 45 (CG)	*Decomm* 29 Apr 47 *Sold* 28 Jan 48
Air Jay (ex-SC 711)	WAVR 431	Dooley's Basin & Drydock Co., Fort Lauderdale, FL	8 Apr 42	17 Oct 42	2 Jan 43 (USN) 9 Oct 45 (CG)	*Decomm* 25 Apr 47 *Sold* 16 Jan 48
Air Kestrel (ex-SC 714)	WAVR 432	Fisher Boat Works, Detroit, MI	24 Apr 42	17 Sep 42	20 Nov 42 (USN) 1 Dec 45 (CG)	*Decomm* 17 Dec 46 *Sold* 19 Jan 48
Air Killdeer (ex-SC 715)	WAVR 433	Fisher Boat Works, Detroit, MI	14 May 42	23 Oct 42	4 Dec 42 (USN) 9 Jan 46 (CG)	*Decomm* 23 Mar 47 *Sold* 19 Jan 48

Name	Hull Number	Builder	Keel Laid	Launched	Commissioned	Disposition
Air Lapwing (ex-SC 717)	WAVR 434	Fisher Boat Works, Detroit, MI	30 Jul 42	14 Dec 42	14 May 43 (USN) 30 Oct 45 (CG)	Decomm 18 Apr 47 Sold 19 Jan 48
Air Linnet (ex-SC 753)	WAVR 435	Robinson Marine Construction Co., Benton Harbor, MI	8 May 42	4 Jan 43	14 Apr 43 (USN) 4 Dec 45 (CG)	Decomm 29 Jan 47 Sold 24 Sep 47
Air Loon (ex-SC 758)	WAVR 436	Robinson Marine Construction Co., Benton Harbor, MI	6 Aug 42	28 Jul 43	14 Sep 43 (USN) 25 Jan 46 (CG)	Decomm 28 Apr 47 Sold 19 Jan 48
Air Mallard (ex-SC 772)	WAVR 437	The Peyton Co., Newport Beach, CA	23 May 42	7 Sep 42	15 Apr 43 (USN) 7 Dec 45 (CG)	Decomm 12 Jan 47 Sold 19 Jan 48
Air Martin (ex-SC 775)	WAVR 438	The Peyton Co., Newport Beach, CA	12 Jun 42	28 Nov 42	30 Jul 43 (USN) 27 Mar 46 (CG)	Decomm 22 Apr 47 Sold 19 Jan 48
Air Merlin (ex-SC 985)	WAVR 439	John E. Matton & Son, Inc., Cohoes, NY	3 Apr 42	18 Sep 42	19 Dec 42 (USN) 30 Oct 45 (CG)	Decomm 4 Feb 47 Sold 26 Sep 47
Air Oriole (ex-SC 987)	WAVR 440	John E. Matton & Son, Inc., Cohoes, NY	15 Jun 42	10 Apr 43	7 Jun 43 (USN) 11 Oct 45 (CG)	Sold 26 Jan 48
Air Owl (ex-SC 988)	WAVR 441	John E. Matton & Son, Inc., Cohoes, NY	7 Nov 42	1 Jun 43	11 Jul 43 (USN) 11 Oct 45 (CG)	Decomm 24 Jan 47 Sold 27 Feb 48
Air Parakeet (ex-SC 989)	WAVR 442	John E. Matton & Son, Inc., Cohoes, NY	9 Dec 42	25 Jun 43	2 Aug 43 (USN) 30 Oct 45 (CG)	Decomm 15 May 47 Sold 8 Apr 48
Air Parrot (ex-SC 996)	WAVR 443	Island Dock, Inc., Kingston, NY	30 Mar 42	7 Sep 42	6 Nov 42 (USN) 30 Oct 45 (CG)	Decomm 4 Feb 47 Sold 19 Jan 48
Air Patridge (ex-SC 1003)	WAVR 444	Fellows & Stewart, Inc., Wilmington, CA	8 Apr 42	25 Jul 42	24 Dec 42 (USN) 21 Nov 45 (CG)	Decomm 17 Mar 47 Sold 5 Mar 47
Air Peacock (ex-SC 1004)	WAVR 445	Fellows & Stewart, Wilmington, CA	8 Apr 42	1 Aug 42	21 Jan 43 (USN) 3 Dec 45 (CG)	Decomm 17 Mar 47 Sold 27 Jan 48
Air Pelican (ex-SC 1009)	WAVR 446	Fellows & Stewart, Wilmington, CA	18 Jul 42	25 Nov 42	25 Jun 43 (USN) 10 Apr 46 (CG)	Decomm 29 Jan 47 Sold 26 Jan 48
Air Penguin (ex-SC 1010)	WAVR 447	Fellows & Stewart, Wilmington, CA	30 Jul 42	12 Dec 42	15 Jul 43 (USN) 6 Dec 45 (CG)	Decomm 29 Jan 47 Sold 18 Jun 47
Air Petrel (ex-SC 1013)	WAVR 448	Luders Marine Construction Co., Stamford, CT	23 May 42	22 Jul 42	21 Sep 42 (USN) 23 Oct 45 (CG)	Decomm 18 Apr 47 Sold 20 Nov 47
Air Pheasant (ex-SC 1015)	WAVR 449	Luders Marine Construction Co., Stamford, CT	4 May 42	30 Aug 42	20 Oct 42 (USN) 19 Oct 45 (CG)	Decomm 24 Jan 47 Sold 14 Jan 48
Air Phoebe (ex-SC 1016)	WAVR 450	Luders Marine Construction Co., Stamford, CT	3 Jun 42	4 Sep 42	15 Dec 42 (USN) 11 Oct 45 (CG)	Decomm 4 Feb 47 Sold 21 Jan 48
Air Pigeon (ex-SC 1017)	WAVR 451	Luders Marine Construction Co., Stamford, CT	8 Jun 42	28 Oct 42	29 Dec 42 (USN) 21 Aug 46 (CG)	Decomm 18 Apr 47 Sold 7 Oct 47
Air Piper (ex-SC 1022)	WAVR 452	Luders Marine Construction Co., Stamford, CT	18 Sep 42	23 Mar 43	9 Jun 43 (USN) 9 Oct 45 (CG)	Decomm 18 Apr 47 Sold 26 Sep 47
Air Plover (ex-SC 1023)	WAVR 453	Mathis Yacht Building Co., Camden, NJ	15 Jun 42	28 Nov 42	18 Dec 42 (USN) 11 Oct 45 (CG)	Decomm 18 Apr 47 Sold 25 Feb 48
Air Puffin (ex-SC 1027)	WAVR 454	Mathis Yacht Building Co., Camden, NJ	7 Sep 42	26 Jan 43	2 Feb 43 (USN) 17 Dec 45 (CG)	Decomm 13 Jan 47 Sold 24 Sep 47
Air Quail (ex-SC 1028)	WAVR 455	Mathis Yacht Building Co., Camden, NJ	21 Oct 42	21 Feb 43	27 Mar 43 (USN) 8 Jan 46 (CG)	Decomm 29 Jan 47 Sold 26 Jan 48
Air Raven (ex-SC 1032)	WAVR 456	Peterson Boat Works, Sturgeon Bay, WI	19 May 42	17 Oct 42	18 Feb 43 (USN) 1 Mar 46 (CG)	Decomm 5 Apr 46 Sold 15 Jan 48
Air Redwing (ex-SC 1033)	WAVR 457	Peterson Boat Works, Sturgeon Bay, WI	17 Jun 42	12 Nov 42	5 Apr 43 (USN) 1 Mar 46 (CG)	Decomm 5 Apr 46 Sold 15 Jun 47
Air Robin (ex-SC 1037)	WAVR 458	Peterson Boat Works, Sturgeon Bay, WI	31 Oct 42	29 May 43	7 Jul 43 (USN) 1 Mar 46 (CG)	Decomm 5 Apr 46 Sold Jun 47
Air Rook (ex-SC 1038)	WAVR 459	Peterson Boat Works, Sturgeon Bay, WI	28 Nov 42	12 Jun 43	28 Jul 43 (USN) 25 Jan 46 (CG)	Decomm 22 Apr 47 Sold 19 Jan 48
Air Ruff (ex-SC 1054)	WAVR 460	Wilmington Boat Works, Inc., Wilmington, CA	11 Apr 42	10 Sep 42	6 Apr 43 (USN) 21 Feb 46 (CG)	Decomm 23 Mar 47 Sold 22 Jan 48

Name	Hull Number	Builder	Keel Laid	Launched	Commissioned	Disposition
Air Skimmer (ex-SC 1063)	WAVR 463	Victory Shipbuilding Corp., Newport Beach, CA	9 Jul 42	16 Jan 43	5 Apr 43 (USN) 30 Oct 45 (CG)	*Decomm* 12 Nov 46 *Sold* 10 Jul 47
Air Skylark (ex-SC 1064)	WAVR 464	Victory Shipbuilding Corp., Newport Beach, CA	9 Jul 42	16 Jan 43	4 May 43 (USN) 30 Oct 45 (CG)	*Decomm* 21 Dec 46 *Sold* 23 Jul 47
Air Snipe (ex-SC 1068)	WAVR 465	Mathis Yacht Building Co., Camden, NJ	10 Dec 42	26 Mar 43	13 Apr 43 (USN) 28 Feb 46 (CG)	*Decomm* 12 Apr 47 *Sold* 27 Jan 48
Air Sparrow (ex-SC 1069)	WAVR 466	Mathis Yacht Building Co., Camden, NJ	30 Dec 42	17 Apr 43	26 Apr 43 (USN) 5 Dec 45 (CG)	*Decomm* 16 Apr 47 *Sold* 8 Jan 48
Air Scaup (ex-SC 1307)	WAVR 481	Daytona Beach Boat Works, Daytona Beach, FL	20 Oct 42	15 Apr 43	3 Oct 43 (USN) 12 Feb 46 (CG)	*Decomm* 15 May 47 *Sold* 4 Aug 47
Air Scoter (ex-SC 1329)	WAVR 482	Simmons Brothers, Dorchester, MA	10 Oct 42	19 Apr 43	8 May 43 (USN) 7 Feb 46 (CG)	N/A
Air Shrike (ex-SC 1062)	WAVR 462	Harris & Parsons, Inc., East Greenwich, RI	3 Jun 42	23 Dec 42	27 Feb 43 (USN) 23 Oct 45 (CG)	*Decomm* 25 Apr 47 *Sold* 11 Mar 48
Air Sheldrake (ex-SC 1055)	WAVR 461	Wilmington Boat Works, Inc., Wilmington, CA	2 May 42	10 Oct 42	10 May 43 (USN) 27 Nov 45 (CG)	*Decomm* 5 Apr 46 *Sold* 15 Jun 48
Air Starling (ex-SC 1070)	WAVR 467	Mathis Yacht Building Co., Camden, NJ	21 Jan 43	3 May 43	24 May 43 (USN) 3 Dec 45 (CG)	*Decomm* 12 Apr 47 *Sold* 19 Jan 48
Air Stork (ex-SC 1296)	WAVR 468	W.A. Robinson Inc., Ipswich, MA	11 Feb 43	20 Aug 43	16 Sep 43 (USN) 14 Aug 45 (CG)	*Decomm* 20 Jan 47 *Sold* 14 Jan 48
Air Swallow (ex-SC 1297)	WAVR 469	W.A. Robinson Inc., Ipswich, MA	19 Mar 43	2 Sep 43	8 Oct 43 (USN) 29 Sep 45 (CG)	*Decomm* 4 Apr 47 *Sold* 14 Jan 48
Air Swan (ex-SC 1339)	WAVR 470	Thomas Knutson Shipbulding Corp., Halesite, L.I., NY	24 Oct 42	21 Aug 43	8 Nov 43 (USN) 15 Nov 45 (CG)	*Decomm* 17 Dec 46 *Sold* 27 Feb 48
Air Swift (ex-SC 1340)	WAVR 471	Thomas Knutson Shipbuilding Corp., Halesite, L.I., NY	7 Nov 42	18 Sep 43	4 Dec 43 (USN) 30 Oct 45 (CG)	*Decomm* 15 May 47 *Sold* 19 Jan 48
Air Tanager (ex-SC 1347)	WAVR 472	Fisher Boat Works Inc., Detroit, MI	15 Feb 43	15 Jul 43	3 Sep 43 (USN) 21 Nov 45 (CG)	*Decomm* 17 Mar 47 *Sold* 13 Feb 48
Air Teal (ex-SC 1348)	WAVR 473	Fisher Boat Works Inc., Detroit, MI	17 Feb 43	12 Aug 43	1 Oct 43 (USN) 31 Oct 45 (CG)	*Decomm* 31 Dec 46 *Sold* 1 Aug 47
Air Tern (ex-SC 1355)	WAVR 474	Luders Marine Construction Co., Stamford, CT	14 Nov 42	12 Apr 43	10 Jul 43 (USN) 16 Sep 45 (CG)	*Decomm* 4 Feb 47 *Sold* 19 Sep 47
Air Thrush (ex-SC 1356)	WAVR 475	Luders Marine Construction Co., Stamford, CT	5 Jan 43	7 Jun 43	18 Aug 43 (USN) 9 Oct 45 (CG)	*Decomm* 21 May 47 *Sold* 26 Jan 48
Air Toucan (ex-SC 1357)	WAVR 476	Luders Marine Construction Co., Stamford, CT	13 Feb 43	21 Jun 43	31 Aug 43 (USN) 12 Feb 46 (CG)	*Decomm* 24 Jan 47 *Sold* 17 Jan 48
Air Warbler (ex-SC 1362)	WAVR 477	The Peyton Co., Newport Beach, CA	7 Nov 42	24 Apr 43	6 Sep 43 (USN) 8 Feb 46 (CG)	*Decomm* 16 Apr 47 *Sold* 19 Jan 48
Air Waxwing (ex-SC 1367)	WAVR 478	Wilmington Boat Works, Inc., Wilmington, CA	25 Nov 42	27 May 43	10 Sep 43 (USN) 10 Jan 46 (CG)	*Decomm* 28 Apr 47 *Sold* 19 Sep 47
Air Willet (ex-SC 1368)	WAVR 479	Wilmington Boat Works, Inc., Wilmington, CA	28 Nov 42	21 Jun 43	13 Oct 43 (USN) 30 Jan 46 (CG)	*Decomm* 1 Apr 47 *Sold* 10 Jan 48
Air Wren (ex-SC 1373)	WAVR 480	Fellows & Stewart, Inc., Wilmington, CA	23 Dec 42	19 Jun 43	1 Nov 43 (USN) 30 Jan 46 (CG)	*Decomm* 28 Apr 47 *Sold* 22 Sep 47

Cost	$355,000		BHP	1,200
Hull			Propellers	2
Displacement (tons)	135 fl; 101 light (1946)		Performance	
Length	111'6" oa		Max Speed	19.3 kts (1946)
Beam	18'9" mb		Max Sustained	17.2 kts 585-mi radius (1946)
Draft	7' max (1946)		Cruising	15.0 kts 735-mi radius (1946)
Machinery			Economic	8.0 kts 1,975-mi radius (1946)
Main Engines	2 GM Model 16-184A diesels (most units)			

Logistics

    Fuel Oil (95%)   4,833 gal.

    Complement   1 officer, 15 men (1946)

Electronics

    Detection Radar   SF-1 (most units)

Armament   small arms

Design

The CG requested that 70 Navy SC 497-class units be permanently transferred from the navy for air-sea-rescue duties. Initially, 36 were provided on a loan basis. Due to the shortage of CG personnel immediately following WWII, few 110-foot SCs became operational and those that did saw little service. Those units placed "in commission in reserve" status were assigned one deck petty officer and one engine-room rate as caretakers.

The Navy SC 497 class was constructed of wood. All armament was removed before transfer to the CG.

Air Brant

20 Aug 45-23 Jan 46 stationed at Stapleton, Staten I., NY, and assigned to the Air Sea Rescue Service; 23 Jan laid up.

Air Cardinal

18 Aug 45-6 May 46 stationed at Stapleton, Staten I., NY, and assigned to the Air Sea Rescue Service; 6 May laid up.

Air Condor

24 Oct 45-6 May 46 stationed at Corpus Christi, TX, and assigned to the Air Sea Rescue Service; 6 May laid up.

Air Cormorant

19 Feb 46-1 Apr 47 stationed at Bellingham, WA, and assigned to the Air Sea Rescue Service—due to a shortage of personnel this craft was maintained in an "in reserve in service" status and was never fully crewed.

Air Crow

4 Dec 45-29 Dec 47 stationed at San Diego, CA, and assigned to the Air Sea Rescue Service—due to a shortage of personnel this craft was maintained in an "in reserve in service" status and was never fully crewed.

Air Curlew

18 Aug 45-9 Nov 46 stationed at Stapleton, Staten I., NY, and assigned to the Air Sea Rescue Service; 9 Nov laid up.

Air Drake

31 Oct 45-30 Jul 46 stationed at Cockspur I., GA, and assigned to the Air Sea Rescue Service—30 Jul placed "out of commission in reserve" because of a shortage of personnel.

Air Eider

19 Oct 45-20 Jan 47 stationed at Cape May, NJ, and assigned to the Air Sea Rescue Service; 19 Oct transported injured crewman from Five Fathom LS to CG Station at Cape May; 4 Jan 46 assisted in search for FV Sea Toy.

Air Egret

20 Jan 46-16 May stationed at Stapleton, Staten I., NY, and assigned to the Air Sea Rescue Service; 16 May placed "in commission in reserve" because of a shortage of personnel.

Air Falcon

30 Oct 45-2 Apr 46 stationed at Palm Beach, FL, and assigned to the Air Sea Rescue Service; Dec 45 rescued overboard crewman from 38' motor launch New Era and towed the disabled craft—tow passed to cutter Ariadne; 2 Apr 46 placed "in commission in reserve" because of shortage of personnel.

Air Finch

17 Jan 46-2 Apr 47 stationed at Neah Bay, WA, and assigned to the Air Sea Rescue Service and maintained "in commission in reserve" because of a shortage of personnel.

Air Gannet

19 Oct 45-16 Apr 46 stationed at Cape May, NJ, and assigned to the Air Sea Rescue Service; 16 Apr placed "in commission in reserve" because of a shortage of personnel.

Air Goose

11 Oct 45-5 Mar 46 stationed at Norfolk, VA, and assigned to the Air Sea Rescue Service; 5 Mar 46 placed "in commission in reserve" because of a shortage of personnel.

Air Grayleg

15 Aug 46 transfer to CG from USN canceled.

Air Grebe

19 Mar 46-2 Apr 47 stationed at Kennydale, WA, "in commission in reserve" because of a shortage of personnel.

Air Hawk

11 Nov 45-12 Aug 46 stationed at Little Creek, VA, and assigned to the Air Sea Rescue Service; 12 Aug placed "in commission in reserve" because of a shortage of personnel.

Air Heron

12 Jan-2 Aug 46 stationed at New Orleans, LA, and assigned to the Air Sea Rescue Service; 2 Aug placed "in commission in reserve" because of a shortage of personnel.

Air Ibis

23 Aug 45-27 Feb 46 stationed at Stapleton, Staten I., NY, and assigned to the Air Sea Rescue Service; 27 Feb 46-27 Apr 47 stationed at CG Yard, Curtis Bay, MD.

Air Jay

9 Oct 45-27 Apr 47 stationed at Bristol, RI, and assigned to the Air Sea Rescue Service; 27 Mar 47 unsuccessfully searched for mine off No Mans Land; Dec 45 towed a disabled FV.

Air Kestrel

1 Dec 45-2 Apr 46 stationed at New Orleans, LA, and assigned to the Air Sea Rescue Service; 2 Aug placed "in commission in reserve" because of a shortage of personnel.

Air Killdeer

9 Jan 46 stationed at Bellevue, WA, and assigned to the Air Sea Rescue Service; due to lack of crew, immediately placed "in commission in reserve."

Air Lapwing

30 Oct 45–12 Aug 46 stationed at Southport, NC, and assigned to the Air Sea Rescue Service; 12 Aug placed "in commission in reserve" because of a shortage of personnel.

Air Linnet

4 Dec 45 stationed at San Diego, CA, and assigned to the Air Sea Rescue Service; due to lack of a crew, immediately placed "in commission in reserve."

Air Loon

26 Jan 46 stationed at Bellevue, WA, and assigned to the Air Sea Rescue Service; due a lack of crew, immediately placed "in commission in reserve."

Air Mallard

7 Dec 45–12 Jan 47 stationed at San Diego, CA, and assigned to the Air Sea Rescue Service.

Air Martin

27 Mar 46 stationed at Bellevue, WA, and assigned to the Air Sea Rescue Service; due to a lack of crew, immediately placed "in commission in reserve."

Air Merlin

30 Oct 45–18 Apr 46 stationed at Miami, FL, and primarily operated from Key West, FL, was assigned to the Air Sea Rescue Service; Nov 45 stood by distressed tanker *Kern Hill* until tug arrived; Dec 45 took part in search for missing naval aircraft; 18 Apr laid up because of a shortage of personnel.

Cutter *Air Lapwing* on 10 Aug 50. Very few of these 110-foot submarine chasers saw active service in the Coast Guard, primarily due to a severe shortage of personnel.

Air Oriole

11 Oct 45–1 Sep 46 stationed at Cockspur I., GA, and assigned to the Air Sea Rescue Service; 29 Oct 45 unsuccessfully searched for downed plane near Altamaha Sound; 25 Oct escorted cruiser *Savannah* during Navy Day celebration; Nov 45 supplied LS *Savannah*; 12–13 Jan 46 escorted ammunition detail while dumping at sea; 1 Sep 46 stationed at Mayport, FL; 23 Apr 47 placed "in commission in reserve" because of a shortage of personnel.

Air Owl

11 Oct 45–6 Feb 46 stationed at Pascagoula, MS, and assigned to the Air Sea Rescue Service; Oct–Dec 45 inoperative due to engine problems; 6 Feb 46 placed "in commission in reserve" because of a shortage of personnel.

Air Parakeet

30 Oct 45–18 Apr 46 stationed at Key West, FL, and assigned to the Air Sea Rescue Service; 18 Apr 46 placed "in commission in reserve" because of a shortage of personnel.

Air Parrot

30 Oct 45–14 Mar 46 stationed at Cockspur I., GA, and assigned to the Air Sea Rescue Service; Jan 46 transported USPHS doctor to MV *Storfonn* to render medical assistance; 14 Mar 46 placed "in commission in reserve" because of a shortage of personnel.

Air Partridge

21 Nov 45–25 Apr 46 stationed at San Francisco, CA, and assigned to the Air Sea Rescue Service; 25 Apr 46 placed "in commission in reserve" because of a shortage of personnel; Nov 47 sustained moderate damage while being towed to Seattle, WA.

Air Peacock

3 Dec 45–22 Jan 46 stationed at San Francisco, CA, and assigned to the Air Sea Rescue Service; 22 Jan 46 placed "in commission in reserve" because of a shortage of personnel; Nov 47 sustained moderate damage while being towed to Seattle, WA.

Air Pelican

10 Apr 46 stationed at San Diego, CA, and assigned to the Air Sea Rescue Service; immediately placed in reserve status.

Air Penguin

6 Dec 45–29 Jan 47 stationed at San Diego, CA, and assigned to the Air Sea Rescue Service—never became fully operational.

Air Petrel

23 Oct 45–15 Mar 46 stationed at Bristol, RI, and assigned to the Air Sea Rescue Service; 15 Mar 46 placed "in commission in reserve" because of a shortage of personnel.

Air Pheasant

19 Oct 45–16 Apr 46 stationed at Cape May, NJ, and assigned to the Air Sea Rescue Service; Dec 45 transported medical case from LS *Overfalls*; 16 Apr 46 placed "in commission in reserve" because of a shortage of personnel.

Air Phoebe

11 Oct 45–16 Mar 46 stationed at Norfolk, VA, and assigned to the Air Sea Rescue Service; 16 Mar 46 placed "in commission in reserve" because of a shortage of personnel.

Air Pigeon

30 Oct 45–12 Aug 46 stationed at Southport, NC, and assigned to the Air Sea Rescue Service; 12 Aug 46 placed "in commission in reserve" due to a shortage of personnel.

Air Piper

9 Oct 45–18 Apr 47 stationed at Boston, MA, and assigned to Air Sea Rescue Service; 2 Dec 45 stood by stranded MV *Fordham Victory* aground on NE point of Spectacle I.

Air Plover

11 Oct 45–26 Apr 46 stationed at Morehead City, NC, and assigned to Air Sea Rescue Service; 26 Apr 46 placed "in commission in reserve" due to a shortage of personnel.

Air Puffin

30 Oct 45 transferred from USN; 21 Aug 46–13 Jan 47 stationed at Santa Barbara, CA, and assigned to the Air Sea Rescue Service; 13 Jan 47 placed "in commission in reserve" due to a shortage of personnel.

Air Quail

8 Jan 46–1 May in training status; 1 May–29 Jan 47 stationed at Santa Barbara, CA, and assigned to the Air Sea Rescue Service.

Air Raven

29 Nov 45 transferred from USN; 1 Mar 46 placed "in commission in reserve" in Ketchikan, AK, due to a shortage of personnel.

Air Redwing

4 Dec 45 transferred from USN; 1 Mar 46 placed "in commission in reserve" in Ketchikan, AK, due to a shortage of personnel.

Air Robin

16 Jan 46 transferred from USN; 1 Mar 46 placed "in commission in reserve" in Ketchikan, AK, due to a shortage of personnel.

Air Rook

16 Jan 46 stationed at Bellevue, WA, and placed "in commission in reserve" due to a shortage of personnel.

Air Ruff

21 Feb 46 stationed at Bellevue, WA, and placed "in commission in reserve" because of a shortage of personnel.

Air Scaup

7 Mar 46 stationed at Miami, FL, and placed "in commission in reserve" due to a shortage of personnel.

Air Scoter

N/A

Air Shrike

23 Oct 45 stationed at Rockland, ME.

Air Sheldrake

8 Mar 46 stationed at Ketchikan, AK; never manned due to a shortage of personnel.

Air Skimmer

30 Oct 45 stationed at Quonset Point, RI; Dec 45 removed crew from a Venezuelan corvette in distress.

Air Skylark

30 Oct 45 stationed at Key West, FL.

Air Snipe

28 Feb 46 placed in reserve in service, stationed in Bellevue, WA.

Air Sparrow

6 Dec 45 placed in reserve in service, stationed at Bellevue, WA.

Air Starling

4 Dec 45 placed in reserve in service, stationed at Port Angeles, WA.

Air Stork

24 Aug 45 stationed at Stapleton, Staten I., NY; 1 Dec placed in reserve in service.

Air Swallow

29 Sep 45 stationed at Morehead City, NC; Jan 46 assisted cutter *Agassiz*; 1 Mar 46 laid up at Berkley, VA.

Air Swan

15 Nov stationed at Galveston, TX.

Air Swift

30 Oct 45 stationed at Cockspur I., GA; 26 Mar 46 placed "in commission in reserve" due to a lack of personnel.

Air Tanager

21 Nov 45 stationed at San Francisco; 25 Apr 46 laid up due to a personnel shortage; Nov 47 sustained moderate damage while being towed to Seattle, WA.

Air Teal

31 Oct 45 stationed at Key West, FL; 2 Apr 46 placed in a caretaker status; 24 Oct 46 fully manned and stationed at San Juan, PR.

Air Tern

16 Sep 46 stationed at Morehead City, NC; Apr 46 placed in caretaker status at CG Yard, Curtis Bay, MD.

Air Thrush

9 Oct 45 assigned to Rockland, ME, but spent most of her time in Boston, MA, under repair; 15 Mar 46 placed in caretaker status due to a shortage of personnel.

Air Toucan

12 Feb 46 stationed at Galveston, TX; 6 May 46 laid up due to a shortage of personnel.

Air Warbler

8 Feb 46 stationed at Bellevue, WA, and placed in reserve.

Air Waxwing

10 Jan 46 stationed at Bellevue, WA, and placed in reserve.

Air Willet

30 Jan 46 stationed at Bellevue, WA, and placed in reserve.

Air Wren

30 Jan 46 stationed at Bellevue, WA, and placed in reserve.

NAVY SC-453

Name	Hull Number	Builder	Keel Laid	Launched	Commissioned	Disposition
Air Avocet (ex-SC 453)	WAVR 411	Fisher Boat Works, Detroit, MI	24 Sep 40	3 May 41	12 Aug 41 (USN) 13 Dec 45 (CG)	*Decomm* 31 Dec 46 *Sold* 1 Aug 47 to Haiti

Cost $355,000

Hull
   Displacement (tons)   135 fl (1946)
   Length   111'6" oa
   Beam   18'9" mb
   Draft   7' (1946)

Machinery
   Main Engines   2 diesels
   BHP   1,200
   Propellers   2

Performance
   Max Speed   19 kts (1946)

Logistics
   Complement   1 officer, 15 men (1946)

Electronics
   Radar   navigation type

Armament   small arms

Design
   Constructed of wood, this craft was not a standard production model. The craft had a narrow beam and lacked sufficient stability for rescue work.

Air Avocet
   24 Dec 45–31 Dec 46 stationed at San Juan, PR, assigned to Air Sea Rescue Service.

EMERGENCY ACQUISITION

Name	Hull Number	Builder	Keel Laid	Launched	Commissioned	Disposition
Colleen	WPYc 27 PYc 27	Pusey & Jones Corp., Wilmington, DE	N/A	N/A	1928 (commercial) 2 Sep 42 (USN) 11 Sep 45 (CG)	*Decomm* 31 Sept 45 *Decomm* 26 Oct 45 *Sold* 25 Mar 47

Cost   N/A

Hull
   Displacement (tons)   250 fl (1944)
   Length   150' oa, 133'4" bp
   Beam   22'
   Draft   8'10"

Machinery
   Main Engines   2 Winton diesels
   BHP   1,200
   Propellers   2

Performance
   Max Speed   14 kts
   Max Sustained   12 kts, 2,000 mi (1944)

Logistics
   Complement   3 officers, 38 men (1944)

Electronics
   Detection Radar   none

Armament   1 3"/50, 2 dc tracks (1944)

Design
   Hull was constructed of steel, and superstructure was composite. *Colleen* was found to be ill-suited to CG needs and was not retained.

83-FOOT PATROL BOAT CLASS

Number	Builder	Commissioned	Disposition
CG 83300–83529 (CG 83399–83383 were originally CG 450–89, 450–99, 600–634, respectively)	Wheeler Shipyard, Brooklyn, NY	1941–1944	By mid-1960s all sold. *See* individual craft histories

Cost $125,000 approx. cost of each unit completely outfitted; See Scheina, *WWII Cutters,* for details.

Hull
Displacement (tons)   65.2 fl (1953); 47 light (1953)
Length   83'2" oa; 78'0" wl
Beam   16'7" max
Draft   5'6" max (1953)

Machinery
Main Engines   CG 83343 through 83348: 2 Hall-Scott Defenders, 1,200 rpm; all others: 2 Sterling Viking II
SHP   all units: 1,200
Propellers   twin

Performance
Max Sustained   13.5 kts, 390-mi radius (1953)
Economic   10.7 kts, 550-mi radius (1953)

Logistics
Fuel Oil (95%)   1,900 gal
Complement   1 officer, 11 men (1953)

Electronics
Detection Radar   SO-2 (most units)

Sonar   QBE series (most units)
Armament   1 20mm/80, 2 mousetraps, 4 dc tracks (1953)

Design*

The 83-footers were wooden-hulled; the hull form was the round-bilge type, single planked. Walter J. McInnis was appointed design agent 6 Dec 40 to develop the plans for the 83-foot class. The design was completed 19 Mar 41, and 40 units were contracted to Wheeler Shipyard, Inc., Brooklyn, NY. War started before this contract was completed, and subsequent contracts for 44, 40, and 106 units were awarded. A total of 230 units were eventually built for the Coast Guard.

Early units (83300–83435) were fitted with an Everdur bronze wheelhouse. These were prefabricated in Boston, MA, and shipped by rail to the Wheeler Yard. Later units (83436–83529) had plywood wheelhouses because of a shortage of bronze. Those 83-footers operating above Cape Henry, VA, were ice-sheathed. All the craft were capable of 20.6 kts full speed at time of delivery, but their performance was degraded by machinery wear as well as the increased displacement from armaments, radar, and sonar. Twelve additional units were built for the USN and transferred to Cuba (4), the Dominican Republic (3), Haiti (1), and Venezuela (4). Nineteen Coast Guard units were also transferred to Latin American navies during the war—the navies of Cuba (8), Colombia (2), Peru (6), and Mexico (3).

*Cost data and design notes prepared and copyrighted by William D. Wilkinson.

CG-83391 on 28 May 53. Following WWII, the 83-footers carried a variety of armaments, SAR equipment, and electronic suites. A sketch and wartime photography of this craft appear in Scheina, *WWII Cutters.*

PATROL CRAFT BUILT OT COAST GUARD SPECIFICATIONS DISPOSED OF SHORTLY AFTER WORLD WAR II*

Class	Numbers	Disposition
80-Foot	80300 thru 80308	1945–46
78-Foot	78300 thru 78305	1945–46
75-Foot	74300 thru 74340	1935–40, 1945–46
72-Foot	72300 thru 72301	1947
65-Foot	65300 thru 65301	1947

*See Scheina, *WWII Cutters,* for details.

Icebreakers

The Coast Guard adopted the Navy's designator for large ice-breakers, WAGB, during the early 1950s. Prior to that time they were classified as miscellaneous auxiliaries (WAGs). The large, or polar, icebreaker was first introduced into the United States Coast Guard in 1944 with the completion of the first *Northwind.* Notwithstanding, the service has had a long history of domestic icebreaking. Since the turn of the century, a few cutters had been rein-forced for domestic icebreaking. The cutter *Northland,* completed in 1927, was classified as an icebreaking gunboat. She was a replacement for the venerable *Bear,* which served in icy Alaskan waters from 1885 to 1929.

During 1965 and 1966 all U.S. Navy icebreakers were turned over to the Coast Guard.

PROJECTED 460-FOOT ICEBREAKERS

Name	Hull Number	Builder	Keel Laid	Launched	Commissioned	Disposition
	WAGB 12				1996	
	WAGB 13				?	

Cost	N/A		Performance	
Hull			Cruising	12.5 kts, 34,500-mi radius (1988)
Displacement (tons)	17,000 fl (1988)		Logistics	
Length	460' oa; 410' wl		Complement	17 officers, 108 men, & 30 scientists (1988)
Beam	94'6″ max		Electronics	
Draft	31' max (1988)		Radar	navigation type
Machinery			Armament	none
Main Engines	diesel electric		Design	
SHP	30,000			
Propellers	twin			

Design

These polar icebreakers will have the largest and heaviest cutter design built for the Coast Guard. They are designed to break 4.5 feet of ice at 3 knots and 7.8 feet of ice by backing and ramming. These icebreakers will have extensive laboratory facilities. Funding for one polar icebreaker has been requested in the FY 90 DoD budget.

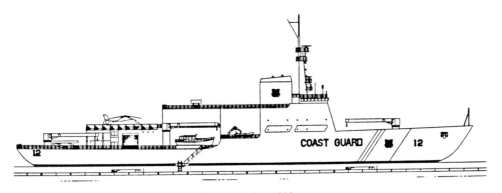

An outboard profile of the projected 460-foot icebreaker, 1988.

399-FOOT ICEBREAKERS (*POLAR STAR* CLASS, "POLAR" CLASS)

Name	Hull Number	Builder	Keel Laid	Launched	Commissioned	Disposition
Polar Star	WAGB 10	Lockheed Shipbuilding Co., Seattle, WA	15 May 72	17 Nov 73	17 Jan 76	Active
Polar Sea	WAGB 11	Lockheed Shipbuilding Co., Seattle, WA	19 Nov 73	24 Jun 75	26 Sep 76 (completed)	Active

Cost — See Appropriations table

Hull
Displacement (tons) — 13,190 fl (1976); 10,430 standard (1976)
Length — 399' oa
Beam — 83'6" max
Draft — 31' max (1976)

Machinery
Main Engines — 6 diesel-electric units or 3 Pratt & Whitney gas turbines
SHP — 6,000 or 20,000
Propellers — triple, CP

Performance
Max Sustained — 18.0 kts, 16,000-mi radius (1976)
Cruising — 13.0 kts, 28,275-mi radius (1976)

Logistics
Fuel Oil (95%) — 1,359,200 gal
Complement — 13 officers, 125 men (1976)

Electronics
Radar — 2 SPS-64

Armament — none

Design

The Polar class is designed to break 6.5 feet of ice at 3 knots. Initially, the Coast Guard had hoped to build a larger number of Polar-class units to replace the aging icebreaker fleet. However, due to financial constraints only two units were built. The most innovative design feature for an icebreaker was the adoption of controllable-pitch propellers. Teething problems with the propellers have been overcome.

Between 1988 and 1992 science support facilities were upgraded. A mid-life reliability improvement project is scheduled for 1993.

399-FOOT ICEBREAKERS (*POLAR STAR* CLASS, "POLAR" CLASS)—APPROPRIATIONS

Name	AC&I Year	Awarded	Scheduled Delivery	Construction Manhours	Costs
Polar Star	1971	24 Aug 71	24 Aug 74	N/A	$52,999,382
Polar Sea	1973	15 Jan 73	15 Jan 76	N/A	$50,873,239

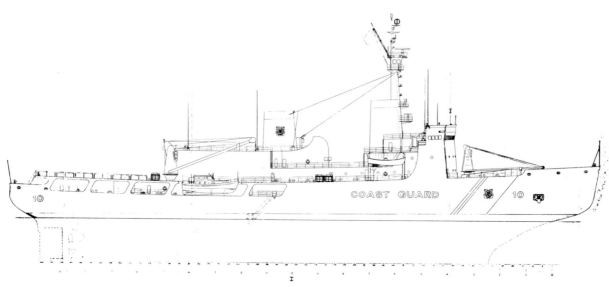

Outboard profile of the *Polar Star,* 1976.

Polar Sea

26 Sep 76–1990 stationed at Seattle, WA, and used primarily for polar icebreaking; 12 Nov 79–12 Apr 80 participated in Operation Deep Freeze in the Antarctic; 27 Aug–17 Oct 80 conducted an oceanographic cruise to the Arctic; 26 Oct 81–31 Mar 82 participated in Op Deep Freeze to the Antarctic; 14 Sep–22 Nov 84 conducted an oceanographic cruise to the Arctic; 19 Oct 83–17 May 84 participated in Op Deep Freeze to the Antarctic; 4 Sep–12 Dec 84 conducted an oceanographic cruise to the Arctic; 2–9 Aug 85 completed E to W passage of Northwest Passage; 8 Nov 86–29 May 87 participated in Op Deep Freeze to the Antarctic; 6 Dec 87–3 Mar 88 participated in Op Deep Freeze to the Antarctic.

Polar Star

17 Jan 76–1990 stationed at Seattle, WA, and used principally for polar icebreaking; 8 Nov 77–8 Feb 78 participated in Operation Deep Freeze to the Antarctic and conducted trials; 8 Nov 78–8 Mar 79 participated in Op Deep Freeze to the Antarctic; 15 Feb–16 Jul 80 used as a scientific platform in the Arctic; 5 Nov 80–10 Mar 81 participated in Op Deep Freeze to the Antarctic; 20 Jun–9 Aug 81 conducted an oceanographic cruise to the Arctic; 19 Oct 82–2 May 83 participated in Op Deep Freeze to the Antarctic; Dec 82–7 Mar 83 circumnavigated Antarctica in Op Deep Freeze 83 during the 32,000-mile tour, taking 69 days to travel the 7,773 mile circle; 20 Feb 84 helicopter medevaced crewman from FV *Daito Maru No 38;* 14 Nov 84–5 May 85 participated in Op Deep Freeze to the Antarctic; 26 Oct 85–5 Apr 86 participated in Op Deep Freeze to the Antarctic; 26 Oct 85 a crewman suffered fatal injuries during a storm off Vancouver I.; 11 Jan 86 rescued 21 from MV *Southern Quest* in the Ross Sea 60 mi N of McMurdo Station; 25 Aug–10 Nov 86 conducted an oceanographic cruise to the Arctic; 28 Oct 87–12 Apr 88 participated in Op Deep Freeze to the Antarctic; Oct–Nov 88 circumnavigated North America W to E after going to the rescue of two Canadian vessels and being trapped E of Point Barrow by heavy ice.

The *Polar Star* and *Polar Sea* during 1978. These icebreakers were constructed to replace the aging seven Wind-class units. However, only two Polar-class units were built, and they will remain America's only heavy icebreakers until the projected 460-foot icebreakers are complete, probably in the late 1990s.

NAVY *GLACIER* CLASS

Name	Hull Number	Builder	Keel Laid	Launched	Commissioned	Disposition
Glacier	WAGB 4 AGB 4	Ingalls Shipbuilding Corp., Pascagoula, MS	3 Aug 53	27 Aug 54	27 May 55 (USN) 30 Jun 66 (CG)	*Decomm* 7 Jul 87

Cost N/A

Hull
  Displacement (tons)   8,449 fl (1966); 6,406 light (1966)
  Length   309′8″ oa; 290′ bp
  Beam   74′4″ max
  Draft   28′3″ max (1966)

Machinery
  Main Engines   6 electric motors driven by 10 Westinghouse generators driven by 10 Fairbanks-Morse diesels
  BHP   21,000
  Propellers   twin

Performance
  Max Sustained   17.0 kts, 16,000-mi radius (1966)
  Economic   10.0 kts, 29,280-mi radius (1966)

Logistics
  Fuel Oil (95%)   822,173 gal
  Complement   12 officers, 3 warrants, 226 men (1966)

Electronics
  Radar   SPS-6C, SPS-10, SPS-46 (1966)
  Sonar   UQN (1966)

Armament   2 5″/38 (twin) (1966)

Design
  The *Glacier* was designed for the USN. She was transferred to the CG on 30 Jun 66 and commissioned the same day.

Glacier

30 Jun 66–May 1988 stationed at Long Beach, CA, and used for ice-breaking; Nov 66–Apr 67 participated in Operation Deep Freeze to the Antarctic; Sep–Nov 67 helped free cutter *Northwind* beset in ice 450 mi NNW of Point Barrow; Dec 67–Mar 68 participated in Op Deep Freeze to the Antarctic; Nov 68–Apr 69 participated in Op Deep Freeze to the Antarctic; Nov 69–Apr 70 participated in Op Deep Freeze to the Antarctic; Jun–Sep 72 conducted oceanographic research in Alaskan waters; Oct 72–Mar 73 participated in Op Deep Freeze to the Antarctic; Jun–Jul 73 conducted oceanographic research in Alaskan waters; Oct 73–Mar 74 participated in Op Deep Freeze to the Antarctic; 17 Nov 74–15 Mar 75 participated in Op Deep Freeze to the Antarctic; 20 Nov 75–27 Mar 76 participated in Op Deep Freeze to the Antarctic; 26 Jul–14 Oct 76 deployed to the Arctic; 8 Jun–17 Sep 77 deployed to the Arctic; 15 Nov 77–5 Apr 78 participated in Op Deep Freeze to the Antarctic; 4 Jul–14 Aug 78 deployed to the Arctic; 15 Nov 78–6 Apr 79 participated in Op Deep Freeze to the Antarctic; 15 Nov 79–2 Mar 80 participated in Op Deep Freeze to the Antarctic; 19 Nov 80–9 Feb 81 participated in Op Deep Freeze to the Antarctic; 17 Oct 81–21 Apr 82 participated in Op Deep Freeze to the Antarctic; 17 Nov 82–10 Apr 83 participated in Op Deep Freeze to the Antarctic; Oct 83–Mar 84 participated in Op Deep Freeze to the Antarctic; 22 Nov 85–7 May 86 participated in Op Deep Freeze to the Antarctic; May 88–7 Jun 87 stationed at Portland, OR, and used for icebreaking; 7 Nov 86–8 Apr 87 participated in Op Deep Freeze to the Antarctic.

The *Glacier*, 12 Jun 72, wears a fresh coat of red paint for the first time. Previously painted white, the Coast Guard changed the color of polar icebreakers to Icebreaker Red in order to help helicopter pilots spot the ships in the ice. The background color of the slash was later changed from red to white to make it more prominent.

290-FOOT ICEBREAKER

Name	Hull Number	Builder	Keel Laid	Launched	Commissioned	Disposition
Mackinaw (ex-*Manitowoc*)	WAGB 83 WAG 83	Toledo Shipbuilding Co., Toledo, OH	20 Mar 43	4 Mar 44	20 Dec 44	Active

Cost	$8,830,198 (hull & machinery)
Hull	
Displacement (tons)	5,253 fl (1965); 3,049 light (1965)
Length	290′ oa; 280′ bp
Beam	74′5″ max
Draft	19′3″ max (1965)
Machinery	
Main Engines	3 electric motors driven by 6 Westinghouse DC generators driven by 6 Fairbanks-Morse diesels
SHP	10,000
Propellers	twin aft, single forward (see Design remarks)
Performance	
Max Sustained	17.9 kts, 9,720-mi radius (1965)
Economic	9.0 kts, 41,000-mi radius (1989)
Logistics	
Fuel Oil (95%)	457,375 gal
Complement	11 officers, 2 warrants, 122 men (1965)
Deck Gear	
Cranes	two 12t

Electronics	
Radar	N/A
Armament	none

Design

Just prior to the United States's entry into World War II, Lieutenant Commander Edward Thiele, USCG (later engineer-in-chief), obtained details on icebreakers while vacationing in Europe. From these materials and details learned from the *Krassin,* the Coast Guard Naval Engineering Division prepared preliminary designs for the *Mackinaw* and the "Winds." The final designs were prepared by Gibbs & Cox of New York.

The *Mackinaw* and the "Winds" were very similar. According to Admiral Thiele, "the *Mackinaw* was nothing but a *Wind*-class ship that was squashed down and pushed out and extended to meet the requirements of the [Great] Lakes." The draft of the then lake-bound *Mackinaw* needed to be considerably less than that of her oceangoing near sisters. Compensation was made by making her a longer and much wider ship. Her engine-cooling system is directly open to the Great Lakes' fresh water. The *Mackinaw* and the "Winds" were built as Baltic-type icebreakers—they were fitted with bow propellers. Bow propellers work well in ice of uniform thickness, as found on the Great Lakes; however, they are a liability in polar ice. For this reason, the "Winds" bow propellers were removable.

There was one major difference in the construction of the *Mackinaw* and the "Winds." The *Mackinaw*'s hull was made of mild steel, since it was to operate against freshwater ice, whereas the hull of the "Winds" was a high tensile steel.

The *Mackinaw* and "Winds" were extremely strong. The frames (spaced about 16″ apart) made up a truss similar to that found in an inverted hangar or gymnasium, and an inner shell was place inside the truss. The volume between the inner and outer plating was divided into many tanks, which were used to store fuel and to carry ballast (seawater) for heeling.

The main engines of the *Mackinaw* consist of six diesel generator sets, each driven by its own Fairbanks-Morse 38D8-1/8 10-cylinder engine. These can be connected in several combinations to the two after DC electric-propulsion motors or to the bow motor. In operation the *Mackinaw* can cruise on two or four generators driving the after screws. In ice, all six generators can be used to drive the two aft shafts (4 generators) and the bow shaft (2 generators). In addition, heeling pumps and trimming pumps were installed to roll the ship or trim it to break free from the ice.

The *Mackinaw* was contracted on 16 Jul 42. Initially, she was to have been named the *Manitowoc*. However, the Navy had assigned this name to a patrol frigate that was under construction. Shortly after the war, her open quarterdeck was used as a helicopter landing area. The *Mackinaw* can break 2.5 ft. of ice continuously and 11 ft. by backing and ramming.

Mackinaw

20 Dec 44–1990 stationed at Cheboygan, MI, and used for icebreaking; 17–18 Mar 48 opened a passage for 12 ice-locked ships at Buffalo, NY—the earliest known date in over 50 years for the movement of shipping from Buffalo, NY; Mar 65 broke ice for car ferry from Detroit, MI, to Drummond I., MI; 10 May 65 served as on-scene commander following collision between U.S. MV *Cedarville* and Norwegian MV *Topdalsfjord* 1 mi NE of Mackinaw City, MI, in which *Cedarville* sank—German MV *Weissenburg* rescued survivors; 30 Oct 66 stood by grounded MV *Halifax* 40 mi S of Sault Ste. Marie, MI; 21 Nov 66 transported 29 crewmen from grounded German MV *Nordmeer* to Alpine, MI; 29 Nov 66 evacuated remaining persons from German MV *Nordmeer*; 5 Apr 68 helped free MV *W. B. Schiller* from heavy ice in Lake Superior; 1 Apr 70 helped free grounded MV *Stadacona* near the Mackinaw Bridge; Sep 86 used as a platform to survey underwater wreck of FV *Razel Brothers*.

Icebreaker *Mackinaw* on 25 Jun 59. This view shows the much finer lines she possesses than the Wind class. The *Mackinaw* is the only icebreaker not to have been painted Icebreaker Red during the 1970s. Extensive plans for this cutter appear in Scheina, *WWII Cutters*.

269-FOOT ICEBREAKERS ("WIND" CLASS)

Name	Hull Number	Builder	Keel Laid	Launched	Commissioned	Disposition
Staten Island (ex-*Northwind*, ex-*Admiral Makarov*, ex-*Severni Veter*, ex-*Northwind*)	WAGB 278 WAG 278 (bn CG-96)	Western Pipe & Steel Co., Los Angeles, CA	9 Jun 42	28 Dec 42	26 Feb 44 (CG) 26 Jan 52 (USN) 1 Feb 65 (CG)	*Trans* to USSR 26 Feb 44 *Decomm* 15 Nov 74 *Sold* 14 May 75

Name	Hull Number	Builder	Keel Laid	Launched	Commissioned	Disposition
Eastwind	WAGB 279 WAG 279 (bn CG-97)	Western Pipe & Steel Co., Los Angeles, CA	23 Jun 42	6 Feb 43	3 Jun 44	*Decomm* 13 Dec 68 *Sold* 31 Jun 72
Southwind (ex-*Atka*, ex-*Kapitan Belusov*, ex-*Southwind*)	WAGB 280 WAG 280 (bn CG-98)	Western Pipe & Steel Co., Los Angeles, CA	20 Jul 42	8 Mar 43	15 Jul 44 (CG) 13 Apr 50 (USN) 31 Oct 66 (CG)	*Trans* to USSR 23 Mar 45 *Decomm* 31 May 74 *Sold* 10 Mar 76
Westwind (ex-*Severni Pulius*, ex-*Westwind*)	WAGB 281 WAG 281 (bn CG-99)	Western Pipe & Steel Co., Los Angeles, CA	24 Aug 42	31 Mar 43	18 Sep 44 (CG) 22 Sep 52 (CG)	*Trans* to USSR 21 Feb 45 *Ret* 19 Dec 51 *Decomm* 29 Feb 88
Northwind	WAGB 282 (bn CG-184)	Western Pipe & Steel Co., Los Angeles, CA	10 Jul 44	25 Feb 45	28 Jul 45	*Decomm* 20 Jan 89
Burton Island	WAGB 283 AGB 1 AG 88	Western Pipe & Steel Co., San Pedro, CA	15 Mar 45	30 Apr 46	28 Dec 46 (USN) 15 Dec 66 (CG)	*Decomm* 9 May 78
Edisto	WAGB 284 AGB 2 AG 89	Western Pipe & Steel Co., San Pedro, CA	15 May 45	29 May 46	20 Mar 47 (USN) 20 Oct 65 (CG)	*Decomm* 15 Nov 74

Cost — $9,891,806 (*Northwind* [II]); $9,880,037 (all others)

Hull
  Displacement (tons) — 6,481 fl (1967); 3,052 light (1967)
  Length — 269' oa; 250' bp
  Beam — 63'10" max
  Draft — 29'1" max (1967)

Machinery
  Main Engines — 3 electric motors driven by 6 Westinghouse DC generators driven by 6 Fairbanks-Morse, 10-cyl 2-cycle diesels (see Design remarks)
  SHP — 12,000
  Propellers — twin aft, single forward (see Design remarks)

Performance
  Max Sustained — 13.4 kts, 30,929-mi radius (1967)
  Economic — 11.6 kts, 32,485-mi radius (1967)

Logistics
  Fuel Oil (95%) — 514,954 gal
  Complement — 11.6 officers, 2 warrants, 205 men (1967)

Electronics
  Radar — SPS-10B; SPS-53A; SPS-6C (*Burton Island*, 1967)

Armament
  1966 — 1 5"/38 (*Edisto* and *Westwind*)
  1967 — none (*Burton Island*)

Design

The "Wind"-class final design—modeled after the Swedish icebreaker *Ymer*—was prepared by Gibbs & Cox of New York. This class was to provide access to military bases in Greenland that would be inaccessible during most of the year without the use of a heavy icebreaker. The first five were contracted on 15 Nov 41; the second *Northwind* was contracted on 9 Oct 43.

These ships were designed with a removable bow propeller. Under certain ice conditions, this bow propeller was advantageous for clearing the hull from ice and dredging broken ice forward; it was not used as a means of propulsion. The *Burton Island* and the *Edisto* were constructed for the Navy and were ultimately transferred to the CG. The *Atka* assumed her former name, *Southwind*, on 18 Jan 67

The *Westwind* and the *Northwind* were reengined with Enterprise diesels in 1973–74 and 1974–75, respectively.

Burton Island

15 Dec 66–mid-77 stationed at Long Beach, CA, and used for icebreaking; Oct 67–Apr 68 participated in Operation Deep Freeze to the Antarctic; Oct 68–Apr 69 participated in Op Deep Freeze to the Antarctic; Nov 69–Apr 70 participated in Op Deep Freeze to the Antarctic—accompanying icebreaker disabled; Nov 70–Apr 71 participated in Op Deep Freeze to the Antarctic—accompanying icebreaker disabled; Aug–Sep 71 conducted oceanographic survey along North Slope, AK; Feb–Mar 72 conducted scientific survey in Cook Inlet, AK; Nov 72–Apr 73 participated in Op Deep Freeze to the Antarctic; Jun–Jul 73 conducted oceanographic research in Alaskan waters; Nov 74–Apr 75 participated in Op Deep Freeze to the Antarctic; 13 Nov 75–26 Feb 76 participated in Op Deep Freeze to the Antarctic; Jul–Sep 76 deployed to the Arctic; 9 Nov 76–7 Apr 77 participated in Op Deep Freeze in the Antarctic; Dec 76 carried out numerous SAR missions at Wellington, New Zealand, following a torrential downpour; 9 Jul–8 Sep 77 undertook cruise to the Arctic; 20 Nov 77–1 Apr 78 participated in Op Deep Freeze to the Antarctic; mid-77–9 May 78 stationed at Alameda, CA, and used for icebreaking.

Eastwind

1946–13 Dec 68 stationed at Boston, MA, and used for icebreaking; 1946–47 made four trips to Greenland supplying bases; 19 Jan 49 collided with tanker *Gulfstream* off New Jersey—13 enlisted men died and cutter sustained extensive damage; Jul–Sep 50 resupplied Arctic bases; Jun–Aug 51 resupplied Arctic bases; May–Sep 52 resupplied Arctic bases; Dec 54–Jan 55 resupplied Narsarssuak AFB, Greenland; Jun–Sep 55 resupplied Arctic bases; Nov 55–Mar 56 participated in Operation Deep Freeze to the Antarctic; May–Nov 58 resupplied Arctic bases; 9 Feb 59 freed icebound MSTS *Chattahoochee* and *Eltanin* off Newfoundland; Nov 59–Mar 60 participated in Op Deep Freeze to the Antarctic; Sep 61–Mar

Icebreaker *Eastwind* on 7 May 63. This and the photograph of the *Westwind* offer an interesting comparison between two ships that were created identical back in 1944. The *Eastwind* mounts a single 3″/50 Mk 33. The radome on the face of the gunhouse is for an SPC-34 fire-control radar.

62 participated in Op Deep Freeze to the Antarctic; Nov 63–Mar 64 participated in Op Deep Freeze to the Antarctic; Nov 64–Apr 65 participated in Op Deep Freeze to the Antarctic; Jun–Aug 65 resupplied Arctic bases; Nov 65–Apr 66 participated in Op Deep Freeze to the Antarctic; Mar 66 helicopter detached to aid in flood relief in Argentina; 7 Feb 67 rescued the Danish Antarctic supply ships *Nella Dan* and *Thala Dan* from heavy ice 40 mi off Budd Coast of Antarctic—*Nella Dan* had been trapped for one month and *Thala Dan* for two weeks; Aug–Oct 67 circumnavigated North Pole to obtain meteorological and oceanographic data; Mar–Apr 68 broke ice on the Great Lakes as part of a project to extend navigational season on the lakes; 18 Jul–8 Aug 68 conducted oceanographic survey along west coast of Greenland; Aug–Nov 68 participated in MSTS resupply cruise to the Arctic.

Edisto

20 Oct 65–Dec 71 stationed at Boston, MA, and used for icebreaking; 29 Jul–1 Sep 66 conducted oceanographic cruise in Baffin Bay and Nares Strait; Nov–Dec 66 assisted cable ship *John Cabbot* repair break in the Thule-Deer Lake ocean cable; Aug–Oct 67 circumnavigated North Pole to obtain meteorological and oceanographic data; 30 Jul 67 helped locate and repair submarine cables 600 mi above the Arctic Circle; Oct 67 conducted oceanographic survey in Labrador Sea; 27 Mar 68 helped fight fire on Long Wharf, Boston, MA; Jul–Nov 68 participated in MSTS resupply cruise to the Arctic; Dec 71–Dec 72 stationed at Milwaukee, WI, and used for icebreaking as part of a study to extend the shipping seasons on the Great Lakes; 5 Oct 72 collided with tow USS *Mizar* in heavy ice off Greenland, lost a propeller and badly damaged her rudder, towed to Reykjavik, Iceland, by cutter *Southwind*, arriving 23 Oct; Dec 72–15 Nov 74 stationed at Baltimore, MD, and used for icebreaking.

Northwind

1945–73 stationed at Seattle, WA, and used for polar ice ops and Bering Sea Patrol; 1945–46 temporarily stationed at Boston, MA, to participate in special Navy ops; 1946–47 participated in Antarctic operation High Jump; May–Aug 48 conducted Bering Sea Patrol—first patrol in eight years; 1953 conducted Bering Sea Patrol; 12 Jul–29 Sep 54 participated in U.S.-Canadian Beaufort Sea Exploration; Feb–Apr 55 conducted Bering Sea scientific expedition; Jul–Sep 55 supported DEW Line ops; Nov 56–Apr 57 participated in Op Deep Freeze to the Antarctic; 5–25 Jul 62 conducted oceanographic experiments in Chukchi Sea in cooperation with northwestern universities; 6–19 Sep 62 conducted oceanographic experiments in Bering Sea in cooperation with northwestern universities; 2–26 Oct 62 conducted oceanographic experiments in East Siberian Sea and Arctic Ocean in cooperation with northwestern universities; 7 Aug–18 Sep 63 conducted oceanographic experiments in Chukchi, East Siberian, and Laptev seas in cooperation with the U. of Southern California; Jul–Oct 64 conducted Bering Sea Patrol, carried out oceanographic experiments in Bering Strait and Chukchi Sea, installed an unmanned oceanographic station in Fairway Rock, and escorted ships resupplying the DEW Line; Jul 65 conducted oceanographic survey between Greenland, Iceland, and Scotland—was first Western vessel to operate in the Kara Sea; mid-Oct 65 escorted disabled Swedish MV *Orion* in North Atlantic to Gulf of St. Lawrence; Jul–Aug 67 conducted a current and hydrographic survey in Bering Strait; Sep–Nov 67 beset by ice 450 mi NNW of Point Barrow—freed by cutters *Glacier*, *Staten Island*, and Canadian icebreaker *John A. MacDonald*; 9 Jun–15 Jul 69 conducted oceanographic survey in Chukchi and Bering seas; 8–22 Sep 69, along with Canadian icebreaker *MacDonald* escorted tanker *Manhattan* from Resolute, AK, to Prudhoe Bay where relieved by cutter *Staten Island* on transit of Northwest Passage—*Northwind* tested ice and returned to Seattle, WA, having transited 14,000 mi and become first vessel to conduct both a W-E and E-W transit of the Northwest Passage in a single season; 20 Jan–9 Apr 70 conducted western Arctic patrol and oceanographic cruise—northernmost penetration 66°35′N, 167°29′W on 13 Mar; 23 Jun–28

The *Northwind* on 17 Jun 63. The aluminum hangar has three retractable sections that telescope one into another. The hangar, which has just been installed on the icebreaker, had been developed by the Canadian Ministry of Transport and used on its icebreakers.

Sep 70 served on Arctic Ops—duties included laying cables, oceanographic studies, and resupplying the DEW Line; 13 Jul 70 rescued two from ditched helicopter near Yukon Delta in Norton Sound; Jun–Jul 73 conducted oceanographic research in Alaskan waters; 1973–75 underwent extensive machinery modernization and electronic modification at the CG Yard, Curtis Bay, MD, and was stationed in Baltimore, MD; summer 1975 conducted Arctic cruise; 6 Oct 76–13 Apr 77 participated on Operation Deep Freeze to the Antarctic; 10 Jul–10 Dec 78 undertook cruise to the Arctic; 3 Nov 79–24 Mar 80 participated in Op Deep Freeze to the Antarctic; 26 Sep–13 Dec 81 undertook cruise to the Arctic; 1978–89 stationed at Wilmington, NC, and used for icebreaking, including the Great Lakes; 16 Feb 84 medevaced a woman from a 33-ft sailboat 200 mi W of Bermuda; 28 Apr 84 assisted USN LCM extinguish a fire in the Caribbean; 5 Aug 84 assisted PC off Kulusuk, Greenland; 4 Nov 84 seized PC *Alexi I* 240 mi SW of Jamaica carrying 20t of marijuana; 2–21 Jul 86 assisted Danish and Greenland governments in reestablishing a musk-ox herd in NW Greenland.

Southwind

31 Oct 66–Dec 72 stationed at Baltimore, MD, and used for icebreaking; 28 May 67 towed disabled yacht *Gytha* from 50 mi N of Bermuda to that island; summer 67 served as an escort and conducted oceanographic research along both coasts of Greenland; 30 Jul 67 helped locate and repair submarine cables 600 mi above the Arctic Circle; Nov 67 assisted in construction of a U.S. scientific station on Anvers I., Antarctica; Dec 67–Apr 68 participated in Operation Deep Freeze to the Antarctic; 21 Mar 68 grounded near Arthur Harbor, Antarctica, and towed; Jul–Aug 69 served as an escort and conducted oceanographic research along the W coast of Greenland; 15 Aug 69 grounded 130 mi ESE of Thule, Greenland, and sustained minor damage—freed on the 17th; Jun–Nov 70 resupplied bases in the Arctic; 15 Aug 70 reached 83°01′N—northernmost penetration into the Arctic Basin by a U.S. icebreaker to date; Jul 71 conducted W Greenland glacier survey; 6 Oct–10 Nov 72 resupplied Arctic bases; 11–23 Oct 72 freed icebound cutter *Edisto* and USS *Mizar* and towed the damaged cutter to Reykjavik, Iceland; Dec 72–31 May 74 stationed at Milwaukee, WI, and used for icebreaking.

Staten Island

1 Feb 66–15 Nov 74 stationed at Seattle, WA, and used principally for icebreaking; 22 Sep 66–6 Apr 67 participated in Operation Deep Freeze to the Antarctic; Sep–Nov 67 helped free cutter *Northwind*, beset in ice after she lost a propeller at 79°02′N, 168°06′W; Oct–Nov 67 helped free cutter *Northwind* beset by ice again 450 mi NNW of Point Barrow; Jul–Aug 68 conducted oceanographic survey of Chukchi Sea-Bering Strait area; 10–11 Mar 69 rescued crew of grounded FV *Martindale* off Akun I.; 7 Sep 69 assisted cutter *Storis* to open water off Point Barrow, AK; 22 Sep–1 Nov 69 relieved cutter *Northwind* and escorted tanker *Manhattan* on transit of Northwest Passage; 6 Jul–20 Aug 70 conducted scientific tests and evaluation of crude-oil spread rate in the Arctic and freed ice-bound convoy of 20 tugs and 40 barges en route to Prudhoe Bay oil fields; 14 Aug 70 freed fouled screw of tug *Active* 30 mi SW of Point Barrow; 3 Feb–7 Apr 73 conducted experiments in the Bering Sea; 5–14 Aug 74 conducted oceanographic survey between Icy Cape and Point Barrow, AK.

Westwind

22 Sep 52–May 66 stationed at Brooklyn, NY, and used for icebreaking; Jun–Sep 53 resupplied Arctic bases; Dec 53–Jan 54 broke ice on Hudson R.; Jun–Sep 54 resupplied Arctic bases—trapped in ice about 450 mi from North Pole, which threatened the possibility of wintering over; summer 55 participated in DEW Line construction; summer 56 participated in DEW Line construction; Dec 57–Mar 58 participated in Operation Deep Freeze to the Antarctic; Jun–Jul 59 resupplied Arctic bases; Jul 60 escorted Danish MV *Julius Thomsen* through ice-clogged water to Thule, Greenland; Jun–Nov 62 resupplied Arctic bases; Jul–Aug 63 resupplied Arctic bases; Jul–Aug 64 resupplied Arctic bases; Jun–Aug 65 resupplied Arctic bases; Nov 65 assisted cable ship *John Cabbot* repair break in the Thule-Deer Lake ocean cable; May 66–1972 stationed at Baltimore, MD, and used for icebreaking; Jul 66 conducted an oceanographic cruise to the Arctic; Dec 67–Mar 68 participated in Op Deep Freeze to the Antarctic; 21 Jan 68 freed grounded Danish MV *Magga* in Winter Quarters Bay; Mar–Apr 69 broke ice on the Great Lakes as part of project to extend navigational season on the lakes; Jul–Nov 69 participated in MSTS resupply cruise to the Arctic; 26 Aug 69 helicopter from cutter rescued expedition of 7 from U. of London near Sermilgaq, Greenland; Mar–Apr 70 broke ice on the Great Lakes; 1972–73 extensively renovated at CG Yard, Curtis Bay, MD; 1974–81 stationed at Milwaukee, WI, and used for icebreaking; May–Oct 79 conducted Arctic cruise; 7 Aug 79 rescued three from a private ac near Kulusuk, Greenland; 29 Aug 79 penetrated to 83°45′N—375 mi from North Pole, the record; 1981–29 Feb 88 stationed at Mobile, AL, and used for LE and icebreaking; 4 Oct 83–25 Feb 84 participated in Op Deep Freeze to the Antarctic; 5 Oct 83 repaired engines on FV *Ocean Hope II* 300 mi S of Mobile, AL; 1 Jan 84 sustained major hull damage while operating in the Weddel Sea—returned to U.S.

The *Westwind* dressed in Icebreaker Red in 1975. The cutter was extensively renovated in 1974–75. Her bow and stern were strengthened, her engines replaced, the shaft diameter was increased from 19 to 22 inches, and her chrome steel propellers were replaced by new ones of alloy steel. The *Westwind* and *Northwind* received taller stacks during the 1970s, distinguishing them from their remaining sisters.

Tugs (WYT, WYTM, and WTGB)

Tug boats have been part of the Coast Guard's fleet since the late nineteenth century. They were primarily used in protected waters, and prior to World War II the Coast Guard frequently maintained an oceangoing tug on each coast for high-seas rescue. The 100-foot classes built in the 1930s and 1940s proved to be more adept at breaking light ice than larger cutters possessing design features for that task; as a result, these tugs were extensively used for this task throughout their careers. During the 1970s and 1980s the Coast Guard constructed replacement tugs, the 140-foot class, for the 110-foot medium harbor tugs. These ships possess a significant increase in icebreaking capabilities over their predecessors. During the construction of the 140-footers, the Coast Guard created a new designator, WTGB, for these tugs.

140-FOOT TUGS

Name	Hull Number	Builder	Keel Laid	Launched	Commissioned	Disposition
Katmai Bay	WTGB 101 WYTM 101	Tacoma Boatbuilding Co., Inc., Tacoma, WA	7 Nov 77	8 Apr 78	8 Jan 79	Active
Bristol Bay	WTGB 102 WYTM 102	Tacoma Boatbuilding Co., Inc., Tacoma, WA	13 Feb 78	22 Jul 78	5 Apr 79	Active
Mobile Bay	WTGB 103 WYTM 103	Tacoma Boatbuilding Co., Inc., Tacoma, WA	13 Feb 78	11 Nov 78	6 May 79	Active
Biscayne Bay	WTGB 104 WYTM 104	Tacoma Boatbuilding Co., Inc., Tacoma, WA	29 Aug 78	3 Feb 79	8 Dec 79	Active
Neah Bay	WTGB 105 WYTM 105	Tacoma Boatbuilding Co., Inc., Tacoma, WA	6 Aug 79	2 Feb 80	18 Aug 80	Active
Morro Bay	WTGB 106 WYTM 106	Tacoma Boatbuilding Co., Inc., Tacoma, WA	6 Aug 79	11 Jul 81	25 Jan 81	Active
Penobscot Bay	WTGB 107	Bay City Marine, Tacoma, WA	1 Jul 83	27 Jul 84	2 Jan 85	Active
Thunder Bay	WTGB 108	Tacoma Boatbuilding Co., Inc., Tacoma, WA	20 Jul 84	15 Aug 85	4 Nov 85	Active
Sturgeon Bay	WTGB 109	Bay City Marine, Tacoma, WA	N/A	12 Sep 87	20 Aug 88	Active

Cost   See Appropriations table

Hull
| | |
Displacement (tons)   662 fl (1979)
Length   140′ oa
Beam   37′6″ max
Draft   12′ mean (1979)

Machinery

Main Engines   2 Fairbanks-Morse diesels driving Westinghouse electric motor

BHP   2,500

Propellers   single

Performance

Max Sustained   14.7 kts, 1,800 nm (1979)

Cruising   12.0 kts, 4,000 nm (1979)

Logistics

Fuel Oil (95%)

Complement   3 officers, 14 men (1979)

Electronics

Radar   SPS-64

Armament   none

Design

The 140-foot class was designed by the Coast Guard to replace the aging 110-foot WYTMs. They are much more versatile than their predecessors. The 140s can break ice up to 20 inches, a significant increase over the capability of the 110s. The 140-foot tugs have a portable bubble-generator system housed in a removable deckhouse on the fantail. This hull air-lubrication (bubbler) system assists the cutter in extracting itself from thicker ice, and, at slow speeds, improves the cutter's icebreaking capabilities.

The 140s are 4 knots faster than the 110s, an important asset in SAR. The 140-foot-class tugs may also be used for A/N; this is accomplished by mating the tug with a work barge, the use of which is a common practice on the Mississippi R. complex. The first barge specifically designed to operate with a 140-footer was constructed in 1989–90.

140-FOOT TUGS—APPROPRIATIONS

Name	Cost
Katmai Bay	$4,709,643
Bristol Bay	$4,706,334
Mobile Bay	$4,728,951
Biscayne Bay	$4,689,786
Neah Bay	$6,799,966
Morro Bay	$6,800,103
Penobscot Bay	N/A
Thunder Bay	N/A
Sturgeon Bay	N/A

Biscayne Bay

1979–90 stationed at St. Ignace, MI, and used for icebreaking, LE, and SAR.

The *Biscayne Bay* during 1979. Shortly after the first few units entered service, the Coast Guard decided to paint the class white because of its multi-mission capabilities. However, this did not prove to be practical. Major tasks for the 140-footers include icebreaking and working with A/N-equipped barges, making the white hull impractical. All except the *Morro Bay,* which serves principally as a training vessel, now have black hulls.

Bristol Bay

1979–90 stationed at Detroit, MI, and used for icebreaking, LE, and SAR.

Katmai Bay

1979–90 stationed at Sault Ste. Marie and used for icebreaking, LE, and SAR.

Mobile Bay

1979–90 stationed at Sturgeon Bay, WI, and used for icebreaking, LE, and SAR; Sep 79 conducted heavy-weather seakeeping trials off Virginia and towing/firefighting trials in New York Harbor; 3–4 Nov 80 towed disabled tanker *Amoco Wisconsin* to safety in Grand Traverse Bay; Feb–Mar 81 participated in WAGB/WTGB comparison icebreaking tests in northern Lake Michigan; Sep–Dec 84 deployed to the Caribbean for LE and SAR—also used to help train Grenadan Coast Guard.

Morro Bay

1981–90 stationed at Yorktown, VA, and used for training and icebreaking.

Neah Bay

1980–90 stationed at Cleveland, OH, and used for icebreaking, LE, and SAR; 18–25 Feb 85 assisted Army Corps of Engineers in preventing possible flooding by breaking up ice-clogged river outlets along Lake Erie.

Penobscot Bay

1985–90 stationed at New York, NY, and used for icebreaking, LE, and SAR.

Sturgeon Bay

1988–90 stationed at New York, NY, and used for LE and SAR.

Thunder Bay

1985–Aug 88 stationed at Portland, ME, and used for icebreaking, LE, and SAR; Aug 88–1990 stationed at Rockland, ME, and used for icebreaking, LE, and SAR.

Cutter *Katmai Bay* in her environment. The first six units were originally classified as WYTMs. While under construction, the Coast Guard decided to give the class a new classification because of its unique icebreaking capabilities. The *Katmai Bay* was reclassified on 5 Feb 79 and the subsequent six were reclassified upon commissioning.

65-FOOT HARBOR TUGS

Name	Hull Number	Builder	Keel Laid	Launched	Commissioned	Disposition
Capstan	WYTL 65601	Gibbs Corp., Jacksonville, FL	N/A	N/A	19 Jul 61	Active
Chock	WYTL 65602	Gibbs Corp., Jacksonville, FL	N/A	N/A	12 Sep 62	Active
Swivel	WYTL 65603	Gibbs Corp., Jacksonville, FL	N/A	N/A	27 Oct 61	Active
Tackle	WYTL 65604	Gibbs Corp., Jacksonville, FL	N/A	N/A	1962	Active
Towline	WYTL 65605	Gibbs Corp., Jacksonville, FL	N/A	N/A	27 Mar 62	Active
Catenary	WYTL 65606	Gibbs Corp., Jacksonville, FL	N/A	N/A	Apr 62	Active
Bridle	WYTL 65607	Barbour Boat Works, New Bern, NC	Mar 62	N/A	3 Apr 63	Active
Pendant	WYTL 65608	Barbour Boat Works, New Bern, NC	Apr 62	N/A	Aug 63	Active
Shackle	WYTL 65609	Barbour Boat Works, New Bern, NC	Apr 62	Jan 63	7 May 63	Active
Hawser	WYTL 65610	Barbour Boat Works, New Bern, NC	Jan 62	N/A	17 Jan 63	Active
Line	WYTL 65611	Barbour Boat Works, New Bern, NC	Jan 62	Jul 62	21 Feb 63	Active
Wire	WYTL 65612	Barbour Boat Works, New Bern, NC	Mar 62	Sep 62	19 Mar 63	Active
Bitt	WYTL 65613	Western Boatbuilding, Tacoma, WA	N/A	N/A	27 May 66	*Decomm* 4 Oct 82
Bollard	WYTL 65614	Western Boatbuilding, Tacoma, WA	N/A	N/A	10 Apr 67	Active
Cleat	WYTL 65615	Western Boatbuilding, Tacoma, WA	N/A	N/A	10 May 67	Active

Cost — $158,366 (first six units)

Hull
  Displacement (tons) — 74 fl (1964); 62 light (1964)
  Length — 64'11" oa; 62'7" bp
  Beam — 19'1" max
  Draft — 9' max (1964)

Machinery
  Main Engines — 1 diesel
  BHP — 400
  Propellers — single

Performance
  Max Sustained — 10.6 kts, 1,130-mi radius (1964)
  Economic — 7.0 kts, 3,690-mi radius (1964)

Logistics
  Fuel Oil (95%) — 1,850 gal
  Complement — 5 men (1964)

Electronics
  Detection Radar — SPN-11 (1964)
  Sonar — none

Armament — none

Design
  These steel-hulled craft were built to replace the wooden-hulled 64-foot harbor tugs built in the 1940s. The 65-footers remained unnamed until the mid-1960s. See the section dealing with small craft.

Bitt

1966–78 stationed at Bellingham, WA, and used for LE and SAR; 5 Jan 69 assisted in evacuation of a stranded person near Nooksack R. when a dike broke; 29 Jul 69 towed disabled FV *Jet Stream* from Admiralty Inlet to safety; 20 Oct 75 rescued two from a capsized sailboat; 1978–82 stationed at Valdez, AK, and used for LE and SAR.

Bollard

1967–70 stationed at Long Beach, CA, and used for LE and SAR; 1971–75 stationed at New York, NY, and used for LE and SAR; 25 Oct 72 fought fire following a barge explosion; 1975–90 stationed at New Haven, CT, and used for LE and SAR.

Bridle

1963–90 stationed at Southwest Harbor, ME, and used for LE and SAR; Jan–Feb 68 freed over 100 lobster boats from ice near Jonesport, ME.

Capstan

1961–90 stationed in the Washington, DC, area and used for LE and SAR; 7 Sep 69 fought fire on houseboat *Lacie C* near Broad Creek; Jan 82 broke ice to permit salvage barges to move to the scene of the Air Florida crash site, Washington, DC.

Catenary

1962–Jun 88 stationed at Gloucester City, NJ, and used for LE and SAR; Jun 88–1990 stationed at Philadelphia, PA, and used for LE and SAR.

Tug *Bridle* on 17 Jun 87. Since the early twentieth century, the Coast Guard has maintained a class of small harbor tugs that have been used for a variety of tasks, including LE, SAR, fire fighting and light icebreaking.

Chock

1962–90 stationed in the Norfolk-Portsmouth, VA, area and used for LE and SAR; 21 Jan 69 helped free a barge pounding against James R. Bridge.

Cleat

1967–69 stationed at New York, NY, and used for LE and SAR; 29 Sep 68 escorted MV *Freetown* up Ambrose Channel following a bomb threat; 1969–Jun 88 stationed at Gloucester City, NJ, and used for LE and SAR; Feb 72 assisted after tanker *Corinthos* disaster off Marcus Hook, PA; Jun 88–1990 stationed at Philadelphia, PA, and used for LE and SAR.

Hawser

1963–90 stationed at New York, NY, and used for LE and SAR; 25 Dec 67 helped fight fire on Norwegian MV *Dianet* in New York harbor; 27 Dec 68 assisted in containing gasoline leak following a collision and fire on barge *Russell 104* in New York harbor; 12 Feb 80 helped fight fire on board tank-cleaning vessel *Peter Frank* 1 mi E of Bayonne Bridge, NJ.

Line

1963–90 stationed at New York, NY, and used for LE and SAR; 3 Mar 80 helped fight fire at Weehawken Pier, NY.

Pendant

1963–70 stationed at Long Beach, CA, and used for LE and SAR; 1971–90 stationed at Boston, MA, and used for LE and SAR.

Shackle

1963–90 stationed at South Portland, ME, and used for LE and SAR; 30 Dec 69–1 Jan 70 fought fire on tanker *Dean Reinauer*, Portland, ME.

Swivel

1961–90 stationed at Rockland, ME, and used for LE and SAR; 25 Mar 70 escorted ferry *Governor Muskie* following a bomb threat.

Tackle

1962–90 stationed in the Baltimore, MD, area and used for LE and SAR; 13 Feb 68 helped fight fire at Pier 5, Baltimore, MD.

Towline

1962–90 stationed at Bristol, RI, and used for LE and SAR; Jan 68 freed eight FVs from ice and assisted residents of Patience I., MA, with food and supplies; late Jan 68 broke up to 14 in. of ice to free four tankers and 28 FVs; late Jan 70 broke ice to aid in delivery of food to Nantucket I.

Wire

1963–90 stationed at New York, NY, and used for LE and SAR; 12 Feb 80 helped fight fire on board tank-cleaning vessel *Peter Frank* 1 mi E of Bayonne Bridge, NJ.

U.S. ARMY HARBOR TUGS

Name	Hull Number	Builder	Keel Laid	Launched	Commissioned	Disposition
Messenger	CG-85009 ST-710	Equitable Equipment, New Orleans, LA	N/A	N/A	5 Sep 45 (USA) mid-1950s (CG)	Active
Research	CG-85010 TD-42	N/A	N/A	N/A	22 Jul 73 (USA) N/A (CG)	*Decomm* 23 May 73 *Trans* to Alabama Civil Defense

Cost	N/A		Logistics	N/A
Hull			Electronics	
Displacement (tons)	N/A		Radar	navigation type
Length	86' oa		Design	

Cost N/A

Hull
Displacement (tons) N/A
Length 86' oa
Beam 23' max
Draft 10' max

Machinery
Main Engines 1 diesel
BHP 650
Propellers single

Performance N/A

Logistics N/A

Electronics
Radar   navigation type

Design
These tugs were constructed of steel for the U.S. Army.

Messenger

Mid-1950s–1987 stationed at CG Yard, Curtis Bay, MD, and used to support yard work.

Research

N/A

Tug *Messenger* 12 Jan 83. She has spent her career at the Coast Guard Yard, Curtis Bay, MD.

NAVY *WOBAN* CLASS

Name	Hull Number	Builder	Keel Laid	Launched	Commissioned	Disposition
Yonaguska	MYT 195 YT 195	Pearl Harbor Navy Yard, Pearl Harbor, HI	21 Jun 42	17 Aug 43	22 Feb 44 (USN) 3 Aug 49 (CG)	*Decomm & returned* to USN 29 Jun 54

Cost   N/A

Hull
   Displacement (tons)   332 fl (1952); 241 light (1952)
   Length   99′10″ oa; 88′4″ bp
   Beam   27′9″
   Draft   11′5″ max (1952)

Machinery
   Main Engines   2 General Electric motors driven by 2 General Motors diesels
   BHP   1,000
   Propellers   single

Performance
   Max Sustained   10.0 kts, 6,100-mi radius (1952)

Cruising   8.0 kts, 7,300-mi radius (1952)

Logistics
   Fuel Oil (95%)   18,000 gal
   Complement   11 men (1952)

Electronics
   Detection Radar   none

Armament   none

Design
   The Navy *Woban* class was constructed of steel.

Yonaguska

3 Aug 49–29 Jun 54 stationed at Honolulu, HI, and used for boardings to inspect inbound ships.

The cutter *Yonaguska* was acquired as an examination ship for Honolulu, HI, during an era when tensions were extremely high between the East and the West. The *Yonaguska* retained her WYT—harbor tug—classification, whereas the *Tahoma,* which performed the same type of duty in the Chesapeake, was given a unique classification—WAGE—miscellaneous auxiliary, examination vessel. The Coast Guard has always attached far less rigidity to the designation of its ships than the U.S. Navy.

110-FOOT TUGS

Name	Hull Number	Builder	Keel Laid	Launched	Commissioned	Disposition
Apalachee	WYTM 71 WYT 71	Ira S. Bushey & Sons, Brooklyn, NY	17 Nov 42	29 Apr 43	26 Nov 43	*Decomm* 11 Apr 86
Yankton	WYTM 72 WYT 72	Ira S. Bushey & Sons, Brooklyn, NY	26 Oct 42	29 Apr 43	26 Jan 44	*Decomm* 28 Sep 84
Mohican	WYTM 73 WYT 73	Ira S. Bushey & Sons, Brooklyn, NY	10 Nov 42	16 Jun 43	29 Feb 44	*Decomm* 26 Jun 86
Chinook	WYTM 96 WYT 96	Ira S. Bushey & Sons, Brooklyn, NY	10 Nov 42	16 Jun 43	24 Mar 44	*Decomm* 1 Jul 86
Ojibwa	WYTM 97 WYT 97	Ira S. Bushey & Sons, Brooklyn, NY	25 Jan 43	10 Sep 43	7 Apr 44	*Decomm* Apr 80 *Sold* 22 Dec 80
Snohomish	WYTM 98 WYT 98	Ira S. Bushey & Sons, Brooklyn, NY	25 Jan 43	10 Sep 43	2 May 44	*Decomm* 4 Apr 86
Sauk	WYTM 99 WYT 99	Ira S. Bushey & Sons, Brooklyn, NY	26 Jan 43	10 Sep 43	25 May 44	*Decomm* 30 Apr 85

Cost $622,677 each (hull & machinery)

Hull
- Displacement (tons)   382 fl (1964); 312 light (1964)
- Length   110'2" oa; 105'1" bp
- Beam   27'3" max
- Draft   12'2" max (1964)

Machinery
- Main Engines   1 electric motor driven by 2 Elliot Electric Co. generators driven by 2 Ingersoll Rand diesels
- SHP   1,000
- Propellers   single

Performance
- Max Sustained   11.2 kts, 1,376-mi radius (1964)
- Economic   8.6 kts, 5,123-mi radius (1964)

Logistics
- Fuel Oil (95%)   10,000 gal
- Complement   1 warrant, 19 men (1964)

Electronics
- Radar   CR-103 (1964)

Armament   none

Design

These 110-foot tugs were contracted on 8 Jun 41. Based on the earlier 110-foot design, the design incorporated characteristics required for Greenland duty and fire fighting.

Apalachee

1943–17 Sep 84 stationed at Baltimore, MD, and used for LE, SAR, and icebreaking; 11–12 Jun 65 helped fight fire on Colombian MV *Ciudad de Nieva* near Baltimore, MD; 13 Feb 68 helped fight fire on Pier 5, Baltimore, MD; 4 Jun 69 helped fight fire on MV *Provence Town* at Baltimore, MD; 17 Sep 84–11 Apr 86 stationed at Portland, ME, and used for LE, SAR, and icebreaking.

Chinook

1946–72 stationed at Baltimore, MD, and used for LE, SAR, and light icebreaking; Mar 60 broke ice in Chesapeake Bay; 11–12 Jun 65 fought fire on Colombian MV *Ciudad de Nieva* near Baltimore, MD, along with other fire fighters; 13 Feb 68 helped fight fire at Pier 5, Baltimore, MD; 4 Jun 69 helped fight fire on MV *Provence Town* at Baltimore, MD; 1973–30 Aug 81 stationed at Baltimore, MD, and used for LE, SAR, and light icebreaking; May–Jun 79 hauled garbage during New York City strike; 31 Aug 81–1 Jul 86 stationed at Portsmouth, VA, and used for LE, SAR, and light icebreaking.

Mohican

1945–47 stationed at New York, NY, and used for LE and SAR; 1948–75 stationed at Norfolk, VA, and used for LE and SAR; 5 Feb 57 assisted Italian MV *Emanuele V. Parodi* following explosion; 26 Feb 65 assisted German MV *Black Swan*, which had fire on board in Hampton Roads; 16 Jun 65 designated on-scene commander following a collision between Norwegian MV *Blue Master* and USS *Hartley* off Cape Henry; 14 Apr 66 escorted Israeli MV *Avadet* following fire off Norfolk, VA; 7 Jul 69 medevaced crewman from MV *Texaco Mississippi* off Hampton Roads; Aug 69 surveyed James R. in cooperation with Civil Defense following flooding; 29 Nov 69 towed disabled PC *Carefree* from Ship Shoal Inlet to Portsmouth, VA; 4 Jul 70 helped fight fire in oil-storage tank, Sewells Point, VA; 1976–84 stationed at Portsmouth, VA, and used for LE and SAR.

Ojibwa

1944–54 stationed at Boston, MA, and used for LE, SAR, and light icebreaking; 29 Nov 51 assisted following collision between MV *Ventura* and FV *Lynn* near Boston, MA; 1954–Aug 79 stationed at Buffalo, NY, and used for LE, SAR, and light icebreaking; Feb 65 broke ice in Buffalo, NY, area during harsh winter; 4 May 65 sustained engine casualty near Buffalo, NY, while breaking ice—towed to port by cutter *Kaw*; Jan 68 experimented with icebreaking plow Alexbow in Great Lakes; Aug 79–Apr 80 converted from fresh- to salt-water ops—plans to be stationed at Yorktown, VA, and used for training cancelled.

Sauk

1944–65 stationed at New York, NY, and used for LE, SAR, and light icebreaking; 4–6 Jan 63 grounded in Hudson R. and sank—raised; 2 Jul 64 delivered incubator to MV *Maasdam* in New York harbor; 1965–68 stationed at Gloucester City, NJ, and used for LE, SAR, and light icebreaking; 1968–30 Apr 85 stationed at New York, NY, and used for LE, SAR, and light icebreaking; 12 Dec 68 assisted following a fire on British MV *Manchester Miller* in New York harbor; Dec 69 directed traffic during salvage of tanker *Princess Bay*, Tremley Point, NJ; 9 Feb 70 assisted in refloating tanker *Desert Princess* aground in Hell Gate; 11 Feb 70 while towing sludge for state of NJ, barge struck RR bridge at Perth Amboy; May–Jun 79 hauled garbage during New York City strike; 3 Mar 80 helped fight fire at Weehawken Pier, NY; 17 Jun 80 along with CG small craft fought fire on tug *Hudson River #4* on the Hudson R.

Snohomish

1944–46 stationed at Boston, MA, and used for wartime duties, LE, SAR, and light icebreaking; 1947–Apr 86 stationed at Rockland, ME, and used for LE, SAR, and light icebreaking; 4 Oct 50 along with cutters *Acushnet* and *Cowslip* freed MV *Berwindale* aground in Kennebec R.; mid-Jul 65 assisted in unsuccessful search for ditched USAF C-121 85 mi E of Nantucket; 24 Oct 67 helped fight fire on Indian MV *Vishva Mangal* near Searsport, ME; Jan 68 broke ice off Maine; 8 Oct 68 towed disabled FV *Halhawk* 25 mi ESE of Matinicus I. to Rockland, ME; May–Jun 79 hauled garbage during New York City strike; 13 Jan 84 damaged after hitting a submerged object while breaking ice in the Penobscot R.

Yankton

1943–47 stationed at Philadelphia, PA, and used for wartime duties, LE and SAR; 1947–28 Sep 84 stationed at Portland, ME, and used for LE, SAR, and light icebreaking; 27 Nov 66 towed disabled FV *Plymouth* from 12 mi S of Grand Manan I. to Boston, MA; Jan 68 broke ice in New Bedford, MA, area; 30 Dec 69–1 Jan 70 relieved commercial tug of towing blazing tanker *Dean Reinauer* from Portland, ME, and towed seaward while fighting fire.

Most Coast Guard tugs stationed along the East Coast, including the *Sauk*, were used to haul garbage during a New York towboat strike in May–Jun 59. The *Sauk* maneuvers through the ice-choked Hudson R. on 1 Feb 71.

110-FOOT TUGS

Name	Hull Number	Builder	Keel Laid	Launched	Commissioned	Disposition
Manitou	WYTM 60 WYT 60	Coast Guard Yard, Curtis Bay, MD	20 May 42	29 Sep 42	15 Feb 43	*Decomm* 19 Nov 80
Kaw (ex-*Kennebec*)	WYTM 61 WYT 61	Coast Guard Yard, Curtis Bay, MD	9 May 42	6 Oct 42	1 Mar 43	*Decomm* 22 Jun 89

Cost $587,209 each (hull & machinery)

Hull
Displacement (tons)   346 fl (1963); 296 light (1963)
Length   110′ oa; 105′ bp
Beam   26′5″ max
Draft   11′11″ max (1963)

Machinery
Main Engines   1 electric motor driven by 2 Elliot Electric Co. generators driven by 2 Ingersoll Rand 8-cyl diesels
SHP   1,000
Propellers   single

Performance
Max Speed   11.6 kts, 1,600-mi radius (1963)
Max Sustained   10.0 kts, 1,800-mi radius (1963)

Logistics
Fuel Oil (95%)   7,700 gal
Complement   1 warrant, 19 men (1963)

Electronics
Radar   SPN-11 (1963)

Armament   none

Design
   The *Manitou*-type 110-foot tugs were contracted on 31 May 41. They differed from the 110-foot *Arundel* type only in machinery installation.

Kaw

1946–48 stationed at Portland, ME, and used for LE, SAR, and light icebreaking; 2 Mar 47 located disabled FV *Lucy and Evelyn*, which had been lost by the *Algonquin* and towed her to New Bedford, MA; 27 Dec 47 fought pier fire in Portland, ME; 1949–51 stationed at Sault Ste. Marie, MI, and used for LE, SAR, and light icebreaking; 1952–79 stationed at Cleveland, OH, and used for LE, SAR, and light icebreaking; 22 Apr–6 May 52 towed *Tahoma* from Cleveland, OH, to 43°48′N, 64°47′W where tow was transferred to *Cherokee*; Feb 65 broke ice in Cleveland, OH, area during harsh winter; 4 May 65 towed disabled cutter *Ojibwa* to Buffalo, NY; Jan 68 broke ice on Huron R.; 31 Jan 69 helped break ice jam below Monroe, MI, thus removing threat of flooding to the city.

Manitou

1946–48 stationed at Philadelphia, PA, and used for LE, SAR, and light icebreaking; 1949–80 stationed at New York, NY, and used for LE, SAR, and light icebreaking; 24 May 57 assisted sightseeing boat aground off Statue of Liberty; 8 Jul 66 helped fight fire at Hess Oil Plant, Perth Amboy, NJ; 7 Sep 66 helped fight fire on German liner *Hanseatic* in New York, NY; Oct 72 helped fight fire when barge *Ocean 80* exploded at Arthur Kill, NJ; Mar–Apr 78 broke ice on Kennebec R.; May–Jun 79 hauled garbage during New York City strike; 12 Feb 80 helped fight fire on board tank-cleaning vessel *Peter Frank* 1 mi E of Bayonne Bridge, NJ; 1 Sep 80 assisted disabled dredge *Hyde* near Rockaway Inlet.

Cutter *Kaw* on 3 Jun 59. The 110-foot tug series were very successful light icebreakers, and most units, including the *Kaw*, were used in this role.

110-FOOT TUGS

Name	Hull Number	Builder	Launched	Commissioned	Disposition
Arundel	WYTM 90 WYT 90	Gulfport Works, Port Arthur, TX	24 Jun 39	6 Jul 39	*Decomm* 1982
Mahoning	WYTM 91 WYT 91	Gulfport Works, Port Arthur, TX	22 Jul 39	7 Aug 39	*Decomm* 1 Oct 84
Naugatuck	WYTM 92 WYT 92	Defoe Boat Works, Bay City, MI	23 Mar 39	12 Apr 39	*Decomm* 15 Jan 79
Raritan	WYTM 93 WYT 93	Defoe Boat Works, Bay City, MI	23 Mar 39	11 Apr 39	*Decomm* 14 May 88

Cost	$309,000 each
Hull	
Displacement (tons)	375 fl (1961); 335 light (1961)
Length	110' oa; 105' bp
Beam	26'5" max
Draft	11'6" max (1961)
Machinery	
Main Engines	1 Westinghouse electric motor connected to 2 Westinghouse generators driven by 2 General Motors 8-cyl diesels
SHP	1,000
Propellers	single
Performance	
Max Sustained	10.0 kts, 1,500-mi radius (1961)
Economic	8.0 kts, 2,000-mi radius (1961)
Logistics	
Fuel Oil (95%)	7,740 gal
Complement	1 warrant, 19 men (1961)
Electronics	
Radar	SPN-11 (1961)
Armament	none

Design

The *Arundel* type was a follow-on to the 110-foot *Calumet* type.

Arundel

1945–46 stationed at New York, NY, and used for LE, SAR, and light icebreaking; 1947 stationed at Portland, ME, and used for LE, SAR, and light icebreaking; 1948–51 stationed at New Bedford, MA, and used for LE, SAR, and light icebreaking; 1952–79 stationed at Chicago, IL, and used for LE, SAR, and light icebreaking; 8–9 Apr 56 towed to Detroit, MI, by cutter *Mesquite*; 20 Aug 65 assisted in search for debris from United Airlines crash in Lake Michigan; 15 Feb 68 helped free tug *Silver Star* from ice and escorted her to Holland, MI; 26 Feb 68 helped medevac crewman from tanker *Meteor* near St. Joseph, MI; 5 Apr 68 helped free grounded MV *Inglehart* in St. Mary's River; 11 Apr 70 helped free grounded MV *Stadacona* near the Mackinaw Bridge; 17 Apr 70 stood by MV *F. R. Denton* following fouling of propeller by buoy chain; 1980–82 stationed at Buffalo, NY, and used for LE, SAR, and light icebreaking.

Mahoning

1939–1 Oct 84 stationed at New York, NY, and used for customs boardings, LE, SAR, and light icebreaking; 11 Nov 65 assisted in fighting fire on board the Liberian tanker *Joan* in Bayonne, NJ; 16 Jun 66 assisted following collision between tankers *Texaco Massachusetts* and *Alva Cape* in Newark Channel; 8 Jul 66 helped fight fire at Hess Oil Plant, Perth Amboy, NJ; 25 Dec 67 helped fight fire on Norwegian MV *Dianet* in New York harbor; 27 Dec 68 assisted in containing gasoline leak following a collision and fire on barge *Russell 104* in New York harbor; 6 Aug 70

Cutter *Raritan* seized the MV *Sarah* off Long Beach, NY, on 28 Jul 87 for illegal commercial broadcasting from a ship.

helped fight fire on tanker *Poling Brothers 11* at Carteret, NJ; May–Jun 79 hauled garbage during New York City strike; 3 Mar 80 helped fight fire at Weehawken Pier, NY.

Naugatuck

1946–50 stationed at Seattle, WA, and used for LE and SAR; 1950–Sep 59 stationed at Port Angeles, WA, and used for LE and SAR; Sep 59–15 Jan 79 stationed at Sault Ste. Marie, MI, and used for LE, SAR, and light icebreaking; 10 May 65 assisted in search for survivors from U.S. MV *Cedarville* and Norwegian MV *Topdalsfjord* collision 1 mi NE of Mackinaw City, MI; Nov 65 assisted in rescue of survivors from tug *Miseford* and barge 8 mi W of Sault Ste. Marie, MI; 28 Nov 65 escorted listing British MV *Algosoo* to Waiska Bay; 14 Sep 66 escorted disabled MV *Lehigh*

to the Soo Canal; 25 Oct 66 assisted in freeing grounded MV *George A. Sloan* on Majors Shoal; 1 Apr 68 helped free MV *Gypsum* aground at Alpena, MI.

Raritan

1945–62 stationed at Portsmouth, VA, and used for LE and SAR; 1963–72 stationed at Milwaukee, WI, and used for LE, SAR, and light icebreaking; 20 Aug 65 assisted in search for debris from United Airlines crash in Lake Michigan; 1973–79 stationed at Grand Haven, MI, and used for LE, SAR, and light icebreaking; 1980–88 stationed at Governors I., NY, and used for LE, SAR, and light icebreaking; 28 Jul 87 seized MV *Sarah* off Long Beach, NY, for illegal commercial broadcasting from a ship.

110-FOOT TUGS

Name	Hull Number	Builder	Launched	Commissioned	Disposition
Calumet	WYTM 86 WYT 86	Charleston Navy Yard, SC	28 Sep 34	3 Dec 34	*Decomm* 29 Sep 67 *Sold* 25 Nov 68
Hudson	WYTM 87 WYT 87	Portsmouth Navy Yard, NH	Oct 34	31 Oct 34	*Decomm* 31 Oct 68 *Trans* to Northwestern University, 8 Jul 70
Navesink	WYTM 88 WYT 88	Charleston Navy Yard, SC	28 Sep 34	5 Jan 35	*Decomm* 30 Oct 68 *Sold* 21 May 70
Tuckahoe	WYTM 89 WYT 89	Charleston Navy Yard, SC	28 Sep 34	30 Jan 35	*Decomm* 14 Nov 68 *Donated* to HEW 16 Apr 69

Cost	$236,000 each
Hull	
Displacement (tons)	291 fl (1961); 274 light (1961)
Length	110′6″ oa; 104′ bp
Beam	24′ max
Draft	10′11″ max (1961)
Machinery	
Main Engines	1 General Electric motor connected to 2 General Electric generators driven by 2 McIntosh Seymour 6-cyl diesels
SHP	800
Propellers	single
Performance	
Max Sustained	11.0 kts, 850-mi radius (1961)
Economic	10.0 kts, 1,200-mi radius (1961)
Logistics	
Fuel Oil (95%)	3,800 gal
Complement	1 warrant, 19 men (1961)
Electronics	
Radar	MR-3A
Armament	none (1961)

Design

The design of the *Calumet*-type 110-foot tugs proved to be so successful that the 3 subsequent classes were only slightly modified. In Jan 40 tests comparing the icebreaking ability of the 110-foot tugs to the 165-foot (B) class were conducted. The tugs proved to be far superior in breaking ability and maneuverability.

Calumet

1945–29 Sep 67 stationed at San Francisco, CA, and used for customs boardings, escorting of ammunition-laden vessels to and from the Naval

Tug *Calumet* on 20 Jan 66. She was frequently used to escort ammunition-laden vessels to and from the Naval Weapons Station, Concord, CA.

Weapons Station, Concord, CA, and LE, and SAR; 26 Sep 66 helped fight fire on barge in San Francisco harbor.

Hudson

1944–58 stationed at New Orleans, LA, and used for customs boardings, LE, and SAR; 1958–62 stationed at Brownsville, TX, and used for customs boardings, LE, and SAR; 1962–68 stationed at Norfolk, VA, and used for customs boardings, LE, and SAR.

Navesink

1944–47 stationed at Norfolk, VA, and used for customs boardings, LE, and SAR; 1947–68 stationed at New York, NY, and used for customs boardings, LE, and SAR; 16 Jun 66 assisted following collision between tankers *Texaco Massachusetts* and *Alva Cape* in Newark Channel; 7 Sep 66

helped fight fire on German liner *Hanseatic* in New York, NY; 25 Dec 67 helped fight fire on Norwegian MV *Dianet* in New York harbor.

Tuckahoe

1945–46 stationed at New Orleans, LA, and used for customs boardings, LE, and SAR; 1946–68 stationed at New York, NY, and used for customs boardings, LE, and SAR; 24 May 57 assisted sightseeing boat aground off Statue of Liberty; 11 Nov 65 assisted in fighting fire on board Liberian tanker *Joan* in Bayonne, NJ; 16 Jun 66 assisted following collision between tankers *Texaco Massachusetts* and *Alva Cape* in Newark Channel; 8 Jul 66 helped fight fire at Hess Oil Plant, Perth Amboy, NJ; 25 Dec 67 helped fight fire on Norwegian MV *Dianet* in New York harbor; 18 Oct 68 assisted following a collision between tanker *Samuel H. Herron* and sludge barge *Newton Creek* in New York harbor.

WAT AND WYT TYPE CUTTERS DISPOSED OF SHORTLY AFTER WORLD WAR II*

Name	Hull Number	Class	Decomm	Sold/Trans
Winnisimmet	WYT 84	96-foot	Oct 45	22 Jul 46
Golden Gate	WYT 94	110-foot	22 Nov 45	8 Apr 47
Carrabasset	WAT 55	EA	26 Jul 46	N/A
Tioga	WYT 74	95-foot	14 Oct 46	22 Mar 47
Shawnee	WAT 54	158-foot	21 Nov 46	28 Nov 47
Manhattan	WYT 95	120-foot	30 Jan 47	28 Jul 47

* See Scheina, *WWII Cutters,* for details.

Miscellaneous Large Cutters

Perhaps due to the multimission nature of the Coast Guard, the service has never enforced the rigidity in ship designators as practiced by the U.S. Navy. Coast Guard Vessels may pass from one designator to another without much fuss. Also, one may find two ships assigned to the same mission but not sharing the same designator. Such is the case of the *Tahoma* (WAGE 10) and the *Yonaguska* (WYT 195).

Many of the cutters in this section concerning miscellaneous large cutters reflect the numerous special tasks the Coast Guard performs from time to time.

NAVY *AUK* CLASS

Name	Hull Number	Builder	Keel Laid	Launched	Commissioned	Disposition
Tanager	WTR 885 MSF 385 AM 385	American Shipbuilding Co., Lorain, OH	29 Mar 44	9 Dec 44	28 Jul 45 (USN) 11 Jul 64 (CG)	*Decomm* 1 Feb 72 *Sold* 15 Nov 72

Cost | N/A
Hull
  Displacement (tons) | 1,112 fl (1966), 788 light (1966)
  Length | 220'7" oa; 215' bp
  Beam | 32'3" max
  Draft | 10'2" max (1966)
Machinery
  Main Engines | 4 generators driven by 4 electric motors driven by 4 Cleveland diesels
  BHP | 3,474
  Propellers | single
Performance
  Max Sustained | 16.0 kts, 4,608-mi radius (1966)
  Economic | 12.0 kts, 7,200-mi radius (1966)
Logistics
  Fuel Oil (95%) | 65,137 gal
  Complement | 5 officers, 1 warrant, 34 men (1966)
Electronics
  Detection Radar | SPS-23 (1966)
  Sonar | SQS-1 (1966)
Armament | 1 3"/50; 1 Mk 11 ASW projector
Design

    The Navy *Auk*-class ships were designed as minesweepers.

Tanager

1964–72 stationed at Yorktown, VA, and used for training; 13 Aug 69 escorted distressed ketch *Arcturus* from Sand Shoal Inlet to Norfolk, VA.

The *Tanager,* photographed on 20 Mar 70, was acquired from the U.S. Navy and served in the Coast Guard between 1964 and 1972 as a training ship. When acquiring ships from the Navy, the Coast Guard has most often retained the original name and hull number. However, in addition to adding the "W" before the ship's designator, frequently it is completely changed to reflect the ship's new Coast Guard mission.

GERMANY NAVY *HORST WESSEL* CLASS

Name	Hull Number	Builder	Keel Laid	Launched	Commissioned	Disposition
Eagle (ex-*Horst Wessel*)	WIX 327	Blohm & Voss, Hamburg, Germany	N/A	13 Jun 36	1936 (Ger. Navy) 15 May 46 (CG)	Active

Cost — N/A

Hull
Displacement (tons) — 1,519 light (1987); 1,816 fl (1987)
Length — 295' oa; 231' wl
Beam — 39'1" max
Draft — 17' max (1987)

Machinery
Main Engines — 1 Caterpillar diesel (early 1980s)
BHP — 1,000
Propellers — single

Performance
Max Speed — 17 kts (under sail)
Max Sustained — 10 kts (under power)
Cruising — 7.5 kts, 5,450-mi-radius (under power—1987)

Logistics
Fuel Oil (95%) — 79t
Complement — 19 officers, 46 men, 175 cadets and instructors (1987)

Electronics
Detection Radar — 1 SPS-64

Armament — none

Design

The *Eagle* was constructed for the German Navy as the *Horst Wessel*. She was acquired by the CG at the end of WWII. Initially, the future *Eagle* was selected by the Soviet Union when the war prizes were divided among the victors. The four available sail ships had been divided into three lots—two large merchant ships being grouped together. The Soviets drew Number 1, Great Britain Number 2, and the United States Number 3. Before the results of the draw were officially announced, the U.S. representative, through quiet diplomacy, convinced the Soviets to trade draws.

The sail area is 21,215 square feet; the height of the fore and main masts are 174'2"; and she carries 344t of ballast. The *Eagle* has over 20 miles of rigging. Over 200 lines must be coordinated during a major maneuver. The sails can provide the equivalent of several thousand through-shaft horsepower.

The *Eagle* 14 Jul 64 in New York harbor. She is the seventh cutter to have this name. The first was among the original ten cutters authorized in 1790 when the service was established. The *Eagle* has sister ships serving in the Portuguese, Romanian, and Soviet navies.

The *Eagle* during May 76. The *Eagle* did not acquire her CG slash until mid-1976, almost ten years after the other cutters. At first, the adoption of the identification marking of this sail-training vessel created quite a stir in the U.S. sailing community.

The *Horst Wessel* in bombed-out Bremerhaven, 16 Apr 46. She is carrying the first of four figureheads to be fitted to the ship. The original eagle figurehead, shown here, is now in the CG Museum at the CG Academy, New London, CT. The second eagle, which was carried from the 1950s until the early 1970s, had been removed from the former training ship *Chase*. It was affectionately known as the "pigeon" because it was too small for a ship the size of the *Eagle*. This was replaced by a fiberglass likeness of the original, which served until damaged in the early 1970s. The present eagle figurehead is a replica of the original, carved from mahogany and mounted in time for the 1976 Bicentennial parade.

Eagle

1946–90 served as training ship for CG Academy, New London, CT; 1946 basically followed Columbus's route across the Atlantic, during which she rode out a hurricane; Sep 54 weathered hurricane Carol while en route to Bermuda; 1964 hosted OpSail in New York as part of the World's Fair; 1976 hosted OpSail during U.S. Bicentennial celebration; 1986 hosted centennial celebration for the Statue of Liberty—for itinerary of cadet cruises see George Putz, *Eagle, America's Sailing Square-Rigger* (Globe Pequot Press, 1986).

MARITIME COMMISSION C1-M-AV1 TYPE

Name	Hull Number	Builder	Keel Laid	Launched	Commissioned	Disposition
Courier (ex-*Coastal Messenger*, ex-*Doddridge*)	WTR 410 WAGR 410 AK 176	Froeming Brothers, Inc., Milwaukee, WI	25 Jan 45	1945	25 Mar 45 (commercial) 15 Feb 52 (CG) 30 Apr 66 (CG)	*Decomm* 25 Aug 64 (CG) *Decomm* 1972 (CG)
Unalga (ex-*Tipton*)	WAK 185 AKA 215 MC 2169	Leatham D. Smith Shipbuilding Co., Sturgeon Bay, WI	28 Dec 44	13 Mar 45	10 Apr 45 (mercantile) 9 Oct 46 (USN) 21 Oct 46 (CG)	*Decomm* 19 Jan 50
Kukui (ex-*Colquitt*)	WAK 186 AK 174	Froeming Brothers, Inc., Milwaukee, WI	1944	1945	11 Mar 45 (commercial) Aug 45 (USN) Mar 46 (CG)	*Decomm & trans* to Philippines 29 Feb 72

Cost   N/A

Hull
  Displacement (tons)   5,650 fl (1966); 3,929 light (1966)
  Length   338'9" oa; 320' bp
  Beam   50'4" max
  Draft   17'3" max (1966)

Machinery
  Main Engines   1 Nordberg diesel
  BHP   1,700
  Propellers   single

Performance
  Max Sustained   10.6 kts, 24,273-mi radius (1966)
  Economic   8.0 kts, 25,230-mi radius (1966)

Logistics
  Fuel Oil (95%)   306,176 gal
  Complement   8 officers, 3 warrants, 101 men (1950); 8 officers,
                             1 warrant, 42 men (1966)

Deck Gear
  Boom Capacity   8 tons
  Hoist Power

Electronics
  Detection Radar   SO-4 (1950); SPS-23 (1966)

Armament   none (1966)

Design
  The C1-M-AV1 type was constructed to Maritime Commission standards.

Courier

15 Feb 52–25 Aug 64 stationed at the island of Rhodes, Greece, and operated for U.S. Information Agency as a relay station for "Voice of America"—the transmitting equipment was the most powerful of its kind ever installed in a ship; 1 Jul 65–1972 stationed at Yorktown, VA, and used for the training of reservists.

Kukui

1946–72 stationed at Honolulu, HI, and used for construction and servicing Loran stations; 15 Jun 53 rendered medical assistance to civilian workman injured at Bataan Loran station; 24 Jul 70 collided with MV *Myoriki Maru No 25* 6 mi from Yokosuka, Japan—minor damage to each vessel.

Unalga

1 Apr 46–19 Jan 50 stationed at Seattle, WA, and used to construct and service Loran stations in Alaska; 28 Nov 48 rendered assistance to MV *Kasilof* at 58°31'N, 138°00'W.

Cutter *Courier* in Jul 63 at Rhodes, Greece. She is serving as a radio-relay broadcasting station for Voice of America. The *Courier* was used in this role from Sep 52 to Jun 64, when she was replaced by a land radio-relay station at Rhodes.

Cutter *Kukui* on 8 Jan 70. She and sister *Unalga* were used to construct and supply Loran stations throughout the Pacific. Landing craft were used to transport building materials ashore at the remote locations.

ARMY 381 DESIGN

Name	Hull Number	Builder	Keel Laid	Launched	Commissioned	Disposition
Nettle (ex-FS 396)	WAK 169	Ingalls Shipbuilding Co., Decatur, AL	N/A	N/A	1945 (USA) 1 Oct 47 (CG)	*Decomm* by USA 18 Jan 46 *Decomm* & *trans* to Philippines 9 Jan 68
Trillium (ex-FS 397)	WAK 170	Ingalls Shipbuilding Co., Decatur, AL	N/A	N/A	1945 (USA) 23 Aug 46 (CG)	*Decomm* 15 Nov 50 *Trans* to USN 7 Jul 55

Cost	$805,494
Hull	
Displacement (tons)	935 fl; 707 light (1945)
Length	176'1" oa; 165' bp
Beam	32' mb
Draft	10' max (1945)
Machinery	
Main Engines	2 General Motors diesels
SHP	1,000
Propellers	twin
Performance	
Max Sustained	13.7 kts, 4,000-mi radius (1945)
Logistics	
Fuel Oil (95%)	70 tons
Complement	4 officers, 26 men (1945)
Deck Gear	
Boom Capacity	15 tons
Electronics	
Detection Radar	SO-8 (1955); SC (1966)
Armament	1 40mm/60 (1945)

Design

The Army 381 type was built for the Transportation Corps. The class was constructed of steel. Both ships had been manned by the Coast Guard for the Army, the *Nettle* between 18 Jan 45 and 18 Jan 46 and the *Trillium* between 20 Feb 45 and 23 Aug 46.

Nettle

1946–52 stationed at Kwajalein Atoll, Marshall I., and 1952–53 stationed at Guam, providing logistics for CG Loran stations at Ulithi, Saipan, Cocos, Kwajalein, and Kwadak islands   also serviced A/N at Tinian and Rota in the Mariana I.; Aug 53–Dec 67 stationed at Sangley Point, Cavite, Philippines, and provided logistics for CG Loran stations at Bataan, Batanes, Naulo Point, Zambales, Talumpulan, Busuanga, Tarumpitao Point, Palawan, and Panay; 1 Sep 58 righted capsized junk *Low Kow Wong How* and rescued crew.

Trillium

23 Aug 46–19 Nov 46 stationed at Honolulu, HI, and provided logistics to Okinawa, Guam, Eniwetok, and among the Hawaiian I.; 19 Nov 47–15 Jun 50 stationed at Guam and provided logistics to Iwo Jima, Okinawa, Kwajalein, and the Philippines; 15 Jun–15 Nov 50 stationed at San Francisco, CA; Sep 50 towed cutter *Hermes* from Pearl Harbor, HI, to Alameda, CA.

On occasion, Coast Guard cutters have been painted gray during peacetime. The *Nettle* sails from Sangley Point, the Philippines, on 9 Jul 57. Tensions were high in Pacific waters due to the confrontation over Quemoy and Matsu islands by the two Chinas. In order to clearly identify the *Nettle* as a military ship, she was painted gray. Previously, she had been painted as a Coast Guard tender—black hull, white superstructure, buff mast, and buff stack with a black cap.

165-FOOT (A) CUTTER

Name	Hull Number	Builder	Keel Laid	Launched	Commissioned	Disposition
Tahoma	WAGE 10 WPG 80	Defoe Works, Bay City, MI	23 Oct 33 contracted	5 Sep 34	22 Oct 34	*Decomm* 1 Jul 53 *Sold* 17 Oct 55

Cost	$525,550
Hull	
Displacement (tons)	1,050 fl (1945)
Length	165' oa; 150' wl
Beam	36' mb; 36' wl
Draft	14' max (1945)
Machinery	
Main Engines	1 DeLaval double-reduction geared turbine
Main Boilers	2 Babcock & Wilcox 310 psi, 200° F superheat
SHP	1,500 total
Propellers	single, 4 blades
Performance	
Max Sustained	12.0 kts, 2,500-mi radius (1945)
Economic	10.0 kts, 3,300-mi radius (1945)
Logistics	
Fuel Oil (95%)	41,500 gal
Complement	2 officers, 34 men (1953)
Electronics	
Detection Radar	SF (1945)
Sonar	QCJ-3 (1945)
Armament	2 3"/50 (single); 2 20mm/80 (single); 2 dc tracks; 4 Y-guns; 2 mousetrap (1942)

Design

The 165-foot-cutter units were the first Coast Guard cutters to employ geared-turbine drive. They were constructed from PWA funds. The hull design was derived from the *Tallapoosa* type of 1915. The 165As were the first flush-deck type with good freeboard. These cutters were designed for light icebreaking. The plating doubled around the bow, the cutaway forefront, short length, and the medium draft made these cutters good ice boats. They had a heavy steel belt around the vessel at the waterline and relatively short bilge kegs, so in a seaway they had a tendency to roll considerably. Also, while in Greenland during WWII they were handicapped by their short cruising range.

The *Tahoma* had five sisters, the *Algonquin, Comanche, Escanaba, Mohawk,* and *Onondaga.* The *Escanaba* was sunk on 13 June 43. The other units were decommissioned shortly after WWII and sold a few years later. The *Tahoma* was redesignated a WAGE—miscellaneous auxiliary, examination vessel—on 1 May 52.

Tahoma

24 Oct 47 decommissioned and placed in storage at Cleveland, OH; 24 Apr–1 Jun 52 towed from Cleveland, OH, to Curtis Bay, MD, by *Kaw* and *Cherokee*; 16 Jul 52 recommissioned and stationed at Norfolk, VA; 31 Aug 52–25 May 53 served as Chesapeake Bay entrance guard ship.

Painted bright yellow with the word "Guard" in black, the *Tahoma* was anchored at the entrance to the Chesapeake Bay on 2 Sep 52 for the purpose of identifying all in-bound ships. This was the height of the Cold War; although the Soviet Union had the atom bomb, it could not effectively deliver it by aircraft. Other means had to be guarded against. Approaching ships identified themselves by radio, giving name, nationality, home port, last port of call, destination, and estimated time of arrival at the entrance to the bay.

WAG-TYPE CUTTERS DISPOSED OF SHORTLY AFTER WORLD WAR II*

Name	Hull Number	Class	Decomm	Sold/Trans
Asterion	WAK 123	EA	20 Jul 44	14 Mar 46
Manasquan	WAG 276	EA	22 Feb 45	11 Mar 46
Menemsha	WAG 274	EA	24 Sep 45	6 Mar 47
Monomoy	WAG 275	EA	12 Oct 45	13 Feb 51
Manhasset	WAG 48	EA	15 Oct 45	16 Oct 46

*See Scheina, *WW II Cutters,* for details.

FERRIES STATIONED AT GOVERNORS ISLAND, NY

Name	Tonnage	Remarks
Major General	est 500	former USA ferry, CG service 1966–70
The Tides	774 fl	former New York City ferry; CG service 1966–90
Lt. Samuel S. Coursen	869	former USA ferry, CG service 1966–90
Pvt. Nicholas Minute	869	former USA ferry, CG service 1966–90
Governor	1,600 fl	former Puget Sound ferry, CG service 1982–90

Tenders

The Coast Guard maintains a large fleet of buoy tenders to serve the tens of thousands of aids-to-navigation that mark our bays, sounds, harbors, and rivers. Since these ships operate under a wide variety of conditions—from placid, shallow water, to deep, heavy seas—and are required to undertake numerous tasks—from driving pilings on rivers to setting large navigation buoys in deep water—their size and capability varies considerably.

PROJECTED SEAGOING BUOY TENDER

Name	Hull Number	Name	Hull Number
Number yet to be determined		Number yet to be determined	

Cost	N/A	Deck Gear	
Hull		Boom Capacity	20t
Displacement (tons)	N/A	Electronics	
Length	N/A	Radar	navigational type
Beam	N/A	Armament	small arms
Draft	14′ max (1988)	Design	

Machinery
Main Engines	N/A
BHP	N/A
Propellers	N/A

Performance
Max (goal)	15 kts (1988)
Economical (goal)	12 kts, 6,000-mi radius (1988)

Logistics
Complement	4 to 6 officers, 32 to 34 men (1988)

Design

The requirements for these tenders call for them to be able to operate in any ocean with a minimum of 30 days' endurance. They are to be able to work aids in at least 6-foot seas and have a minimum 15-ton side-loading capacity. Their buoy deck is to have a minimum 50-ton capacity. At a minimum, a design specification calls for a continuous 14-inch icebreaking capacity at 3 knots and a minimum ramming capacity of 2 feet. The minimum towing requirement is for a like-size vessel at 8 knots in 8-foot seas. They are to be able to remain afloat with any two compartments flooded.

75-FOOT RIVER TENDER CLASS

Name	Hull Number	Builder	Commissioned
Kankakee	WLR 75500	Avondale Industries, Small Boat Division, New Orleans, LA	Building
Greenbrier	WLR 75501	Avondale Industries, Small Boat Division, New Orleans, LA	Building

Cost	N/A	Performance	N/A
Hull		Logistics	
Displacement (tons)	est. 150 fl (1989)	Fuel Oil (95%)	3,487 gal
Length	75′ oa; 73′ wl	Complement	13 (1989)
Beam	24′ molded	Electronics	N/A
Draft	4′8″ max (1989)	Design	

Machinery
Main Engines	2 diesels
BHP	1,000
Propellers	twin

Design

These units are designed to work in tandem with a barge. Both are to commission by mid-1990.

160-FOOT INLAND CONSTRUCTION TENDERS

Name	Hull Number	Builder	Keel Laid	Launched	Commissioned	Disposition
Pamlico	WLIC 800	Coast Guard Yard, Curtis Bay, MD	1 Jun 74	13 Dec 75	11 Aug 76	Active
Hudson	WLIC 801	Coast Guard Yard, Curtis Bay, MD	6 Jun 75	29 May 76	14 Oct 76	Active
Kennebec	WLIC 802	Coast Guard Yard, Curtis Bay, MD	9 Jan 76	11 Dec 76	6 Apr 77	Active
Saginaw	WLIC 803	Coast Guard Yard, Curtis Bay, MD	5 Jul 76	11 Jun 77	22 Sep 77	Active

The *Pamlico* on 21 Jun 76 at the Coast Guard Yard, Curtis Bay, MD, prior to commissioning.

Cost — See Appropriations table

Hull
  Displacement (tons)   459 fl; 413 light (1976)
  Length   160' oa
  Beam   30' max
  Draft   3'10" max (1976)

Machinery
  Main Engines   2 Cummins diesels
  BHP   1,000 total
  Propellers   twin

Performance
  Max Sustained   11 kts, 1,400-mi radius (1967)
  Cruising   6.5 kts, 2,200-mi radius (1976)

Logistics
  Complement   13 men (1976)

Deck Gear
  Boom Capacity   9t

Electronics
  Radar   Raytheon 1900

Armament   none

Design
  The 160-foot inland construction tender is designed to fulfill the primary requirements for construction, maintenance, repair, and alterations of fixed A/N structures. The hull and superstructure are constructed of steel.

160-FOOT TENDERS—APPROPRIATIONS

Name	AC&I Year	Awarded	Scheduled Delivery	Construction Manhours	Costs (Contracted)
Pamlico	1974	22 Feb 74	1 Oct 75	N/A	$2,447,000
Hudson	1974	22 Feb 74	1 Dec 75	N/A	$2,000,000
Kennebec	1975	7 Jul 75	6 Apr 77	N/A	$3,182,000
Saginaw	1976	N/A	N/A	N/A	$3,635,000

Hudson

14 Oct 76–1990 stationed at Miami, FL, and used for A/N.

Kennebec

6 Apr 77–mid-1980 stationed at Fort Macon, NC, and used for A/N; mid-1980–1990 stationed at Portsmouth, VA, and used for A/N.

Pamlico

4 Jun 76–1990 stationed at New Orleans, LA, and used for A/N.

Saginaw

22 Sep 77–1990 stationed at Mobile, AL, and used for A/N.

75-FOOT RIVER TENDER CLASS

Name	Hull Number	Builder	Keel Laid	Launched	Commissioned	Disposition
Gasconade	WLR 75401	St. Louis Shipbuilding & Drydock Co., St. Louis, MO	N/A	N/A	15 Jan 64	Active
Muskingum	WLR 75402	Maxon Construction Co., Tell City, IN	1964	Mar 65	25 Mar 65	Active
Wyaconda	WLR 75403	Maxon Construction Co., Tell City, IN	1964	7 Mar 65	30 May 65	Active
Chippewa	WLR 75404	Maxon Construction Co., Tell City, IN	Nov 64	N/A	5 Oct 65	Active
Cheyenne	WLR 75405	Maxon Construction Co., Tell City, IN	N/A	N/A	3 Oct 66	Active
Kickapoo	WLR 75406	Halter Marine Services Inc., New Orleans, LA	N/A	N/A	20 May 69	Active
Kanawha	WLR 75407	Halter Marine Corp., New Orleans, LA	N/A	N/A	22 Sep 69	Active
Patoka	WLR 75408	Halter Marine Corp., New Orleans, LA	N/A	N/A	9 Feb 70	Active
Chena	WLR 75409	Halter Marine Corp., New Orleans, LA	N/A	N/A	27 May 70	Active

Cost $374,423 (*Muskingum* & *Wyaconda*)
            $510,000 (*Chippewa*)

Hull
   Displacement (tons)   141 fl (1966); 127 light (1965)
   Length   75' oa; 73' bp
   Beam   22'1" max
   Draft   4'6" max (1966)

Machinery
   Main Engines   2 Caterpillar diesels
   BHP   600
   Propellers   twin

Performance
   Max Speed   10 kts (1966)
   Cruising   8.5 kts, 7,250-mi radius (1965)

Logistics
   Fuel Oil (95%)   6,700 gal

Complement   10 men (1966)
Electronics
   Navigation Radar   CRM
Armament   none
Design

The 75-foot river-tender class is designed to work in tandem with a 90-foot barge. Typically, a 75-foot tender services 250 buoy stations.

Chena

27 May 70–1983 stationed at Natchez, TX, and used for A/N; 1983–89 stationed at Hickman, KY, and used for A/N.

Cheyenne

15 Oct 65–70 stationed at Leavenworth, KS, and used for A/N; 1970–90 stationed at St. Louis, MO, and used for A/N.

Tender *Patoka,* 10 Aug 71, with her work barge.

Chippewa

5 Oct 65–1971 stationed at Omaha, NE, and used for A/N; 1971–78 stationed at Hickman, KY, and used for A/N; 1978–90 stationed at Owensboro, KY, and used for A/N.

Gasconade

15 Jan 64–Jul 65 stationed at St. Louis, MO, and used for A/N; Jul–27 Sep 65 stationed at Florence, NE, and used for A/N; 27 Sep 65–1990 stationed at Omaha, NE, and used for A/N.

Kanawha

22 Sep 69–1989 stationed at Memphis, TN, and used for A/N.

Kickapoo

20 May 69–1976 stationed at Pine Bluff, AR, and used for A/N; 1976–90 stationed at Vicksburg, MS, and used for A/N.

Muskingum

25 Mar 65–1973 stationed at Brunswick, MD, and used for A/N; 1973–78 stationed at Memphis, TN, and used for A/N; 1978–90 stationed at Sallisaw, OK, and used for A/N.

Patoka

9 Feb 70–1978 stationed at Sallisaw, OK, and used for A/N; 1978–90 stationed at Greenville, MS, and used for A/N; 18 Dec 84 helped recover barges after a towboat with 40 barges collided with a bridge near Port Memphis, TN.

Wyaconda

30 May 65–Jun 73 stationed at Leavenworth, KS, and used for A/N; Jun–Jul 70 assisted cleanup following an oil spill on Missouri R.; Jun 73–1990 stationed at Dubuque, IA, and used for A/N.

80-FOOT TENDER

Name	Hull Number	Builder	Keel Laid	Launched	Commissioned	Disposition
Tern	WLI 80801	Coast Guard Yard, Curtis Bay, MD	15 Jan 68	15 Jun 68	7 Feb 69	*Decomm* Jul 77

Cost — $1,169,419

Hull
Displacement (tons) — 173 fl (1969); 133 light (1969)
Length — 81'3" oa; 80' bp
Beam — 24'7" max
Draft — 5'9" max (1969)

Machinery
Main Engines — 2 diesels
BHP — 500
Propellers — twin

Performance
Max Speed — 10 kts (1969)

Logistics
Complement — 7 men (1969)

Deck Gear
Crane Capacity — 5 tons

Electronics
Navigation Radar — N/A

Armament — none

Design

The *Tern* was designed as a stern-loading tender. The greatest value of this design was its capability of hoisting a large buoy as compared to the size of the tender. The *Tern* could handle a 7 x 17 buoy; the smallest side-loading tender capable of handling this buoy was the 122-foot *Narcissus*. The *Tern* had a number of shortcomings, principally excessive noise on the deck caused by the gantry crane driver, poor visibility of the crane operator, inadequate complement, numerous blind spots on the bridge that interfered with the conn of the vessel, and an overly complicated propulsion and control system. Qualities includes excellent maneuverability and habitability. The two 250-hp diesels were fitted to right-angle drive train. The *Tern* had a 125-hp bow-thruster.

Tern

1969 used for test and evaluation; 1970–77 stationed at Governors I., NY, and used for A/N.

The *Tern*, 5 Feb 69. The first two digits in her hull number indicate that she is 80 feet long. This system is somewhat casual; sometimes it refers to the overall length and other times, as in this case, to the length between perpendiculars.

157-FOOT TENDERS

Name	Hull Number	Builder	Keel Laid	Launched	Commissioned	Disposition
Red Wood	WLM 685	Coast Guard Yard, Curtis Bay, MD	1 Jul 63	4 Apr 64	4 Aug 64	Active
Red Beech	WLM 686	Coast Guard Yard, Curtis Bay, MD	14 Oct 63	6 Jun 64	20 Nov 64	Active
Red Birch	WLM 687	Coast Guard Yard, Curtis Bay, MD	6 Jul 64	19 Feb 65	7 Jun 65	Active
Red Cedar	WLM 688	Coast Guard Yard, Curtis Bay, MD	1 Jul 69	1 Aug 70	18 Dec 70	Active
Red Oak	WLM 689	Coast Guard Yard, Curtis Bay, MD	26 Oct 70	19 Jun 71	10 Dec 71	Active

Cost	See Appropriations table		Logistics	
Hull			Fuel Oil (95%)	17,000 gal
Displacement (tons)	525 fl		Complement	5 officers, 29 enlisted (1964)
Length	157' oa		Deck Gear	
Beam	31' max		Boom Capacity	10 tons
Draft	7' max (1964)		Electronics	
Machinery			Navigation Radar	N/A
Main Engines	2 Caterpillar diesels		Armament	none
BHP	1,800		Design	
Propellers	twin			
Performance				
Max Speed	13 kts (1964)			
Cruising	11 kts, 3,000-mi radius (1964)			

Design

The hulls of these 157-foot coastal buoy tenders are reinforced for icebreaking. The conventional ship's wheel is absent, being replaced by a simple tiller. The hydraulic steering system provides a change from full left to full right rudder in 6 seconds.

157-FOOT TENDERS—APPROPRIATIONS

Name	AC&I Year	Awarded	Scheduled Delivery	Construction Manhours	Costs (Contracted)
Red Wood	1963	10 Aug 62	N/A	209,494	$2,779,624
Red Beech	1964	5 May 63	N/A	167,555	$2,382,984
Red Birch	1965	23 May 64	N/A	147,250	$2,181,506
Red Cedar	1969	5 Dec 68	15 Aug 70	206,028	$3,402,176
Red Oak	1970	10 Feb 70	22 Nov 71	N/A	$3,328,077

Red Beech

20 Oct 64–1990 stationed at New York, NY, and used for A/N; 15 Jul 66 assisted in refloating cutter *Arbutus* in Long Island Sound; 1 Jun 70 recovered downed private ac in Long Island Sound; May–Jun 79 hauled garbage during New York City strike.

Red Birch

7 Jun 65–Jul 76 stationed at San Francisco, CA, and used for A/N; early Oct 65 escorted Japanese MV *Louisiana Maru* and U.S. tug *Las Plumas* to port following a collision off Yerba Buena I.; 30 Apr 70 recovered downed USA helicopter 5 mi W of Golden Gate Bridge; Jul 76–1990 stationed at Baltimore, MD, and used for A/N and light icebreaking.

Red Cedar

18 Dec 70–1990 stationed at Portsmouth, VA, and used for A/N.

Red Oak

10 Dec 71–88 stationed at Gloucester City, NJ, and used for A/N; 1988–90 stationed at Philadelphia, PA, and used for A/N.

Red Wood

4 Aug 64–1990 stationed at New London, CT, and used for A/N and light icebreaking; 24 Aug 65 assisted cutter *Owasco* off Little Goshen Reef.

The *Red Birch* on 23 May 76. This class was designed to service A/N up to 10 tons and to operate in shallow waters often encountered on sides of dredged harbor channels.

100-FOOT C TENDER

Name	Hull Number	Builder	Keel Laid	Launched	Commissioned	Disposition
Buckthorn	WLI 642 WAGL 642	Mobile Ship Repair, Inc., Mobile, AL	Dec 62	N/A	17 Jul 64	Active

Cost | N/A

Hull
  Displacement (tons) | 196 fl (1964); 158 light (1964)
  Length | 100′ oa; 96′ bp
  Beam | 24′ max
  Draft | 4′8″ max (1964)

Machinery
  Main Engines | 2 Caterpillar Tractor diesels
  BHP
  Propellers | twin

Performance
  Max Sustained | 10.6 kts, 1,441-mi radius (1964)
  Economic | 9.4 kts, 1,881-mi radius (1964)

Logistics
  Fuel Oil (95%) | 4,742 gal
  Complement | 1 warrant, 13 men (1964)

Deck Gear
  Boom Capacity | 5 tons

Electronics
  Detection Radar | CR-103 (1964)

Armament | none

Design
  The *Buckthorn* was designed as a large inland buoy tender. She has a steel hull and aluminum superstructure.

Buckthorn

17 Jul 64–26 Nov 67 stationed at Detroit, MI, and used for A/N; 26 Nov 67–1970 stationed at Buffalo, NY, and used for A/N; 1970–1990 stationed at Sault Ste. Marie, MI, and used for A/N.

Tender *Buckthorn* on 11 Jun 75. If you compare this 100-foot C tender with the 100-ft B *Azalea* you will conclude that they share the same length overall and little else.

100-FOOT B TENDER

Name	Hull Number	Builder	Keel Laid	Launched	Commissioned	Disposition
Azalea	WLI 641 WAGL 641	Coast Guard Yard, Curtis Bay, MD	1 Oct 57	4 Mar 58	23 May 58	*Decomm* 31 Oct 78

Cost — $550,000

Hull
Displacement (tons) — 178 fl (1966); 140 light (1966)
Length — 100' oa; 100' bp
Beam — 24' max
Draft — 5'7" max (1967)

Machinery
Main Engines — 2 General Motors diesels
BHP — 220
Propellers — twin

Performance
Max Sustained — 9.0 kts, 2,273-mi radius (1966)
Economic — 6.0 kts, 5,244-mi radius (1966)

Logistics
Fuel Oil (95%) — 4,074 gal
Complement — 1 warrant, 13 men (1966)

Deck Gear
Boom Capacity — 5 tons

Electronics
Detection Radar — none (1966)

Armament — none

Design
The *Azalea* was designed as a large inland buoy tender. She had a steel hull, aluminum superstructure, and mounted a pile driver on the bow. The machinery was cooled through the hull by a skin system using treated waters. The living spaces were air-conditioned.

Azalea
23 May 58–31 Oct 78 stationed at Charleston, SC, and used for A/N.

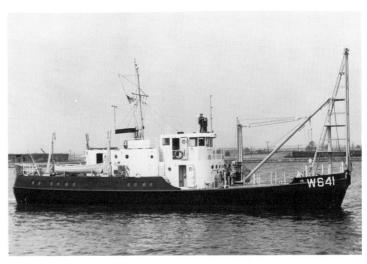

The *Azalea*, 1 Jun 58, was the only member of the 100-foot B tender class. Coast Guard classes were denoted by length. When there was more than one class of a given length, a letter was assigned to each to distinguish among them. Frequently, classes of the same length bore little relationship to each other. The *Azalea* mounts a pile driver on her bow.

75-FOOT INLAND CONSTRUCTION TENDERS

Name	Hull Number	Builder	Keel Laid	Launched	Commissioned	Disposition
A TYPE						
Anvil	WLIC 75301	Gibbs Shipyard, Jacksonville, FL	N/A	N/A	14 May 62	Active
Hammer	WLIC 75302	Gibbs Shipyard, Jacksonville, FL	N/A	N/A	20 Nov 62	Active
B TYPE						
Sledge	WLIC 75303	McDermott Fabricators, Morgan City, LA	N/A	N/A	5 Dec 62	Active
Mallet	WLIC 75304	McDermott Fabricators, Morgan City, LA	N/A	N/A	1 Feb 63	Active
Vise	WLIC 75305	McDermott Fabricators, Morgan City, LA	N/A	N/A	14 Mar 63	Active
D TYPE						
Clamp	WLIC 75306	Sturgeon Bay Shipbuilding & Dry Dock Co., Sturgeon Bay, WI	N/A	N/A	24 Nov 64	Active
Wedge	WLIC 75307	Sturgeon Bay Shipbuilding & Dry Dock Co., Sturgeon Bay, WI	N/A	N/A	10 Dec 64	Active

Name	Hull Number	Builder	Keel Laid	Launched	Commissioned	Disposition
Spike	WLIC 75308	Dorchester Shipbuilding Corp., Dorchester, NJ	29 Mar 65	15 Jan 66	13 Apr 66	*Decomm* 30 May 86
Hatchet	WLIC 75309	Dorchester Shipbuilding Corp., Dorchester, NJ	1 May 65	15 Feb 66	23 Jun 66	Active
Axe	WLIC 75310	Dorchester Shipbuilding Corp., Dorchester, NJ	29 Mar 65	1 Aug 66	17 Oct 66	Active

Cost   N/A

Hull
  Displacement (tons)   129 fl (1966)
  Length   76'1" oa; 73' bp
  Beam   22'5" max
  Draft   4'6" max (1966)

Machinery
  Main Engines   2 Waukesha Motor Co. (*Axe*)
  BHP   630
  Propellers   twin

Performance
  Max Sustained   10 kts, 1,000-mi radius (1966)

Logistics
  Fuel Oil (95%)   2,616 gal
  Complement   1 warrant, 8 men (1966)

Electronics
  Navigation Radar   CR-103 (1966)

Armament   none

Design

These inland construction tenders can drive pilings in depths of water from 4 to 20 feet. These tenders are also used to set and recover medium-size buoys. They usually work in conjunction with a barge.

Anvil

25 Sep–Oct 76 stationed at Miami Beach, FL, and used for A/N; 1 Aug 70 salvaged wreckage of private ac off Miami Beach, FL; Oct 76–1990 stationed at Corpus Christi, TX.

Axe

17 Oct 68–1990 stationed at Mobile, AL, and used for A/N.

Clamp

24 Nov 64–1990 stationed at Galveston, TX, and used for A/N.

Hammer

20 Nov 62–May 86 stationed at Ft. Pierce, FL, and used for A/N; May 86–1990 stationed at Jacksonville, FL, and used for A/N.

The *Hatchet* on 17 May 71 with her work barge.

Hatchet

23 Jun 66–1990 stationed at Galveston, TX, and used for A/N; 26 Nov 69 helped salvage private ac from Galveston Bay.

Mallet

1 Feb 63–1990 stationed at Corpus Christi, TX.

Sledge

5 Dec 62–1980 stationed at Portsmouth, VA, and used for A/N; 1980–90 stationed at Baltimore, MD, and used for A/N.

Spike

13 Apr 66–30 May 86 stationed at Mayport Beach, FL, and used for A/N.

Vice

14 Mar 63–1990 stationed at St. Petersburg, FL, and used for A/N.

Wedge

10 Dec 64–1990 stationed at New Orleans, LA, and used for A/N; 2 Jan 68 helped salvage Beechcraft ac from Lake Pontchartrain; 7–8 Dec 68 searched for survivors from cutter *White Alder.*

65-FOOT RIVER TENDER CLASS

Name	Hull Number	Builder	Keel Laid	Launched	Commissioned	Disposition
Ouachita	WLR 65501	Platzer Shipyard, Houston, TX	N/A	N/A	22 Jul 60	Active
Cimarron	WLR 65502	Platzer Shipyard, Houston, TX	N/A	N/A	30 Sep 60	Active
Obion	WLR 65503	Gibbs Corporation, Jacksonville, FL	N/A	N/A	5 Jan 62	Active
Scioto	WLR 65504	Gibbs Corporation, Jacksonville, FL	N/A	N/A	27 Mar 62	Active
Osage	WLR 65505	Gibbs Corporation, Jacksonville, FL	N/A	N/A	15 May 62	Active
Sangamon	WLR 65506	Gibbs Corporation, Jacksonville, FL	N/A	N/A	16 Jun 62	Active

Cost	$287,759 (*Ouachita* & *Cimarron* each)
Hull	
Displacement (tons)	145 fl
Length	65'8" oa
Beam	21' max
Draft	5' max (1962)
Machinery	
Main Engines	2 Caterpillar diesels
BHP	600
Propellers	twin
Performance	
Max Sustained	12.5 kts (1962)
Logistics	
Fuel Oil (95%)	5,300 gal
Complement	8 men (1962)
Electronics	
Radar	navigation
Armament	none

Design

The 65-foot pusher tenders were designed to service aids on the western rivers. The class was designed to work with a barge, which had served as a work platform, storage area, and machine shop.

Cimarron

30 Sep 60–18 Sep 62 stationed at Old Hickory, TN, and used for A/N; 6–13 Feb 61 used to train Vietnamese officials; 9 Aug 61 escorted NASA missile barge *Compromise*; 17 Feb 62 escorted NASA barge *Promise*; 9–13 Sep 62 escorted NASA barge *Promise*; 18 Sep 61–1978 stationed at Paris Landing, TN, and used for A/N; Jul–Aug 63 escorted NASA barge *Promise*; 1978–90 stationed at Buchanan, TN, and used for A/N.

Osage

15 May 62–1982 stationed at Sheffield, AL, and used for A/N; 9–13 Sep 62 escorted MV *Bob Fugua* with Saturn missile barge *Promise* in tow; 20–21 Jan 63 escorted MV *Bob Fugua* with missile barge *Promise*; 4–6 Apr 63 escorted MV *Bob Fugua* with Saturn missile barge in tow; 14 Jul 63 escorted Saturn missile barge *Promise* in tow; 11 Aug 63 escorted *Bob Fugua* with Saturn missile barge in tow; 1982–90 stationed at Sewickley, PA, and used for A/N.

Obion

5 Jan–16 May 63 stationed at Memphis, TN, and used for A/N; 16 May 63–1 Aug 69 stationed at Gasconade, MO, and used for A/N; 1 Aug 69–Jun 73 stationed at Louisville, KY, and used for A/N; Jun 73–May 77 stationed at Memphis, TN, and used for A/N; May 77–1990 stationed at St. Louis, MO, and used for A/N.

Ouachita

22 Jul 60–1990 stationed at Chattanooga, TN, and used for A/N; Aug 61 escorted tug *Ace* and barge *Palaemon* down Tennessee, R.; Feb 62 escorted tug *Ace* and barge *Palaemon* down Tennessee R.; Aug 69 assisted following derailment of railroad cars into Tennessee R.

Sangamon

16 Jun–25 Aug 62 stationed at Paris, TN, and used for A/N; 25 Aug 62–Apr 66 stationed at Old Hickory, TN, and used for A/N; Apr 66–1990 stationed at Peoria, IL, and used for A/N.

Scioto

25 Aug 61–3 Sep 65 stationed at St. Joseph, MO, and used for A/N; 3 Sep 65–1970 stationed at St. Louis, MO, and used for A/N; 31 Mar 68

assisted following fire on barge at Cahokia, IL; 1970–83 stationed at Leavenworth, KS, and used for A/N; 3 Mar 79 heavy flowing ice and strong current broke cutter loose from winter mooring—grounded and sank; 1983–90 stationed at Keokuk, IA, and used for A/N.

The *Osage* photographed circa 1972. The barge is equipped with a 3-ton telescopic, hydraulic-powered crane with a 43-ft boom.

65-FOOT TENDER CLASS

Name	Hull Number	Builder	Keel Laid	Launched	Commissioned	Disposition
Bayberry	WLI 65400	Reliable Welding Works, Olympic, WA	N/A	2 Jun 54	28 Jun 54	Active
Elderberry	WLI 65401	Reliable Welding Works, Olympic, WA	N/A	2 Jun 54	28 Jun 54	Active

Cost $150,000
Hull
  Displacement (tons)   71 fl (1954)
  Length   65'4" oa
  Beam   17' max
  Draft   4'9" max (1954)
Machinery
  Main Engines   2 General Motors diesels
  BHP   400
  Propellers   twin
Performance
  Max Sustained   11.5 kts, 590-mi radius (1954)
  Cruising   10.0 kts, 720-mi radius (1954)
Logistics
  Complement   5 men (1954)
Deck Gear
  Boom Capacity   7 tons
Electronics
  Navigational Radar   N/A

The *Elderberry* on 10 Sep 68 underway near Petersburg, AK, shortly after her slash was added.

Armament   N/A

Design

These 65-foot inland buoy tenders had steel hulls. They were initially designed to operate in fresh water, intended for the western rivers, and had to be modified for saltwater operations.

Bayberry

28 Jun 54–3 Apr 61 stationed at San Francisco, CA, and used for A/N; 3 Apr 61–12 Jun 63 stationed at Rio Vista, CA, and used for A/N; 12 Jun

63–Sep 71 stationed at San Francisco, CA, and used for A/N; Sep 71–1990 stationed at Seattle, WA, and used for A/N.

Elderberry

28 Jun 54–1990 stationed at Petersburg, AK, and used for A/N; 19 Jul 54 towed FV *Shafto* to Ketchikan, AK; 9 Aug 54 towed FV *Thora* to Petersburg, AK; 19 Jun 56 towed FV *Monroe* to Petersburg, AK.

65-FOOT TENDER CLASS

Name	Hull Number	Builder	Keel Laid	Launched	Commissioned	Disposition
Blackberry	WLI 65303	Dubuque Boat & Boiler Co., Dubuque, IA	N/A	N/A	24 Aug 46	Active
Chokeberry	WLI 65304	Dubuque Boat & Boiler Co., Dubuque, IA	N/A	23 May 46	30 Aug 46	Active
Loganberry	WLI 65305	Dubuque Boat & Boiler Co., Dubuque, IA	N/A	N/A	29 Aug 46	*Decomm* early 77

Cost   N/A

Hull

  Displacement (tons)   68 fl (1966); 50 light (1966)

  Length   65′ oa; 63′ bp

  Beam   17′ max

  Draft   3′6″ max (1966)

Machinery

  Main Engines   1 General Motors diesel

  BHP   220

  Propellers   single

Performance

  Max Sustained   10 kts, 830-mi radius (1966)

  Cruising   8 kts, 913-mi radius (1966)

Logistics

  Fuel Oil (95%)   914 gallons

  Complement   5 men (1966)

Electronics

  Radar   none (1966)

Armament   none

Design

The 65-foot-class tenders were designed as inland buoy tenders. These tenders remained unnamed until 1963.

Blackberry

7 Jul 46–1 Apr 50 stationed at Sheffield, AL, and used for A/N; 1 Apr 50–1 Oct 62 stationed at Paris, TN, and used for A/N; 1 Oct 62–1990 stationed at Southport, NC, and used for A/N.

Chokeberry

30 Aug 46–1 Jul 60 stationed at Chattanooga, TN, and used for A/N; 1 Jul 60–9 Jun 62 stationed at Sheffield, AL, and used for A/N; 9 Jun 62–30 Mar 82 stationed at Hatteras Inlet, NC, and used for A/N; Jan 79

removed wreck of *Trio* 6 mi NW of Buxton, NC; 30 Mar 82–1990 stationed at Crisfield, MD, and used for A/N.

Loganberry

1946–11 Nov 51 stationed at Paducah, KY, and used for A/N; 16–17 Feb 50 assisted in flood relief at Smithland, KY; 12 Nov 51–31 Jun 60 stationed at Nashville, TN, and used for A/N; 1 Jul 60–early 77 stationed at New Orleans, LA, and used for A/N; 20 Oct 62 assisted following collision between MV *Boheme* and tug *Bonnie D* at mile 148 above Head of Passes; 3 Dec 68 sank in 6 feet of water after she sprang a leak and the pumps failed in Lake Pontchartrain—refloated on 4 Dec by cutter *White Alder* and utility boats.

The *Loganberry*, Aug 65, underway on Lake Pontchartrain, LA. Some of this class had bulwarks added around the bow.

NAVY YF 257 CLASS

Name	Hull Number	Builder	Keel Laid	Launched	Commissioned	Disposition
White Sumac	WLM 540 WAGL 540 YF 416	Niagara Shipbuilding Corp., Buffalo, NY	31 Aug 42	14 Jun 43	6 Nov 43 (USN) 19 Sep 47 (CG)	Active
White Alder	WLM 541 WAGL 541 YF 417	Niagara Shipbuilding Corp., Buffalo, NY	31 Aug 42	30 Jun 43	1943 (USN) 19 Sep 47 (CG)	Sank 7 Dec 68
White Bush	WLM 542 WAGL 542 YF 339	Basalt Rock Co., Napa, CA	2 Apr 43	5 Feb 44	1944 (USN) 1 Nov 47 (CG)	*Decomm* 16 Sep 85
White Holly	WLM 543 WAGL 543 YF 341	Basalt Rock Co., Napa, CA	3 Aug 43	8 Apr 44	6 Jun 44 (USN) 1 Dec 47 (CG)	Active
White Sage	WLM 544 WAGL 544 YF 444	Erie Concrete & Steel Supply Co., Erie, PA	28 Mar 43	9 Jun 43	29 May 44 (USN) 9 Aug 47 (CG)	Active
White Heath	WLM 545 WAGL 545 YF 445	Erie Concrete & Steel Supply Co., Erie, PA	4 Jun 43	21 Jul 43	9 Aug 44 (USN) 9 Aug 47 (CG)	Active
White Lupine	WLM 546 WAGL 546 YF 446	Erie Concrete & Steel Supply Co., Erie, PA	28 Apr 43	28 Jul 43	31 May 44 (USN) 5 Sep 47 (CG)	Active
White Pine	WLM 547 WAGL 546 YF 448	Erie Concrete & Steel Supply Co., Erie, PA	12 Jun 43	28 Aug 43	11 Jul 44 (USN) 3 Aug 48 (CG)	Active

Cost	N/A
Hull	
Displacement (tons)	600 fl (1948)
Length	132'10" oa
Beam	30' max
Draft	8'9" max (1948)
Machinery	
Main Engines	2 diesels
BHP	600
Propellers	twin
Performance	
Max Sustained	10.5 kts, 2,450-mi radius (1948)
Economic	7.5 kts, 2,830-mi radius (1948)
Logistics	
Complement	1 warrant, 20 enlisted (1948)
Electronics	
Navigational Radar	N/A
Armament	none

Design

The Navy YF 257 class was built entirely of steel.

White Lupine

5 Sep 47–20 Jun 58 stationed at Detroit, MI, and used for A/N; 18 Oct 51 assisted following collision between MVs *George F. Rand* and *Harvey H. Brown* off Port Huron, MI; 24 May 52 assisted yacht *Judy Lane*; 20 Apr 56 assisted following collision between MVs *A. M. Byers* and *E. M. Ford* off Sans Souci, MI; 20 Jun 58–Nov 67 stationed at Ogdensburg, NY, and

used for A/N on Lake Ontario; 28 Sep 62 assisted tug *Russel* towing a barge 10 mi NE of Rochester, NY; Nov 67–1990 stationed at Rockland, ME, and used for A/N; 16 Jan 70 touched bottom near Whaleback Ledge, ME, and sustained minor damage.

White Pine

3 Aug 48–1 Sep 61 stationed at Memphis, TN, and used for A/N; 3 Apr 60 patrolled Miss R. Marathon race; 13 May 61 assisted with flood relief at Olive Branch, TN; 1 Sep 61–Jul 76 stationed at Baltimore, MD, and

The *White Pine,* photographed in the 1950s. During the early 1960s, this unusual bow configuration was rebuilt to a more conventional form. The above configuration permitted the tender to push a work barge more easily.

used for A/N; May 64 installed automatic generator at Baltimore LH; 11–12 Jun 65 assisted to fight fire on Colombian MV *Ciudad de Nieva* near Baltimore, MD; Jul 76–1990 stationed at Mobile, AL, and used for A/N; 13 Mar 83 sustained engine-room fire; Dec 84 rescued four from sunken PC in Gulf of Mexico.

White Sage

9 Aug 47–1 Feb 50 stationed at Bristol, RI, and used for A/N and ice-breaking; 1 Feb 50–1988 stationed at Woods Hole, MA, and used for A/N; 7–9 Sep 52 salvaged capsized boat near Nantucket I.; 16–17 Jan 54 freed icebound FVs near East Greenwich, RI; 30 Jul 59 assisted following collision between MVs *Francisville* and *Luckenback* at 41°27′N, 71°04′W; 4 Mar 60 assisted disabled tug *M. Moran* 2 mi E of Cape Cod Canal; 28 Aug 71 collided with MV *Edgar M. Queeny* in Delaware Bay; Jul 88–1990 stationed at Bristol, RI, and used for A/N.

White Sumac

19 Sep 47–1969 stationed at Key West, FL, and used for A/N; 6 Dec 52 assisted FV *Commodore Perry* off Dry Tortugas; 2 Feb 54 assisted FV *Elliot* near Key West, FL; 4 Mar 54 towed disabled FV *Vkelpie* to Key West; 10 Jul 68 rescued 47 Haitian refugees from a distressed sloop 40 mi E of Andros I.; 1969–Aug 76 stationed at Miami, FL, and used for A/N; Aug 76–1990 stationed at St. Petersburg, FL, and used for A/N.

White Alder

1947–7 Dec 68 stationed at New Orleans, LA, and used for A/N; mid-Nov 65 escorted raised barge carrying chlorine to a chemical plant; 4 Dec 68 refloated cutter *Loganberry*, which had been beached on 3 Dec; 7 Dec 68 collided with Formosan MV *Helena* near White Castle, LA, and sank—17 Coast Guardsmen were lost and 3 were rescued.

White Bush

1 Nov 47–16 Sep 85 stationed at Astoria, OR, and used for A/N; 4 Aug 51 assisted MVs *Adventure* and *Tullahoma* following a collision near Astoria, OR; 20 Dec 51 helped fight fire on MV *Erria* off Tongue Point; 26 Dec 51 assisted FV *Susan* at 45°10′N, 125°00′W; 7 May 52 repaired cable to Tillamook Rock; 23 Sep 54 repaired cable to Destruction I.; 4 Sep 55 patrolled salmon derby; 6 May 59 repaired cable to Destruction I.; 8–9 Jun 61 assisted with flood relief in Vancouver-Longview area; Aug 65 fought fire on dredge *MacLeod* at Vancouver.

White Heath

9 Aug 47–1990 stationed at Boston, MA, and used for A/N; 4–5 Oct 60 assisted after an Eastern Airlines crash near Boston, MA.

White Holly

1 Dec 47–fall 71 stationed at Ketchikan, AK, and used for A/N; 31 Oct 48 assisted Navy tug *ATA-196* near Ketchikan; 27 Aug 49 collided with FV *Deborah* near Ballenas I.—sustained no damage and escorted damaged FV to Nanaimo, British Columbia; 24 Aug 50 assisted FV *Carolen Dixon* at 55°00′N, 131°47′W; 26 Aug 50 assisted FV *Vermay* at 55°17′N, 131°59′W; 8 Sep 50 assisted FV *31-G-180* at Fanshaw Bay; 10 Sep 50 assisted FV *Burnett* aground near Streets I.; 16–17 Nov 50 provided medical assistance in Sitka, AK; 19 May 51 struck rock near Keku Strait and holed—escorted to Ketchikan by the cutter *Citrus*; 22 Mar 52 fought fire in Wrangell, AK; 27 Jul 52 assisted yacht *Travelore* near Ketchikan; 22 Sep 53 assisted MV *Silver Wave* at 55°30′N, 131°58′W; 26 Sep 53 assisted grounded FV *Valiant Maid* off Wales I.; 4 Oct 53 transported National Guard from Metlakahtla to Ketchikan, AK; 8 Nov 53 assisted FV *Irene J* near Tyee, AK; 6 Dec 53 assisted tug *Keumalong* aground on Hump I.; 22 Feb 54 assisted MV *James Lick*; 29 Dec 54 assisted FV *Barney* in Otter Sound; Feb 65 transported aviation fuel to mouth of Chickmin R. in support of relief of avalanche disaster 43 mi NW of British Columbia; early Oct 68 refloated FV *Evie*—towed her and FV *Waldine* toward Ketchikan, AK—*Evie* swamped and sank en route; early 72–1990 stationed at New Orleans, LA, and used for A/N.

U.S. ARMY *CHIMO* CLASS

Name	Hull Number	Builder	Keel Laid	Launched	Commissioned	Disposition
Magnolia (ex-*Barricade*, ex-*Colonel John Storey*)	WLB 328 WAGL 328 ACM 3	Marietta Manufacturing Co., Point Pleasant, WV	10 Oct 41	1942	7 Nov 42 (USA) 7 Apr 44 (USN) 3 Sep 46 (CG)	*Decomm* 13 Aug 71
Ivy (ex-*Barbican*, ex-*Colonel George Armistead*)	WLB 329 WAGL 329 ACM 5	Marietta Manufacturing Co., Point Pleasant, WV	1941	1942	1942 (USA) 24 Mar 45 (USN) 21 Apr 47 (CG)	*Decomm* 26 Nov 69
Jonquil (ex-*Bastian*, ex-*Henry J. Hunt*)	WLB 330 WAGL 330 ACM 6	Marietta Manufacturing Co., Point Pleasant, WV	N/A	1942	1942 (USA) 9 Apr 45 (USN) 29 Aug 46 (CG)	*Decomm* 15 Sep 69
Heather (ex-*Obstructor*, ex-*First Lieutenant William G. Sylvester*)	WLB 331 WAGL 331 ACM 7	Marietta Manufacturing Co., Point Pleasant, WV	N/A	1942	1942 (USA) 1 Apr 45 (USN) 1 Feb 47 (CG)	*Decomm* 15 Dec 67 *Trans* to Seattle, WA, 12 Apr 68

Name	Hull Number	Builder	Keel Laid	Launched	Commissioned	Disposition
Willow (ex-*Picket*, ex-*General Henry Knox*)	WLB 332 WAGL 332 ACM 8	Marietta Manufacturing Co., Point Pleasant, WV	1941	1942	15 Apr 42 (USA) 6 Mar 45 (USN) 20 Sep 47 (CG)	*Decomm* 10 Oct 69

Cost	N/A
Hull	
Displacement (tons)	1,323 fl (1964); 868 light (1964)
Length	188'8″ oa; 168'8″ bp
Beam	37' max
Draft	12'10″ max (1964)
Machinery	
Main Engines	Skinner Engine Co. reciprocating steam
Main Boilers	2 Combustion Engineering
SHP	1,200
Propellers	twin
Performance	
Max Sustained	11.5 kts, 2,375-mi radius (1964)
Economic	8.5 kts, 3,000-mi radius (1964)
Logistics	
Fuel Oil (95%)	48,131 gal
Complement	3 officers, 2 warrants, 47 men (1964)
Electronics	
Detection Radar	Sperry MK 3 (*Magnolia* & *Ivy*, 1964); SPS-53 (*Jonquil*, 1966)
Sonar	none
Armament	none

Design

The *Chimo* class was a minelayer type constructed for the Army Coastal Artillery Corps. The class was built of steel. When transferred to the CG the buoy deck was reinforced with armor plating.

Heather

23 Jul 47–5 Dec 49 stationed at Mobile, AL, and used for A/N; 23 Jul 49 assisted sinking barge off Isle aux Herbes; 6 Dec 49–15 Dec 67 stationed at San Pedro, CA, and used for A/N; 26 Jan 51 assisted disabled USNS *Cache* near San Pedro, CA; 9 Feb 53 escorted MV *Greece Victory* into San Francisco, CA; 23 Apr 56 escorted PC *Avalon* to San Pedro, CA; May–Jun 57 patrolled outboard races in Los Angeles harbor; 19 Jul 60 assisted following collision between USS *Ammen* (DD 527) and USS *Collette* (DD 730) near Newport Beach; 15–16 Mar 61 assisted Greek MV *Dominator* off Palos Verdes Pt. and transported survivors to San Pedro, CA; 19 May 61 assisted in raising CG 40453; 22 May 66 salvaged a CG helicopter 96 mi off San Diego, CA.

Ivy

25 Jul 47–14 Jun 49 stationed at Miami, FL, and used for A/N; 15 Jun 49–26 Nov 69 stationed at Astoria, OR, and used for A/N; 29 Jun 51 assisted MVs *Alan Seeger* and *Audrey* following a collision at 43°50′N, 124°40′W; 23 Oct 52 assisted MV *Paul T Seafarer* at 46°12′N, 124°07′W; 12 Feb 54 assisted FV *Western Fisherman* at 46°12′N, 127°07′W; 27 Mar 54 dragged for sunken FV off Lower Columbia R.; 1 Aug 58 grounded

near Lake Washington—no damage; Aug 59 served on law-enforcement patrol off Puget Sound; 15 Jan 61 assisted FV *Mermaid* off Columbia River Bar; 1 Mar 68 assisted following collision between Japanese MV *Suwaharu Maru* and Liberian MV *Mandoil II* off Oregon.

Jonquil

1 May 47–31 Aug 60 stationed at Portsmouth, VA, and used for A/N; 14 Mar 50 escorted disabled trawler to Thimble Shoal; 7 Apr 50 assisted barge that was adrift at 36°00′N, 74°40′W; 19 Oct 51 assisted MV *Theofano Livano* aground near Cape Henry; 11–12 Dec 51 towed disabled MV *McKittrick Hills* to Chesapeake LS where she was transferred to a commercial tug; 26–27 Feb 52 assisted grounded tug *Mary Sheridan* near York Spit LH; 11 Mar 52 assisted disabled FV *Elizabeth* 2 mi SE of Turner Lump; 14 May 54 assisted grounded barge near Diamond Marsh; Oct 54

The *Ivy* on 11 Apr 69 shortly before decommissioning. Following both world wars, Army mine planters were converted to buoy tenders. Following WWI, six 172-ft ships were taken into the USLHS and served throughout WWII except for the *Acacia* (WAGL 200), which was sunk by a U-boat. Following WWII, five 188-ft mine planters were taken into the Coast Guard, one of which was the *Ivy,* and she served until the late 1960s.

assisted disabled ferry *Princess Ann* near Kiptopeke Beach, VA; 11 Apr 56 assisted MV *Paraporti* aground near Lynnhaven Inlet; 1 Sep 60–15 Sep 69 stationed at Morehead City, NC, and used for A/N; 27 Sep 61 helped fight fire on USNS *Potomac* at Beaufort, NC; 9 Mar 62 stood by stern section of tanker *Gem* following her breakup at 33°33′N, 75°18′W; 6–7 Dec 62 towed disabled yacht *Cid* for 185 mi to Morehead City, NC; 14 Nov 68 towed disabled yacht *Xanadu* to Morehead City, NC; 28 Jul 69 dewatered schooner *Chauve Souris* 19 mi W of Frying Pan Light Tower.

Magnolia

25 Jul 47–31 Aug 65 stationed at San Francisco, CA, and used for A/N; 28–29 Apr 51 assisted Japanese MV *Kenkoju Maru* at 38°41′N, 123°28′W; 21 Aug 58 escorted MV *Flyer* to San Francisco, CA; 9 Feb 60 assisted disabled MV *Angelo Petri* 2 mi S of San Francisco Bar; 5 Jun 63 assisted following collision between USNS *Asterion* and Japanese MV *Kokoku Maru*

at 37°55′N, 123°2′W—transported 19 crew members from Japanese vessel to San Francisco, CA; 21–24 Jun 65 escorted damaged catamaran *Judy Al* 165 mi SW of Eureka, CA, to that port—hull was too weak to permit towing; 1 Sep 65–13 Aug 71 stationed at Astoria, OR, and used for A/N; 6 Dec 67 escorted distressed MV *David E. Day*, which had grounded on Columbia R. Bar; 10 Aug 68 assisted following collision between *Seatrain Washington* and *Rose S* 17 mi E of Cape Flattery in fog.

Willow

23 Jul 47–20 Jun 49 stationed at San Juan, PR, and used for A/N; 20 Jun 49–10 Oct 69 stationed at San Francisco, CA, and used for A/N; 14 Aug 55 assisted MV *Tancred* 80 mi W of Farallon I.; 2 Feb 60 assisted tanker *Angelo Petri* 2 mi S of San Francisco Bar; 2 Feb 63 assisted the USS *Coral Sea* aground in Alameda Channel; 31 Jul 65 assisted passengers overcome by fumes on PC 2 mi off Point Ano Nuevo.

ARMY 106-FOOT BARGE

Name	Hull Number	Builder	Keel Laid	Launched	Commissioned	Disposition
Aster	WAGL 408	Martinolinch Shipbuilding Corp., San Francisco, CA	N/A	1943	Apr 44 (CG)	*Decomm* 15 Aug 62
Thistle	WAGL 409 BSP 1049	Martinolinch Shipbuilding Corp., San Francisco, CA	20 Jun 43	N/A	1 Sep 43 (USA)	*Decomm* 1 Aug 57 *Sold* 25 Mar 58

Cost	N/A
Hull	
Displacement (tons)	450 fl (1956); 250 light (1956)
Length	106′3″ oa; 85′8″ bp
Beam	30′9″
Draft	8′ (1956)
Machinery	
Main Engines	2 Caterpillar diesels
BHP	270
Propellers	twin
Performance	
Max Sustained	7.5 kts, 2,915-mi radius (1956)
Logistics	
Fuel Oil (95%)	46,620 gal
Complement	10 men (1956)
Deck Gear	
Boom Capacity	1 ton
Electronics	
Detection Radar	Bendix Marine
Armament	none

Design
These barges were constructed of wood for the U.S. Army. The *Thistle* was fitted out as a diving platform.

Thistle

1946–57 stationed at Ketchikan, AK, and used for A/N; 17 Sep 49 assisted FV *Chomley* in Dall Bay; 25 May 55 engaged in recovery of crashed helicopter in Bradfield Canal.

Aster

Apr 44–15 Aug 62 stationed at Seattle, WA, and used for A/N.

The *Aster* on 5 Apr 49. She and her sister were former Army barges. Over the years the Coast Guard has employed numerous ships and craft constructed for the Army and Navy.

114-FOOT TENDER

Name	Hull Number	Builder	Keel Laid	Launched	Commissioned	Disposition
Foxglove	WLR 285 WAGL 285	Dubuque Boat & Boiler Works, Dubuque, IA	9 Nov 44	19 Jul 45	1 Oct 45	*Decomm* 8 Jul 77

Cost $191,595

Hull
  Displacement (tons)   338 fl (1962); 308 light (1962)
  Length   114′ oa; 114′ bp
  Beam   26′ mb; 30′ max
  Draft   6′ max (1962)

Machinery
  Main Engines   3 General Motors diesels
  BHP   1,200
  Propellers   triple

Performance
  Max Sustained   13.5 kts, 2,738-mi radius (1962)
  Ecomomic   12.0 kts, 3,012-mi radius (1962)

Logistics
  Fuel Oil (95%)   12,048 gal
  Complement   1 warrant officer, 23 men (1962)

Deck Gear
  Boom Capacity   1 ton
  Hoist Power   air

Electronics   none (1962)

Armament   none

Design
  Designed by the builder, the river tender *Foxglove* had a steel hull, decks, and superstructure. The tender was reengined in 1961. The fuel capacity does not include the capacity of the barge (CGB 58) associated with the tender, which can be interconnected with the tender's piping system.

Foxglove

1 Oct 45–8 Jul 77 stationed at St. Louis, MO, and used for A/N; May 61 assisted in flood relief in Olive Branch area; 31 Mar 68 assisted after a fire on a barge at Cahokia, IL.

The *Foxglove* on 31 Aug 61 working with a construction barge.

114-FOOT TENDER

Name	Hull Number	Builder	Keel Laid	Launched	Commissioned	Disposition
Sumac	WLR 311 WAGL 311	Peterson & Haecker Ltd., Blair, NE	13 Mar 44	14 Oct 44	11 Nov 44	Active

Cost	$356,372
Hull	
Displacement (tons)	350 fl (1944)
Length	114'6" oa
Beam	30'6" max
Draft	9' max (1944)
Machinery	
Main Engines	3 General Motors diesels
BHP	2,250
Propellers	triple
Performance	
Max Speed	11.0 kts (1975)
Logistics	
Fuel Oil (95%)	26,260 gal
Complement	1 officer, 23 men (1945)
Electronics	none
Armament	none

Design

The *Sumac* was designed by A. M. Deering, Chicago, IL, as a river tender.

Sumac

1 Nov 44–1 Jul 46 stationed at Owensboro, KY, and used for A/N and light icebreaking; 1 Jul 46–12 Nov 51 stationed at Paducah, KY, and used for A/N and light icebreaking; 12 Nov 51–1 Aug 62 stationed at Owensboro, KY, and used for A/N and light icebreaking; 21 Nov 58 assisted MV *Barbara Lee* towing three barges afire at mile 896 on Ohio R.; 13 May 61 assisted in flood relief in Carmi area; 1 Aug 62–May 66 stationed at Peoria, IL, and used for A/N and light icebreaking; May 66–late 68 stationed at Cairo, IL, and used for A/N and light icebreaking; late 68–1

Oct 70 stationed at Hickman, KY, and used for A/N and light icebreaking; 1 Oct 70–12 May 73 stationed at Dubuque, IA, and used for A/N and light icebreaking; 12 May 73–1978 stationed at Keokuk, IA, and used for A/N and light icebreaking; 1978–90 stationed at St. Louis, MO, and used for A/N and light icebreaking.

The *Sumac* below Ice Gorge on the Mississippi R. at Wittenburg Ferry Landing. In the mid-1970s the tender was re-engined with three General Motors diesels totaling 2,250hp. As built, she had been fitted with three Fairbanks-Morse diesels totaling 960hp. Note the ice plow attached to the bow of the tender.

73-FOOT TENDERS

Name	Hull Number	Builder	Keel Laid	Launched	Commissioned	Disposition
Clematis	WLI 74286 WAGL 286	Peterson & Haecker Ltd., Blair, NE	20 Jul 43	15 May 44	28 Jul 44	*Decomm* 17 Oct 76 *Trans* TVA Feb 77
Shadbush	WLI 74287 WAGL 287	Peterson & Haecker Ltd., Blair, NE	20 Jul 43	15 May 44	28 Jul 44	*Decomm* 24 Feb 76 *Sold* Oct 76

Cost	$185,450 each (hull & machinery)
Hull	
Displacement (tons)	86 fl (1956); 84 light (1966)
Length	73'6" oa; 70' bp
Beam	18'10" max
Draft	4'6" max (1966)
Machinery	
Main Engines	2 General Motors diesels
BHP	165
Propellers	twin
Performance	
Max Speed	10 kts (1966)
Economic	8 kts, 1,200-mi radius (1966)

Logistics	
Fuel Oil (95%)	2,400 gal
Complement	0 officers, 9 men (1966)
Deck Gear	
Boom Capacity	1.5 tons
Hoist Power	electricity
Electronics	none
Armament	none

Design

Designed by Coast Guard with detail drawings by A. M. Deering, Chicago, IL, the *Clematis* and *Shadbush* had their pilothouses raised four feet, and the spaces beneath the pilothouses were used for storage in the mid-1960s.

Clematis

28 Jul 44–22 Aug 66 stationed at Galveston, TX, and used for A/N; 27 Feb 52 marked wreck of tug *Ahepa* and tanker *Dubelly* in Texas City Channel; 15 Apr 58 collided with tug *Crochet No. 2* in Houston Ship Channel; 23 Aug 66–17 Oct 76 stationed at Corpus Christi, TX, and used for A/N.

Shadbush

28 Jul 44–27 Apr 67 stationed at Mobile, AL, and used for A/N; 28 Apr 67–late 1975 stationed at New Orleans, LA, and used for A/N; 7–8 Dec 68 searched for survivors from cutter *White Alder*; late 1975–24 Feb 76 stationed at Galveston, TX, and used for A/N.

The *Clematis* on 2 Jun 64. As built, her pilothouse was at the buoy-deck level; the new one was added in 1964.

80-FOOT TENDER

Name	Hull Number	Builder	Keel Laid	Launched	Commissioned	Disposition
Lantana	WLR 80310 WAGL 310	Peterson & Haecker Ltd., Blair, NE	21 Mar 43	18 Oct 43	6 Nov 43	Active

Cost — $201,143 (hull & machinery)
Hull
  Displacement (tons) — 235 fl (1965); 205 light (1965)
  Length — 80' oa; 75' bp
  Beam — 30' max
  Draft — 5'10" max (1965)
Machinery
  Main Engines — 3 Cummins diesels
  BHP — 945
  Propellers — triple
Performance
  Max Speed — 10 kts (1965)
  Ecomomic — 9 kts, 3,636-mi radius (1965)
Logistics
  Fuel Oil (95%) — 12,424 gal
  Complement — 1 warrant, 21 men (1965)
Electronics — none (1965)
Armament — none

Design

The river tender *Lantana* was designed by A. M. Deering, Chicago, IL. She was designed to accommodate an ice plow. The *Lantana* normally employed barge CGB-41, which had been built by Jones & Loughlin Steel Corp. in 1929. *Lantana*'s pilothouse was reconstructed in the early 1960s. She was also reengined at that time.

Lantana

1 May 45–1 Aug 62 stationed at Keokuk, IA, and used for A/N; Feb 61 used to train Vietnamese officials; 1 Aug 62–1978 stationed at Owensboro, KY, and used for A/N; early Nov 68 assisted following a grounding by MV *Nelson M. Broadfoot* towing two gasoline barges at Mile 533 on the Ohio R.; 1978–83 stationed at Hickman, KY, and used for A/N; 1983–90 stationed at Natchez, MS, and used for A/N.

Tender *Lantana* on 9 May 49. The design of this type of tender is based upon a pusher towboat.

EMERGENCY ACQUISITION

Name	Hull Number	Builder	Keel Laid	Launched	Commissioned	Disposition
Blackrock (ex-*The Boys*)	WAGL 367	Morehead City, NC	N/A	1924	17 Jun 43 (CG) 23 Feb 45 (*recomm in CG*)	*Decomm* 31 Mar 44 *Decomm* 24 Aug 54 *Sold* 2 Nov 55

Cost   Acquisition $56,079; conversion $86,689

Hull
  Displacement (tons)   230 fl (1953); 190 light (1953)
  Length   114' oa; 112' bp
  Beam   19'6" mb
  Draft   8'4" max (1953)

Machinery
  Main Engines   1 Atlas diesel
  BHP   300
  Propellers   single

Performance
  Max Speed   12.0 kts, 2,948-mi radius (1953)
  Cruising   10.0 kts, 3,240-mi radius (1953)

Logistics
  Fuel Oil (95%)   3,900 gal
  Complement   1 warrant, 14 men (1953)

Deck Gear
  Boom Capacity   5 tons
  Hoist Power   electricity

Electronics   none

Armament   none

Design
  Constructed of wood, the *Blackrock* was a former fishing craft.

Blackrock

1946–54 stationed at Portsmouth, VA, and serviced A/N in the Chesapeake Bay; 28 Feb 51 assisted in salvage of CGB-52027 and towed barge to Portsmouth.

100-FOOT TENDERS (*COSMOS* TENDERS, *BLUEBELL* TENDERS)

Name	Hull Number	Builder	Keel Laid	Launched	Commissioned	Disposition
Cosmos	WLI 293 WAGL 293	Dubuque Boat & Boiler Works, Dubuque, IA	19 Feb 42	11 Nov 42	21 Dec 42	*Decomm* 16 Aug 85
Barberry	WLI 294 WAGL 294	Dubuque Boat & Boiler Works, Dubuque, IA	20 Apr 42	14 Nov 42	3 Jan 43	*Decomm* 1 Sep 70 *Donated* 23 Feb 71
Rambler	WLI 298 WAGL 298	Dubuque Boat & Boiler Works, Dubuque, IA	7 Dec 42	6 May 43	26 May 43	Active
Brier	WLI 299 WAGL 299	Dubuque Boat & Boiler Works, Dubuque, IA	5 Aug 42	6 May 43	2 Jul 43	*Decomm* 9 Nov 67 *Trans* to USN 10 Mar 69
Bluebell	WLI 313 WAGL 313	Birchfield Boiler, Inc., Tacoma, WA	20 Mar 44	28 Sep 44	24 Mar 45	Active
Smilax	WLI 315 WAGL 315	Dubuque Boat & Boiler Works, Dubuque, IA	26 Nov 43	18 Aug 44	1 Nov 44	Active
Primrose	WLI 316 WAGL 316	Dubuque Boat & Boiler Works, Dubuque, IA	26 Nov 43	18 Aug 44	23 Oct 44	Active
Verbena	WLI 317 WAGL 317	Dubuque Boat & Boiler Works, Dubuque, IA	20 Mar 44	2 Oct 44	13 Nov 44	*Decomm* 1 Sep 77 *Sold* Feb 78

Cost   Hull & machinery ranged between $173,557 and $194,238 per unit—see Scheina, *WWII Cutters,* for details.

Hull
  Displacement (tons)   178 fl (1965); 153 light (1965)
  Length   100' oa; 96' bp
  Beam   24'7" max
  Draft   5'4" max (1965)

Machinery
  Main Engines   2 Waukesha diesels
  BHP   600
  Propellers   twin

Performance
  Max Sustained   9.5 kts, 1,130-mi radius (1965)
  Economic   8.5 kts, 1,241-mi radius (1965)

Logistics

| Fuel Oil (95%) | 3,800 gal |
| Complement | 1 warrant, 14 men (1965) |

Deck Gear

Boom Capacity	5 tons
Hoist Power	air
Electronics	SPN-11X (1962—*Barberry*)
Armament	none

Design

These 100-foot bay and sound tenders were designed by the Coast Guard with detail drawings by Dubuque Boat & Boiler Works, Dubuque, IA. These units were reengined in the 1960s.

Barberry

6 Jan 45–16 May 50 stationed at Coinjock, NC, and used for A/N; 17 May 50–1 Sep 70 stationed at Portsmouth, VA, and used for A/N; 12 Sep 55 patrolled President's Cup Regatta, Washington, DC; 26 Apr 56 assisted in search for a Navy F9F aircraft off Stingray Point; 2 Dec 58 assisted yacht grounded near Wilkerson Creek, NC; Jan 59 used for icebreaking near Crisfield, MD; Feb 61 used for icebreaking near Crisfield, MD.

Bluebell

3 Apr 45–1973 stationed at Vancouver, WA, and used for A/N; 22 Jul 51 assisted barge adrift in Columbia R.; 6 Apr 68 assisted following capsizing of an oil barge in Columbia R.; 1973–90 stationed at Portland, OR, and used for A/N; 15 Feb 82 fought fire on a grain ship at Kalama, WA— 2 CG men injured.

Brier

21 Oct 43–15 Jan 52 stationed at Charleston, SC, and used for A/N; 16 Jan 52–9 Nov 65 stationed at Brunswick, GA, and used for A/N; 17–18 Jul 53 salvaged USAF B-29 at Rockfish Creek, GA; 17 Sep 55 assisted in hurricane evacuation on Frederica River; 25 May 56 escorted MV *Busy Bee* to Isle of Hope; 17 May 62 collided with FV *Two Brothers Second* in Creighton Narrows; 9 Nov 65–10 Nov 66 stationed at Atlantic City, NJ, and used for A/N; 10 Nov 66–25 Apr 67 placed in reserve at St. George, Staten I., NY; Jun 67–9 Nov 67 stationed at Boston, MA, and used for A/N.

Cosmos

21 Dec 42–16 Aug 85 stationed at St. Petersburg, FL, and used for A/N; 3 Jan 57 assisted CG HO4S helicopter in Tampa Bay; 25 Feb 65 escorted German MV *Schanenberg*, which had a fire on board, into Tampa, FL.

Primrose

23 Sep 44–1 Mar 46 stationed at Charleston, SC, and used for A/N; 1 Mar 46–1 Jun 46 stationed at Corpus Christi, TX, and used for A/N; 1 Jun 46–1 Aug 49 stationed at Galveston, TX, and used for A/N; 1 Aug 49–22 Sep 66 stationed at Corpus Christi, TX, and used for A/N; 30 Jul 52 assisted a PBY5A ac 3 mi S of Baffin Bay, TX; 21 Apr 54 towed disabled tender *Myrtle*; 19–20 Oct 57 assisted disabled tender *Iris*; 22 Sep 66–28 Aug 80 stationed at Baltimore, MD, and used for A/N; 28 Aug 80–1990 stationed at Atlantic Beach, NC, and used for A/N.

Rambler

26 May 43–1978 stationed at Mobile, AL, and used for A/N; 15 Feb 53 assisted grounded tug *Coyle* in Pascagoula Channel; 27–28 Mar 53 dragged for wreckage of National Flight 470 S of Sand I. LH; 2 Aug 55 assisted in hurricane evacuation near Mobile, AL; 17 Nov 59 assisted following Freeport Co. sulphur barge explosion; 1978–90 stationed at Charleston, SC, and used for A/N.

Smilax

1 Nov 44–1 Jun 54 stationed at Ft. Pierce, FL, and used for A/N; 15 Nov 50 assisted grounded FV *Ava Maria* near St. Augustine, FL; 1 Jan 53 assisted disabled yacht *Mimosa* at New Smyrna Beach, FL; 1 Jun 54–9 Nov 65 stationed at New Smyrna Beach, FL, and used for A/N; 17 Jan 56 assisted yawl *Quest* aground at St. Augustine; 9 Nov 65–1990 stationed at Brunswick, GA, and used for A/N.

Verbena

13 Nov 44–6 Jun 45 stationed at Coinjock, NC, and used for A/N; 6 Jun 45–1 May 53 stationed at Morehead City, NC, and used for A/N; 20 Sep 51 patrolled President's Cup Regatta, Washington, DC; 3 Mar 53 assisted fighting fire at Wilmington, NC; 1 May 53–1 Mar 63 stationed at Washington, NC, and used for A/N; 10 Feb 55 assisted cutter *Linden* aground at 35°10′N, 76°07′W; 7 Jan 59 assisted CG-30456 aground at Briery Hall Point; 17 Feb 59 searched for downed Navy blimp near Pinetown, NC; 1 Mar 63–1964 stationed at Morehead City, NC, and used for A/N; 1964–1 Sep 77 stationed at Ft. Macon, NC, and used for A/N.

The *Bluebell*, Oct 60. She has spent her entire career in the Pacific Northwest.

115-FOOT TENDER

Name	Hull Number	Builder	Keel Laid	Launched	Commissioned	Disposition
Fern	WLR 304 WAGL 304	Peterson & Haecker Ltd., Blair, NE	1 Jul 42	6 Nov 42	19 Nov 42	*Decomm* 1 Sep 71 *Sold* 19 Jun 72
Ice plow		Peterson & Haecker Ltd., Blair, NE	Jun 42	23 Oct 42	7 Nov 42	*Sold* 19 Jun 72

Cost	$256,369 (hull, machinery, and ice plow)
Hull	
Displacement (tons)	440 fl (1963); 350 light (1963)
Length	114′6″ oa; 109′6″ bp
Beam	31′ max
Draft	8′3″ max (1963)
Machinery	
Main Engines	3 Fairbanks-Morse diesels
BHP	960
Propellers	triple
Performance	
Max Sustained	10.7 kts, 3,400-mi radius (1963)
Economic	9.5 kts, 3,880-mi radius (1963)
Logistics	
Fuel Oil (95%)	16,940 gal
Complement	1 warrant, 22 men (1963)
Electronics	none (1963)
Armament	none

Design

In May 1942 Coast Guard engineering was ordered to outline a contract for an icebreaking river tender to be in service on the upper Mississippi complex by the end of the year. The *Fern*'s final design and the design of her ice plow were executed by Peterson & Haecker, Ltd., Blair, NE. The *Fern* was contracted within two weeks and delivered in November before the freeze-up. She was patterned on a conventional river towboat. Icebreaking was achieved by means of a detachable "Amsterdam"-type ice plow. The *Fern* normally employed barge CGB-36.

Fern

1 Nov 44–31 Nov 45 stationed at Burlington, IA, and serviced A/N; 1 Dec 45–9 Sep 47 stationed at St. Louis, MO, and serviced A/N; 10 Sep 47–25 Feb 52 stationed at Cincinnati, OH, and serviced A/N; 26 Feb 52–1 Sep 71 stationed at Dubuque, IA, and serviced A/N; late Apr 65 assisted with flood relief near LaCrosse, WI.

The *Fern* on 26 Dec 51 with the Amsterdam bow attached. She spent her career working on the Illinois and Mississippi rivers and Lake Peoria.

180-FOOT TENDERS *IRIS* (180 [C]) CLASS

Name	Hull Number	Builder	Keel Laid	Launched	Commissioned	Disposition
Basswood	WLB 388 WAGL 388	Marine Iron & Shipbuilding Corp., Duluth, MN	21 Mar 43	20 May 43	12 Jan 44	Active
Bittersweet	WLB 389 WAGL 389	Zenith Dredge Co., Duluth, MN	16 Sep 43	11 Nov 43	11 May 44	Active
Blackhaw	WLB 390 WAGL 390	Marine Iron & Shipbuilding Corp., Duluth, MN	16 Apr 43	18 Jun 43	17 Feb 44	Active
Blackthorn	WLB 391 WAGL 391	Marine Iron & Shipbuilding Corp., Duluth, MN	21 May 43	20 Jul 43	27 Mar 44	Sank 28 Jan 80
Bramble	WLB 392 WAGL 392	Zenith Dredge Co., Duluth, MN	2 Aug 43	23 Oct 43	22 Apr 44	Active
Firebush	WLB 393 WAGL 393	Zenith Dredge Co., Duluth, MN	12 Nov 43	3 Feb 44	20 Jul 44	Active
Hornbeam	WLB 394 WAGL 394	Marine Iron & Shipbuilding Corp., Duluth, MN	19 Jun 43	14 Aug 43	14 Apr 44	Active

Name	Hull Number	Builder	Keel Laid	Launched	Commissioned	Disposition
Iris	WLB 395 WAGL 395	Zenith Dredge Co., Duluth, MN	10 Dec 43	18 May 44	11 Aug 44	Active
Mallow	WLB 396 WAGL 396	Zenith Dredge Co., Duluth, MN	10 Oct 43	9 Dec 43	6 Jun 44	Active
Mariposa	WLB 397 WAGL 397	Zenith Dredge Co., Duluth, MN	25 Oct 43	14 Jan 44	1 Jul 44	Active
Redbud	WLB 398 WAGL 398	Marine Iron & Shipbuilding Corp., Duluth, MN	21 Jul 43	11 Sep 43	2 May 44	*Trans* to Philippines 1 Mar 72
Sagebrush	WLB 399 WAGL 399	Zenith Dredge Co., Duluth, MN	15 Jul 43	30 Sep 43	1 Apr 44	*Decomm* 26 Apr 88
Salvia	WLB 400 WAGL 400	Zenith Dredge Co., Duluth, MN	24 Jun 43	15 Sep 43	19 Feb 44	Active
Sassafras	WLB 401 WAGL 401	Marine Iron & Shipbuilding Corp., Duluth, MN	16 Aug 43	5 Oct 43	23 May 44	Active
Sedge	WLB 402 WAGL 402	Marine Iron & Shipbuilding Corp., Duluth, MN	6 Oct 43	27 Nov 43	5 Jul 44	Active
Spar	WLB 403 WAGL 403	Marine Iron & Shipbuilding Corp., Duluth, MN	13 Sep 43	2 Nov 43	12 Jun 44	Active
Sundew	WLB 404 WAGL 404	Marine Iron & Shipbuilding Corp., Duluth, MN	29 Nov 43	8 Feb 44	24 Aug 44	Active
Sweetbrier	WLB 405 WAGL 405	Marine Iron & Shipbuilding Corp., Duluth, MN	3 Nov 43	30 Dec 43	26 Jul 44	Active
Acacia (ex-*Thistle*)	WLB 406 WAGL 406	Zenith Dredge Co., Duluth, MN	16 Jan 44	7 Apr 44	1 Sep 44	Active
Woodrush	WLB 407 WAGL 407	Zenith Dredge Co., Duluth, MN	4 Feb 44	28 Apr 44	22 Sep 44	Active

Cost
Hull & machinery range between $861,589 and $927,156 per unit—see Scheina, *WWII Cutters,* for details.

Hull
Displacement (tons)	1,025 fl (1962); 694 light (1962)
Length	180' oa; 170' bp
Beam	37' max
Draft	13'11" max (1962)

Machinery
Main Engines	1 electric motor connected to 2 Westinghouse generators driven by 2 Cooper-Bessemer diesels
SHP	1,200
Propellers	single

Performance
Max Sustained	13.5 kts, 10,000-mi radius (1962)
Economic	10.5 kts, 13,000-mi radius (1962)

Logistics
Fuel Oil (95%)	67,225 gal
Complement	3 officers, 2 warrants, 42 men (1962)

Deck Gear
Boom Capacity	20 tons
Hoist Power	electricity

Electronics
Detection Radar	SPS-23 (*Acacia*, 1962; *Blackhaw*, 1964; *Firebush*, 1965)
Sonar	UNQ-1 (*Acacia*, 1962; *Blackhaw*, 1964; *Firebush*, 1965)

Armament
1 3"/50 (*Blackhaw*, 1964); none (*Acacia*, 1962; *Firebush*, 1965)

Design
The preliminary design for the third set of 180-foot coastwise tenders was prepared by the Coast Guard, and the final design was prepared by Marine Iron & Shipbuilding Corp., Duluth, MN. *See* 180-foot tenders, *Cactus* (180 [A]) class for additional details.

Acacia

5 Sep 44–1 Jul 58 stationed at Detroit, MI, and used primarily for A/N and icebreaking; 17–18 Mar 48 assisted cutter *Mackinaw* to open port of Buffalo, NY, from ice; 18 Oct 51 assisted MVs *George F. Rand* and *Harvey H. Brown* off Black River, St. Clair River, following a collision; 13–14 Dec 51 unsuccessfully searched for a missing Cessna aircraft in Lake Erie; 24 Dec 51 assisted tug *Atomic* and MV *Carl W. Meyers* through ice near Toledo, OH; 11 Sep 52 assisted MVs *Kulas* and *Fink* aground in Livingstone Channel; 12 Jun 53 assisted MV *Maryland* aground at Poe's Reef; 18 Jun 53 assisted MV *Colonel J. M. Schoonmacker* aground in Lake St. Clair; 19 Mar 54 assisted icebound MVs *Conneaut* and *S. T. Crapo*; 2 Sep 56 patrolled Detroit River Race; 29 Jan 57 assisted MV *Diamond I* in Livingstone Channel; 5 Apr 57 assisted car ferry *Vacationland* aground near Mackinac I. city dock; 16 Apr 57 assisted MV *George A. Sloan* damaged by ice off North End Isle Parisienne, Lake Superior; 1 Jul 58–1975 stationed at Port Huron, MI, and used primarily for A/N and icebreaking; 25 Jun 59 provided assistance to Canadian MV *Royalton* and Liberian MV *Monrovia* on Lake Huron; 17 Aug 64 assisted Canadian tug *G. W.*

Rogers in Lake Huron; Feb 65 broke ice between Detroit, MI, and Toledo, OH, during harsh weather; 12 Mar 69 struck by MV *S. T. Crapo* while breaking ice in Lake Huron—slight damage; 5 Jan 70 aided Canadian MV *Yankcanuck* beset by ice in St. Clair R.; 1976 underwent a major renovation, including habitability improvements, improved handling system, new electric distribution system, and bow-thruster at CG Yard, Curtis Bay, MD; stationed at South Portland, ME, and primarily for A/N and icebreaking; 1977–79 stationed at Sturgeon Bay, WI, and used primarily for A/N and icebreaking; Jun 79–1990 stationed at Grand Haven, MI, and used primarily for A/N and icebreaking; winter 1987–88 conducted LE patrols in the Caribbean; Mar 88 intercepted a 50-ft boat carrying Haitians—transferred them to cutter *Vigorous*, which returned them to Haiti.

Bittersweet

1 Mar 45–27 Aug 47 stationed at Kodiak, AK, and used for A/N and LE; 19 May 47 assisted MV *Square Knot* near Dutch Harbor, AK; 27 Aug–2 Dec 47 stationed at Ketchikan, AK, and used for A/N and LE; 2 Dec 47–30 Jun 64 stationed at Kodiak, AK, and used for A/N and LE; 15 Jul 48 assisted MV at 56°10′N, 145°10′W; 7–10 Nov 48 searched for lost plane near Portage Bay; 10 Jun 49 assisted MV *Bogosof Island* in Unalaska Bay; 15 Jun 49 searched for FV *Sunset Bodies* in Cold Bay; 30 Oct 49 assisted tug *Eek* near Cape St. Elias; 15 Jun 50 rendered medical assistance at Squaw Harbor, AK; 6 Sep 50 assisted PC aground in Monashaka Bay; 27–29 Nov 50 stood by sinking barge near Kodiak; 9 Jan 51 towed log raft in Clarence Strait; 22 Feb 51 rendered medical assistance at Chignik, AK; 2 May 51 towed disabled FV to Akutan, AK; 13 May 51 assisted FV *CSF* in Lenard Harbor; 26–28 Jun 51 on halibut patrol near Kodiak, AK; 23–25 Jul 51 searched for Canadian DC-4 ac near Yakutat, AK; 14–19 Jul 52 assisted USS *Mahopac* near Pasagshak Point; 24–27 Nov 52 searched for MATS flights 1105 and 1107; 18 Mar 53 rendered medical assistance at Karluk Village, AK; 23 Mar 53 assisted FV *Wafko 21* near Kodiak, AK; 30 Jun 53 towed disabled FV *Socol* to Kodiak, AK; 4 Jul 53 refueled Navy PBM near Kodiak, AK; 13 Jul 53 assisted cutter *Sweetbrier* in Graves Harbor; 25–26 Feb 54 assisted MV *James Lick* at Dundas Bay; 3 Jul 54 towed disabled FV *Recruit* to Kodiak; 11–12 Jun 55 assisted FV *Flint* at 55°55′N, 153°30′W and towed her to Kodiak, AK; 12 Mar 57 rendered medical assistance at Nikoloski Village, AK; 3 Mar 58 assisted following Aero Commander flight 41458 crash at 57°15′N, 151°42′W; 10 Jun 59 escorted MV *Galena* to Kodiak, AK; 30 Jun 64–mid-76 stationed at Ketchikan, AK, and used for A/N and LE; 29 Jan 66 salvaged CG HH52A helicopter at Lancaster Cove, AK; 12 Apr 68 struck a submerged object off Alaska while on an SAR mission—intentionally grounded to effect temporary repairs; 7 Jul 68 helped fight fire at Ketchikan, AK; early Oct 68 salvaged a 32-foot FV 20 mi S of Ketchikan, AK; 4 Oct 68 dewatered and towed disabled FV *Inkosi* 10 mi SW of Annette I. to Ketchikan, AK; 5 May 70 seized foreign-operated fixed fishing gear for territorial violation; mid-1976 underwent major renovation; late 1976–1990 stationed at Woods Hole, MA, and used for A/N and icebreaking; Dec 76 assisted following tanker *Argo Merchant* grounding; Nov 78 recovered marijuana as evidence from *Traveller III* off Maine; Sep 80 patrolled America's Cup Race, Newport, RI; Nov 81 assisted in cleanup off Maine following *Christian Rienauer* grounding; as part of IIP, May 87 collected hydrographic and drift buoy data off the Grand Banks using a mobile laboratory.

Blackthorn

1944–Dec 49 stationed at San Pedro, CA, and used for A/N; 17 Nov 48 salvaged a USN helicopter; 4 Jul 49 assisted distressed PC; 1950–76 stationed at Mobile, AL, and used for A/N; 27 Jul 51 assisted distressed MV *Ocean Pride*; 20 Oct 51 assisted distressed MV *Kerry Mae*; 27 Jun 52 assisted distressed MV *Mission Carmel*; May–Jul 53 salvaged wreckage from National Airlines crash; 16 Apr 54 assisted distressed MV *Beatrice*; Apr 54 salvaged USAF ac; Oct 57 assisted cutter *Iris*, which was beached; 16 Jun 65 established a marker buoy at crash site of AF F-105 off Florida; late Aug 65 provided men and equipment to fight fire on Liberian MV *Arctic Reefer* off Choctaw Point, Mobile, AL; 1972 underwent an austere renovation; 1976–80 stationed at Galveston, TX, and used for A/N; 28 Jan 80 sank after collision with tanker *Capricorn* at mouth of Tampa Bay Channel—23 CG men died.

Basswood

15 Sep 44–1 Feb 46 stationed at Astoria, OR, and used for A/N; 2 Feb–21 Aug 46 stationed at San Francisco, CA, and used for A/N; 22 Aug 46–1968 stationed at Honolulu, HI, and used for A/N throughout the Pacific, including Eniwetok, French Frigate Shoal, Kwajalein, Midway, and Okinawa, and paid numerous annual visits to Jarvis, Baker, and Howland islands in support of title and sovereignty claims; 4 Sep 49 towed sampan *Broadbill*; 12–21 Mar 51 assisted disabled MV *Andrea F. Luckenbach* off Kanala Point; 18–21 Apr 54 unsuccessfully searched for missing aircraft N5613W; 19–23 Jan 56 towed disabled Japanese FV *Taihei Maru* from 23°24′N, 167°47′W to Honolulu, HI; 27–30 Nov 56 searched for sinking Japanese MV *Towa Maru Sitsum Nr 1* near 20°05′N, 128°50′E; 18 Jan 57 medevaced crewman from Japanese FV *Fuku Maru* to Guam; 4–5 Aug 58 assisted disabled MV *Oceanic* near Necker I.; 14–17 Sep 60 patrolled Billfish Tournament, Kona, HI; 8 Mar 61 assisted ketch *Marinac* near Honolulu, HI; 6 Jan 62 assisted grounded FV *Hiroshima Maru* at 21°17′N, 157°51′W; 16 Jan 65 escorted disabled Liberian MV *African Monarch* to Midway I.; 1968–90 stationed at Guam and used for A/N.

The *Basswood* on 16 Mar 61. She was one of four buoy tenders to serve in Vietnam, the others being *Blackhaw, Ironwood,* and *Planetree*.

Blackhaw

17 Feb 44–1 Aug 54 stationed at Charleston, SC, and used for A/N; 19–20 Dec 51 assisted tanker *Bulkfuel* at 32° N, 76°09′W, due to casualty to main-engine fuel pump, and along with cutter *Koiner* escorted tanker to Jacksonville, FL; 7–9 Sep 52 searched for survivors from MV *Foundation Star* near 32°20′N, 77°40′W; 19–20 Nov 52 discovered and recovered wreck of F8F-2 ac near 31°46′N, 81°01′W; 21 Sep 53 unsuccessfully searched for AF SA-16 ac off Charleston, SC; 29 Oct 53 assisted vessel *T. N. Gill* off Charleston, SC; 1 Aug 54–1967 stationed at Honolulu, HI, and used for A/N throughout the Pacific, including American Samoa, the Marshalls, the Marianas, the Carolines, and the Philippines; 11 Oct 54 medevaced a sailor from USS *Kearsarge* off Honolulu, HI; Jun–Aug 57 operated off Alaska on Special Arctic Operation, including icebreaking; 9–14 Nov 57 searched for Pan American Flight 944 off Hawaii; 24 Dec 57 assisted FV *Hawaiian Fisherman* off Kahului, HI; 15 Oct 58 assisted FV *Flying Fish Victor 3* at 22°05′N, 156°17′W; 23–24 Nov 58 escorted MV *Nicoline Maersk* to Honolulu, HI, following on-board fire; 18 Jul 59 relieved cutter *Dexter* of tow of FV *Cloud Nine* at 21°38′N, 155°21′W and proceeded to Hawaii; 19 Jul 59 towed sailboat *Trans-Pac*; 1967–71 stationed at Sangley Pt., Philippines, and used to service A/N; Mar 68–May 71 performed numerous tours in Vietnamese waters servicing A/N: 13 Mar–6 May 68; 24 Jun–18 Jul 68; 9 Sep–11 Oct 68; 16 Jan–4 Mar 69; 16 Apr–3 May 69; 16 Jun–3 Jul 69; 24 Oct–7 Dec 69; 23 Apr–18 May 70; 24 Oct–10 Nov 70; 13 Jan–7 Mar 71; 25 Apr–17 May 71; 1971–90 stationed at San Francisco, CA, and used for A/N; Jul 83 replaced destroyed Blunts Reef LNB with new ELB.

Firebush

1 Nov 45–26 Oct 48 stationed at New London, CT, and used for A/N; 1946 placed "in commission in reserve" due to a shortage of personnel; 26 Oct 48–12 Apr 78 stationed at St. George, Staten I., NY, and used for A/N and icebreaking; Dec 49 broke ice in Hudson R. near Albany, NY; 28–30 Mar 50 assisted Ambrose LS (LS-533) and served on temporary relief; Jan 51 broke ice in Hudson R., near West Point, NY; 29–31 Oct 52 assisted in salvage of a ditched C-45 ac near Newburgh; 15 Jan 53 stood by grounded *Esso Wilmington* in Ambrose Channel; Jan–Feb 54 assisted icebound vessels in Hudson R., including tanker *Flying A*; Jan–Feb 55 assisted icebound vessels in Hudson R.; Dec 55 assisted icebound vessels in Hudson R.; 1 Dec 56 helped fight fire at foot of 35th St., Brooklyn, NY; Jan 57 assisted icebound vessels in Hudson R.; 22–23 Mar 57 towed dead whale from Belmar, NJ, to sea; Jul–Sep 57 served under orders of the USN off Greenland and Iceland; Jan–Feb 58 assisted icebound vessels in Hudson R.; Dec 58–Jan 59 assisted icebound vessels in Hudson R.; Jul 61 transported Continental Navy gunboat *Philadelphia* from New York, NY, to Washington, DC; 4–6 Jan 63 assisted grounded cutter *Sauk*; 8 Oct 68 dumped confiscated weapons at sea; 12 Apr 78–22 Jun 79 underwent major renovation at CG Yard, Curtis Bay, MD; 22 Jun 79–1990 stationed at Kodiak, AK, and used for A/N; Jan 87 participated in Op Brimfrost 87, an exercise to defend against sabotage.

Bramble

22 Apr 44–1 Mar 45 stationed at San Pedro, CA, and used for A/N; 1 Mar 45–1 Feb 46 stationed at Juneau, AK, and used for A/N; 1 Feb–22 Aug 46 stationed at San Francisco, CA, and used for A/N; 22 Aug 46–28

Jul 47 stationed at Honolulu, HI, and used for A/N; 28 Jul 47–20 Jul 49 stationed at San Francisco, CA, and used for A/N; 20 Jul 49–1 Jul 53 stationed at San Juan, PR, and used for A/N; 23 Sep 49 towed disabled schooner *Ramon B* to St. Barthelemy; 9 Feb 50 towed disabled PC *Iorana* to San Juan, PR; 15 Nov 50 assisted grounded sloop *Mayflower* at 17°59′N, 65°52′W; 20 Mar 51 assisted MV *Esso Pineridge* at San Juan, PR; 11–12 Apr 52 transported 10 survivors from DC-4 crash to San Juan; 1 Jul 53–1 Aug 62 stationed at Miami Beach, FL, and used for A/N; 25 May 54 assisted grounded USS *Catawba* at Triumph Reef; 16–17 Jul 54 towed disabled MV *Lucky* from 19°09′N, 68°12′W to San Juan, PR; 7 Dec 54 assisted FV *Commander* at 24°38′N, 82°53′W; Oct 56 visited Ecuadoran and Colombian ports; 18 Dec 56 assisted FV *Sarah J* at 27°50′N, 80°11′W; May–Sep 57 transited the Northwest Passage circumnavigating North America, starting and ending at Miami, FL—joined by cutters *Spar* and *Storis* en route; 17–18 Sep 57 searched for survivors of B-47 near 47°15′N, 58°05′W; 9 Dec 57 assisted PC *Happy Three* off Miami, FL; 23–24 Dec 57 assisted tug *William G. Osborne* towing MV *Humula* at 25°14′N, 80°11′W; 1 Mar 58 assisted MV *African Duke* at 25°07′N, 80°17′W; 29–30 Sep 59 performed Hurricane Gracie evacuation in Charleston, SC, and Savannah, GA, areas; 28 Jan 60 escorted MV *Kori*, which was towing MV *Evangeline* from 25°47′N, 77°20′W, to Miami, FL; 31 Mar 60 searched for AF KC-97 ac at 28°25′N, 79°40′W; 13 Jan 61 attempted to assist barge *Arizona Sword* 10 mi E of Palm Beach; 12–14 Aug 61 escorted Saturn missile barge *Compromise* from 24°35′N, 83°04′W to Ft. Pierce, FL; 12 Sep 61 assisted grounded Greek MV *Doric* at 25°34′N, 80°06′W; 19 Nov 61 searched for survivors from ketch *Blue Bell* at 25°55′N, 77°27′W; 1 Aug 62–Aug 74 stationed at Detroit, MI, and used for A/N and icebreaking; 4–5 May 63 assisted Canadian MV *Orefax* aground on Summer I.; 25 Jan 65 struck in stern by MV *Robert S. McNamara* while breaking ice for the MV; 27 Nov 65 retrieved U.S. barge *Tampico*, which had broken her moorings and grounded in Detroit R.; 12 Dec 68 helped fight fire on Corps of Engineers tug *Anchor Bay* on Lake Erie; 5 Jan 70 aided Canadian MV *Yankcanuck* beset by ice in St. Clair R.; 1974 underwent major renovation, including rebuilding engines, improved berthing, a new boom; Sep 75–1990 stationed at Port Huron, MI, and used for A/N and icebreaking; 1986–87 deployed during winter months to Caribbean on LE patrols; 4 Feb 87 seized a PC and arrested crew 80 mi E of Miami, FL, after liquid from a 100-gal. portable water tank tested positive for morphine and codeine.

Hornbeam

14 Apr 44–Jul 76 stationed at Woods Hole, MA, and used for A/N and icebreaking; 26 Nov 50 assisted USS *Manners,* adrift off Cape Cod; 19 Feb 52 assisted FV *Flamingo* near Pollock Rip; 17 Feb 54 assisted FV *Shannon* aground at No Mans Land; 12–14 Sep 54 assumed duties temporarily on Nantucket LS station; 21 Nov 55 towed disabled FV *Midway*; 22 Nov 55 towed disabled FV *Ballard*; 26 Feb 56 assisted LS regain station; 10 Jun 56 escorted MV *Chelsea* to New Bedford; 26 Jul 56 assisted following collision between passenger ships *Andrea Doria* and *Stockholm* at 40°30′N, 69°53′W—carried two lifeboats to Woods Hole; 8–9 Jul 57 assisted MV *American Packer* off Buzzards Bay; 25 Oct 57 assisted MV *Nicolos* aground at Hog I.; 4 Apr 58 assisted MV *Fort Fetterman* at 40°33′N, 69°26′W; 30 Apr 58 assisted FV *Venture 1* at 40°20′N, 68°38′W; 7 Aug 58 assisted following collision between MVs *Graham* and *Gulf Oil* in E passage of

Narragansett Bay; 29 Jan 61 assisted cutter *Spar* aground in Narragansett Bay; Mar–Apr 65 escorted USS *Atka*, which was taking on water off New Bedford, MA; late Nov 65 assisted U.S. MVs *American Pilot* and *Maumee Sun* following their collision W of the Cape Cod Canal; Jan 68 freed research ship *Gosnold* from ice near Woods Hole, MA; 24 May 72 collided with British MV *Docelago* at 40°41′N, 69°19′W—sustained damage to starboard side, no personal casualties; Jul 76–29 Apr 77 underwent job overhaul at CG Yard, Curtis Bay, MD; 29 Apr 77–1990 stationed at Cape May, NJ, and used for A/N.

Iris

14 Oct 44–15 Mar 72 stationed at Galveston, TX, and used for A/N; 16–17 Apr 77 evacuated injured and dead from Texas City, TX, following devastating explosion—later fought fire once she could get close enough to be effective; 11–14 Feb 50 unsuccessfully searched for missing Navy PBM ac; 8–9 Jan 51 towed FV *Barto No 1* to Port Isabel, TX; 2–3 Mar 51 escorted disabled FV *John R. Speed* to Sabine Pass; 10 May 51 towed FV *Que* to Galveston, TX; 18–19 Dec 53 assisted MV *Florida Sword* off Galveston, TX; 11 Feb 55 assisted FV *Fish Hawk*; 22 Mar 55 assisted barge *Mr. Gus* in Galveston Bay; 13 Oct 56 assisted FV *Texas Explorer* at 29°5′N, 94°52′W; 2–5 Jan 57 disabled and towed to New Orleans, LA, by cutter *Dione*; 26 Mar 57 assisted FV *Six Kids* at 29°5′N, 94°40′W; 27 Jun 57 assisted FV *Parker* in distress due to hurricane; 24 Sept 57 assisted USS *Navajo* at 29°35′N, 93°51′W; 19 Oct 57 intentionally beached at Aransas Pass after being holed during dragging operation for a sunken buoy—refloated and repaired at New Orleans, LA; 23 Nov 57 towed FV *Captain George Hamilton* to Aransas Pass; 4 Jan 58 escorted FV *Thunderbolt* to Port Isabel, TX; 15 Feb 58 assisted CG-40459 off Galveston, TX; 3 Jul 58 assisted FV *John and Mary* at 29°6′N, 94°35′W; 6 Jul 59 fought fire on MV *Anvers* at 29°41′N, 92°20′W; 29–30 Jan 60 assisted FV *Gannet* near Sabine Pass; Aug 61 escorted Saturn missile barge *Compromise*; 29 Jan 63 assisted MV *Diversity* at 29°30′N, 93°W; 30 Oct 66 stood by heavily damaged MV *Gulfstag* 50 mi S of Marsh I.; May–Jun 70 assisted following explosion and fire on oil rig 10 mi off Galveston, TX; 15 Mar 72–1990 stationed at Astoria, OR, and used for A/N; 24 Apr 80 disabled by engine-room fire—assisted by cutters *Citrus, White Bush, Intrepid,* a 44-footer, 2 HHS2s from CG air station North Bend, OR, and commercial tug *Umpqua.*

Mallow

6 Jun 44–16 Sep 46 stationed at San Francisco, CA, and used for A/N; 16 Sep 46–11 Oct 65 stationed at Astoria, OR, and used for A/N; 7 Jun 48 towed disabled FV *Fearless* to Astoria, OR; 13 Aug 49 towed disabled FV *Haven;* 3 Jan 51 assisted a loose barge in lower Columbia R., 29 Jun 51 assisted following collision between MVs *Alan Seeger* and *Audrey* at 43°50′N, 124°40′W; 8 Aug 51 assisted FV *Bobby First* at 48°37′N 125°07′W; 13–14 Mar 52 searched for derelict in Coos Bay; 10 Sep 52 assisted FV *Rogue* at 43°35′N, 124°30′W; 21 Jan 53 assisted disabled MV *Toni-B* off Columbia Bar; 4–5 Sep 55 patrolled salmon derby, Astoria, OR; 19 Feb 58 assisted USS *Yuma* towing USS *Tinian* 6 mi S of Swiftsure Bank; 4 Dec 59 collided with MV *Meiko Maru* off Astoria dock in fog; 21 Nov 60 assisted dismasted PC *Yawl* in Coos Bay; 17 Apr 61 assisted Army tug at 48°10′N, 122°44′W; 11 Oct 65–1967 stationed at Honolulu, HI, and used for A/N; 1967–75 stationed at Guam and used for A/N in American Samoa, Wake, Midway, Kwajalein, and Johnson islands; 10 Sep 67 assisted grounded tanker *R. C. Stoner* at Wake I.; 2–6 Jul 70 towed disabled MV *Makua* 1,140 mi SW of Hawaii to Majuro; 1975–90 stationed at Honolulu, HI, and used for A/N; 7 Apr 84 seized FV *Jin Ruey Yng* for violating 200-mi Fisheries Conservation Zone; 9 Jul 87 helped medevac crewman from FV *Miyagi Maru* 350 mi N of Oahu I; Feb 88 helped seize *Christina M* 800 mi SE of Hawaii carrying 13t of marijuana; Feb 89 recovered debris from United Airlines Flight 811 off Hawaii.

Mariposa

1 Jul 44–15 Jun 54 stationed at St. George, Staten I., NY, and used for A/N; Oct 46 broke ice near Albany, NY; Oct 46 assisted FV *Rainbow*; Dec 49–Jan 50 broke ice in Hudson R.; 28 May 50 assisted and towed LS-533 (Ambrose); 23 Jun 53 assisted tug *Sheridan* in Long I. Sound; Jan–Feb 54 broke ice in Hudson R.; 15 Jun 54–11 Apr 73 stationed at New London, CT, and used for A/N; 8 Sep 54 assisted FV *Major Casey* off Shelter I.;

A white buoy tender—*Iris* on 17 Sep 63. She may have been painted white for crew comfort since she was stationed at Galveston, TX, at the time.

Jan–Feb 55 broke ice in Hudson R.; 12 May 55 assisted yacht *Whiteson* 58 mi ENE of Winter Quarter; 20 Aug 55 aided with flood relief on Housatonic R.; Jan 56 broke ice in Hudson R.; Jan 57 broke ice in Hudson R.; Feb 58 broke ice in Hudson R.; Jan–Feb 59 broke ice in Hudson R.; 30 Jul 59 assisted following collision between MVs *Francisville* and *Luckenback*; Jan 60 broke ice in Hudson R.; 7–9 Jan 62 assisted MV *Leif Viking* aground off Watch Hill Pt.; 15 Feb 65 assisted in recovery of bodies and debris from Eastern DC-7 crash off Long I.; 1973–74 underwent a major overhaul at CG Yard, Curtis Bay, MD; 23 Oct 74–1990 stationed at Detroit, MI, and used for A/N; Oct 81 helped restore Ashtabula Harbor LH.

Redbud

1944–49 stationed at Miami, FL, and used for LE and SAR; 1949–52 loaned to USN and operated in the Arctic; 1952–70 loaned to MSTS and operated in the Arctic with a civilian crew; Aug 68 rescued eight Swiss explorers in a small boat beset in ice off Kulusuk, Greenland, during 50-knot winds; Nov 70–Mar 72 inactive.

Sagebrush

1944–88 stationed at San Juan, PR, and used for A/N and SAR; 31 Mar–1 Apr 51 towed dredge *San Pedro* to Santiago, Cuba; 28–29 May 51 assisted stranded MV *Monte Sollube*; 1 Jul 53 assisted MV *Dodecanese* near San Juan, PR; 14 Dec 54 assisted MV *Fensal* at 20°25′N, 68°08′W; 22–23 Sep 56 assisted Greek tanker *Ioannis Zafirakis* near San Juan, PR; 6–9 Sep 60 rendered assistance to Anegada, British Virgins, following hurricane Donna; 23 Mar 62 assisted MV *Michalikis* near San Juan, PR; 10 Aug 62 assisted MV *Heinrich Schulte* 90 mi N of San Juan, PR; 13 Sep 62 assisted MV *Marlene* off Cape San Juan; 21 Dec 62 assisted MV *Catalina* aground at San Juan entrance; 1 May 63 assisted MV *Transcaribbean* aground at San Juan entrance; 26–29 May 65 towed disabled Venezuelan Navy cargo ship 120 mi NW of San Juan, PR, to that port; mid-Dec 65 fought fire on Norwegian MV *Norseman* at Guayanilla, PR; 15 Nov 66 rescued two from liferaft from a ditched Cessna ac off Puerto Rico; 8 Mar 69 rescued three of five from houseboat *Stand Pat* 35 mi E of West Palm Beach, FL, and took in tow—tow passed to cutter *Cape Fox*; 14 Aug 69, responding to SAR case, fabricated a rudder for sailboat *Brendan*, which had refused to take a tow 600 mi ENE of Puerto Rico; 6 Jan 70 assisted in escorting leaking tanker *Antonatos* to safety; 6–10 Oct 70 evacuated refugees during flooding in Puerto Rico; Aug 78 assisted in seizure of MV *Heidi* carrying 120t of marijuana; 20 Sep 83 seized FV *Endeavor* carrying 20t of marijuana; Dec 83–Jan 84 assigned to Grenada as tender for 95-foot cutters and performed patrol and training duties; 20 Aug 84 intercepted 34 on a 30-foot sailboat 50 mi W of Great Inagua and returned them to Haiti; 14 Jan 85 seized FV *Carey* 155 mi NW of San Juan, PR, with 5t of marijuana on board.

Salvia

1 Nov 45–1990 stationed at Mobile, AL, and used for A/N; 30 Apr 48 towed disabled MV *Gulf Light* to Mobile, AL; 12 Mar 49 stood by grounded MV *Kulukundis* in Gulfport Channel; 11 Aug 50 towed disabled FV *Ocean Bridge*; 12 Mar 51 towed disabled FV *Marietta* to Mobile, AL; 20–23 Apr 51 assisted following collision between tankers *Esso Suez* and *Esso Greensboro*; 27–30 Apr 51 disabled in Calasieu Pass—towed to Mobile

by cutter *Tampa*; 25 Jun 52 assisted MV *Mission Carmel* at 28°03′N, 88°54′W; 24 Sep 52 helped fight fire on MV *Maplebank* at Depot Point; 4–6 Jan 53 assisted USNS *Marine Fiddler* aground in Gulfport Channel; 5–9 Apr 53 searched for wreck of National Flight 47 off Mobile Point; 19–20 Jan 55 assisted FV *Buccaneer*; 1 Jun 55 assisted FV *Colleen* at 29°19′N, 93°54′W; 15 Oct 56 assisted disabled MV *Hummel Elvn*; 27 Aug 58 assisted FV *Minorcan* at 29°28′N, 93°15′W; 30 Oct–2 Nov 58 assisted USS *Instill* at 28°55′N, 89°13′W; 17–18 Nov 59 searched for National Flight 967; 5 Dec 62 assisted FV *Doria* at 29°20′N, 85°03′W; 9 Feb 64 collided with dredge *Duplex* in Mobile Channel; late Aug 65 provided men and equipment to fight fire on Liberian MV *Arctic Reefer* off Choctaw Point, Mobile, AL; 7–8 Dec 68 searched for survivors from cutter *White Alder*.

Sassafras

15 Apr 45–23 Aug 46 stationed at San Francisco, CA, and used for A/N; 23 Aug 46–22 Aug 47 stationed at Honolulu, HI, and used for A/N; 22 Aug 47–1977 stationed at Cape May, NJ, and used for A/N; 30 Apr 48 assisted MV *Berwindglen*; 18–19 Jan 49 assisted cutter *Eastwind* following collision; 31 Oct 49 assisted FV *Marjorie M* off Delaware; 7 Mar 50 assisted disabled FV *Mayflower* at 38°24′N, 73°49′W; 21 Dec 51 assisted MV *Burco Trader* near Cape May; 22 Feb 52 assisted FV *Theresa and Jean* near Cape May; 7 Mar 52 escorted distressed FV *Carol Ann* to Cape May; 27 Apr 52 escorted distressed MV *Monte Brazil*; 16 Jan 53 temporarily assumed Overfalls Station; 18 Aug 53 assisted FV *Lefrancais* at 38°10′N, 73°40′W; 22 Oct 53 towed disabled FV *Sea Rambler* to Cape May; 30 Dec 53 assisted following collision between MVs *Atlantic Dealer* and *Atlantic Engineer* in Delaware R.; 27 Feb 54 assisted disabled FV *Mayflower* at 38°37′N, 73°56′W; 3 May 55 assisted FV *Captain Deebold* near Cape May; 17 Nov 56 assisted FV *Emila Anna* at 38°59′N, 74°44′W; 11 Jan 57 recovered drifting barge *Elizabeth H Graham* in Delaware Bay; 8–20 Mar 57 assisted following collision between Liberian MV *Elna II* and USNS *Mission of San Francisco* near Patch I.; 4 Sep 57 assisted following a mid-air collision between two USAF F89 ac in Delaware Bay; 11 Oct 57 assisted FV *Pamnico* off Cape May; 19 Feb 58 assisted tanker *Tydol Flying A*, icebound in the Chesapeake and Delaware Canal; 20 Nov 58 assisted FV *Sea Hawk* near Cape May; 17–20 Feb 62 assisted following collision between MVs *Pinemore* and *American Archer* at 38°47′N, 75°W; 20 Nov 62 helped fight fire on MV *Sarpeon* at 35°58′N, 75°29′W; 1–2 Jan 63 towed disabled FV *Angie Irene* to Cape May; 30 Apr 67 rescued five from FV *Mockingbird*, which sank 130 mi SE of New York City; 12 Jan 69 grounded on a pinnacle in the Hudson R. N of Bear Mountain Bridge—refloated 16 Jan; 1977–78 underwent a major renovation at the CG Yard, Curtis Bay, MD; 1978–81 stationed at Governors I., NY, and used for A/N; 1981–90 stationed at Honolulu, HI, and used for A/N; 27 Mar 83 seized *Shinei Maru No 21* 165 mi NW of Midway I. for illegal fishing; 21 Feb 86 seized Taiwanese FV *Huey Shyang 31* near Pago Pago for fisheries violation; 5 Dec 86 rescued two from sailboat *Joie de Mer* 550 mi SW of Honolulu, HI; Feb 89 helped recover debris from United Airlines Flight 811 off Hawaii.

Sedge

11 Aug 44–26 Feb 47 stationed at Honolulu, HI, and used for A/N throughout the Pacific; 26 Feb 47–14 Apr 50 out of commission due to a shortage of personnel; 1 May 50–15 Jul 57 stationed at Kodiak, AK, and used primarily for A/N and SAR; 30 Apr–1 May 51 towed disabled FV

Lillian Wizard to Kodiak, AK; 20 Nov 52 assisted MV *Alaska Spruce* at Phipps Point and medevaced crewman from FV *Evening Star* at 58°02′N, 148°16′W; 11 May 55 assisted FV *Hunky Dory* at 59°13′N, 151°16′W; 24–26 May 55 towed disabled CGS *Surveyor* from Popof I. to Kodiak, AK; 9 Jun 55 helped remove casualties from private ac at Montague I.; 11 Jun 55 stood by distressed FV *Marinet*; 15 Jul 57–28 Apr 73 stationed at Cordova, AK, and used for A/N; 13 Jul 58 medevaced crewman from FV *Unimak* at 60°01′N, 144°26′W; 9–10 Aug 58 patrolled salmon derby at Seward, AK; 10 May 59 assisted USNS *Mission San Rafael* aground on Fire I., Cook Inlet; 1–2 Oct 62 rescued survivors from MV *Roustabout* at 60°06′N, 146°41′W; 2 May 63 helped fight fire in Cordova, AK; 10 May 65 medevaced a seaman from Russian FV *Dozorny* at Seward, AK; 29–30 Mar 66 escorted disabled Russian FV *Bess* while in U.S. waters off Alaska; 5 Feb 67 medevaced an injured seaman from Russian FV *Arseniew*; Mar 67 assisted and watched disabled Russian MV *Shkery*, which had sought shelter in Icy Bay; 4 Apr 68 helped fight fire at Cordova docks, AK; 31 Mar 69 towed disabled FV *Camaano Sound* 400 mi SE of Kodiak, AK, to Sitka; 24–26 May 70 towed disabled FV *Irene C* to Cordova, AK; 28 Apr 73–25 Jun 74 underwent major rehabilitation at CG Yard, Curtis Bay, MD; 6 Nov 74–1990 stationed at Homer, AK, and used primarily for A/N; 18 Feb 76 seized South Korean FV *Dong Won 109* near Sitka, AK, for fisheries violation; 2 Nov 84 extinguished fire and towed crabber 12 mi to Homer, AK.

Spar

21 Aug 44–1 Dec 46 stationed at Boston, MA, and used for A/N and icebreaking; 1 Dec 46–1 Jun 51 stationed at Woods Hole, MA, and used for A/N and icebreaking; 5 Feb 47 assisted MV *Amelia* near Woods Hole, MA; 6 Jul 47 assisted FV *M. J. Hayes* near Woods Hole, MA; 16 Jan 51 assisted FV *Mary Ann* 30 mi off Block I.; 1 Jun 51–Feb 76 stationed at Bristol, RI, and used for A/N and icebreaking; 9 Jan 53 assisted FV *Noreen* off Bristol, RI; 20 Jan 56 escorted distressed USNS *Sagita* to Boston, MA; 18 May–24 Sep 57 departed from and returned to Bristol, RI, circumnavigating North American continent via the Panama Canal and the Northwest Passage in company with cutters *Bramble* and *Storis*; 29 Jul 59 assisted following collision between *Francisville* and *Luckenbach* at 41°27′N, 71°01′W; late Nov 65 medevaced a crewman and towed disabled FV *John F. Kennedy* from 170 mi E of Cape Cod to Gloucester, MA; 29 Jan 71 grounded in Narragansett Bay and sustained minor damage; Feb–Oct 76 underwent a major renovation at the CG Yard, Curtis Bay, MD; Jan 81 broke ice and delivered urgently needed supplies to Mount Hope Bay area following record-setting freeze; Oct 1976–1990 stationed at South Portland, ME, and used for A/N and icebreaking.

Sundew

1 Nov 45–15 Jun 53 stationed at Milwaukee, WI, and used for A/N and icebreaking; 8 Jul 48 stood by stranded MV *Edgewater* near Milwaukee, WI; 15 Jul 53–1 Jun 58 stationed at Sturgeon Bay, WI, and used for A/N and icebreaking; 14 Jan 54 freed icebound FVs in Green Bay, Ellison Bay, and Jackson Harbor; 1 Jun 58–Aug 77 stationed at Charlevoix, MI, and used for A/N and icebreaking; 12 Jul 58 patrolled Port Huron-Mackinac I. Race; 18–20 Nov 58 rescued two from MV *Carl D. Bradley* in northern Lake Michigan; 10 May 65 assisted in search for survivors from U.S. MV *Cedarville* and Norwegian MV *Topdalsfjord* collision 1 mi NE of Mackinaw City, MI; 24 Jun 69 located and escorted lost tug *Wright* to Alpena, MI, following equipment failure; 29 Apr 70 towed disabled 17-foot PC to St. Ignace, MI; Aug 77–Aug 78 underwent major renovation at CG Yard, Curtis Bay, MD; Aug 78–1980 stationed at Charlevoix, MI, and used for A/N and icebreaking; 1980–90 stationed at Duluth, MN, and used for A/N and icebreaking; winter 1987–88 conducted LE patrols in Caribbean.

Sweetbrier

11 Aug 44–1 Apr 46 stationed at Eureka, CA, and used for A/N; 1 Apr 46–1 Feb 48 stationed at Honolulu, HI, and used for A/N; 1 Feb 48–5 May 50 temporarily out of commission due to a shortage of personnel; 5 May 50–15 Jul 57 stationed at Ketchikan, AK, and used for A/N and icebreaking; 13 Dec 50 aided FV *Tyde* off Ketchikan; 5 Jan 51 assisted FV *Linda B* aground at Port Chester, AK; 5 Aug 51 towed disabled FV *Patricia Joan* to Ketchikan, AK; 25 Nov 51 assisted MV *Dart* off Ketchikan; 20 Nov 52 assisted grounded MV *Alaska Spruce* at Phipps Point; 30 May 53 assisted FV *Maradol* near Monte Carlo I.; 11 Jul 53 holed after striking a rock off Sugar Loaf I.—damage moderate; 15 Apr 55 towed disabled FV *Five Brothers II* from 55°16′N, 131°28′W, to Ketchikan; 15 Jul 56–1974 stationed at Juneau, AK, and used for A/N and icebreaking; 1–2 Sep 58 rescued two from private ac near Juneau, AK; 5 Jun 63 assisted following Northwest Airlines crash near 54°16′N, 134°41′W; 26 Apr 67 assisted in medevac from Soviet MV *Tuloma* 60 mi SW of Ketchikan, AK; 30 Jul 67 crew party rescued two from crashed ac on Admiralty I.; 28 Oct 68 helped repair fuel leak on MV *Sunde* off Kayak I.; 6 Feb 69 medevaced a patient from FV *Wrangell* to Juneau, AK; 1974–31 Oct 75 received extensive renovation at the CG Yard, Curtis Bay, MD; 1975–90 stationed at Cordova, AK, and used for A/N and icebreaking; 26 Jul 84 stabilized flooding in FV *Ironhead* and escorted her to Cordova, AK.

Woodrush

22 Sep 44–31 Jul 78 stationed at Duluth, MN, and used for A/N and icebreaking; 4 Jun 51 assisted MV *A. B. Wolvin* aground off Houghton Point; 5 Jul 51 escorted distressed yacht *Buccaneer* to Grand Haven, MI; 29 Oct 51 refloated MV *Leonard C. Hanna* off Ashland; 25 Apr 53 assisted MV *J. H. Brown* near Superior, WI; 11–13 May 53 unsuccessfully searched for survivors from MV *Henry Steinbrenner* 15 mi off Passage I.; 12 Sep 53 assisted MV *Maryland* near Marquette, MI; 5 Dec 61 towed disabled MV *Second* in Lake Superior until relieved by commercial tug; Aug 62 salvaged USAF F-101B ac near Marquette, WI; 11 Apr 70 helped free grounded MV *Stadacona* near Mackinac Bridge; 31 Jul 78–Mar 80 underwent major renovation at CG Yard, Curtis Bay, MD; 3 Jun 80–1990 stationed at Sitka, AK, and used for A/N, LE, SAR, and icebreaking; 4–5 Nov 80 assisted during rescue of passengers and crew from cruise ship *Prinsendam*.

180-FOOT TENDERS *MESQUITE* (180 [B]) CLASS

Name	Hull Number	Builder	Keel Laid	Launched	Commissioned	Disposition
Ironwood	WLB 297 WAGL 297	Coast Guard Yard, Curtis Bay, MD	2 Nov 42	16 Mar 43	4 Aug 43	Active
Mesquite	WLB 305 WAGL 305	Marine Iron & Shipbuilding Corp., Duluth, MN	20 Aug 42	14 Nov 42	27 Aug 43	Stranded 5 Dec 89
Buttonwood	WLB 306 WAGL 306	Marine Iron & Shipbuilding Corp., Duluth, MN	5 Oct 42	30 Nov 42	24 Sep 43	Active
Planetree	WLB 307 WAGL 307	Marine Iron & Shipbuilding Corp., Duluth, MN	4 Dec 42	20 Mar 43	4 Nov 43	Active
Papaw	WLB 308 WAGL 308	Marine Iron & Shipbuilding Corp., Duluth, MN	16 Nov 42	19 Feb 43	12 Oct 43	Active
Sweetgum	WLB 309 WAGL 309	Marine Iron & Shipbuilding Corp., Duluth, MN	21 Feb 43	15 Apr 43	20 Nov 43	Active

Cost   Hull & machinery range between $870,836 and $1,388,227 per unit—see Scheina, *WWII Cutters,* for details.

Hull
  Displacement (tons)   1,028 fl (1964); 768 light (1964)
  Length   180' oa; 170' bp
  Beam   37' max
  Draft   14' max (1964)

Machinery
  Main Engines   1 electric motor connected to 2 Westinghouse generators driven by 2 Cooper-Bessemer diesels
  SHP   1,200
  Propellers   single

Performance
  Max Sustained   12.5 kts, 7,000-mi radius (1964)
  Economic   9.0 kts, 9,000-mi radius (1964)

Logistics
  Fuel Oil (95%)   47,360 gal
  Complement   5 officers, 2 warrants, 46 men (1964)

Deck Gear
  Boom Capacity   20 tons
  Hoist Power   electricity

Electronics
  Detection Radar   SPS-23 (*Basswood*, 1964; *Ironwood*, 1965)
  Sonar   UNQ-1 (*Basswood*, 1964); UQU-1 (*Ironwood*, 1965)

Armament   1 3"/50 (*Basswood*, 1964); none (*Ironwood*, 1964)

Design
The preliminary design for the second set of 180-foot coastwise tenders was prepared by the Coast Guard, and the final design was prepared by A. M. Deering of Chicago, IL. *See* 180-foot tenders, *Cactus* (180 [A]) class for additional details.

Buttonwood

22 Aug 46–1981 stationed at Honolulu, HI, and used for A/N and to carry supplies throughout the Pacific, including Okinawa, Guam, the Philippines, Kwajalein, Bikati, and Eniwetok; 4–10 Jul 54 escorted damaged cutter *Iroquois* from Midway I. to Honolulu, HI; 6 Mar 58 unsuccessfully searched for overboard crew member from sampan *Fuji Maru* at

21°15'N, 158°00'W; 14 Mar 58 assisted MV *Hawaiian Trader* aground at 21°08'N, 157°38'W; 27 Jul–1 Aug 58 towed disabled FV *Taihei Maru* from 24°38'N, 167°22'W, to Honolulu, HI; 26 Nov 65 medevaced an injured seaman from Japanese FV *Taineu Maru* to Honolulu, HI, and rescued 18 from stranded FV *Kaiyo Maru No 25* at Laysan I.; Aug 71 patrolled Transpacific Yacht Race; 1981–90 stationed at Galveston, TX, and used for A/N; Jan 89 fought fire on FV *Gulf Cloud* off Louisiana.

Ironwood

25 Jul 47–9 May 50 stationed at Monterey, CA, and used for A/N; 28 Mar 48 searched for reported mine; 12 Oct 49 assisted FV *Victory* at 36°40'N, 123°45'W; 9 May 50–12 Jul 54 stationed at Guam and used for A/N and to service Loran stations throughout Pacific, including those at Okinawa, the Philippines, and Kwajalein; 12 Jul 54–26 Oct 69 stationed at Honolulu, HI, and used for A/N and to service Loran stations throughout Pacific, including Okinawa, Kwajalein, and French Frigate Shoal; 9–14 Nov 57 unsuccessfully searched for missing Pan American Flight

Tender *Buttonwood* on 27 Dec 60. Note the unique crest adorning the stack.

994—returned to Honolulu, HI, due to cracked hull weld, escorted by cutter *Planetree*; 8 Jan 59 assisted grounded sampan *Bellatrix* at Molokai Beach, HI; 19 Mar 59 towed becalmed French small craft *La Cle de Sol* off Barber's Point, HI; 1 Dec 60 towed disabled yacht *Endymion* to Honolulu, HI; 6 Jan 62 rescued crew of FV *Hiroshima Maru* aground at 21°17′N, 157°51′W; 23–25 May 63 escorted disabled MV *Oianna* to Honolulu, HI; 18 Feb 69 towed disabled FV *Widgeon* from Augustine I. to Homer, AK; early Apr 69 escorted distressed tanker *Yukon,* which was holed by a submerged object in Cook Inlet; 29 Apr 69 fought fire on Shell Oil drilling platform in Cook Inlet; 26 Oct 69–13 Jul 74 stationed at Homer, AK, and used for A/N; 26 Dec 69 hoisted disabled FV *Arctic Fox* on board at MacArthur Cove and carried her to Seward, AK; 13 Jul 74–early 75 underwent major overhaul at CG Yard, Curtis Bay, MD; early 75–1 May 79 stationed at Adak, AK, and used for A/N; 1 May 79–1990 stationed at Kodiak, AK, and used for A/N; 23 Oct 83 seized FV *Kiyo Maru No 55* for underlogging catch.

Mesquite

1 Sep 47–15 Sep 59 stationed at Sault Ste. Marie, MI, and used for A/N and icebreaking; 30–31 May 49 assisted USS *PC 782* off Isle Royale; 10 May 52 assisted disabled MV *Outarde* 11 mi W of Great Duck I.; 2 Jun 52 assisted MV *James Watt* aground in St. Marys R.; 17–18 Apr 53 assisted and escorted tug *Favorite* and barge *Krupp* 32 mi NW of Whitefish Pt.; 8–9 Apr 56 towed disabled cutter *Arundel* to Detroit, MI; 2 Jul 56 assisted grounded MV *Angeline* at Soo Canals; 7 Oct 56 assisted barge *Delkote* in Lake Superior; 3 May 57 assisted MV *Jay C Morse* aground near Lake Nicolet; 15 Sep 59–1977 stationed at Sturgeon Bay, WI, and used for A/N and icebreaking; 30 Apr 60 assisted following crash of Canadian B-25 ac off Cadahy, WI; 30 Nov 60 assisted grounded Liberian MV *Francisco Morazan* in Lake Michigan; 10 Apr 64 grounded on Eleven Foot Shoal; 1 Dec 66 recovered barge adrift and towed it to Milwaukee; 8 Apr 70 freed tanker *Mercy* from ice near Green Bay, WI; 15 Apr 70 medevaced crewman from MV *Leon Falk Jr* off Escanaba, MI; 19 Nov 70 medevaced crewman from MV *George R. Fink* off Escanaba, MI; Jan 73 fought fire on board tanker *Venus* near Escanaba, MI; 1977–89 stationed at Charlevoix, MI, and used for A/N and icebreaking; 3 Mar 85 seized Cayman MV *Cruz del Sur* carrying three pounds of marijuana.

Papaw

1 Feb 46–15 Jun 49 stationed at Astoria, OR, and used for A/N; 15 Jun 49–21 Sep 54 stationed at Miami, FL, and used for A/N; 27–28 Mar 50 unsuccessfully attempted to free cutter *Mocoma* aground on Star Reef; 8 May 52 stood by MV *James Lykes* following stranding at 27°23′N, 78°50′W; 24–25 Oct 52 assisted in hurricane evacuation in Jacksonville area; 21 Jan 53 assisted MV *Little Women* aground on Loose Key; 7 Jul 53 salvaged wreckage of CG PBY ac in North Pass, Mississippi R.; 21 Sep 54–1990 stationed at Charleston, SC, and used for A/N; 18 Jun 56 assisted tug *Eugene F. Moran* at 32°32′N, 79°50′W; 7–8 Aug 56 assisted following mid-air collision between two USAF F-84 ac off Savannah; 10 Jun 58 towed disabled FV *Mikelbet* to Charleston, SC; 30 Sep–1 Oct 59 assisted in hurricane evacuation for Charleston and Savannah areas; 1–2 Oct 59 helped fight fire at Standard Oil Co., Charleston, SC; 10 Jan 60 assisted MV *Bill* at 30°14′N, 72°32′W; 1 Mar 60 assisted following a mid-air collision of USAF ac off Charleston, SC; 28–30 Jun 60 rescued crew from MV *George MacDonald* at 32°25′N, 78°50′W; 25–27 Nov 61

assisted following collision between MVs *Caravan* and *Haiti Trader* at 23°24′N, 78°58′W; 31 May 62 towed disabled PC *Linda M* to Savannah; 31 Oct–2 Nov 62 towed disabled tanker *N. W. Gokey* from 32°14′N, 80°17′W to Charleston, SC; 31 Jan 63 struck overhanging flight deck of USS *Saratoga* at Mayport, FL, collapsing mast; Feb 64 transported NOMAD, first atomic-powered weather buoy, to Gulf of Mexico; mid-Nov 65 rescued three from FV *Ocean Queen* after she had collided with German MV *Lutzenburg* off Charleston, SC; 29 Mar 66 helped fight fire on Norwegian MV *Noorwijk* in Charleston, SC; 8 Feb 68 towed disabled FV *Sandra Dean* 100 mi S of Charleston, SC, to Savannah, GA; 9 Oct 68 escorted distressed sailboat *Quest* 38 mi E of Charleston, SC, to Port Royal Sound; Dec 85 rescued 43 Dominican refugees in an overloaded 30-ft boat adrift for four days without food or water 20 mi N of Mona I.

Planetree

1 Jun 44–1947 stationed at Pearl Harbor, HI, and used for A/N; 1947–1 Sep 49 decommissioned due to shortage of personnel; 1 Sep 49–1 Oct 54 stationed at Guam, Mariana I., and used for A/N at Eniwetok, French Frigate Shoal, Guam, Okinawa, Philippines, Saipan, and other islands; 10–21 Jan 54 assisted MV *Metomkin* aground at Ponape Passage; 1 Oct 54–7 Aug 74 stationed at Honolulu, HI, and continued to service A/N in Western Pacific; 9–14 Nov 57 searched for missing Pan American Flight 944; 12–14 Nov 57 escorted cutter *Ironwood* to Honolulu, HI; 15 Oct 58 assisted FV *Flying Fish* at 22°00′N, 156°29′W; 25 Aug 59 towed disabled PC *Diablo* 150 mi N of Oahu, HI; 18–20 Jan 65 escorted disabled cutter *Matagorda* from 90 mi NE of Midway I. to Midway; 22 Jan 65 escorted disabled Liberian MV *African Monarch* from Midway to Honolulu, HI; late Sep 65 towed disabled ketch *Kate* during a typhoon from 50 mi NW of Saipan to that island; 18 Jul 67 towed disabled yacht *Rampage*; 30 Nov 67 escorted distressed MV *Hongkong Amber* 150 mi N of Honolulu, HI, to that port; Dec 69 made extensive repairs to French Frigate Shoal, which sustained storm damage; 21 Jul 70 gave medical assistance to FV *Katrusa Maru No 28* 930 mi S of Honolulu, HI; 25 Jul 70 medevaced crewman from FV *Katrusa Maru No 28* off Hawaii; 23–26 Oct 70 towed disabled yacht *Redwing* from 200 mi off Honolulu, HI, to that port; 7 Aug 74–1985 stationed at Juneau, AK, and used for A/N; Jan 83 sustained damage during a storm and was escorted to Hawaii by the cutter *Munro*; 1985–90 stationed at Ketchikan, AK, and used for A/N.

Sweetgum

15 Mar 44–1 Sep 46 stationed at Miami, FL, and used for A/N; 1 Sep 46–1990 stationed at Mayport, FL, and used for A/N; 27 May 50 assisted disabled FV *Johnny Boy* at 29°55′N, 81°02′W; 21–22 Oct 52 escorted disabled MV *Rio Escondido* to Mayport; 8 Oct 53 towed disabled FV *Amelia*; 20 Dec 53 helped refloat MV *Port Lyttleton* near Mayport; 7 Dec 54 assisted FVs *American Eagle* and *Wanderer* at 29°56′N, 81°07′W; 4 Apr 55 assisted PC *Nola Sergent* off Mayport; 17–18 Sep 55 assisted with hurricane evacuation of Jacksonville area; 25 Oct 55 assisted tug *Moultrie* near St. Simon Sound; 30 Apr 57 towed disabled yacht *Quail* to Brunswick, GA; Aug–Sep 67 participated in sunken tanker project to determine potential of pollution from tankers sunk in WW II; 27 Dec 67 towed disabled yacht *Pinafore* 170 mi E of Jacksonville, FL, to Mayport, FL; 21 Jul 68 stood by disabled tanker *Transhudson* until commercial tug arrived; Aug 75 carried 43 tons of marijuana seized at Deep Water Cay, Bahamas, to Miami, FL; Jan 86 assisted in recovery of debris from space shuttle Challenger.

180-FOOT TENDERS *CACTUS* (180 [A]) CLASS

Name	Hull Number	Builder	Keel Laid	Launched	Commissioned	Disposition
Balsam	WLB 62 WAGL 62	Zenith Dredge Co., Duluth, MN	25 Oct 41	15 Apr 42	14 Oct 42	*Decomm* 6 Mar 75 *Sold* 13 Sep 77
Cactus	WLB 270 WAGL 270	Marine Iron & Shipbuilding Corp., Duluth, MN	31 Mar 41	25 Nov 41	1 Sep 42	*Decomm* 23 Nov 71 *Sold* 9 Oct 73
Cowslip	WLB 277 WAGL 277	Marine Iron & Shipbuilding Corp., Duluth, MN	16 Sep 41	11 Apr 42	17 Oct 42 *Recomm* 9 Nov 81	*Decomm* and *sold* 29 Mar 73 *Repurchased* 19 Jan 81; active
Woodbine	WLB 289 WAGL 289	Zenith Dredge Co., Duluth, MN	2 Feb 42	3 Jul 42	17 Nov 42	*Decomm* 15 Feb 72 *Donated* 19 Jun 72
Gentian	WLB 290 WAGL 290	Zenith Dredge Co., Duluth, MN	3 Oct 41	23 May 42	3 Nov 42	Active
Laurel	WLB 291 WAGL 291	Zenith Dredge Co., Duluth, MN	17 Apr 42	4 Aug 42	24 Nov 42	Active
Clover	WMEC 292 WLB 292 WAGL 292	Marine Iron & Shipbuilding Corp., Duluth, MN	3 Dec 41	25 Apr 42	8 Nov 42	Active
Evergreen	WMEC 295 WLB 295 WAGO 295 WAGL 292	Marine Iron & Shipbuilding Corp., Duluth, MN	15 Apr 42	3 Jul 42	30 Apr 43	Active
Sorrel	WLB 296 WAGL 296	Zenith Dredge Co., Duluth, MN	26 May 42	28 Sep 42	15 Apr 43	Active
Citrus	WMEC 300 WLB 300 WAGL 300	Marine Iron & Shipbuilding Corp., Duluth, MN	29 Apr 42	15 Aug 42	30 May 43	Active
Conifer	WLB 301 WAGL 301	Marine Iron & Shipbuilding Corp., Duluth, MN	6 Jul 42	3 Nov 42	1 Jul 43	Active
Madrona	WLB 302 WAGL 302	Zenith Dredge Co., Duluth, MN	6 Jul 42	11 Nov 42	30 May 43	Active
Tupelo	WLB 303 WAGL 303	Zenith Dredge Co., Duluth, MN	15 Aug 42	28 Nov 42	30 Aug 43	*Decomm* 30 Sep 75 *Sold* 13 Sep 77

Cost	Hull & machinery range between $782,381 and $952,103 per unit—see Scheina, *WWII Cutters,* for details.
Hull	
Displacement (tons)	1,026 fl (1966); 700 light (1966)
Length	180′ oa; 170′ bp
Beam	37′1″ max
Draft	14′7″ max (1966)
Machinery	
Main Engines	1 electric motor connected to 2 Westinghouse generators driven by 2 Cooper-Bessemer-type GND-8, 4-cycle, diesels
SHP	1,000
Propellers	single
Performance	
Max Sustained	11.9 kts, 12,800-mi radius (1966)
Economic	8.5 kts, 27,000-mi radius (1966)
Logistics	
Fuel Oil (95%)	69,650 gal
Complement	4 officers, 2 warrants, 47 men (1966)

Deck Gear	
Boom Capacity	20 tons
Hoist Power	electricity
Electronics	
Detection Radar	SPS-23 (*Balsam*, 1966; *Clover*, 1967)
Sonar	UNQ-1 (*Balsam*, 1966); SQS-2 (*Clover*, 1967)
Armament	none (*Balsam*, 1966; *Clover*, 1967)

Design

The preliminary design of the 180-foot coastwise tenders was initiated by the USLHS prior to its amalgamation into the Coast Guard. The final design was executed by Marine Iron & Shipbuilding Corp., Duluth, MN. This design was intended to replace all large or class "A" tenders. For the first time it added search-and-rescue features to those designed for tending buoys or servicing lighthouses. Following the amalgamation of the USLHS into the Coast Guard, ice-breaking features were added to the design. The final design produced a single-screw ship with considerable slack bilges and a cutaway forefront. In addition, the deckhouse aft of the buoy deck was extended to the ship's side, increasing interior space. The search-and-rescue requirement caused a reduction in the beam-to-length ratio, and also gave the ship finer lines at the bow and stern.

The *Balsam*, 30 Mar 73. Although classified as a tender throughout her career, the *Balsam*, like all buoy tenders stationed in the Pacific Northwest, undertook numerous law-enforcement and search-and-rescue missions.

Balsam

1942–47 assigned to 12th District and SERVPAC providing A/N, logistics, and fire fighting in South Pacific; 21 Oct 47–14 Aug 53 stationed at Astoria, OR, and used for A/N; 23 May 48 sank a mine off Astoria, OR; 19–22 Jul 48 towed MV *Colima*; 17–19 Nov 48 assisted MV *Herald of Morning*; 20 Nov 58 towed disabled FV; 26 Jul 49 assisted FV *Destiny* at 47°42′N, 126°29′W; 1 Aug 49 assisted FV *Mirn* at 46°47′N, 124°11′W; Aug 49 served on tuna patrol in Neah Bay; 16 Aug 49 towed disabled FVs *Prowler* and *Yellow Fin* to Astoria, OR; 23 Aug 49 assisted dredge *Kingman* off Columbia R. Bar; Sep–Oct 49 served on tuna patrol; 20 Jan 50 broke ice in Columbia R.; 24 Mar 50 assisted tug *Klihyan* and barge at 46°19′N, 124′W; 27 Jul 50 assisted FV *Suzanne* at 44°22′N, 124°20′W; 29 Jul 51 patrolled International Yacht Race, Vancouver, Canada; 4 Aug 51 patrolled Gold Cup Races, Lake Washington, WA; 14 Mar 52 assisted FV *Jimmy Boy* at 48°23′N, 124°36′W; 30 Apr 52 assisted MV *Beloit Victory* at 48°07′N, 124°56′W; 25 May 52 towed disabled FV *Scarlet Queen* to Astoria, OR; 8–9 Jun 52 assisted grounded MV *Cynthia Olson* at Columbia R. Bar; Jul 52 served on sockeye salmon patrol; 14–15 Sep 52 towed disabled FV *Kennfalls* to Astoria, OR; 24 Oct 52 assisted tug *Winquatt* and MV *Seafarer*; 13–18 Dec 52 assisted grounded MV *Yorkmar* at Grays Harbor; 23 Apr 53 assisted MV *Shawnee Trail*; 15 Aug 53–30 Sep 56 stationed at Eureka, CA, and served A/N; 26–27 Sep 53 towed disabled FV *Defiant* to Humboldt Bay; 19 Oct 53 assisted FV *Jenus* at 40°41′N, 124°25′W; 21–22 May 54 assisted tug *Hercules* in towing MV *William Carson* 18 mi NW of Point Cabrillo; 22 Sep 55 escorted disabled Army dredge *Davidson* to San Francisco; 15 May 56 assisted MVs *Flomar* and *Thorvald* following a collision at 40°34′N, 124°40′W; Jul–Aug 56 resupplied DEW Line in Alaska; Oct 56–29 Jun 58 stationed at Honolulu, HI, and served A/N; Feb 57 towed disabled USFWS *Hugh Smith* from 14°18′S, 114°45′W to Hawaii; Jul–Aug 57 resupplied DEW Line in Alaska; 10–14 Nov 57 searched for missing Pan American Flight 944; 3–4 Dec 57 assisted FV *Setsu Maru* at 21°50′N, 160°08′W; 9 Apr 58 supplied MV *Vagabond* with food and water at 28°N, 179°21′W; 30 Jun 58–29 Jun 64 stationed at Ketchikan, AK, and serviced A/N; 30 Jun 64–6 Mar 75 stationed at Adak, AK, and serviced A/N; 27 Apr 65 medevaced seaman from Russian FV *Sakhalin* at Dutch Harbor, AK; Jun 65 served on Alaska Patrol; Nov 65 escorted Russian MV *Ivan Kuliban*, which had entered U.S. waters to make emergency repairs; 9 Nov 66 evacuated survivors of FV *Bettles* from Aleutian I.; 26 Jul 68 assisted and escorted British MV *Welsh Minstrel* to Adak, AK; 29 Sep 68 rescued three from FV *Marsha Ann* in Atka Pass; 14 Oct 69 medevaced crewman from FV *Shintoko Maru* off Dutch Harbor, AK.

Cactus

1942–67 stationed at Boston, MA, and used for A/N and SAR; 2 Mar 52 assisted FV *Dorothy and Mary* 20 mi S of Nantucket; 16 Nov 53 fought fire on FV *Jane and Patricia*; 26 Aug 54 assisted grounded FV *Western Pride* near Provincetown, MA; 10 Feb 57 assisted grounded MV *Franco Lisi* near Salem, MA; 27 Jul 57 moved a 450-ft Norwegian MV away from burning pier in Boston, MA, and helped fight fire; 21–22 Feb 59 assisted FV *Jo-Ann*; 16 Nov 62 assisted FV *Barbara M* 20 mi SE of Nantucket; 8 Feb 63 assisted FV *Clipper* at 40°50′N, 68°30′W; 24–25 Jan 66 escorted disabled MV *South African Victory* to Boston, MA; 1967–69 stationed at Bristol, RI; 4 Feb 69 towed disabled FV *Chrisway* 140 mi SE of Cape Henry to safety; 1970–71 stationed at Astoria, OR.

Citrus

1 Mar 45–29 Jun 64 stationed at Ketchikan, AK, and used for A/N; 9 Sep 48 assisted MV *Caledonia* in Idaho Inlet; 29–31 Oct 48 assisted USNS *Mission Santa Cruz* at 57°6′N, 134°40′W; 13–19 Feb 50 searched for missing USAF plane near Wrangell Narrows; 25 Aug 50 assisted barge *Bisco 3* near Ratz Harbor; 26 Aug 50 assisted FV *Vermay* near Cape Muzon; 27 Aug 50 towed power scow *Chichagof* near Cape Chacon; 19 May 51 escorted cutter *White Holly* to Ketchikan after cutter struck a rock and was holed; 25 May 51 assisted FV *Dolores* near Point Gardner; 21–27 Jul 51 searched for a Canadian DC-4; 15–19 Jan 52 escorted cutter *Cahoone* to Sitka, AK; 8 Jun 52 towed FV *Pioneer* to Ketchikan, AK; 13 Aug 52 assisted FV *Hobo* near Lincoln I.; 23 Aug 52 assisted FV *Unuk* in Behm Canal; 24 Aug 53 helped tug *Saturn* recover lost tow at 56°25′N, 140°28′W; 25–30 Aug 53 searched for, found, and towed scow to Ketchikan, AK; 13 Oct 53 assisted grounded APL-55 near Dangerous R.; 7 Apr 55 assisted FV *Jo Darlin* near Ketchikan, AK; 30 May–1 Jun 58 patrolled salmon derby; 30 Jun 64–1979 stationed at Kodiak, AK, and used for A/N; 12 Feb 65 located two Russian FVs 3.4 mi from U.S. territory, notified them of proximity to U.S. territory, and they departed; 8 Mar 65 fought fire on MV *Kalaikh* off Alaska and towed to Kodiak, AK; 28 Apr 65 discovered a Russian FV 2 mi SE of Marmot I., AK—FV refused to answer signals and proceeded to sea; 3 May 65 medevaced a seaman from Russian FV *Churkin* at Kodiak I., AK; late Oct 65 escorted two Japanese FVs from U.S. waters; 24–26 Jan 68 fought fire on Japanese MV *Seifu Maru* in Dutch Harbor, AK; 12 Apr 68 rescued two from MV *MPE-110* in Cook Inlet; 9 Aug 68 assisted and escorted distressed MV *Dantzler*, following a grounding, from Cook Inlet to Homer, AK; 1 Apr 69 medevaced patient from FV *Zuiyo Maru* off Alaska; 8 May 70 towed disabled FV *Shirley Rose* to Kodiak, AK; 20 Oct 70 removed 31 from grounded ferry *Tustumena* near Kodiak, AK; 19 Jan 74 searched for missing crew members from trawler *John and Olaf* in Gulf of Alaska; 27 Feb 79 struck a submerged object at 57°54′N, 152°31′W and sustained significant flooding—no personal casualties; 1979–82 underwent extensive repairs;

Mar 82-1990 stationed at Coos Bay, OR, and used primarily for LE and SAR; 1 Jan 85 rammed by MV *Pacific Star* 680 mi SW of San Diego, CA, while attempting to board—1,000 lbs of marijuana recovered from debris.

Clover

22 Aug 46-17 Oct 48 stationed at Dutch Harbor, AK, and used for A/N; 18 Oct 48-30 Jan 58 stationed at Kodiak, AK, and used for A/N; 7 May 50 assisted FV *Evolution* in Warm Springs Bay; 14 Aug 50 assisted grounded barge in Hooper Bay; 12 Jan 51 assisted grounded MV *Lady Jape* at Valdez Arm; 25 Jan 51 rendered medical assistance at Cold Bay, AK; 8 Aug 51 towed disabled aircraft from 64°30'N, 164°14'W to Nome, AK; 15 Feb 52 rendered medical assistance at Cold Bay, AK; 27-29 Mar 52 assisted disabled MV *Garland* at 56°24'N, 154°40'W; 5 Aug 52 assisted FV *Alice I* near Chugach I.; 15 Aug 52 towed disabled FV *Renabel* from 59°15'N, 148°47'W to Seward, AK; 12 Oct 53 assisted APL-55 aground at 59°21'N, 139°19'W; 23 May 55 assisted USCGS ship *Surveyor* off Popof I.; 21 Jan 56 rescued three marooned survivors from Amaniuliak I.; 22-23 Jan 56 medevaced patient from Akutan to Dutch Harbor, AK; 18-19 Apr 56 towed disabled FV *Shamrock* from 57°00'N, 135°30'W to Yakutat, AK; 3-15 Feb 58 held joint exercise with USN; 1 Jul 58-30 Jun 64 stationed at Adak, AK, and used for A/N; 23-25 Dec 59 assisted and escorted disabled Japanese MV *Hokyo Maru* from Nazan Harbor to Adak, AK; 24 Apr 60 towed disabled Canadian FV *Norprince* to Dutch Harbor, AK; 27 Nov 61 escorted two tugs and barges to Dutch Harbor, AK, after they experienced problems with tow; 28-30 Apr 60 discovered Japanese FVs in U.S. territorial waters and escorted them to international waters; 1 Jul 64-30 Jun 65 stationed at Ketchikan, AK, and used for A/N; 1 Jul 65-Dec 69 stationed at Sitka, AK, and used for A/N; 2 Jan 66 helped fight fire in Sitka, AK; Apr 66 assumed tow of disabled FV *Astronaut* from Russian FV *Churkin* 200 mi NW of Ketchikan, AK; 27 Nov 67 medevaced crewman from FV *Kirishima Maru* in Sitka Sound; 20 May 68 escorted distressed FV *Freeland* 300 mi S of Cordova, AK, to Cape St. James, AK; 12 Sep 68 escorted FV *Marutomo Maru* with injured seaman on board to Sitka, AK; 29 Sep 68 towed disabled FV *Miss Georgia* from Salisbury

Sound to Sitka, AK; 13 Oct 68 escorted FV *Fukuyofhi Maru No 55* carrying injured crewman to Sitka, AK; 11 Nov 68 escorted FV *Matuei Maru No 53* carrying injured crewman to Sitka, AK; 2 Jan 69 salvaged a Champion ac in Rodman Bay; 6 Jan 70 assisted distressed FV *Irene G* off Sitka, AK; 21 Feb 70 rescued five from tug *Intrepid* 15 mi S of Ocean Cape; 5 May 70 escorted distressed FV *Oceanic* to Ketchikan, AK; 27 Jun 70 seized FV *Akebono Maru No 11* for fishing inside U.S. Contiguous Zone; 10 Sep 75 seized Taiwanese FV *Tong Hong 3* W of Sitka, AK, for fisheries violation; 9 Feb 77 seized FV *Fukuyoshi Maru 75* for violating U.S. waters; Dec 79-1990 stationed at Eureka, CA, reclassified as WMEC, and used for SAR and LE patrols; Mar-Apr 83 assisted in attempted salvage of Blunts Reef LNB; Aug 83 conducted fisheries patrol off WA, OR, and CA.

Conifer

1 May 45-4 Aug 52 stationed at Portsmouth, VA, and used for A/N; 4 Dec 48 assisted cutter *Pontchartrain*; 14 Mar 50 assisted barge under tow at 30°21'N, 76°39'W; 25 Nov 50 assisted FV *Cavalier* near Cape Henry; 14 Jun 51 assisted PC *Evening Star* 15 mi SE of Diamond Shoal; 4 Oct 51 assisted MV *Marose* aground near Cape Henry; 4-5 Dec 51 assisted tug *Fort Sumter* with MV *Johnny Appleseed* in tow 4 mi E of Cape Romain; 10 Jan 52 assisted FV *Sea Dog* near Wimble Shoals; May 52 escorted SS *United States*; 4 Aug 52-1 Sep 60 stationed at Morehead City, NC, and used for A/N; 31 Dec 52-1 Jan 53 towed disabled MV *Hydra*; 2 Jan 53 assisted disabled FV *Miss Carry* 90 mi ENE of Cape Henry; 8-11 Feb 53 assisted MV *Seaconnet* aground off Beaufort Inlet; 31 Aug 54 towed disabled tug *Ocean Prince*; 23 Sep 54 grounded in Ocracoke Inlet—no damage; 14-15 Dec 54 searched for MV *Southern Districts*; 11 Jan 55 assisted and escorted MV *Flying Cloud* 25 mi S of Frying Pan Shoal; 14 Jan 55 towed FV *Stephen Margo* to Morehead City, NC; 24 Jan 55 escorted disabled MV *Steelore*; 14 Jan 56 assisted PC *Manitou*; 11 Apr 56 assisted tug *Barney Turecamo* off Morehead City; 11 Sep 56 assisted MV *Michael* off Cape Fear R.; 13 Oct 56 towed disabled tug *Hila* and towed tanker *Alpha X*; 19 Feb 58 freed icebound tanker *Trinity* and MV *Berylstone* in Chesapeake Bay; 4 Dec 59 assisted MV *Gulf Tiger* following an explosion at 34°40'N, 75°30'W; 1 Sep 60-11 Jun 75 stationed at Portsmouth, VA, and used for A/N; 12 Sep 60 assisted following hurricane Donna; 3 Feb 61 freed icebound tanker *Pacific* in the Chesapeake; 29 Jan 67 assisted following a collision between MVs *Bodoro* and *Beaver State* on Potomac R.; Feb 69 maintained surveillance over 12 foreign FVs that sought a haven off the Chesapeake during a storm; 11 Jun 75-Jul 83 stationed at Morehead City, NC, and used for A/N; Jul 83-11 Jul 86 underwent major overhaul; 11 Jul 86-1990 stationed at San Diego, CA, and used for A/N; 21 Sep 87 assisted following collision between *Pacharoness* and *Atlantic Wing* 15 mi SW of Point Conception.

Cowslip

1 May 44-29 Mar 73 stationed at Portland, ME, and used for A/N and icebreaking; 12 Feb 46 fought fire on cutter *Modoc*; 1 May 46 assisted cutter *Shrub* to Portland, ME; 21 May 46 assisted disabled FV *Gertrude Decosta* to Boston, MA; 26 Jun 46 assisted disabled FV *Yankee* to Gloucester, MA; 29 Jun 46 assisted disabled FV *Heidi* to New Bedford; 1 Jul 46 assisted disabled FV *Gay Head* to Boston, MA; 27 Aug 46 assisted disabled FV *Skillogilee* to Gloucester, MA; 24 Sep 46 assisted disabled FV *Francis C. Denekey* to Portland, ME; 10 Oct 46 assisted disabled FV *Magellan*; 2 Nov 46 towed disabled tug *Florence W* and its tow, the tug *Sundew*, with the

Icing has the capacity to sink any ship by endangering its stability. The *Citrus* searches for a missing crew member off the trawler *John and Olaf* in the Gulf of Alaska, 19 Jan 74.

cutter's motor launch to Portland, ME; 22 Feb 47 fought fire on tug CG-64301; 3 Mar 47 stood by MV *Oakey S. Alexander*, which had beached at Cape Elizabeth, ME, while crew was rescued by CG station; 4 Mar 47 towed LS to Portland, ME; 14 Mar 47 assisted by CG ac, found two men adrift from Halfway Rock LH and returned them to LH; 19 Apr 47 towed FV *Rita B* to Gloucester, MA; 11 May 47 crew fought fire on Boston pier; 10 Jun 47 towed disabled FV *Florence and Lee* to Gloucester, MA; 30 Jun–1 Jul 47 towed disabled FV *Venture I* to New Bedford, MA; 4 Jul 47 towed disabled FV *Geraldine and Phyllis* to Boston, MA; 14 Aug 47 towed disabled FV *Roma II* to Portland, ME; 15 Aug 47 transported water to Monhegan I. due to shortage; 22–23 Oct 47 crew helped fight forest fire at Waldoboro, ME; 18 Nov 47 freed CG-50004D which had grounded; 25–26 Jan 54 fought fire in Portland harbor; 5 Aug 55 transported water to Monhegan I. due to shortage; 22–23 Nov 55 towed disabled FV *Connie Breaker* from 42°55'N, 66°23'W to Portland, ME; 3 Feb 59 assisted FV *Araho* near Portland, ME; 7 May 59 assisted tug *J. M. Hathaway* near Portland, ME; 25 Aug 59 assisted tug *Jake* at 43°44'N, 69°41'W; 30 Dec 69–1 Jan 70 fought fire on tanker *Dean Reinauer*, Portland, ME; 29 Mar 73 decommissioned and sold; 19 Jan 81 repurchased at Miami, FL, for $1.6 M; 9 Nov 81 recommissioned and stationed at Governors I., NY; 13 Jan 83–25 Jun 84 underwent major renovation at CG Yard, Curtis Bay, MD; 25 Jun 84–1990 stationed at Portsmouth, VA, and used for A/N.

Evergreen

1944–69 stationed at Boston, MA, and used for A/N and oceanographic research; 27 Mar–24 Aug 50 shared IIP with cutters *Acushnet* and *Tampa*; 7 Jul–11 Aug 50 conducted oceanographic survey from N of Grand Banks to Baffin Bay; 21 Jan 54 stood by and escorted MV *Hess Bunker* following grounding at E entrance to Cape Cod Canal; 13 Feb 56 towed disabled FV *Annie Luce* to Boston, MA; 5 Mar–10 Aug 57 shared IIP with cutter *Acushnet*; 27 Jul–4 Aug 63 conducted Labrador Sea survey and observations in the Kane Basin and Smith Sound made possible by unprecedented blockage of Kennedy Channel by an ice island; Mar–Jul 64 conducted oceanographic experiments in the Grand Banks-Newfoundland area in support of IIP; Oct–Nov 65 conducted oceanographic survey between the North Atlantic and Arctic oceans from Greenland to Iceland to Scotland; Jan–Feb 66 conducted an oceanographic survey between Fortaleza, Brazil, and St. Peter and Paul Rocks; Apr 67 served on IIP; Jul 67 conducted oceanographic survey off New England; Aug 67 conducted oceanographic survey in Labrador Sea; 23 Oct 67 helped fight rekindled fire on Indian MV *Vishva Mangal* at Boston, MA; 11–22 Dec 67 conducted hydrographic survey between Cape Cod and Cape Hatteras; 15–26 Jan 68 conducted oceanographic survey between Nova Scotia and Long Island; 7–16 Sep 68 conducted oceanographic survey between Nova Scotia and Long Island; 23–27 Sep 68 conducted survival craft drift project off Nantucket; 23 Dec 68 sustained a fire, main motor and main generators flooded; 1969–1 Apr 70 placed in storage; 1969–73 stationed at Curtis Bay, MD, and used for oceanographic research; Sep 70 conducted SAR research 125 mi E of Norfolk, VA; 14 Oct–9 Nov 70 conducted oceanographic research between Nova Scotia and Cape Hatteras; May 71 conducted Grand Banks research cruise; 14 Sept–14 Oct 71 conducted oceanographic research between Nova Scotia and Cape Hatteras; Nov 71 conducted surface-current research cruise off Sanibel I., FL; 3–23 Apr 72, 5–21 May 72, and 3–22 Jun 72, conducted ice-patrol survey; 1974–90

The *Evergreen* leaves the CG Yard, Curtis Bay, MD, in Feb 73 with a new superstructure, bow-thrusters, and improved electronics. She hardly resembles any of her sister 180-foot tenders. *Evergreen* has served as a buoy tender (1943–63), an oceanographic vessel (1963–82), and a medium-endurance cutter (1982–90).

stationed at New London, CT, and used for oceanographic research; Apr–May 74 conducted ice surveys off Grand Banks; Jul 74 conducted SAR research off New York Bight; 17–26 Sep 74 conducted SAR research off the Carolinas and Georgia; Sep 75 conducted SAR research in South Atlantic Bight; Feb 76 conducted SAR research in South Atlantic Bight; Jun 76 conducted Labrador Current Survey; 17 Aug–7 Sep 76 conducted SAR research in mid-Atlantic Bight; May 83 seized FV *Glenda Lynn* off Long I. with 27t of marijuana on board; 25 Sep 84 seized yacht *Margie* 150 mi SE of Nantucket I. carrying 4t of marijuana; Jul 86 seized FV *Sao Marcos* off Nantucket I. for using illegal liner in nets.

Gentian

3 Feb 44–1 Oct 56 stationed at Cape May, NJ, and used for A/N; 1 Apr 48 assisted tug *Ivanhoe* near Cape May; 3 Jul 48 evacuated 42 persons from disabled Swedish MV *Dagmar Salen* 20 mi from Overfalls LS and brought engine-room fire under control; Jul 48 towed seven CG vessels from Cape May to CG Yard, Curtis Bay, MD; 6 Nov 48 assisted FV *Mary Ann* at 39°32'N, 73°35'W; Nov 48 towed cutter *Tamaroa* from Cape May to CG Yard, Curtis Bay, MD; 9 Jan 49 assisted FV *Cecile W* at 30°31'N, 71°30'W; 16–19 Jan 49 assisted cutter *Eastwind* following collision; 2 Feb 49 assisted FVs *Beatrice* and *Ida* off Cape May, NJ; 16 Feb 49 assisted FV *Jennia Lucia*; 18 Sep 49 assisted FV *New Bedford* 33 mi E of Fire I.; 16 Dec 49 broke ice in Hudson R.; 5 Jan 50 assisted FV *Madona* off Delaware; 8 Jan 50 assisted FV *Carol Ann* off Delaware; 27 Jan 50 assisted FV *Viking* at 40°28'N, 71°W; 18–19 Feb 50 assisted disabled USS *Ludlow* at 38°49'N, 73°41'W; 22 Feb 50 broke ice in Hudson R.; 11–12 Jun 50 assisted FV

Mark K at 39°27'N, 73°49'W; 21 Jun 50 assisted downed USN F2H ac 49 mi from Atlantic City, NJ; 28 Jun 50 assisted FV *Richard Lance* in Gravesend Bay; 4 Sep 50 assisted FV *Reid*; Jan–Feb 51 broke ice in Hudson R.; 9 Mar 51 assisted USN boat L-71 aground at Cape Henlopen; Mar 51 towed CG-83490 from Cape May to CG Yard, Curtis Bay, MD; 26 May 51 assisted FV *New Dawn*; May 51 towed cutters *Calypso* and *Crawford* from Cape May to CG Yard, Curtis Bay, MD; 18 Jul 51 assisted FV *Jenny* off New Jersey; 27 Aug 51 assisted MV *M. L. Mother* off Long I.; 15–16 Sep 51 towed disabled LS 510; 25 Oct 51 assisted FV *Benjamin Brothers* off Cape May; 19 Nov 51 assisted PC *Islamorada* off Cape May; Jan 52 broke ice in Hudson R.; 26–28 May 52 assisted following collision between tanker *Michael* and motor barge *A. C. Dodge* in Delaware R.; 3 Dec 52 assisted FV *Katherine Brown*; 14 Jan 53 assisted FV *Catherine C* off Cape May; 4 Feb 53 assisted FV *Lady of Fatima* in Swash Channel; 15 Jul 54 assisted FV *Nora V* off Bowers Beach, DE; 26–27 Nov 54 assisted FV *Nancy S* at 40°39'N, 72°10'W; 28 Nov 54 assisted FV *Star of the Sea*; 14 Dec 54 assisted tug *Anne Moran* and barge off Cape May; 18–21 Dec 54 assisted following collision between tanker *Atlantic Capetown* and MV *Maya*; 1 Feb 55 assisted FV *Diana Janet*; 12–13 Feb 55 towed disabled FV *North Star* to Cape May; 14 Feb 55 assisted MV *Tynefield*; 21 Feb 55 assisted FV *Carol and Dennis* at 39°55'N, 71°49'W; 3 Jul 55 towed FV *Ana* to Cape May; 7 Jul 55 assisted FV *Blue Star* at 39°26'N, 73°41'W; 8 Jul 55 assisted FV *Hustler*; 16 Jul 55 assisted FV *Serina II*; 21 Jul 55 assisted FV *Anna Maersk* at 39°N, 74°39'W; 15 Sep 55 assisted following collision between MVs *Edith* and *Josefina Thorden* 9 mi N of Ship John Shoal; 21–23 Nov 55 towed PC *Victoria* to Cape May; 5 Feb 53 assisted FV *Sally and Eileen*; 20 Feb 53 towed FV *Richard Lance* to Gravesend Bay; 21 Feb 53 towed FV *Evelyn G. Stars*; 22 Feb 53 assisted FV *Clipper*; 4 Mar 53 assisted FV *Serline II* 70 mi E of Five Fathom LS; 14–15 Mar 53 assisted FV *Thelma* 20 mi S of Montauk Pt.; 16 Mar 53 assisted FV *Gaspin*; 26 Mar 53 towed FV *Villanova* to New York, NY; 3 Apr 53 took on board survivors from FV *Eric*; 16 Apr 53 assisted FV *Catherine L. Brown*; 29 Jun 53 assisted following collision between MVs *Gulftrader* and *Sol de Panama* 4 mi SE of Barnegat LS; 28 Aug 53 towed FV *Vagabond* to Absecon Inlet; 20 Sep 53 assisted FV *Rosley* 35 mi from Ambrose LS; 7 Nov 53 towed FV *Helen M* to Cape May; 30 Nov 53 assisted FV *Ocean Spray* at 38°20'N, 75°50'W; 31 Jan 54 assisted FV *Hiwal*; 19 Feb 54 assisted FV *Patricia* at 39°4'N, 72°53'W; 5 Mar 54 assisted FV *Positive* at 36°16'N, 73°26'W; 13–14 Jun 54 assisted MV *Robert Barnes Fiertz* off Little Egg Inlet; 28–29 Jun 54 towed disabled PC *Victory Chimes* to Cape May; 12 Apr 56 assisted tug *North Point* and tow; 28 Apr 56 assisted FV *Hazel B* off Sandy Hook; 16–18 May 56 assisted schooner *Victoria* at 39°46'N, 69°11'W; 28 May 56 assisted capsized barge *YRB 9*; 1 Oct 56–15 Jul 60 stationed at Miami, FL, and used for A/N; 14 Oct 56 towed FV *Pamlico* to Cape May; 25 Oct 56 assisted barge *Turecamo* at 30°1'N, 74°44'W; 2 Jan 57 assisted disabled MV *Helmar* near Great Isaac LH; 26 Jan 57 patrolled yacht race; 27 Jan 57 assisted *Zuider Zee* at 25°35'N, 79°13'W; 12 Mar 57 assisted grounded railroad car ferry *Grand Haven* at Molasses Reef; 1 Jul 57 assisted grounded tanker *Windward Island* at 25°48'N, 80°05'W; 28 Feb–2 Mar 58 assisted grounded MV *African Duke* at 25°6'N, 80°17'W; 14–16 Jul 58 assisted and towed grounded LCT-456 at Samanan Cay; 3 Sep 58 towed MV *Erikboye* to Miami, FL; 29 Apr 59 assisted and towed *Sunshine Development* at 25°57'N, 79°52'W; 14 May 59 assisted YP 245; 25 Jun 59 towed tug *Charles E. Dunlap* to San Juan, PR; 29–30 Sep 59 assisted in hurricane

Gracie evacuation from Charleston and Savannah areas; 12–20 Mar 60 participated in Operation Big Slam; 15 Jul 60–2 Sep 76 stationed at Galveston, TX, and used for A/N; 9 Nov 61 rammed by FV *Islander* at 28°43'N, 95°6'W—FV sank; 2 Sep 76–27 Jul 83 decommissioned and stored at CG Yard, Curtis Bay, MD—subsequently underwent a major overhaul; 27 Jul 83–1990 stationed at Morehead City, NC, and used for A/N; Feb 84 assigned to Grenada as tender for 95-foot cutters and performed patrol and training duties; 27 Nov 84 helped seize vessel *Princess* carrying 17.5t of marijuana.

Laurel

8 Oct 43–3 Sep 46 stationed at Boston, MA, and used for A/N; 3 Sep–8 Dec 46 stationed at Portland, ME, and used for A/N; 8 Dec 46–21 May 69 stationed at Rockland, ME, and used for A/N; 27 Oct 50 assisted FV *Schoodic*; Jan 52 broke ice in Penobscot R.; 4–5 Jan 53 towed FV *Estrella* from 43°20'N, 66°28'W, to Gloucester, MA; Feb 54 broke ice in Penobscot R.; 8 Apr 54 stood by stranded FV *Consolidated* at Bakers I., ME; 22 Dec 54 towed FV *Courier* to Southwest Harbor, ME; 27 May 57 towed FV *Regina Maria* to Rockland, ME; 7–8 Aug 58 directed on-scene operation following collision between tanker *Gulfoil* and *S. E. Graham* at entrance to Narragansett Bay during heavy fog; 10 Jan 59 assisted FV *Bobby and Harvey* off Rockland, ME; 13–14 Mar 59 assisted lobster boat *Betty Lu* at 43°57'N, 68°02'W; 6 Jul 59 assisted sardine carrier *The Oquirrh*; 25 Nov 59 assisted tug *Alta May* and barge near Rockland, ME; 4 Jul 67 recovered wreckage and bodies from private ac crash off Moose Point, ME; 21 May 69–Jun 75 stationed at Morehead City, NC, and used for A/N; 22–28 Jan 70 helped fight fire on Norwegian MV *Thordis Prethus* off North Carolina; Jan 75–Sep 86 stationed at Ketchikan, AK, and used for A/N; Sep 83–28 Apr 86 stationed at San Pedro, CA, and used for A/N; May 84 sustained main motor casualty and was towed to Pt. Loma by cutter *Confidence*; 12 Jul 86–1990 underwent major renovation at CG Yard, Curtis Bay, MD.

Madrona

20 Apr 43–22 Sep 47 stationed at Miami, FL, and used for A/N; 25 Feb 47 stood by damaged MV *David B. Johnson*, which had grounded at Matanilla Shoal, Bahamas; 22 Sep 47–Apr 84 stationed at Portsmouth, VA, and used for A/N; 25 Jan 48 escorted tug *Coral Sea* and oil barge *NR16*; 27 Apr 49 searched for mine near Chesapeake LS; 6 May 50 assisted grounded ship near Cape Fear R.; 4–6 Nov 50 towed disabled MV *Atlantic Explorer* until relieved by commercial tug; 14 May 51 assisted following collision between MV *Thomas Tracey* and naval vessel; 4 Oct 51 assisted MV *Marose*, which had grounded near Cape Henry; 11 Mar 52 medevaced crew member from MV *Esso Guyenne* at 36°48'N, 73°03'W; Feb 55 broke ice in Chesapeake Bay; 26 Jul 57 assisted in fighting fire on MV *Havmoy* in Lynnhaven Roads; 12 Jan 58 assisted FV *Pameleica* near Cape May, NJ; Feb 58 broke ice in the Chesapeake; 2 Apr 59 assisted MV *Terra Nova* in lower Chesapeake; 12 Sep 60 provided assistance in Portsmouth, VA, area following hurricane Donna; 4 Feb 63 assisted following collision between MV *Skaustrand* and tanker *P. W. Thirtle* in Baltimore harbor; 27–28 Feb 67 helped fight fire on MV *Caldas* 50 mi E of Chincoteague, VA; 24 May 80 escorted disabled tanker *Esso Portland* to Hampton Roads; Jan 82 broke ice to permit salvage barges to move to the scene of the Air Florida crash site, Washington, DC; 1984–90 underwent major renovation at CG Yard, Curtis Bay, MD.

Sorrel

18 Mar 43–25 Jul 47 stationed at Boston, MA, and used for A/N and icebreaking, frequently working out of Argentia, Newfoundland; 25 Jul 47–25 Oct 48 stationed at Rockland, ME, and used for A/N and icebreaking, frequently working out of Argentia; 8 Dec 48 freed USS *Whitewood* from ice at 60°00′N, 45°54′W; 25 Oct 48–1 May 54 stationed at Boston, MA, and used for A/N and icebreaking, frequently working out of Argentia; 23–24 Oct 50 rescued eight survivors from MV *North Voyager* at 45°40′N, 52°17′W; 29 Nov 51 assisted following collision between MV *Ventura* and FV *Lynn* near Boston, MA; 12 Jun 52 assisted FV *Sunapee* at 41°42′N, 66°37′W; 20–21 Jul 52 towed disabled FV *Richard J Nunan* to Portland, ME; 19 Feb 53 towed disabled FV *Geraldine and Phyllis*; 14–15 Mar 53 towed disabled FV *Neptune* from 42°10′N, 66°35′W to Boston, MA; 4 Apr 53 towed FV *John J Nagle* from 43°15′N, 68°47′W to Portland, ME; 25 Apr 53 assisted FV *Serafina* off Boston; 9–10 Sep 53 escorted distressed FV *St. Anthony* to Boston; 16 Nov 53 fought fire on FV *Jane and Patricia*; 23 Nov 53 assisted FV *California* at 41°54′N, 69°55′W; 18–19 Dec 53 towed FV *Adelek* to Portland, ME; 1 May 54–1 Jul 65 stationed at Sitka, AK, and used primarily for A/N; 12–13 Sep 56 assisted FV *Valencia* near Sitka, AK; 18 Jun 58 assisted FV *Guardian* 120 mi W of Sitka; 10–11 Jul 58 assisted following earthquake at Lituya Bay and Yakutat Bay; 9 Jun 59 towed FV *Galena* to Kodiak; 10 Jul 59 assisted FV *Edrie* in Lisianski Inlet; 6 Apr 61 medevaced crewman from MV *Martha Bakke*; 22 Oct 62 assisted after the ditching of DC-7 ac 1 mi N of Biorka I., Sitka Sound— 102 survivors; 5 Jun 63 unsuccessfully searched for survivors of Northwest Orient aircraft crash; 1 Jul 65–18 Apr 73 stationed at Seward, AK, and used primarily for A/N; 13 Sep 66 assisted towing distressed FV *Jo Ann* to Cordova, AK; 6 Nov 67 fought fire at Shelter Cove, AK; 4 Nov 69 medevaced two crewmen following a fire on FV *Koshin Maru 5*; 11 Feb 70 towed disabled FV *Mermaid* to Ketchikan, AK; 21 Nov 70 medevaced crewman from FV *Lee Ann* to Seward, AK; 18 Apr 73–31 Mar 76 stationed at Cordova, AK, and used for A/N; 31 Mar 76–1982 underwent a major renovation at the CG Yard, Curtis Bay, MD; 2 Dec 82–1990 stationed at Governors I., NY, and used primarily for A/N and icebreaking.

Tupelo

1 Jul 46–1969 stationed at Toledo, OH, and used for A/N and icebreaking; 25 Jun 50 patrolled Mills Trophy Race off Kelly I.; 27 Nov 50 assisted tug *Whitney* and two scows 1.5 mi from Toledo, OH; 9–11 Jan 51 escorted disabled tug *Sherman H. Serre* from Erie, PA, to Cleveland, OH; 24 Jun 51 patrolled Mills Trophy Race off Kelly I.; 20 Oct 51 assisted MV *George F. Rand* off Port Huron; 13–14 Dec 51 searched for missing Cessna

ac in western Lake Erie; 11 Sep 52 assisted grounded MVs *Kulas* and *Fink* in Livingstone Channel; 23–25 Sep 52 searched for overdue PC in western Lake Erie; 21 Apr 53 assisted grounded MV *J. H. Hillman* in St. Clair R.; 23–25 Aug 53 patrolled Rochester Race in Lake Ontario; 24 Jan 55 assisted ice-bound tug and barges near Detroit, MI; 13 Jun 55 searched for missing PC in western Lake Erie; 20 Apr 56 assisted following collision between MVs *A. M. Byers* and *E. M. Ford* off Sans Souci; 14 Jul 57 patrolled International Trophy Race, St. Clair, MI; 12 Nov 57 assisted grounded MV in Amherstburg Channel; 1 Mar 58 assisted in restoring power to Marblehead, OH; 4–5 Oct 58 patrolled Cleveland Race; 25–26 Jul 59 patrolled Mackinac I. Race; 1961 salvaged PC J-3776; 1 Aug 62 assisted following wreck of MV *Montrose* in Detroit R.; 12 Jan 63 assisted in rescue of 154 persons stranded on an ice floe adrift 10 mi E of Toledo, OH; 25 Jan 65 escorted damaged cutter *Bramble* to Toledo, OH; mid-Sep 65 salvaged USN helo from Lake Erie; 31 Jan 69 broke ice jam below Monroe, MI, thus removing threat of flooding in the city; 1969–30 Sep 75 stationed at Astoria, OR, and used for A/N; 9–11 Oct 69 stood by grounded British MV *Hawthorne Enterprise* on Mona I. until relieved by cutter *Point Warde*.

Woodbine

15 Feb 46–2 Mar 47 stationed at Toledo, OH, and used for A/N and icebreaking; 2 Mar–19 Sep 47 stationed at San Juan, PR, and used for A/N; 19 Sep 47–15 Feb 72 stationed at Grand Haven, MI, and used for A/N and icebreaking; 20 Jun–8 Jul 48 assisted MV *Edgewater* near Grand Haven, MI; 4 Apr 49 assisted MV *Benson Ford* in Neebish Bay; 25 Apr 53 assisted MV *J. H. Brown* near Superior, WI; 29 Dec 53 salvaged USAF ac near Chicago, IL; 22 Jul 56 patrolled Mackinac I. Race; 5 Dec 57 assisted MV *Saugatuck* near Grand Haven, MI; 16–18 Apr 57 assisted MV *George A. Sloan*, which had been damaged by ice in Lake Superior; 6 Apr 58 assisted tanker *Clark Milwaukee* beset in ice in Sturgeon Bay Canal; 20 Jul 58 patrolled Mackinac I. Race; 19 Jul 59 patrolled Mackinac I. Race; 28 Aug 59 patrolled Chicago Regatta; 30 Apr 60 searched for downed Canadian B-25 ac off Cadahy, WI; 23 Nov 62 assisted MV *Makefjell* aground near Muskegon, MI; 19 Apr 65 slightly damaged in a collision with MV *Meteor* while breaking ice off Green Bay, WI; 18–20 Aug 65 recovered debris from United Airlines crash in Lake Michigan; 15 Feb 68 helped free tug *Silver Star* from ice and escorted her to Holland, MI; 2 Apr 68 salvaged private ac afloat near Muskegon, MI; 22 May 68 escorted distressed MV *Joseph Bloc* to Manitowoc, WI; Jan 71 salvaged USAF B-52 ac in upper Lake Michigan.

65-FOOT INLAND TENDER

Name	Hull Number	Builder	Keel Laid	Launched	Commissioned	Disposition
Blueberry	WLI 65302	Birchfield Boiler Co., Tacoma, WA	1941	1942	1942	*Decomm* 1975–76

Cost   N/A

Hull
- Displacement (tons)   68 fl (1966)
- Length   65′ oa; 63′9″ bp
- Beam   14′5″ max
- Draft   4′ max (1966)

Machinery
- Main Engines   2 General Motors diesels
- BHP   330
- Propellers   twin

Performance
- Max Sustained   12 kts, 800-mi radius (1966)
- Cruising   10 kts, 1,000-mi radius (1966)

Logistics
- Fuel Oil (95%)   800 gal
- Complement   5 men (1966)

Electronics
- Radar   none (1966)
- Armament   none (1966)

Design

The *Blueberry* was designed as an inland buoy tender; she remained unnamed until 1964. She is constructed entirely of steel. Numbers 65300 and 65301 were not assigned.

Blueberry

1942–76 stationed in the Pacific Northwest and used for A/N.

73-FOOT TENDER

Name	Hull Number	Builder	Keel Laid	Launched	Commissioned	Disposition
Oleander	WLR 73264 WAGL 264	Jeffersonville Boat & Machine Co., Jeffersonville, IN	N/A	24 May 41	20 Sep 41	*Decomm* 31 Jul 77

Cost $65,922

Hull
- Displacement (tons)   80 fl (1940)
- Length   73′ oa
- Beam   18′ max
- Draft   5′ max (1940)

Machinery
- Main Engines   2 Gray Marine diesels
- BHP   300
- Propellers   twin

Performance
- Cruising   7.5 kts, 1,160-mi radius (1945)

Logistics
- Fuel Oil (95%)   1,300 gal
- Complement   0 officers, 9 men (1945)

Deck Gear
- Boom Capacity   3 tons
- Hoist Power   electricity

Electronics   none

Armament   none

Design

The *Oleander* was designed to serve A/N on the Mississippi River and to render aid during floods.

Oleander

13 Oct 42–12 Sep 50 stationed at Peoria, IL, and used for A/N; 13 Sep 50–31 Jul 60 stationed at Kansas City, MO, and used for A/N; 1 Aug 60– 14 Oct 61 stationed at St. Joseph, MO, and used for A/N; 15 Oct 61–31 Jul 77 stationed at Point Pleasant, WV, and used for A/N; Dec 67–Feb 68 marked temporary channel following collapse of Point Pleasant bridge and supported reconstruction operations; Jul 69 assisted following a chlorine gas leak, South Charleston, WV.

Tender *Oleander,* 14 Mar 61, at Leavenworth, KS, nearing the completion of a major reconstruction. She received a new pilothouse, rudder, and galley among other improvements. See Scheina, *WWII Cutters,* for a view of the old configuration.

114-FOOT TENDERS

Name	Hull Number	Builder	Keel Laid	Launched	Commissioned	Disposition
Forsythia	WLR 63 WAGL 63	Avondale Marine Ways, Westwego, LA	24 Nov 41	15 Apr 42	15 Feb 43	*Decomm* 12 Aug 77
Dogwood	WLR 259 WAGL 259	Dubuque Boat & Boiler Works, Dubuque, IA	Jul 40 (contracted)	16 Jun 41	17 Sep 41	*Decomm* 11 Aug 89
Sycamore	WLR 268 WAGL 268	Dubuque Boat & Boiler Works, Dubuque, IA	Jul 40 (contracted)	16 Jun 41	9 Sep 41	*Decomm* 30 Jun 77

Cost $159,000 (*Dogwood* and *Sycamore*); $176,450 (*Forsythia*)

Hull
  Displacement (tons)   280 fl (1964); 240 light (1964)
  Length   113′9″ oa; 113′9″ bp
  Beam   26′ max
  Draft   5′6″ max (1964)
Machinery
  Main Engines   2 General Motors diesels
  BHP   800
  Propellers   twin
Performance
  Max Sustained   11.0 kts, 1,325-mi radius (1964)
  Economic   8.0 kts, 1,766-mi radius (1964)
Logistics
  Fuel Oil (95%)   5,310 gal
  Complement   1 warrant, 19 men (1964)
Electronics   none (1964)
Armament   none

Design
This class was designed to replace the aging sternwheeler steamers such as the *Cottonwood* and *Wakerobin* used on the Mississippi River. The new class was much more versatile and much less expensive to maintain. These tenders were reengined in the 1960s.

Dogwood
18 Mar 45–1977 stationed at Vicksburg, MS, and used for A/N; Feb 61 trained Vietnamese officials; Jan 63 escorted NASA missile barge *Promise* in lower Mississippi R. to Baton Rouge, LA; Apr 63 escorted NASA barge *Promise*; Jul 63 escorted NASA barge *Palaemon* in lower Mississippi R. to Baton Rouge, LA; Aug 63 escorted NASA barge *Promise*; Sep 65 assisted in cleanup operation in the Gulf of Mexico following hurricane Betsey; 1977–90 stationed at Pine Bluff, AR.

Forsythia
15 Feb 43–15 May 63 stationed at Sewickley, PA, and used for A/N; 16 May 63–12 Aug 77 stationed at Memphis, TN, and used for A/N.

Sycamore
1 Apr 44–25 Feb 52 stationed at Dubuque, IA, and used for A/N; 26 Feb 52–7 Jan 58 stationed at Cincinnati, OH, and used for A/N; 8 Jan 58–7 Feb 64 stationed at New Richmond, OH, and used for A/N; 8 Feb 64–Jan 66 stationed at Cincinnati, OH, and used for A/N; Jan 66–19 Jun 73 stationed at Memphis, TN, and used for A/N; assisted in fighting fire on MV *Ouachita* 24 mi S of Memphis, TN; 19 Jun 73–30 Jan 77 stationed at Sewickley, PA, and used for A/N.

The *Forsythia* on 1 Mar 49. An outboard profile and deck plans appear in Scheina, *WWII Cutters*.

177-FOOT TENDER

Name	Hull Number	Builder	Keel Laid	Launched	Commissioned	Disposition
Juniper	WLM 224 WAGL 224	John H. Mathis Co., Camden, NJ	N/A	18 May 40	1 Oct 40	*Decomm* 15 Jul 75 *Sold* Dec 75

Cost   N/A

Hull
  Displacement (tons)   790 fl (1945)
  Length   177' oa
  Beam   32' mb
  Draft   8'7" max (1945)

Machinery
  Main Engines   2 electric motors connected to 2 generators driven by 2 Cooper-Bessemer diesels
  SHP   900
  Propellers   twin

Performance
  Max Speed   12.5 kts (1945)
  Cruising   11.0 kts, 7,000-mi radius (1945)

Logistics
  Fuel Oil (95%)   18,000 gal
  Complement   1 officer, 3 warrants, 34 men (1945)

Deck Gear
  Boom Capacity   20 tons
  Hoist Power   electricity

Electronics
  Detection Radar   SPN-11 (1964)

Armament   none (1964)

Design

The *Juniper* was the last tender begun for the USLHS. She was under construction when that service was amalgamated into the CG. The *Juniper* was the prototype for the 180-foot tenders and was the first all-welded steel and diesel-electric-propelled coastwise tender. A distinguishing feature was the turtle-back forecastle.

Juniper

24 Oct 45–15 Jul 75 stationed at St. Petersburg, FL, and used for A/N; 3 Oct 51 rescued survivors from PC near St. Petersburg, FL; 3 May 52 assisted recovery of bodies from USAF B-29 crash near Cedar Keys, FL; 16–19 May 52 rescued three survivors from FV *Parnell* at 23°31'N, 88°16'W; 22–24 Nov 52 helped free tender *Birch* and barge aground on Gasparilla Pass; 5–6 Jan 53 assisted PBM aircraft at 27°25'N, 82°58'W; 15 Feb 53 searched for survivors from National Flight 470 at 28°30'N, 88°W; 18 Jul 54 salvaged Navy SNB aircraft off Tampa Bay; 4 Oct 54 searched for overdue Navy Hellcat aircraft near Tampa, FL; 5–6 Feb 55 assisted FV *Southsea* off St. Petersburg, FL; 8 Feb 55 towed disabled trawler *Bluebonnet* from 27°16'N, 83°07'W to St. Petersburg, FL; 29 Mar 55 assisted Navy LST 287 off FL; 17 Jul 55 searched for overdue MV *Fay* off FL; 12 Dec 55 towed disabled FV *Edward T* to St. Petersburg, FL; 4 May 56 towed disabled tug *Do All 3* to St. Petersburg, FL; 17 Oct 56 assisted disabled FV *Eleanor Singleton* at 26°22'N, 83°25'W; 23 Jan 57 towed disabled FVs *Cola II* and *Spray* to Crystal R., FL; 5–6 Feb 57 assisted disabled FVs *Gulf Defender* and *Gulf Trader* at 26°16'N, 84°35'W; 3 Jan 58 assisted FVs *Noahs Ark* and *Miss Jan* off Key West, FL; 31 Jan 58 assisted FV *Miss Mary* near Tampa Bay; 22 Sep 59 assisted FV *Echo* near St. Petersburg, FL; 27 Sep 59 assisted PC *Capadoo* at 26°33'N, 82°18'W; 9–12 Nov 59 assisted FV *Bonita* at 28°55'N, 85°59'W; 7–8 Mar 62 towed disabled FV *Amber Jack* from 27°00'N, 83°20'W to Tampa Bay; 29 Nov–6 Dec 62 salvaged CG HUS1-G helicopter that had crashed into Gulf of Mexico; 28 Jan 63 escorted NASA missile barge *Promise* from 29°14'N, 85°16'W to Ft. Pierce, FL; 11–20 Apr 63 escorted NASA barge *Promise*; 17–19 Aug 63 escorted NASA barge *Promise*; 2–3 Nov 64 towed disabled FV *Mystery* from 90 mi W of Ft. Myers, FL, to Charlotte Harbor; 27 Nov 69 salvaged remains of CG HH52A helicopter near Tarpon Springs, FL.

The *Juniper,* 18 Feb 49. Like most tenders designed by the USLHS, she spent her entire career in one geographical area.

72-FOOT TENDER

Name	Hull Number	Builder	Keel Laid	Launched	Commissioned	Disposition
Birch	WAGL 256	General Ship & Engine Works, Boston, MA	N/A	N/A	1939	*Decomm* 24 Feb 63 *Sold* 31 Jul 64

Cost	$74,000
Hull	
Displacement (tons)	137 fl (1945)
Length	72'4" oa
Beam	18' max
Draft	3'8" max (1939); 4'1" max (1945)
Machinery	
Main Engines	2 Winton diesels
BHP	300
Propellers	twin
Performance	
Max Speed	9.0 kts (1939)
Cruising	8.0 kts, 1,000-mi radius (1945)
Logistics	
Fuel Oil (95%)	1,300 gal
Complement	0 officers, 9 men (1945)
Deck Gear	
Boom Capacity	2 tons
Hoist Power	electricity
Electronics	none
Armament	none

Design

The *Birch* was designed as a bay and sound tender.

Birch

1946–24 Feb 63 stationed at St. Petersburg, FL, and used for A/N; 14–18 Sep 55 assisted in hurricane evacuation of St. Petersburg and Tampa, FL; 5 Jul 57 assisted FV *King Shrimper* off Sarasota, FL; Mar 58 towed by a CG HO4S helicopter to show feasibility of towing disabled FVs by helicopter.

The *Birch* on 24 Mar 58 is under tow by a CG HO4S-3 helicopter (not in view), successfully testing the feasibility of towing fishing vessels that are a similar size.

122-FOOT TENDER

Name	Hull Number	Builder	Keel Laid	Launched	Commissioned	Disposition
Maple	WLI 234 WAGL 234	Marine Iron & Shipbuilding Co., Duluth, MN	15 Apr 38 (contracted)	29 Apr 39	Jun 39	*Decomm* 1 Jun 73 *Trans* to USN 8 Aug 73

Cost	$190,000	Machinery	
Hull		Main Engines	2 General Motors diesels
Displacement (tons)	350 fl (1962)	BHP	800
Length	122'3" oa; 113'9" bp	Propellers	twin
Beam	27' max	Performance	
Draft	7'6" max (1962)	Max Sustained	10 kts, 1,200-mi radius (1962)

Logistics
  Fuel Oil (95%)   4,600 gal
  Complement   1 warrant, 19 men (1962)
Deck Gear
  Boom Capacity   10 tons
  Hoist Power   electricity
Electronics
  Detection Radar   SPN-11 (1962)
Armament   none

Design

The *Maple* was designed as a bay and sound tender, and she was constructed entirely of steel. The tender was reengined, probably in the early 1960s.

Maple

1946-19 Jun 58 stationed at Ogdensburg, NY, and used for A/N; 23-24 Aug 49 patrolled Rochester Race; 15 Aug 51 assisted tanker *A. C. Dodge* aground near Excelsior Shoal; 20 Aug 51 patrolled Rochester Race; 26 Apr 52 assisted tanker *Bruce Hudson* aground at Wells I.; 3-4 Aug 52 patrolled Freeman Cup Races at Toronto, Canada; 24 Aug 52 patrolled Rochester Race; 27 Jul 53 patrolled Freeman Cup Race at Toronto; 23 Aug 53 patrolled Rochester Race; 20 Jun 58-14 Sep 59 stationed at Detroit, MI, and used for A/N; 15 Sep 59-1967 stationed at Buffalo, NY, and used for A/N; 1967-1 Jun 73 stationed at Ogdensburg, NY, and used for A/N.

The *Maple* on 16 Feb 49. She does not yet wear a hull number, which will be added in a few years. By the late 1950s, her forecastle and hull will be painted black to the 01 deck. In this photograph, her boat bears the letter M. By 1959 this will be changed to Map. Cutter boats have been identified by a simple letter code since the late nineteenth century.

122-FOOT TENDERS

Name	Hull Number	Builder	Keel Laid	Launched	Commissioned	Disposition
Narcissus	WLI 238 WAGL 238	John H. Mathis Co., Camden, NJ	15 Apr 38 (contracted)	4 Feb 39	1939	*Trans* to Guyana, 5 May 71
Zinnia	WLI 255 WAGL 255	John H. Mathis Co., Camden, NJ	15 Apr 38 (contracted)	4 Feb 39	1939	*Decomm* 14 Jan 72 *Trans* to USAF 1 Mar 72

Cost $220,023 each
Hull
  Displacement (tons)   355 fl (1939)
  Length   122'2" oa
  Beam   27' max
  Draft   7' max (1939); 7'6" max (1945)
Machinery
  Main Engines   2 Superior diesels
  BHP   430
  Propellers   twin
Performance
  Max Speed   9.0 kts (1939)
  Max Sustained   8.0 kts, 3,000-mi radius (1945)
  Economic   6.0 kts, 3,500-mi radius (1945)
Logistics
  Fuel Oil (95%)   4,800 gal
  Complement   3 officers, 40 men (1945)

Tender *Narcissus* in Sep 53. Note the large number of skylights (which are propped open), doors, windows, and portholes, revealing that she was built before the days of air conditioning.

Deck Gear
    Boom Capacity   10 tons
    Hoist Power   electricity
Electronics (1945)
    Detection Radar   SO-8 (*Narcissus* only)
Armament   none
Design
    The *Narcissus* and *Zinnia* were the first tenders to be extensively welded; initially they were classified as bay and sound design.

Narcissus

28 Feb 41–5 May 71 stationed at Portsmouth, VA, and used for A/N; 16 Oct 54 searched for survivors from tug *Indian* in James R.; 12–18 Sep 55 patrolled President's Cup Regatta; 24 Jan 56 medevaced crew member from CG-23067 off Smith Point; 1 Jul 61 collided with Liberian MV *World Challenger* while moored at Portsmouth and sustained topside damage.

Zinnia

5 Dec 40–1 May 47 stationed at Edgemoor, DE, and used for A/N; 1 May 47–2 Feb 67 stationed at Gloucester City, NJ, and used for A/N; 21 Dec 51 assisted CG-64304 icebound in Delaware R.; 22 May 52 assisted tugs *Patco* and *Atlantic Dealer* in Delaware R.; 26–27 May 52 assisted following collision between tanker *Michael* and motor barge *A. C. Dodge* near Reedy I.; 6–10 Jun 53 assisted following collision between tankers *Phoenix* and *Pan Massachusetts* at entrance to Chesapeake and Delaware Canal; 18 Dec 54 assisted following collision between tanker *Atlantic Capetown* and MV *Maya* in Delaware R.; 7–8 Mar 57 assisted following collision between Liberian MV *Elna Second* and USNS *Mission of San Francisco* near Pea Patch I.—26 survivors taken on board from tug *Kraft Houler*; 19 Mar 59 assisted in debris recovery following mid-air collision off Dover, DE; 21 Dec 62 assisted following collision between tanker *Olympic Rock* and tug *Princess* in Delaware R.; 2 Feb 67–Apr 69 stationed at New York, NY, and used for A/N; Apr 69–14 Jan 72 stationed at New Orleans, LA, and used for A/N.

104-FOOT TENDERS

Name	Hull Number	Builder	Keel Laid	Launched	Commissioned	Disposition
Goldenrod	WLR 213 WAGL 213	Dubuque Boat & Boiler Works, Dubuque, IA	21 Jun 37 (contracted)	N/A	2 Jun 38	*Decomm* 26 May 73 *Trans* to NSF 26 Sep 73
Poplar	WLR 21 WAGL 241	Dubuque Boat & Boiler Works, Dubuque, IA	N/A	N/A	1939	*Decomm* 17 Jun 73 *Trans* to NSF 26 Sep 73

Cost $115,375 (*Goldenrod*); $123,200 (*Poplar*)
Hull
    Displacement (tons)   235 fl (1964); 162 light (1964)
    Length   103'6" oa; 99'7"
    Beam   24' max
    Draft   4'5" max (1964)

Machinery
    Main Engines   2 General Motors diesels
    BHP   800
    Propellers   twin
Performance
    Max Sustained   10.5 kts, 1,432-mi radius (1964)

The *Goldenrod* with a work barge on 4 Jun 71. Note that she is flying the Union Jack at her jackstaff while underway. By late twentieth century custom, the Union Jack should be flown only while at anchor.

Logistics

Fuel Oil (95%)	4,300 gal
Complement	1 warrant, 16 men (1964)

Deck Gear

Boom Capacity	2.5 tons
Hoist Power	electricity

Electronics

Detection Radar	GRM

Armament   none

Design

The 104-foot river tenders were constructed of steel except for the top of the pilothouse and Texas deck, which were wood. Their propellers were mounted in tunnels for operation in shallow waters. Both tenders were reengined in early 1960. Radius does not include fuel in the barge that usually operated with the tenders. *Goldenrod* used barge CGB-89002.

Goldenrod

1945–12 Sep 50 stationed at Kansas City, MO, and used for A/N; 13 Sep 50–31 Jul 62 stationed at Peoria, IL, and used for A/N; Feb 61 used to train Vietnamese officials; 1 Aug 62–26 May 73 stationed at Keokuk, IA, and used for A/N; 29 Apr 65 assisted in flood relief near Keokuk, IA; 3 May 65 assisted in flood relief near Niota, IA; mid-May 69 assisted following large fire at La Grange, MO.

Poplar

1946–15 May 63 stationed at St. Louis, MO, and used for A/N; 27 Jan 55 assisted in fighting fire on barge belonging to Federal Barge Lines at St. Louis, MO; 15 May 63–17 Jun 73 stationed at Sewickley, PA, and used for A/N.

72-FOOT TENDER

Name	Hull Number	Builder	Keel Laid	Launched	Commissioned	Disposition
Elm	WLI 72260 WAGL 260	Defoe Boat & Motor Works, Bay City, MI	N/A	N/A	1 Apr 38	*Decomm* 30 Jul 69 *Donated* 23 Oct 70

Cost	$77,177

Hull

Displacement (tons)	78 fl (1964); 59 light (1964)
Length	72'4" oa; 70' bp
Beam	17'6" max
Draft	4'6" max (1964)

Machinery

Main Engines	2 General Motors diesels
BHP	230
Propellers	twin

Performance

Max Sustained	9.4 kts, 900-mi radius (1964)

Logistics

Fuel Oil (95%)	1,300 gal
Complement	0 officers, 9 men (1964)

Deck Gear

Boom Capacity	3.0 tons
Hoist Power	electricity

Electronics   none (1964)

Armament   none

Design

The *Elm* was built as a bay and sound tender. She had a steel hull and a wooden superstructure. *Elm* had been reengined in approximately 1960.

Elm

1946–30 Jul 69 stationed at Atlantic City, NJ, and used for A/N.

The *Elm* on 15 May 59. The tender's radio call sign, NPWM, is painted atop the bridge, a standard practice on CG ships. This view exaggerates the length of this 72-ft inland buoy tender.

175-FOOT TENDERS

Name	Hull Number	Builder	Keel Laid	Launched	Commissioned	Disposition
Fir	WLM 212 WAGL 212	Moore Dry Dock Co., Oakland, CA	16 Aug 38	N/A	1 Oct 40	Active
Hollyhock	WLM 220 WAGL 220	Defoe Boat & Motor Works, Bay City, MI	13 Apr 36	24 Mar 37	7 Aug 37	*Decomm* 31 Mar 82
Walnut	WLM 252 WAGL 252	Moore Dry Dock Co., Oakland, CA	N/A	N/A	27 Jun 39	*Decomm* 1 Jul 82 *Trans* to Honduras

Cost | $389,746 (*Fir, Walnut*); $347,800 (*Hollyhock*)

Hull
Displacement (tons) | 993 fl (1966); 811 light (1966)
Length | 174′10″ oa; 163′6″ oa
Beam | 34′ max
Draft | 12′5″ max (1966)

Machinery
Main Engines | 2 Fairbanks-Morse diesels
BHP | 1,350
Propellers | twin

Performance
Max Sustained | 11.9 kts, 9,920-mi radius (1966)
Economic | 7.5 kts, 13,400-mi radius (1966)

Logistics
Fuel Oil (95%) | 34,700 (*Fir*), 40,000 (*Hollyhock, Walnut*)
Complement | 3 officers, 2 warrants, 33 men (1966)

Deck Gear
Boom Capacity | 20 tons
Hoist Power | hydraulic

Electronics
Detection Radar | CS (*Fir*, 1966); SPM-11 (*Hollyhock*, 1967; *Walnut*, 1967)
Sonar | UNQ-1 (1966)

Armament | none (1966)

Design

The 175-foot-class ships were designed as coastwise tenders by the USLHS. These units were constructed entirely of steel. Originally they were fitted with triple-expansion steam engines and were reengined with diesels in the early 1950s.

Fir

1940–90 stationed in Seattle, WA, and used for A/N and servicing telephone cables; 4 Nov 49 removed 18 from disabled MV *Andalucia* off Waada I. and transported them to port; 30 Apr 52 assisted MV *Beliot Victory* near Destruction I.; 22 Mar 54 patrolled Maritime Day tugboat races in Elliott Bay; 19 Feb 58 escorted USS *Yuma* (ATF-94), which developed trouble while towing USS *Tinian* (CVHE-123) 6 mi S of Swiftsure Bank; 9–11 Aug 58 patrolled Lake Washington Gold Cup Regatta; 11 Nov 62 salvaged CG HO4S helicopter and delivered it to Port Angeles, WA; 14 Mar 63 assisted in search following a crash of a Navy aircraft in Guemes Channel; 16 Jul 65 grounded in Drayton Harbor—no damage sustained; Jan 66 assisted in recovery of USAF T-34 ac; 28 Nov 68 helped fight fire at Todd Shipyard, Seattle, WA.

Walnut

1 Jun 41–31 Aug 54 stationed at Honolulu, HI, and used for A/N; 2 Jun 53 assisted sampan *Sunfish* 18 mi S of Honolulu, HI; 8–9 Mar 54 searched for ketch *Novia* between Hilo and Honolulu, HI; 1 Sep 54–Dec 67 stationed at Miami, FL, and used for A/N; 3 Jul 55 towed disabled MV *Antwerpen* from 18°32′N, 66°13′W to San Juan, PR; 30 Dec 56 assisted sinking yacht *Melody* at 27°01′N, 79°43′W; Feb 58 patrolled Miami to Nassau Race; 14 Jun 59 assisted disabled MV *Johann Ahlers* at 22°03′N, 77°20′W; 25 Nov 59 assisted disabled PC at 25°06′N, 80°15′W; 6 Aug 60 assisted disabled PC *Snow* in Old Bahama Channel; 28–29 Apr 61 escorted NASA Saturn barge *Palaemon* from 24°42′N, 82°43′W to Ft. Pierce Inlet; 15–16 Nov 61 searched for ketch *Blue Bell* near 25°55′N, 77°27′W; 12–13 Mar 62 assisted MV *Flying Trader* aground near Matanilla Shoal; 6 Jan 63 stood by MV *Ermoupolis* aground 4 mi off Elliot Key; 22 Mar 63 recovered USAF drone 17 mi off Nassau; 28 Apr 63 assisted MV *Capri Koch* aground NE of Molasses Reef; 1 Sep 65 collided with MV *American Leader*; 4 Oct 66 unsuccessfully attempted to prevent *Point Thatcher* from grounding off Miami; Dec 67–1 Jul 82 stationed at San Pedro, CA, and used for A/N; 25 Mar 68 assisted following collision

In 1988 tender *Fir* earned the right to paint her name in gold, indicating that she was the oldest ship in the Coast Guard. She has spent her entire service life in Seattle. WA.

between MVs *Atlantic Trader* and *Steel Designer* 2 mi off Point Fermin, CA; 1980–82 assisted NOAA setting weather information buoys; 4 Mar 82 fought fire on board a FV off Malibu, CA.

Hollyhock

1946–30 Jun 58 stationed at Milwaukee, WI, and used for A/N; 15 Oct 54 assisted following a collision between Dutch MV *Prins Willem V* and tug

Sinclair No 12 with barges at Milwaukee, WI; 1 Jul 58–14 Sep 59 stationed at Sturgeon Bay, WI, and used for A/N and icebreaking; 19–21 Nov 58 assisted disabled MV *Carl D. Bradley* in northern Lake Michigan; 15 Sep 59–31 Jul 62 stationed at Detroit, MI, and used for A/N and icebreaking; 1 Aug 62–31 Mar 82 stationed at Miami, FL, and used for A/N; Mar 64 refueled USAF seaplane 140 mi E of Great Abaco I., Bahamas.

91-FOOT TENDERS

Name	Hull Number	Builder	Keel Laid	Launched	Commissioned	Disposition
Bluebonnet	WLI 257 WAGL 257	Dubuque Boat & Boiler Works, Dubuque, IA	N/A	N/A	4 Nov 39	*Decomm* 18 Jan 65 *Sold* 19 May 66
Jasmine	WLI 261 WAGL 261	The Dravo Construction Co., Neville Island, Pittsburgh, PA	N/A	26 Mar 35	May 35	*Decomm* 18 Jan 65 *Sold* 19 May 66

Cost $132,500 each

Hull
  Displacement (tons)   184 fl (1958); 171 light (1958)
  Length   91′4″ oa; 82′ bp
  Beam   23′ max
  Draft   6′6″ max (1958)

Machinery
  Main Engines   2 Cooper-Bessemer diesels (*Bluebonnet*)
  Main Boilers   2 General Motors diesels (*Jasmine*)
  BHP   440 (*Bluebonnet*); 295 (*Jasmine*)
  Propellers   twin

Performance
  Max Sustained   9.0 kts, 1,400-mi radius

Logistics
  Fuel Oil (95%)   1,920 gal
  Complement   0 officers, 11 men (1958)

Electronics
  Radar   CR-103 (1958)

Armament   none

Design
  These 91-foot units were designed as bay and sound tenders. They had steel hulls, and their superstructure was a combination of wood and steel. Each tender was fitted with a pile driver.

Bluebonnet

1946–18 Jan 65 stationed at Galveston, TX, and used for A/N; 27 Jun–1 Jul 57 provided disaster relief to Cameron-Lake Charles area following a hurricane.

The *Jasmine* hoists a temporary buoy marker from the waters of Louisiana's Rigolets in Sep 55 after having put a permanent one in place. Her boom was extended to 37 ft by adding a 10-ft section—the dark area.

Jasmine

1946–18 Jan 65 stationed at New Orleans, LA, and used for A/N; 11 Jan 54 attempted recovery of bodies from crashed Piper Pacer in Lake Pontchartrain; 30 Jun–1 Jul 57 assisted in relief from Hurricane Audrey in Pecan I. area.

81-FOOT TENDER

Name	Hull Number	Builder	Keel Laid	Launched	Commissioned	Disposition
Rhododendron	WAGL 267	Commercial Iron Works, Portland, OR	N/A	16 Mar 35	12 Apr 35	*Decomm* 20 Aug 58 Donated to state of WA 20 Apr 59

Tender *Rhododendron* holds the speed boat *Such Crust* to prevent her from sinking. The boat was disabled while taking a turn during the Gold Cup Race, at Seattle, WA, 7 Aug 55.

Cost	$75,000
Hull	
Displacement (tons)	140 fl (1935 and 1945)
Length	81' oa
Beam	20' max
Draft	6' max (1935 and 1945)
Machinery	
Main Engines	2 Imperial diesels
BHP	240
Propellers	twin
Performance	
Max Speed	9.0 kts (1935)
Logistics	
Fuel Oil (95%)	N/A
Complement	0 officers, 10 men (1945)
Deck Gear	
Boom Capacity	1.5 tons
Hoist Power	electricity
Electronics	none
Armament	none

Design
The *Rhododendron* was designed as a bay and sound tender.

Rhododendron
1948–6 Jul 49 stationed at Vancouver, WA, and used for A/N; 6 Jul 49–20 Aug 58 stationed at Seattle, WA, and used for A/N.

124-FOOT TENDER

Name	Hull Number	Builder	Keel Laid	Launched	Commissioned	Disposition
Tamarack	WLI 248 WAGL 248	Manitowoc Shipbuilding Corp., Manitowoc, WI	11 Dec 33 (contracted)	N/A	Nov 34	*Decomm* 27 Oct 70 *Sold* 2 Aug 71

Cost	$233,917
Hull	
Displacement (tons)	400 fl (1966); 290 light (1966)
Length	124'4" oa; 111'8" bp
Beam	30'3" mb
Draft	8' max (1966)
Machinery	
Main Engines	1 General Motors diesel
BHP	520
Propellers	single
Performance	
Max Sustained	10 kts, 3,505-mi radius (1966)
Logistics	
Fuel Oil (95%)	13,300
Complement	1 warrant, 19 men (1966)
Deck Gear	
Boom Capacity	15 tons
Hoist Power	electricity

Tender *Tamarack* on 28 Aug 61 sports a new stack. Note how little freeboard she has off the buoy deck.

Electronics
  Detection Radar   CR-103 (1966)
Armament   none
Design
  The *Tamarack* was designed as a bay and sound tender. She was constructed entirely of steel.

Tamarack

3 Dec 42–27 Jan 46 stationed at Manitowoc, WI, and used for A/N and icebreaking; 28 Jan 46–28 Feb 47 stationed at Detroit, MI, and used for A/N and icebreaking; 29 Feb 47–27 Oct 70 stationed at Sault Ste. Marie, MI, and used for A/N and icebreaking; Oct 60 assisted MV *John Sherwin* near Round I.; 6 May 61 assisted British MV *Crystal Jewel* in Whitefish Bay.

175-FOOT TENDER

Name	Hull Number	Builder	Keel Laid	Launched	Commissioned	Disposition
Hemlock	WAGL 217	Berg Shipbuilding Co., Seattle, WA	12 Jan 33 (contracted)	23 Jan 34	1934	*Decomm* 17 Jun 58 *Sold* 2 Aug 61

Cost $228,480
Hull
  Displacement (tons)   1,005 fl (1957); 770 light (1957)
  Length   174'6" oa; 163'6" bp
  Beam   32' max
  Draft   13'1" max (1957)
Machinery
  Main Engines   2 triple-expansion steam
  Main Boilers   2 Foster-Wheeler watertube
  SHP   1,000
  Propellers   twin
Performance
  Max Sustained   12.0 kts, 1,050-mi radius (1967)
  Economic   10.5 kts, 1,500-mi radius (1957)
Logistics
  Fuel Oil (95%)   26,000
  Complement   2 officers, 4 warrants, 41 men (1957)
Electronics
  Detection Radar   Sperry Mk-3 (1957)
Armament   none (1957)
Design
  The *Hemlock* was designed for operations in Alaskan waters and was constructed entirely of steel. She was given a double bottom and a larger fuel and water capacity than are normally found on a coastwise tender.

Hemlock

1941–17 Jun 58 stationed at Ketchikan, AK, and used for A/N.

The *Hemlock*, 1 Mar 55. Notice the life raft and the life-raft canisters abeam the main mast. Tenders serving in Alaskan waters are frequently called upon to perform search and rescue.

175-FOOT TENDER

Name	Hull Number	Builder	Keel Laid	Launched	Commissioned	Disposition
Arbutus	WLM 203 WAGL 203	Pusey & Jones Co., Wilmington, DE	21 Jul 32 (contracted)	25 Mar 33	1933	*Decomm* 27 Feb 67 *Sold* 24 Mar 69

Cost	$239,800

Hull

Displacement (tons)	997 fl (1945)
Length	174'7" oa
Beam	33' mb
Draft	14' max (1945)

Machinery

Main Engines	2 triple-expansion steam
Main Boilers	2 Foster-Wheeler watertube
SHP	1,000
Propellers	twin

Performance

Max Speed	11.3 kts (1945)
Max Sustained	11.0 kts, 1,950-mi radius (1945)

Logistics

Fuel Oil (95%)	29,800 gal
Complement	1 officer, 3 warrants, 37 men (1945)

Deck Gear

Boom Capacity	20 tons
Hoist Power	steam

Electronics

Detection Radar	SO-8 (1958)
Armament	none (1958)

Design

The *Arbutus* was designed as a coastwise tender for the USLHS. An inboard profile, deck plans, and launch photograph appear in Scheina, *WWII Cutters.*

Arbutus

1945–27 Feb 67 stationed at St. George, Staten I., NY, and used for A/N; 2 Jun 50 assisted grounded yacht *Hurricane* off Copps Rock; 29 Feb 56 towed CGB-70017 to Barnegat, NJ; Feb 65 recovered bodies and debris from Eastern DC-7 crash off Long I., NY; 15 Jul 66 grounded in Long Island Sound—refloated without damage.

131-FOOT TENDER

Name	Hull Number	Builder	Keel Laid	Launched	Commissioned	Disposition
Hickory	WLI 219 WAGL 219	Bath Iron Works, Bath, ME	13 Apr 32 (contracted)	9 Feb 33	Mar 33	*Decomm* 10 Jan 67 *Sold* 28 Apr 69

Cost	$152,480 each

Hull

Displacement (tons)	438 fl (1962); 332 light (1962)
Length	131'4" oa; 121'4" bp
Beam	24'6" mb
Draft	9'5" max (1962)

Machinery

Main Engines	1 triple-expansion steam
Main Boilers	1 Babcock & Wilcox watertube
SHP	500
Propellers	single

Performance

Max Sustained	10.4 kts, 1,450-mi radius (1962)
Economic	9.5 kts, 1,700-mi radius (1962)

Logistics

Fuel Oil (95%)	16,690 gal
Complement	1 warrant, 22 men (1962)

Deck Gear

Boom Capacity	10 tons
Hoist Power	steam

Electronics

Detection Radar	CR-103 (1962)
Armament	none (1962)

Design

The *Hickory* was designed as a coastwise tender by the USLHS. She had a steel hull, steel and wood decks, and a wooden superstructure.

Hickory

1946–10 Jan 67 stationed at St. George, Staten I., NY, and used for A/N; 2 Jul 50 assisted MVs *Sandcraft* and *Melrose* following their collision in New York harbor; 9 Mar 57 assisted MV *Steel Admiral*, tanker *Val T*, and water taxi *Oscar Gordon* following their collision off Brooklyn, NY.

The *Hickory* on 3 Oct 47. With the exception of the addition of modern electronics and a hull number, she has changed little since her commissioning in 1933.

81-FOOT TENDER

Name	Hull Number	Builder	Keel Laid	Launched	Commissioned	Disposition
Dahlia	WAGL 288	Great Lakes Engineering Works, River Rouge, MI	25 Feb 33 (contracted)	N/A	Aug 33	*Decomm* 9 Oct 64 *Sold* 20 May 65

Cost $66,566

Hull
  Displacement (tons)   188 fl (1955); 160 light (1955)
  Length   81′2″ oa; 72′ bp
  Beam   21′4″ max
  Draft   7′10″ max (1962)

Machinery
  Main Engines   1 General Motors diesel
  BHP   500
  Propellers   single

Performance
  Max Sustained   10.0 kts, 390-mi radius (1962)

Logistics
  Fuel Oil (95%)   1,045 gal
  Complement   0 officers, 10 men (1962)

Deck Gear
  Boom Capacity   3.0 tons
  Hoist Power   electricity

Electronics
  Radar   SPN-11 (1962)

Armament   none (1962)

Design
  The *Dahlia* was designed as a bay and sound tender by the USLHS. She was constructed entirely of steel. *Dahlia* was reengined following WWII.

Dahlia

1946–9 Oct 64 stationed at Detroit, MI, and used for A/N; 20 Apr 56 assisted *A. M. Byers* and *E. M. Ford* following their collision in St. Clair R. Channel; 5 Oct 62 assisted MVs *Richard V. Lindaberry* and *Hutchcliff Hall* following their collision in lower St. Clair R.

Tender *Dahlia* on 4 Aug 50. The Coast Guard was created on this date in 1790. An inboard profile and deck plans appear in Scheina, *WWII Cutters*.

93-FOOT TENDER

Name	Hull Number	Builder	Keel Laid	Launched	Commissioned	Disposition
Myrtle	WAGL 263	Dubuque Boat & Boiler Works, Dubuque, IA	15 Feb 32 (contracted)	30 Sep 32	1932	*Decomm* 8 Feb 63 *Sold* 19 May 64

Cost $95,000

Hull
  Displacement (tons)   186 fl (1932)
  Length   92′8″ oa
  Beam   23′ mb
  Draft   6′ max (1945)

Machinery
  Main Engines   2 Cummins diesels
  BHP   220
  Propellers   twin

Performance
  Max Speed   6.0 kts (1945)
  Cruising   5.0 kts, 980-mi radius (1945)

Logistics
  Fuel Oil (95%)   800 gal
  Complement   0 officers, 11 men (1945)

Deck Gear
  Boom Capacity   3 tons
  Hoist Power   gasoline

Electronics   none

Armament   none

Design
  The *Myrtle* was designed as a bay and sound tender by the USLHS.

Myrtle
1946–19 Jun 53 stationed at Galveston, TX, and used for A/N; 17 Dec 52 assisted tug *Astral* towing barges in San Antonio Bay Channel; 20 Jun 53–8 Feb 63 stationed at Corpus Christi, TX, and used for A/N.

The *Myrtle* on 22 Jun 60. A pile driver is mounted on the starboard side of her buoy deck. The use of the "W" to denote Coast Guard ships appears to be an outgrowth of the fact that this letter was used as the routing symbol for the Service during the 1930s in the Treasury Department.

86-FOOT TENDER

Name	Hull Number	Builder	Keel Laid	Launched	Commissioned	Disposition
Cherry	WAGL 258	Leathem D. Smith Dock Co., Sturgeon Bay, WI	2 Jan 31 (contracted)	N/A	19 May 32	*Decomm* 1 Dec 64 *Sold* 20 May 65

Cost $109,017

Hull
  Displacement (tons)   254 fl (1958); 197 light (1958)
  Length   86′3″ oa; 77′ bp
  Beam   23′6″ max
  Draft   9′6″ max (1958)

Machinery
  Main Engines   1 General Motors diesel
  BHP   500
  Propellers   single

Performance
  Max Sustained   11.0 kts, 800-mi radius (1958)
  Economic   9.0 kts, 1,000-mi radius (1958)

Logistics
  Fuel Oil (95%)   3,000 gal
  Complement   0 officers, 10 men (1958)

Deck Gear
  Boom Capacity   5 tons
  Hoist Power   electricity

| Electronics | none (1958) |
| Armament | none (1958) |

Design

The *Cherry* was designed as a bay and sound tender. She had a steel hull and wood and steel superstructure. *Cherry* was reengined in Jul 50.

Cherry

1946–14 Sep 59 stationed at Buffalo, NY, and used for A/N; 22 Oct 51 carried Marine Board of Investigation to site of raising of tug *Sachem* off Dunkirk, NY; 15 Sep 59–1 Dec 64 stationed at Sault Ste. Marie, MI, and used for A/N.

The *Cherry* on 3 Aug 50. A photograph taken from the same angle prior to 1 Sep 39 appears in Scheina, *WWII Cutters*. By comparing the two photographs you can see the numerous modifications that were made over the years, including the addition of a new stack.

121-FOOT TENDERS

Name	Hull Number	Builder	Keel Laid	Launched	Commissioned	Disposition
Columbine	WLI 208 WAGL 208	Moore Dry Dock Co., Oakland, CA	19 Jan 31 (contracted)	23 Jul 31	21 Oct 31	*Decomm* 8 Oct 65 *Sold* 29 Jun 67
Linden	WLI 228 WAGL 228	Merrill Stevens Shipbuilding & Dry Dock Co., Jacksonville, FL	26 Sep 30	7 Mar 31	22 Jul 31	*Decomm* 29 May 69 *Sold* 22 May 70
Wisteria	WLI 254 WAGL 254	United Dry Dock, Inc., New York, NY	21 Jul 32 (contracted)	3 Feb 33	Mar 33	*Decomm* 7 Oct 66 *Sold* 6 Dec 68

Cost $179,434 (*Columbine*); $169,110 (*Linden*); $129,800 (*Wisteria*)

Hull

Displacement (tons)	328 fl (1965); 268 light (1965)
Length	121'4" oa; 111'8" bp
Beam	26'4" max
Draft	7'2" max (1965)

Machinery

Main Engines   1 electric motor driven by 2 General Electric generators driven by 2 Winton diesels

SHP   240

Propellers   single, 4-bladed

Performance

Max Sustained   9.0 kts, 1,200-mi radius (1965)

Cruising   8.0 kts, 1,600-mi radius (1965)

Logistics

Fuel Oil (95%)	3,400 gal
Complement	1 warrant, 19 men (1965)

Deck Gear

Boom Capacity	10 tons; 8 tons (*Linden* only)
Hoist Power	electricity; air (*Linden* only)

Electronics

Detection Radar	SPN-11 (1965)

Armament   none (1965)

Design

This class was designed as bay and sound tenders for the USLHS. These tenders had steel hulls and a combination of wood and steel superstructures. The *Linden* was the first U.S. tender powered by diesel-electric drive.

Columbine

1946–8 Oct 65 stationed at San Francisco, CA, and used for A/N.

Linden

28 Feb 41–30 Apr 53 stationed at Washington, NC, and used for A/N; 17 May 50 towed disabled converted LCI off New River to Morehead City, NC; 1 May 53–31 Dec 62 stationed at Portsmouth, VA, and used for A/N; 10 Feb 55 grounded near Portsmouth, VA, no damage sustained; 21 Nov 55 assisted grounded MV near Alligator R.; 7 Mar 58 assisted tanker *Paul Dana* aground near North R.; 1 Jan 63–29 May 69 stationed at St. George, Staten I., and Governors I., NY, and used for A/N.

Wisteria

31 Oct 39–7 Oct 66 stationed at Baltimore, MD, and used for A/N and light icebreaking; 23 Apr 49 assisted grounded barge in Pocomoke Sound;

Tender *Columbine*, 18 Mar 60. Note her low freeboard. An 18 Oct 62 report noted that "although *Columbine* was designed for operation in inside waters, the last inclination experiment conducted on this vessel on 22 Jun 48 . . . states . . . that the vessel . . . would have satisfactory stability under all normal operating conditions as a buoy tender on coastwise waters." The report went on to say that "normal conditions" rarely existed outside the Golden Gate. An outboard profile of *Linden* appears in Scheina, *WWII Cutters.*

11–12 Jun 65 fought fire on Colombian MV *Ciudad de Neiva* near Baltimore, MD, along with other firefighters.

173-FOOT TENDERS

Name	Hull Number	Builder	Keel Laid	Launched	Commissioned	Disposition
Lilac	WLM 227 WAGL 227	Pusey & Jones Co., Wilmington, DE	16 Aug 32 (contracted)	26 May 33	1933	*Decomm* 3 Feb 72 *Donated* 6 Jun 72
Mistletoe	WLM 237 WAGL 237	Pusey & Jones Co., Wilmington, DE	N/A	N/A	15 Sep 39	*Decomm* 27 Sep 68 *Sold* 14 Aug 69
Violet	WAGL 250	Manitowoc Shipbuilding Corp., Manitowoc, WI	6 Sep 29 (contracted)	21 Aug 30	1930	*Decomm* 2 Jan 62 *Sold* 8 Mar 63

Cost	$334,900 (*Lilac*); $378,800 (*Mistletoe*); $337,745 (*Violet*)	Performance		
		Max Sustained	11.0 kts, 1,444-mi radius (1961)	
Hull		Economic	10.0 kts, 1,734-mi radius (1961)	
Displacement (tons)	799 fl (1961); 770 light (1961)	Logistics		
Length	173'4" oa; 163'9" bp	Fuel Oil (95%)	29,000 gal	
Beam	34' max	Complement	2 officers, 2 warrants, 34 men (1961)	
Draft	11' max (1961)	Deck Gear		
Machinery		Boom Capacity	20 tons	
Main Engines	2 triple-expansion steam	Hoist Power	steam	
Main Boilers	2 Babcok & Wilcox watertube	Electronics		
SHP	1,000	Detection Radar	SPN-11 (1961)	
Propellers	twin	Sonar	UNQ-1 (1961)	

The *Mistletoe,* photographed in the 1950s. The large deckhouse aft was used to accommodate the USLHS district inspector as he traveled between lighthouses in his district. Note the skylights abaft the stack.

| Armament | none (1961) |

Design

This class was designed as coastwise tenders by the USLHS. They were constructed entirely of steel.

Lilac

1946–2 Dec 48 stationed at Edgemoor, DE, and used for A/N; 3 Dec 48–3 Feb 72 stationed at Gloucester City, NJ, and used for A/N; 15–17 May 52 assisted following collision between MVs *Barbara Lykes* and *F. L. Hayes* in Chesapeake and Delaware Canal; 22 May 52 assisted tug *Pateo* and *Atlantic Dealer* in Delaware R.; 26 May 52 assisted following collision between tanker *Michael* and motor barge *A. C. Dodge* near Ready I.; 30 Jan 53 assisted FV *Benjamin Brothers* in Delaware R.; 6–12 Jun 53 assisted following collision between tankers *Pan Massachusetts* and *Phoenix* in Chesapeake and Delaware Canal; 24–25 Jul 53 fought fire on tanker *Pan Georgia* and searched for survivors in Christina R.; 30 Dec 53 assisted MVs *Atlantic Dealer* and *Atlantic Engineer* in Delaware R.; 13 Jul 55 assisted yacht *Nip and Tuck* in Delaware R.

Mistletoe

1946–27 Aug 68 stationed at Portsmouth, VA, and used for A/N; 8 Sep 50 patrolled President's Cup Regatta; 31 May 51 assisted dragging for plane near Langley Field; 25 Jul 51 assisted refloating *PC 572* near Cedar Point LH; 16 Sep 51 patrolled President's Cup Regatta; 19 Sep 52 patrolled President's Cup Regatta; 24 Feb 53 refloated and towed tug *Fortuna* from Horn Harbor, VA, to Portsmouth, VA; 17 Jul 53 towed *CG-95304* from Windmill Point LH to Portsmouth, VA; 17–18 Jan 57 broke ice in Upper Potomac R.; 7 Jan 59 assisted cutter *Madrona* aground at Point Lookout; 26 Aug 59 assisted in a search for survivors following a mid-air collision off Old Plantation Flats; 28 Sep 61 assisted two skin divers off Stingray Point; 6–7 Mar 63 dragged for Piper Cherokee near 37°N, 76°W.

Violet

1941–2 Jan 62 stationed at Baltimore, MD, and used for A/N.

80-FOOT TENDERS

Name	Hull Number	Builder	Keel Laid	Launched	Commissioned	Disposition
Althea	WAGL 233	New London Ship & Engine Co., Groton, CT	N/A	24 Feb 30	30 Apr 30	*Decomm* 10 Nov 62 *Sold* 26 Nov 63
Poinciana	WAGL 266	Electric Boat Co., Groton, CT	N/A	7 Jun 30	8 Jul 30	*Decomm* 17 Aug 62 *Sold* 26 Nov 63

Cost	$70,608 (*Althea*); $82,743 (*Poinciana*)
Hull	
Displacement (tons)	120 max (1945)
Length	80'9" oa
Beam	19' mb
Draft	3'8" mean draft (1930)
Machinery	
Main Engines	2 Cummins diesels
BHP	220
Propellers	twin, 4-bladed
Performance	
Max Speed	7.0 kts (1930)
Cruising	6.0 kts, 875-mi radius (1945)

Logistics	
Fuel Oil (95%)	1,000 gal
Complement	0 officers, 9 men (1945)
Deck Gear	
Boom Capacity	1.5 tons
Hoist Power	electricity
Electronics	none
Armament	none

Design

This were small shallow-draft bay and sound tenders for service in inland waters of the South Atlantic coast. Their hulls were steel.

Althea

1945–10 Nov 62 stationed at Ft. Pierce, FL, and used for A/N; 24–25 Oct 52 aided in hurricane evacuation; 29 Nov 52 transported plane wreckage to Patrick AFB.

Poinciana

Dec 43–17 Aug 62 stationed at Miami, FL, and used for A/N; 25 Oct 52 assisted in hurricane evacuation in Dania, FL; 19 Nov 53 salvaged ordnance from wrecked USMC ac in Biscayne Bay.

Tender *Poinciana* on 10 Feb 49. Note the typical white sailor uniforms of the Coast Guardsmen forward of the bridge. The CG uniform paralleled that of the USN in appearance until 1974, when the current Coast Guard blue uniform was adopted.

103-FOOT TENDER

Name	Hull Number	Builder	Keel Laid	Launched	Commissioned	Disposition
Beech	WAGL 205	Southern Shipyard Corp., Newport News, VA	16 Aug 26 (contracted)	N/A	Jan 28	*Decomm* 23 Jan 63 *Sold* 28 Aug 64

Cost	$133,306		Deck Gear	
Hull			Boom Capacity	10 tons
Displacement (tons)	255 fl (1959); 226 light (1959)		Hoist Power	electricity
Length	103′ oa; 96′ bp		Electronics	
Beam	21′8″ max		Detection Radar	Raytheon 1500 (1959)
Draft	9′ max (1959)		Armament	none
Machinery			Design	
Main Engines	1 Cooper-Bessemer diesel			
BHP	300			
Propellers	single			
Performance				
Max Sustained	8.0 kts, 2,000-mi radius (1959)			
Cruising	7.5 kts, 2,600-mi radius (1959)			
Logistics				
Fuel Oil (95%)	3,150 gal			
Complement	2 warrants, 11 men (1959)			

Design

A bay and sound tender, the *Beech* was originally fitted with a steam plant, which was removed in 1940. She was built entirely of steel except for her boat deck, which was wood. An outboard profile, inboard profile, lines, and deck plans and a photograph appear in Scheina, *WWII Cutters*.

Beech

1946–23 Jan 63 stationed at St. George, Staten I., NY, and used for A/N; 16 Sep 58 assisted Jersey Central Railroad, Newark Bay, NJ, in SAR; 12 Jan 63 assisted FV *Saint Anthony* on fire 3 mi SW of Peaked Hill Bar, MA.

182-FOOT TENDER

Name	Hull Number	Builder	Keel Laid	Launched	Commissioned	Disposition
Wakerobin	WAGL 251	The Dravo Constructing Co., Neville Island, Pittsburgh, PA	9 Oct 25 (contracted)	N/A	15 Apr 27	*Trans* to Arm Corps of Engineers, 20 Apr 55

Cost $187,500

Hull
Displacement (tons)   622 fl (1948); 575 light (1948)
Length   182′ oa; 129′8″ bp
Beam   43′ max
Draft   5′8″ max (1948)

Machinery
Main Engines   2 horizontal steam
Main Boilers   2 Babcock & Wilcox sectional header, 200 psi
SHP   550
Propellers   stern paddlewheel, 11′4″ diameter

Performance
Max Sustained   9.0 kts, 1,470-mi radius (1947)
Economics   5.0 kts, 1,690-mi radius (1947)

Logistics
Fuel Oil (95%)   Coal
Complement   1 officer, 1 warrant, 34 men (1947)
Electronics   none (1948)
Armament   none (1948)

Design
The *Wakerobin* was a stern-wheel river steamer. She had a steel hull and wood and steel superstructure.

Wakerobin

17 Mar 45–18 Dec 48 stationed at Memphis, TN, and used to service A/N; 18 Dec 48 decommissioned for storage; 18 Apr 49 temporarily loaned to Army Corps of Engineers.

The *Wakerobin* lies near St. Louis, MO, on 3 May 45. She remained in CG service for only a few more years. As a 1948 report noted, "the cost of operation of the *Wakerobin* is approximately twice that of diesel cutter *Foxglove* engaged in similar, but more arduous duties." A starboard view of *Wakerobin* appears in Scheina, *WWII Cutters*.

160-FOOT TENDERS

Name	Hull Number	Builder	Keel Laid	Launched	Commissioned	Disposition
Hawthorne	WAGL 215	Consolidated Shipbuilding Corp., Morris Heights, NY	14 Jan 20	18 Jul 21	28 Dec 21	*Decomm* 24 Jul 64 *Sold* 29 Nov 65
Oak	WAGL 239	Consolidated Shipbuilding Corp., Morris Heights, NY	14 Jan 20	28 Jun 21	31 Dec 21	*Decomm* 6 Nov 64 *Trans* to Smithsonian 3 Mar 67

Cost	$357,250 each
Hull	
Displacement (tons)	875 fl (1961); 740 light (1961)
Length	160′ oa; 149′ bp
Beam	30′ max
Draft	10′6″ max (1961)
Machinery	
Main Engines	1 triple-expansion steam
Main Boilers	1 Scotch Marine, 200 psi
SHP	675
Propellers	single
Performance	
Max Sustained	7.0 kts, 1,300-mi radius (1961)
Cruising	6.5 kts, 1,500-mi radius (1961)
Logistics	
Fuel Oil (95%)	21,300 gal
Complement	2 officers, 2 warrants, 34 men (1961)
Deck Gear	
Boom Capacity	20 tons
Hoist Power	steam

Electronics

Detection Radar   CR-103

Armament   none (1961)

Design

These ships were built as bay and sound tenders by the USLHS. They had steel hulls and wood and steel superstructures. A port view of the *Oak* appears in Scheina, *WWII Cutters.*

Hawthorne

1946–24 Jul 64 stationed at New London, CT, and used for A/N; 28 Jun 55 assisted FV *Natican* near Fishers I.; 26 Jul 56 assisted following collision between Italian liner *Andrea Doria* and Swedish liner *Stockholm* off Nantucket; 27 Dec 56 assisted in search for Navy A-D4 aircraft 8 mi E of Fishers I.

Oak

1946–6 Nov 64 stationed at St. George, Staten I., NY, and used for A/N; 21 May 46 placed "in commission in reserve" because of a shortage of personnel; 19 Aug 49—returned to active service; 17 Mar 55 searched for sunken tug *Justine McAllister* in Lower Bay, New York harbor.

201-FOOT TENDER

Name	Hull Number	Builder	Keel Laid	Launched	Commissioned	Disposition
Cedar	WAGL 207	Craig Shipbuilding Co., Long Beach, CA	4 May 15 (contracted)	27 Dec 16	30 Jun 17	*Decomm* 29 Jun 50 *Sold* 27 Jun 55

Cost	$248,189
Hull	
Displacement (tons)	1,970 fl (1950); 1,245 light (1950)
Length	200′8″ oa; 188′ bp
Beam	36′6″ max
Draft	17′6″ max (1950)
Machinery	
Main Engines	California Shipbuilding triple-expansion reciprocating, 3-cyl steam
Main Boilers	2 Scotch Marine, 190 psi
SHP	1,250
Propellers	single
Performance	
Max Sustained	10.0 kts, 4,000-mi radius (1950)
Logistics	
Fuel Oil (95%)	110,403 gal
Complement	2 officers, 4 warrants, 44 enlisted (1950)

Deck Gear

Boom Capacity   20 tons

Electronics

Detection Radar   SO-8 (1950)

Armament   none (1950)

Design

The *Cedar* was designed to operate in Alaskan waters. Her hull and superstructure were steel, and she had a double bottom. The *Cedar* was the largest tender built for the USLHS.

Cedar

1 Mar 45–8 Sep 47 stationed at Kodiak, AK, and serviced A/N; 8 Sep–2 Dec 47 stationed at Ketchikan, AK, and serviced A/N; 2 Dec 47–29 Jun 50 stationed at Kodiak, AK, and serviced A/N; 25 Feb–1 Mar 49 assisted survivors of PC *Lady Jane* at Orca Inlet, AK; 18 May 49 assisted tug *Adak*.

90-FOOT TENDER

Name	Hull Number	Builder	Keel Laid	Launched	Commissioned	Disposition
Palmetto	WAGL 265	Merrill-Stevens Dry Dock & Repair Co., Jacksonville, FL	3 Sep 15 (contracted)	30 Jun 16	19 Mar 17	*Decomm* 23 May 58 *Sold* 13 Apr 59

Cost $28,975

Hull
  Displacement (tons)   200 fl (1954); 190 light (1954)
  Length   90′ oa; 80′6″ bp
  Beam   22′ max
  Draft   5′ max (1954)

Machinery
  Main Engines   2 Superior diesels
  BHP   350
  Propellers   twin

Performance
  Max Sustained   8.5 kts, 500-mi radius (1954)
  Cruising   7.0 kts, 600-mi radius (1954)

Logistics
  Fuel Oil (95%)   1,368 gal
  Complement   13 men (1954)
Electronics   none (1954)
Armament   none (1954)

Design
The *Palmetto* was constructed for shoal-water service in the Jacksonville, FL, area. She had a steel hull, wooden deck and superstructure; her original machinery was two 4-cylinder internal-combustion engines.

Palmetto
1947–23 May 58 stationed at Charleston, SC, and used for A/N.

AIDS TO NAVIGATION TYPE CUTTERS DISPOSED OF SHORTLY AFTER WORLD WAR II*

Name	Hull Number	Class	Decomm	Sold/Trans
Kickapoo	WAGL 56	157-foot	24 Aug 45	7 Jul 47
Amaranth	WAGL 201	166-foot	29 Sep 45	19 Oct 46
Marigold	WAGL 235	160-foot	3 Oct 45	19 Oct 46
Hydrangea	WAGL 236	164-foot	8 Oct 45	8 Oct 45
Hyacinth	WAGL 221	221-foot	15 Nov 45	19 Oct 46
Orchid	WAGL 240	190-foot	1 Dec 45	1 Dec 45
Tulip	WAGL 249	190-foot	1 Dec 45	5 Jul 47
Larkspur	WAGL 226	169-foot	10 Jan 46	19 Feb 46
Sunflower	WAGL 247	174-foot	10 Jan 46	19 Feb 47
Aster	WAGL 269	75-foot	24 Jan 46	2 Oct 46
Kukui	WAGL 225	190-foot	1 Feb 46	8 Apr 47
Chaparral	WAGL 178	EA	8 Feb 46	N/A
Azalea	WAGL 262	EA	6 May 46	14 Nov 46
Cottonwood	WAGL 209	152-foot	25 May 46	1 May 47
Spruce	WAGL 246	EA	28 Jun 46	17 May 50
Crocus	WAGL 210	165-foot	13 Jul 46	N/A
Cypress	WAGL 211	190-foot	20 Aug 46	18 Mar 47
Mangrove	WAGL 232	164-foot	22 Aug 46	6 Mar 47
Hibiscus	WAGL 218	190-foot	3 Sep 46	26 Jun 47
Lotus	WAGL 229	EA	5 Nov 46	11 Jun 47

Name	Hull Number	Class	Decomm	Sold/Trans
Manzanita	WAGL 233	190-foot	29 Nov 46	30 Apr 47
Pequot	WARC 58	160-foot	8 Dec 46	5 Sep 47
Lupine	WAGL 230	EA	7 Jan 47	28 Nov 47
Aspen	WAGL 204	126-foot	25 Jan 47	26 Jan 48
Ilex	WAGL 222	EA	17 Apr 47	14 Oct 47
Speedwell	WAGL 245	EA	19 Jun 47	30 Dec 47
Anemone	WAGL 202	190-foot	1 Jul 47	1 Jul 47
Sequoia	WAGL 243	190-foot	1 Jul 47	1 Jul 47
Shrub	WAGL 244	EA	1 Jul 47	29 Dec 47
Camellia	WAGL 206	110-foot	18 Aug 47	29 Dec 47
Forward	WAGL 160	99-foot	18 Aug 47	9 Sep 47
Pine	WAGL 162	99-foot	25 Aug 47	15 Jul 48
Phlox	WAGL 161	99-foot	26 Aug 47	20 Jan 49
Greenbrier	WAGL 214	164-foot	19 Sep 47	19 Apr 48
Rose	WAGL 242	138-foot	15 Oct 47	14 Jun 48
Alder	WAGL 216	EA	11 Dec 47	14 Jun 48

* See Scheina, *WWII Cutters,* for details.

Lightships (WLV and WAL)

The post–World War II era represented the twilight years of lightships. These vessels were an expensive solution to marking a navigational hazard. Following World War II, technological advances permitted replacing these ships with large navigation buoys and "Texas Tower" light platforms.

128-FOOT LIGHTSHIP

Name & Hull Number	Builder	Keel Laid	Launched	Commissioned	Disposition
Nantucket I WLV 612 WAL 612	Coast Guard Yard, Curtis Bay, MD	N/A	1950	1950	*Decomm* 29 Mar 85 *Sold* to Boston Educational Marine Exchange
Nantucket II WLV 613 WAL 613	Coast Guard Yard, Curtis Bay, MD	4 Feb 52	4 Aug 52	12 Sep 52	*Decomm* 7 Jul 84 *Sold* to New England Historic Seaport

Cost $500,000

Hull
  Displacement (tons)   490 fl (1953)
  Length   128' oa; 112' bp
  Beam   30'2" max
  Draft   10' max (1953)

Machinery
  Main Engines   1 General Motors diesel
  BHP   520
  Propellers   single

Performance
  Max Sustained   10.5 kts, 12,500-mi radius (1953)

Logistics
  Diesel (95%)   45,000 gal
  Complement   1 warrant, 16 men (1953)

Electronics
  Radar   CR-103 (1953)

Design
  This was the last lightship class constructed in the U.S.

WLV 612

1951–69 served on San Francisco LSS; 1969–71 served on Blunts Reef LSS; 1971–75 served on Portland LSS; 1975–83 served on Nantucket Shoals LSS; 1983–85 served on LE patrols.

WLV 613

1952–67 served on Ambrose Channel LSS; 1967–79 served as a relief in the First District; 1979–83 served on Nantucket Shoals LSS.

Nantucket I underway on an LE patrol, accounting for her non-traditional paint scheme. She and her sister were the only two lightships to be formally named. This was done in 1979 when they were the only lightships remaining in service and Nantucket Shoals was the only remaining lightship station.

129-FOOT LIGHTSHIP

Hull Number	Builder	Keel Laid	Launched	Commissioned	Disposition
WLV 604 WAL 604	Rice Brothers, East Boothbay, ME	N/A	1950	19 Dec 50	*Decomm* 13 Dec 79 *Sold* 1980 to Columbia R. Maritime Museum
WLV 605 WAL 605	Rice Brothers, East Boothbay, ME	1 Mar 49	4 Mar 50	15 Dec 51 (completed)	*Decomm* 1 Jan 76

Cost $500,000 (WLV 604)
        $651,000 (WLV 605)

Hull
 Displacement (tons) 617 fl (1964); 335 light (1964)
 Length   128′ oa; 112′ bp
 Beam   30′2″ max
 Draft   10′2″ max (1964)

Machinery
 Main Engines 1 Atlas Imperial diesel
 BHP   550
 Propellers   single

Performance
 Max Sustained 10.0 kts, 11,000-mi radius (1964)

Logistics
 Diesel (95%) 47,000 gal
 Complement 1 warrant, 16 men (1964)

Electronics
 Radar   SPN-11 (1964)

Design
 The 129-foot lightships were similar in design to their immediate predecessors, the 128-foot lightships.

WLV 604

1951–79 served on Columbia River LSS.

WLV 605

1951–60 served on Overfalls LSS; 1960–69 served on Blunts Reef LSS; 1969–75 served as Relief for the West Coast.

WLV 605 replaces WLV 523 on Blunts Reef LSS in 1960. Except for *Nantucket I* and *Nantucket II,* lightships did not have names, only numbers. Whenever a lightship permanently took over a new station, the name of that station was painted on her hull. WLV 523 was acquired by the U.S. Lighthouse Society and is now on exhibit in the San Francisco Bay area.

128-FOOT LIGHTSHIP

Hull Number	Builder	Keel Laid	Launched	Commissioned	Disposition
WLV 189 WAL 189	Defoe Shipbuilding Co., Bay City, MI	N/A	16 Oct 46	Nov 46	*Decomm* 17 May 75
WLV 196 WAL 196	Defoe Shipbuilding Co., Bay City, MI	N/A	16 Oct 46	Nov 46	*Decomm* 30 Sep 71

Cost   N/A

Hull
  Displacement (tons)   630 fl (1946)
  Length   128′ oa
  Beam   30′ max
  Draft   11′ max (1946)
Machinery
  Main Engines   1 General Motors diesel
  BHP   500
  Propellers   single
Performance
  Max Speed   10 kts (1946)
Logistics
  Complement   1 warrant, 16 men (1946)
Electronics
  Radar   navigation type
Design
  These were the first lightships built by the Coast Guard. They were also the first lightships in which welding was used.

WLV 189

1947–66 served on Diamond Shoal LSS; 1966–71 served on New Orleans LSS; 1971–72 served on Five Fathom Bank LSS; 1972–75 served on Boston LSS.

WLV 196

1946–58 served on Pollock Rip LSS; 1958–60 served on Nantucket Shoals LSS; 1961–71 served on Umatilla Reef LSS.

WLV 196 on 30 Sep 61 in passage from the East Coast to the West. Note the ship does not bear a station name on her hull. Typical of the six lightships built for the CG, she has a high breakwater forward and an oval stack.

115-FOOT LIGHTSHIP

Hull Number	Builder	Keel Laid	Launched	Commissioned	Disposition
WLV 539 WAL 539 LS 118	Rice Brothers Corp., East Boothbay, ME	1 May 37	4 Jun 38	11 Sep 38	*Decomm* 7 Nov 72 Donated to Lewes, DE, Historical Soc. 9 Aug 73

Cost $223,900

Hull
  Displacement (tons)   449 fl (1963)
  Length   114′9″ oa
  Beam   26′ mb
  Draft   11′1″ max (1946)

Machinery
  Main Engines   Hill diesel (as completed)
                         1 Cooper-Bessemer diesel (1945)
  BHP   300
  Propellers   single

Performance
Max Sustained   8.0 kts, 7,000-mi radius (1963)

Logistics
Diesel (95%)   12,500 gal
Complement   1 warrant, 14 men (1963)

Electronics
Radar   SPN-11 (1963)

Design
     The WLV 539 was constructed entirely of steel and patterned after WLV 534.

WLV 539

1938–57 served on Cornfield Point LSS; 1958–62 served on Cross Rip LSS; 1962–72 served on Boston LSS.

WLV 539 during the 1950s. She was the last lightship built by the USLHS. The lightship designator changed from LS to WAL in 1942 and from WAL to WLV in 1965. WLV 539 is flying a red small-craft warning pennant from her starboard yard and the CG ensign from the port yard—these in fact should be reversed.

149-FOOT LIGHTSHIPS

Name & Hull Number	Builder	Keel Laid	Launched	Commissioned	Disposition
WLV 534 WAL 534 LS 112	Pusey & Jones Co., Wilmington, DE	N/A	N/A	1936	*Decomm & trans* to Dept. of Labor, NY, 28 May 75

Cost $300,956

Hull
Displacement (tons)   1,050 fl (1946)
Length   148'10" oa
Beam   31' mb
Draft   16'3" max (1946)

Machinery
Main Engines   Compound reciprocating steam
Main Boilers   2 Babcock & Wilcox
BHP   600
Propellers   single

Performance

Max Sustained	12.0 kts, 2,000-mi radius (1946)

Logistics

Fuel Oil (95%)	37,300 gal
Complement	1 officer, 18 men (1946)

Electronics

Radar	SO-1 (1945)

Design

Built specifically for the Nantucket station following the sinking of LS 117 by the SS *Olympic*. The hull was divided into watertight compartments; six different exits were provided to the upper deck, and other safety design features were incorporated.

WLV 534

1945–58 served on Nantucket Shoals LSS; 1958–60 underwent major renovation; 1960–75 served on Nantucket Shoals LSS.

WLV 534 on 4 Dec 74. Nantucket Shoals was the last U.S. lightship station in service, ending in 1983. WLV 534, retired in 1975, now serves as a museum at South Portland, ME.

133-FOOT LIGHTSHIPS

Hull Number	Builder	Keel Laid	Launched	Commissioned	Disposition
WLV 523 WAL 523 LS 100	Albina Marine Iron Works, Portland, OR	28 Mar 28	N/A	10 Feb 30	*Decomm* 12 May 71 *Trans* to USN 6 Aug 71
WLV 535 WAL 535 LS 113	Albina Marine Iron Works, Portland, OR	28 Mar 28	N/A	15 Jun 30	*Decomm* 1 Oct 68 Donated 7 Jun 69
WLV 536 WAL 536 LS 114	Albina Marine Iron Works, Portland, OR	28 Mar 28	N/A	1930	*Decomm* 5 Nov 71
WLV 537 WAL 537 LS 115	Charleston Dry Dock & Machine Co., Charleston, SC	4 Oct 28	N/A	14 Jul 30	*Decomm* 4 Nov 65 Donated 5 Sep 67
WLV 538 WAL 538 LS 116	Charleston Dry Dock & Machine Co., Charleston, SC	4 Oct 28	N/A	14 Aug 30	*Decomm* 5 Jan 71 *Trans* to NPS 25 Aug 71

Cost between $741,090 & 744,833

Hull

Displacement (tons)	630 fl (1958)
Length	133'3" oa; 108'9" wl
Beam	30' mb
Draft	13'3" max (1958)

Machinery

Main Engines	1 General Electric motor driven by 4 generators driven by 4 Winton diesels
SHP	350
Propellers	single

Performance

Max Sustained	6.0 kts, 4,000-mi radius (1958)

Logistics

Diesel (95%)	21,000 gal
Complement	1 warrant, 16 men (1959)

Electronics

Radar	SPN-11 (1959)

Design

Constructed of steel, a sister ship, LS 117, was run down by the liner *Olympic* on 15 May 34.

WLV 523

1930–59 served on Blunts Reef LSS; 1959–69 served as Relief on the West Coast; 1969–71 served on San Francisco LSS.

WLV 535

1930–61 served on Swiftsure Bank LSS; 1961 served on Umatilla Reef LSS; 1961–69 served as Relief in the 13th District.

WLV 536

1930–42 served on Fire Island LSS; 1942–45 served as an Examination Vessel; 1945–58 served as Relief in the 1st District; 1959–69 served on Pollock Rip LSS; 1969–71 served on Portland LSS.

WLV 537

1930–64 served on Frying Pan Shoal LSS; 1964–65 served as Relief in the 5th District.

WLV 538

1930–33 served on Fenwick Island Shoal LSS; 1933–65 served on Chesapeake LSS; 1965–70 served on Delaware LSS.

WLV 537 on 20 Feb 49. During WWII most lightships were taken off station and served as Examination Vessels to monitor vessels entering and leaving port. WLV 537 served as the Examination Vessel at Cristobal, the Canal Zone (1942–44), and Charleston, SC (1944–45). After the war, she returned to her prewar station, Frying Pan Shoal.

132-FOOT LIGHTSHIPS

Hull Number	Builder	Keel Laid	Launched	Commissioned	Disposition
WLV 528 WAL 528 LS 106	Bath Iron Works, Bath, ME	8 Jul 21	N/A	14 Jun 23	*Decomm* 17 Oct 67 *Trans* to Surinam 4 Jun 68
WLV 529 WAL 529 LS 107	Bath Iron Works, Bath, ME	8 Jul 21	N/A	22 Feb 24 delivered	*Decomm* 15 Apr 68 *Trans* to Hampton, VA, as a museum 21 Nov 68
WLV 530 WAL 530 LS 108	Bath Iron Works, Bath, ME	8 Jul 21	N/A	17 Sep 23 delivered	*Decomm* 31 Aug 70 Donated 29 Dec 71
WLV 531 WAL 531 LS 109	Bath Iron Works, Bath, ME	8 Jul 21	N/A	10 Nov 23 delivered	*Decomm* 8 Dec 66 *Trans* AID 20 Feb 67
WLV 532 WAL 532 LS 110	Bath Iron Works, Bath, ME	8 Jul 21	N/A	22 Jan 24 delivered	*Decomm* 3 Nov 71 Donated 30 Mar 72
WLV 533 WAL 533 LS 111	Bath Iron Works, Bath, ME	14 Jun 24	N/A	20 Dec 26	*Decomm* & *trans* to USN 11 Jul 69

Cost $200,000 (WAL 528, 529, 530); $160,000 (WAL 531 & 532); $90,000 (WAL 533)

Hull
Displacement (tons)   770 fl (1961)
Length   132′4″ oa
Beam   30′ mb
Draft   15′ max (1961)

Machinery
Main Engines   1 General Motors diesel
BHP   400–500
Propellers   single

Performance
Max Sustained   6.5 kts, 8,750-mi radius (1961)

Logistics
Diesel (95%)   46,000 gal
Complement   1 warrant, 14 men (1961)

Electronics
Radar   CR-103 (1961)

Design
This class was constructed of steel. Standard Oil paid for WAL 533 to replace a lightship sunk in a collision with one of its barges. All units were completed with

compound steam engines except for WAL 533, which was built with a diesel. All were reengined in the 1950s with diesels.

WLV 528

1945–67 served as Relief in 1st District.

WLV 529

1945–60 served on Winter Quarter Shoal LSS; 1960–65 served on Delaware LSS.

WLV 530

1947–50 served on Five Fathom Bank LSS.

WLV 531

1924–54 served as Relief in 6th District; 1954–64 served on Savannah LSS; 1965–66 served on New Orleans LSS.

WLV 532

1945–54 served on Vineyard Sound LSS; 1954–59 served on Cross Rip LSS; 1959–61 served on Buzzards Bay LSS; 1961–71 served as Relief in 5th District.

WLV 533

1932–52 served on Ambrose Channel LSS; 1952–69 served on Portland, ME, LSS.

WLV 530, 2 Oct 63, on Five Fathom Banks LSS. Whether at anchor or underway, lightships frequently flew the national ensign from the flagstaff astern and the Coast Guard ensign from the foremast.

96-FOOT LIGHTSHIP

Hull Number	Builder	Keel Laid	Launched	Commissioned	Disposition
WLV 526 WAL 526 LS 103	Consolidated Shipbuilding Corp., Morris Heights, NY	5 Jun 18	1 May 20	22 Dec 20	*Decomm* 25 Aug 70 Donated to Port Huron, MI, 5 Jun 71

Cost	$161,074
Hull	
Displacement (tons)	335 freshwater fl (1962)
Length	96′5″ oa
Beam	24′ mb
Draft	10′ max (1962)
Machinery	
Main Engines	1 General Motors diesel
BHP	340
Propellers	single
Performance	
Max Sustained	9.0 kts, 2,570-mi radius (1962)
Logistics	
Diesel (95%)	8,680 gal
Complement	11 men (1962)
Electronics	
Radar	CR-103 (1962)

Design

WLV 526 was built with a steel hull and superstructure. She was the only lightship to be painted black, all others having red hulls. As a "black light station," she was passed to port like a black buoy would be passed. As built, she had a reciprocating steam engine that was replaced by a diesel in the 1950s.

WLV 526

1936–70 served on Lake Huron LSS.

This 1962 photograph of WLV 526 shows how small a pre-WWII lightship could be. A crew of about a dozen would spend three weeks or more isolated off a port bobbing up and down and dodging shipping.

92-FOOT LIGHTSHIP

Hull Number	Builder	Keel Laid	Launched	Commissioned	Disposition
WAL 522 LS 99	Rice Brothers Corp., East Boothbay, ME	10 Jul 17	7 Nov 19	20 Dec 20	*Decomm* 24 May 56 *Sold* 5 Nov 56

Cost	$97,220
Hull	
Displacement (tons)	215 at mean draft (1921)
Length	91'1"
Beam	22' mb
Draft	10'7" max (1920)
Machinery	
Main Engines	1 compound reciprocating steam
Main Boilers	1 heating
SHP	350
Propellers	single
Performance	
Max Sustained	N/A
Logistics	
Fuel	coal
Complement	13 men (1945)
Electronics	
Radar	SO-1 (1945)

Design

WAL 522 was contracted on 29 Jul 16. Shortly after being laid down a fire swept the yard. The original keel was badly damaged and cut up for scrap. The contract was renegotiated on Jul 18. Constructed for service on the Great Lakes, originally she was not fitted with an engine but was towed from place to place.

WAL 522, 12 Apr 50, at Curtis Bay, MD. She was converted into an experimental unattended lightship.

WAL 522

1945–53 stationed at the CG Yard, Curtis Bay, MD, and developed as an experimental, unattended lightship.

102-FOOT LIGHTSHIP

Hull Number	Builder	Keel Laid	Launched	Commissioned	Disposition
WAL 524 LS 101	Pusey & Jones Co., Wilmington, DE	6 Mar 15 (contracted)	12 Jan 16	25 Sept 16	*Decomm* 23 Mar 64 Donated 3 Sep 64
WAL 525 LS 102	Pusey & Jones Co., Wilmington, DE	6 Mar 15 (contracted)	27 Nov 25	3 Jan 17	*Decomm* 25 Oct 63 *Sold* 2 Mar 65

Cost	$108,507 WAL 524; $110,065 WAL 525
Hull	
Displacement (tons)	360 fl (1963)
Length	101'10" oa; 91'6" bp
Beam	25' max
Draft	12'1" max (1963)
Machinery	
Main Engines	1 Cooper-Bessemer diesel
BHP	300
Propellers	single
Performance	
Max Speed	8.5 kts, 1,600-mi radius (1963)

Logistics	
Complement	2 warrants, 12 men (1963)
Electronics	
Radar	CR-103 (1963)

Design

Constructed of steel, these ships were originally fitted with steam plants. They were reengined in the 1950s.

WAL 524

1926–51 served on Overfalls LSS; 1951–63 served on Stonehorse Shoal LSS.

WAL 525

1935–62 served on Brenton Reef LSS; 1962–68 served on Cross Rip LSS.

WAL 524, probably during WWII. She remained on Overfalls LSS throughout WWII. The WLV designator did not come into use until 1965; therefore, this ship and her sister, WAL 525, were never designated WLVs.

WAL 521 in Jan 49. Typical of lightships built in the early part of the twentieth century, the deck edges were rounded or turtled to improve water run-off.

101-FOOT LIGHTSHIPS

Hull Number	Builder	Keel Laid	Launched	Commissioned	Disposition
WAL 520 LS 96	Racine-Truscott-Shell Lake Boat Co., Muskegon, MI	24 Apr 13 (contracted)	21 Apr 14	24 Apr 15	*Decomm* 18 Jan 55 *Sold* 28 Jul 55
WAL 521 LS 98	Racine-Truscott-Shell Lake Boat Co., Muskegon, MI	24 Apr 13 (contracted)	9 Jun 14	12 Jun 15	*Decomm* 18 Jan 55 *Sold* 28 Jul 55

Cost	$71,292 WAL 520; $87,025 WAL 521	Electronics	
Hull		Radar	SO-1 (1945)
Displacement (tons)	195 gross (1952)	Design	
Length	101′ oa; 83′ bp		Constructed of steel, these ships were originally fitted with internal-combustion engines. They were reengined in the 1950s.
Beam	23′6″ max		
Draft	11′ max (1952)		
Machinery		*WAL 520*	
Main Engines	1 Cooper-Bessemer diesel	1937–54 served on the Cross Rip LSS.	
BHP	315		
Propellers	single	*WAL 521*	
Performance		1931–51 served on the Handkerchief Shoal LSS; 1951–55 served as Relief in 1st District.	
Max Speed	5.0 kts, 1,400-mi radius (1945)		
Logistics			
Complement	2 warrants, 14 men (1952)		

108-FOOT LIGHTSHIP

Hull Number	Builder	Keel Laid	Launched	Completed	Disposition
WAL 519 LS 95	Muskegon, MI	14 Jun 10	N/A	30 Nov 12	*Decomm* 15 Jan 65 Donated 12 May 66

Cost	$74,558
Hull	
Displacement (tons)	382 fl (1964)
Length	108'5" oa
Beam	23' max
Draft	11'6" max (1964)
Machinery	
Main Engines	1 National Superior diesel
BHP	200
Propellers	single
Performance	
Max Speed	6.0 kts, 6,000-mi radius (1964)

Logistics	
Diesel (95%)	10,321 gal
Complement	1 warrant, 14 men (1964)
Electronics	
Radar	SO-1

Design

With a steel hull and wooden deckhouses, WAL 519 sank four days before delivery and had to be rebuilt. On 4 Jul 12, WAL 519 was delivered unfinished and was completed at the government depot at Staten Island, NY, on 27 Sep 12. First date on station was 30 Nov 12.

WAL 519

1934–65 served as Relief in 3rd District.

136-FOOT LIGHTSHIP

Hull Number	Builder	Keel Laid	Launched	Completed	Disposition
WAL 518 LS 94	Racine Boat Manufacturing Co.	28 May 09	N/A	13 Jun 11	*Decomm* 15 Dec 54 *Sold* 16 Nov 55

Cost	$104,604
Hull	
Displacement (tons)	660 fl (1952)
Length	135'6" oa; 112'11" bp
Beam	29' max
Draft	12'9" (1952)
Machinery	
Main Engines	1 Atlas Imperial diesel
BHP	375
Propellers	single
Performance	
Max Speed	8.0 kts, 7,000-mi radius (1952)
Logistics	
Diesel (95%)	17,950 gal
Complement	1 officer, 14 men (1952)
Electronics	
Radar	SO-1 (1945)

Design

Hull is constructed of steel, deckhouses of wood.

WAL 518

1930–54 served on Savannah LSS.

WAL 518 on 23 Feb 49. When she entered service in 1911, WAL 518 was equipped with two recently developed electronic aids, the radio and the submarine bell.

135-FOOT LIGHTSHIPS

Hull Number	Builder	Completed	Disposition
WLV 509 WAL 509 LS 84	New York Shipbuilding Co., Camden, NJ	1907	*Decomm* 26 Oct 65 Donated for museum 7 Aug 68
WAL 510 LS 85	New York Shipbuilding Co., Camden, NJ	1907	*Decomm* 15 Nov 62 *Sold* 17 Oct 63

Hull Number	Builder	Completed	Disposition
WAL 511 LS 86	New York Shipbuilding Co., Camden, NJ	1907	*Decomm* 28 Feb 59 *Sold* 30 Dec 59
WLV 512 WAL 512 LS 87	New York Shipbuilding Co., Camden, NJ	1907	*Decomm* 4 Mar 66 Donated for museum 4 Aug 68
WAL 513 LS 88	New York Shipbuilding Co., Camden, NJ	1908	*Decomm* 23 Nov 60 *Sold* 25 Jul 62
WAL 514 LS 90	Fore River Shipbuilding Co., Quincy, MA	1908	*Decomm* 30 Sep 52 *Sold* 21 Jul 55
WAL 515 LS 91	Fore River Shipbuilding Co., Quincy, MA	1908	*Decomm* 30 Nov 61 *Sold* 11 Mar 63
WAL 516 LS 92	Fore River Shipbuilding Co., Quincy, MA	1908	*Decomm* 28 Jun 51 *Sold* 7 Dec 54
WAL 517 LS 93	Fore River Shipbuilding Co., Quincy, MA	1908	*Decomm* 9 Apr 51 *Sold* 2 Nov 55

Cost	between $99,000 & $107,213
Hull	
Displacement (tons)	575 fl (1958)
Length	135′5″ oa; 112′ bp
Beam	29′1″ max
Draft	12′ max (1958)
Machinery	
Main Engines	1 diesel
BHP	300
Performance	
Max Sustained	9 kts, 5,400-mi radius (1958)
Logistics	
Diesel (95%)	18,500 gal
Complement	2 warrants & 12 men (1958)
Electronics	
Radar	Bendix Mk 3 (1958)

Design

These lightships were constructed with steel hulls and wooden superstructure.

WLV 509

1929–54 served on St. John's LSS; 1954–60 served as Relief in 6th District; 1960–65 served as Relief in 3rd District.

WAL 510

1944–51 served as Relief in 1st District; 1952–62 served on Boston LSS.

WAL 511

1934–54 served on Hen and Chickens LLS; 1954–59 served on Buzzard Bay LLS.

WLV 512

1945–62 served on Scotland LLS.

WAL 513

1945–49 served on Umatilla LLS; 1959–60 served as Relief on West Coast.

WAL 514

1944–52 served on Portland LSS.

WAL 515

1945–61 served as Relief.

WAL 516

1909–51 served as Relief on West Coast.

WAL 517

1939–51 served on Columbia River LSS.

WAL 510, Jan 49, serving as Relief in the First District. A sistership, WAL 516, spent her entire 42-year career as a Relief, never to wear the name of a station. The hand-operated bell on the forecastle was the standard fog signal on board lightships built prior to WWII.

129-FOOT LIGHTSHIPS

Hull Number	Builder	Completed	Disposition
WAL 504 LS 76	Burles Drydock Co., Port Richmond, NY	26 May 04	*Decomm* 16 Sep 60 *Sold* 9 Oct 61
WAL 505 LS 78	New York Shipbuilding Co., Camden, NJ	1904	*Sank* 24 Jun 60
WLV 506 WAL 506 LS 79	New York Shipbuilding Co., Camden, NJ	1904	*Decomm* 3 Mar 67 Donated 13 Oct 67
WAL 507 LS 81	Camden, NJ	1904	*Decomm* 4 Apr 51 *Sold* 21 Jul 55
WAL 508 LS 83	Camden, NJ	1904	*Decomm* 18 Jul 60 Donated 1 Oct 63

Cost $89,000 (WAL 505 & 506)

Hull
   Displacement (tons)   558 fl (1952)
   Length   129′6″ oa; 114′ bp
   Beam   28′8″ max
   Draft   11′9″ max (1952)

Machinery
   Main Engines   1 diesel
   BHP   300
   Propellers   single

Performance
   Max Sustained   6.0 kts, 4,600-mi radius (1952)

WAL 506 on 21 Aug 63. Note the television antenna atop her aft deckhouse.

Logistics
    Diesel (95%)   16,000 gal
    Complement   1 warrant, 14 men (1952)
Electronics
    Radar   SO-1 (1945)
Design
    The 129-foot lightships had steel hulls and wooden superstructures. All were built with compound reciprocating-steam engines except LS 507, which had a diesel. Following WWII all received new diesels. These class numbers were disposed of before WWII—LS 77, 80, and 82.

WAL 504
1945–60 served as Relief on the West Coast.

WAL 505
1945–60 served as Relief in the 3rd District.

WLV 506
1946–51 served on Boston LSS.

WAL 507
1945–51 served on Boston LSS.

WAL 508
1945–51 served on San Francisco LSS; 1951–60 served as Relief on West Coast.

119-FOOT LIGHTSHIPS

Hull Number	Builder	Completed	Disposition
WAL 501	West Bay City, MI	1892	*Decomm* 15 Jun 51
LS 53			*Sold* 19 Jul 55
WAL 502	West Bay City, MI	1892	*Decomm* 23 Jul 46
LS 54			*Sold* 15 Sep 47

Cost $61,538 (WAL 501)
                    $62,030 (WAL 502)
Hull
    Displacement (tons)   325 fl (1949)
    Length   118'10" oa
    Beam   26'6" max
    Draft   11' max (1945)
Machinery
    Main Engines   1 diesel
    BHP   150
    Propellers   single
Performance
    Max Sustained   6.0 kts, 1,500-mi radius (1949)

Logistics
    Diesel (95%)   3,200 gal
    Complement   14 men (1949)
Electronics
    Radar   SO-1 (1945)
Design
    Designed by W. Sylven. LS 54 had a steel hull, and both units had wooden superstructures.

WAL 501
1934–51 served on Stonehorse Shoal LSS.

WAL 502
1940–46 served as Relief in 1st District.

Search-and-Rescue Craft

The United States Coast Guard and its predecessors actively pursued the design and construction of small craft from their earliest days. Due to the multimission nature of the service, boats were designed to perform a wide variety of tasks from rescuing those in distress, to setting small aids to navigation, and much more. One unique type among the hundreds of designs that have been used over the decades was the search-and-rescue craft. The U.S. Life-Saving Service, and its successor, the U.S. Coast Guard, have designed and built this type for almost a century. A number of Coast Guard designs have influenced those used by other coast guard–type agencies throughout the world.

47-FOOT MOTOR LIFEBOAT

Number	Completed	Remarks
Approx. 100	1991	Jul 90 for prototype

Cost	N/A
Hull	
Displacement (lbs)	40,000 fl (1988)
Length	47' oa
Beam	14' max
Draft	4' max
Machinery	
Main Engines	N/A
BHP	N/A
Propellers	N/A
Performance	
Max Sustained	25 kts (1989)
Logistics	
Fuel Oil (95%)	N/A
Complement	4 plus 5 survivors
Electronics	
Radar	N/A

Design

The 47-foot MLB is being designed to replace the aging 44-foot MLB as the primary inshore and surf and bar rescue craft under the worst environmental conditions. The craft will be self-righting, designed to be operated in 20-foot seas and 20-foot surf.

The hull and superstructure of the craft are made of aluminum. The hull form is a single chine, deep-V planing hull. The size was determined by existing station moorings, haulout facilities, and manning levels. The primary improvements over the 44-footer are increased speed, greater crew protection, and improved seakeeping.

The production process calls for the construction of a prototype, five pre-production boats, and approximately 100 production models.

A preliminary sketch of the new 47-foot MLB.

30-FOOT SURF RESCUE CRAFT

Number	Completed	Remarks
30201 thru 30220	1986–90	

Cost	N/A
Hull	
Displacement (lbs)	11,500 fl; 10,300 operational (1980)
Length	30′4″ max
Beam	9′4″ max
Draft	3′8″ max
Machinery	
Main Engines	N/A
BHP	N/A
Propellers	N/A
Performance	
Max Speed	31 kts
Cruising	25 kts, 150-mi radius (1988)
Logistics	
Fuel Oil (95%)	77 gal
Complement	2 men (1980)

Design

The 30-foot SRB was designed for close-in rescue work under moderately heavy sea and surf conditions. The boat is self-bailing and self-righting and can accommodate six survivors. It can tow boats up to 40 feet. Prior to the development of this boat, standard shipboard MSBs were modified for limited duty and assigned to some shore stations.

The 30-foot SRB is constructed of solid glass-reinforced plastic from the chine down. Above the chine, the boat is foam core glass-reinforced plastic.

CG-30201 on 17 Oct 79.

CG-253312 on 16 Jun 67 off New York. This is the inshore version of the 25-footer.

25-FOOT MOTOR SURF BOAT (SHORE VERSION)

Number	Completed	Remarks
253301 thru 253317	1969–70	Stationed throughout the U.S.; most units active

Cost	$16,300 (1967)
Hull	
Displacement (lbs)	7,410 fl (1980)
Length	25′8″
Beam	7′1″
Draft	2′1″ max (1980)
Machinery	
Main Engines	1 General Motors diesel
BHP	80
Propellers	single
Performance	
Max Sustained	11 kts, 60-mi radius (1980)
Logistics	
Fuel Oil (95%)	30 gal
Complement	3 (1980)

Design

The 25-foot MSB (SV) is a standard shipboard boat designed for use in moderately heavy seas. It has also been modified for shore-station use. Is is used under moderate conditions and is not self-righting. The boat can carry 13 in addition to its crew, or 2,340 lbs.

The boat is constructed of fiberglass. The short-station modifications include a semi-enclosed cabin over the forward third of the boat, lifelines, a towing line and bitt, and a marine radio.

The 25-footer's slow speed and its bottom configuration with a weak skeg make it less than ideal for shallow-water operations in rough surf. However, the boat is rugged and reliable. During the 1960s the Coast Guard had evaluated 22-foot and 26-foot Bartender designs for rescue work in moderate surf but concluded that neither was sturdy enough for the task.

CG-38101 passes Alcatraz I. in 1970. The observation bubble forward of the radar antenna was installed by the CG.

38-FOOT AIR-CUSHION VEHICLE

Number	Completed	Remarks
38101 thru 38103	1969 (USN) Oct 70 Dec 70 Feb 71 (CG)	Tested for use in SAR, A/N, LE, Marine Safety & logistics; 2 stationed in San Francisco & 1 in Alaska—later *trans* to Great Lakes; 38101 & 38102 *trans* to USA Mobility Equipment Research & Development Center on 25 Apr 75; 38103 sank.

Cost
Hull
  Displacement (lbs)   20,000 fl (1971)
  Length   38'10" oa
  Beam   23'9" max
  Obstacle Clearance   3'6" solid wall (1971) 5–6' vegetation
Machinery
  Main Engines   1 General Electric marine gas turbine
  SHP   1,150
  Propellers   single
Performance
  Max Speed   70 kts (1971)
  Max Sustained   50 kts, 300-mi radius (1971)
Logistics
  Kerosene   484 gal
  Complement   3 (1971)
Electronics
  Radar   navigation type

44-FOOT MOTOR LIFEBOAT

Number	Completed	Remarks
44300 thru 44409	7 Jan 63 thru Nov 72	Stationed throughout the U.S.; 105 units active

Cost $125,000 (1967); $225,000 (1972)
Hull
  Displacement (lbs)   20 fl (1972)
  Length   44'2" oa
  Beam   12'8" max
  Draft   3'2" max (1972)
Machinery
  Main Engines   2 Detroit diesels
  BHP   370
  Propellers   twin
Performance
  Max Sustained   14 kts, 164-mi radius (1980)
  Economic   8 kts, 550-mi radius (1980)
Logistics
  Fuel Oil (95%)   330 gal
  Complement   4 men (1980)
Electronics
  Radar   SPS-57
Design

The 44-foot MLB was designed for inshore and surf and bar rescue under the worst environmental conditions. It is self-righting and self-bailing and can carry up to 25 survivors. It was built to replace the aging 36-foot MLB.

The 44-footer is constructed of steel and is divided into seven watertight compartments. It is equipped with a 120-gal.-per-minute pump for dewatering and fire fighting.

The 44-footer was designed by the Coast Guard, and all units were constructed at the Coast Guard Yard, Curtis Bay, MD. One hundred and ten units have been built—106 for the Coast Guard (one of which has been disposed of) and four for foreign governments.

CG-44300, the first 44-foot MLB to be built, runs trials in Apr 62.

CG-35090.

35-FOOT LAND AMPHIBIOUS RESCUE CRAFT

Number	Completed	Remarks
35086 thru 35100	1963 thru	Stationed between Massachusetts
35112 thru 35113	1967	& North Carolina; disposed of
35738, 35747		between 1968 & 1979.

Cost $47,850 (1963)
Hull
  Displacement (lbs)   20,063 (1963)
  Length   35′
  Beam   10′ max
  Draft   N/A
Machinery
  Main Engines   1 diesel
  BHP   300
Performance
  Max Speed   30 mph (short distance on land)
                                8 kts (in water)
  Max Sustained   18 mph (10 hrs, on land)
Logistics
  Complement   3 men
Design

The 35-Foot LARC was designed for the U.S. Army to carry men and supplies from offshore ships to the beach or to an inland area. It can carry a maximum load of five tons on either land or water. The Coast Guard used the LARC primarily for shallow-water flood-relief rescue and as a platform for underwater searches.

The amphibian is constructed of aluminum. It is fitted with four low-pressure tires that permit it to travel over soft surfaces, such as sand or mud. It can ascend and descend grades of up to 60 degrees.

Due to the extremely high maintenance cost associated with these amphibians, LARCs were used only when the task could not be accomplished by another type of craft.

52-FOOT STEEL-HULLED MOTOR LIFEBOAT

Number	Completed	Remarks
52312	Jun 56	*Victory:* stationed at Yaquina Bay, OR; active
52313	Sep 60	*Invincible:* stationed at Grays Harbor, WA; active
52314	Dec 61	*Triumph II:* stationed at Cape Disappointment, WA; active
52315	1963	*Intrepid:* stationed at Coos Bay, OR; active

Cost $235,927
Hull
  Displacement (lbs)   75,715 (1974)
  Length   52′ oa
  Beam   14′7″ max
  Draft   6′11″ normal (1974)
Machinery
  Main Engines   2 General Motors diesels
  BHP
  Propellers   twin
Performance
  Max Sustained   11 kts, 495-mi radius (1974)
Logistics
  Complement   5 men (1974)
Electronics
  Radar   navigation type
Design

The steel-hulled 52-foot MLB was designed for offshore rescue under the worst conditions. This 52-foot MLB is self-righting and self-bailing and can carry up to 40 survivors. The boat was designed to replace the 52-foot wooden-hulled MLB and to complement the shorter-legged 36-foot and 44-foot MLBs.

The 52-footer is constructed of steel. Among other features that increase the range and endurance, the craft is fitted with a complete galley. The boat is equipped with 250-gal.-per-minute pump for dewatering and fire fighting.

The 52-footer was designed by the Coast Guard, and all units were constructed at the Coast Guard Yard, Curtis Bay, MD.

The 52-foot steel-hulled MLB 52312 during trials at CG Yard, Curtis Bay, MD, 6 Jul 56.

38-FOOT DUKW AMPHIBIANS

Number	Completed	Remarks
31300 thru 31327	1944 & 1948	Also bore numbers in T-4000, T-5000, & T-13000 series; T-4000 & T-5000 acquired in 1944 & stationed at lifeboat stations between Long Island, NY, & Cape Hatteras, NC; T-13000 acquired in 1948 & stationed on East & West coasts; all units disposed of by 30 Sep 70.

Cost	$8,460 per unit (1947)
Hull	
Displacement (lbs)	16,380 fl
Length	38′
Beam	8′4″
Draft	3′10″ max
Machinery	
Main Engines	gasoline 6-cyl.
BHP	90
Propellers	single (for water)
Performance	
Max Sustained	55 mph (on land)
	12 mph (across beaches)
	6 mph (in water)
Logistics	
Complement	2 men

Design

The 38-foot DUKW was designed for the U.S. Army to carry men and supplies from offshore ships and across a beach. The term DUKW is a manufacturer's code designation. It translates to D for 1942, U for utility vehicle, K for front-wheel drive, and W for two rear-drive axles. The nickname "Duck" grew out of this code and the amphibious capability of the craft.

The DUKWs acquired from the U.S. Army were constructed of sheet steel. The following modifications were made by the Coast Guard: installation of an aluminum alloy cover over the driver's area and extending aft over the forward part of the cargo space; a self-bailing cockpit in the after part of the cargo space; a walkway along each side of the cover; towing bitts and tow rail; and navigational lights.

In 1948 the Coast Guard constructed additional units at the Coast Guard Yard, Curtis Bay, MD. These had aluminum bodies and incorporated the experience learned from using the Army model.

DUKWs were most useful in flood relief. However, the craft suffered from high maintenance costs, rapid deterioration due to salt water, and a lack of watertight subdivisions.

52-FOOT WOODEN-HULLED MOTOR LIFEBOATS

Number	Completed	Remarks
52300	12 Apr 35	*Invincible:* 1935–67, stationed at Point Adams, OR; *trans* to USN 15 Aug 67

A CG DUKW from Kill Devil Hills, NC, comes ashore carrying a load of Boy Scouts, 27 Jul 53.

The 52-foot wooden-hulled MLB 52300 during the 1930s. A starboard bow view appears in Scheina, *WWII Cutters and Craft.*

Number	Completed	Remarks
52301	30 Jul 35	*Triumph I:* 1935–41, stationed at Sandy Hook, NJ; 1941–? stationed at Grays Harbor, WA; ?–12 Jan 61 stationed at Coos Bay, OR; 12 Jan 61 lost.

Cost	N/A
Hull	
Displacement (tons)	30 fl (1936)
Length	52′ oa; 50′ wl
Beam	14′4″ max
Draft	6′8″ max (1936)
Machinery	
Main Engines	1 Buda diesel
BHP	150
Propellers	single
Performance	
Max Speed	10.5 kts (1936)
Logistics	
Complement	4 men (1936)

Design

The 52-foot wooden-hulled MLB was designed for offshore rescue under the worst conditions. It is not self-righting or self-bailing. The boat can carry up to 60 survivors. It was designed to complement the shorter-legged 36-foot MLB.

The superstructure, including the wheelhouse, engine-room trunk, companionway, and the survivor compartments are constructed of bronze. The hull is divided into six watertight compartments, any two of which may be flooded and the boat would remain afloat. The watertight bulkheads are bronze, all welded construction.

The 52-footer was designed by the Coast Guard, and both units were constructed at the Coast Guard Yard, Curtis Bay, MD.

For data concerning design evolution, see material authored by William D. Wilkinson, in Scheina, *WWII Cutters.*

36-FOOT MOTOR LIFEBOAT (TRS TYPE)

Number	Completed	Remarks
36416 thru 36474, 36479 thru 36554	1937 thru 30 Aug 56	Stationed throughout the U.S.; last unit removed from service in 1987.

Cost	N/A

Hull

Displacement (lbs)	20,170 operational (1968)
Length	36′10″ oa
Beam	10′9″ max
Draft	3′4″ (1968)

Machinery

Main Engines	1 diesel (General Motors, Buda, or Cummins)
BHP	between 75 and 100
Propellers	single

Performance

Max Sustained	9.0 kts, 202-mi radius (1968)

Logistics

Fuel Oil (95%)	194 gal
Complement	3 men (1968)

Design

The 36-foot MLB was designed for inshore and surf and bar rescue under the worst conditions. It is self-righting and self-bailing and can carry up to 20 survivors. The evolution of its design dates from the early part of the century.

Most boats in service after WWII were the TRS model, constructed between 1937 and 1956. All of these units were built at the Coast Guard Yard, Curtis Bay, MD.

For data concerning design evolution and earlier models, see material authored by William D. Wilkinson, in Scheina, *WWII Cutters.*

CG-36535 was the last 36-foot MLB retired from the CG. The craft is now on display at The Mariners Museum, Newport News, VA.

Harbor Craft

U.S. ARMY 65-FOOT HARBOR TUG

Number	Completed	Remarks
65024-D thru 65028-D	1944–45	First four *trans* to CG in 1945–46 and fifth in 1957; all *decomm* 1963–65.

Cost $50,000

Hull
   Displacement (tons)   46 fl (1957)
   Length   65′ oa
   Beam   14′1″ max
   Draft   4′1″ max (1957)

Machinery
   Main Engines   diesel or gasoline
   BHP   160
   Propellers   single

Performance
   Max Sustained   9.0 kts, 675-mi radius (1946)

Logistics
   Fuel Oil (95%)   1,000 gal
   Complement   5 men (1957)

Electronics   N/A

Design
   These were wooden harbor tugs constructed for the USA and used as buoy boats by the CG.

CG-65027-D, 1 Dec 60.

CG-64313 on 20 Aug 60. A 1944 photo of 64312 appears in Scheina, *WWII Cutters*.

64-FOOT HARBOR MOTOR/BOAT/TUG

Number	Completed	Remarks
64300 thru 64314	24 Nov 43 thru 10 Aug 44	64300 thru 05 built by Patchogue Yacht Basin, NY; 64306 thru 11 built by Elscot Boat, Inc., NY; 64312 thru 14 built by Nunes Brothers, Sausalito, CA, disposed of between 1963 and 1974.

Cost $43,591 each (1945)

Hull
  Displacement (tons)   65 fl (1945)
  Length   64'11" oa
  Beam   18'6" max
  Draft   6'6" max (1945)

Machinery
  Main Engines   1 Murphy diesel
  BHP   160
  Propellers   single
Performance
  Max Speed   11 kts (1945)
Logistics
  Fuel Oil (95%)   1,120 gal
  Complement   5 men (1945)
Electronics
  Radar   navigation type

Aids-to-Navigation Boats

55-FOOT AIDS-TO-NAVIGATION BOAT

Number	Completed	Remarks
55100 thru 55112	1976–77	Built by Robert E. Derecktor, Inc., Mamaroneck, NY; all active

Cost $330,000 (1980)

Hull
- Displacement (lbs)   68,620
- Length   58′ oa; 55′ bp
- Beam   17′ max
- Draft   5′ operational diesels (1980)

Machinery
- Main Engines   2 General Motors diesels
- BHP   900
- Propellers   twin

Performance
- Max Speed   22 kts (1980)
- Max Sustained   18 kts, 350-mi radius (1980)

Logistics
- Fuel Oil (95%)   1,045 gal
- Complement   4 men (1980)

Deck Gear   1,000-lb crane

Electronics
- Radar   navigation type

Design

The 55-foot ANB was designed to respond quickly to aids-to-navigation needs in moderately rough weather in all coastal and inland waters. The design was based upon a prototype 63-foot ANB that was evaluated at Coast Guard Base, Buffalo, NY.

The boat is made of steel. It has a secondary control station on the main deck aft, which has a complete set of engine and rudder controls, plus the controls for the crane and deck winches. Each boat is equipped with a workshop for servicing buoy components. The 55-footer has live-aboard features so that it can be used in areas where few shore facilities are available. The 55-footer has a 4,000-lb cargo capacity and is fitted with a 500-gallon-per-minute fire pump.

CG-55101 on 18 Nov 76.

46-FOOT BUOY BOAT STERN LOADER

Number	Completed	Remarks
46301 thru 46315	1966 & 1969	46301–06 built by Hunt Shipyard in 1966; 46307–15 built by CG Yard, Curtis Bay, MD, in 1969; all active

Cost	$154,000 (1969)
Hull	
Displacement (lbs)	59,500
Length	46'4″ oa
Beam	16'2″ max
Draft	5'1″ operating deep (1980)
Machinery	
Main Engines	1 General Motors diesel
BHP	180
Propellers	Schottel rudder-propeller
Performance	
Max Sustained	9 kts, 440-mi radius
Logistics	
Fuel Oil (95%)	440 gal
Complement	4 men (1980)
Deck Gear	4,000-lb lift capacity
Electronics	
Radar	navigational type

Design

The 46-foot BUSL has essentially the same operating capacity as the 45-foot BU and differs principally in physical layout and power train. The buoy hoist is located on the stern, and two winches provide a two-point lifting capability of 4,000 pounds.

The hull of the boat is constructed of steel, and the crews' berthing is air-conditioned and equipped with showers. The 46-footer has an 8-ton cargo capacity.

CG-46307 off New York, 16 Jun 71.

CG-45308 off New York, 16 Jun 71.

45-FOOT BUOY BOAT

Number	Completed	Remarks
45302 thru 45316	1957 thru 1962	Built by CG Yard, Curtis Bay, MD; all active

Cost	$132,625 (1959)
Hull	
Displacement (lbs)	68,800 fl (1980)
Length	45'4″ oa
Beam	15'1″ max
Draft	3' max (1980)
Machinery	
Main Engines	1 General Motors diesel (see design)
BHP	150 or 180
Propellers	single
Performance	
Max Sustained	8.5 kts, 550-mi radius (1980)
Logistics	
Fuel Oil (95%)	508 gal
Complement	4 men (1980)
Electronics	
Radar	navigational type
Deck Gear	4,000-lb lift capacity

Design

The 45-foot BU was designed to operate in sheltered and semi-protected areas of relatively shallow water. The 45-footer has a hydraulically powered A-frame for hoisting buoys and weights over the bow with a 4,000-lb capacity.

The hull of the boat is constructed of steel, and the crews' quarters contain berthing and sanitary facilities. The 45-footer has a 10-ton cargo capacity.

40-FOOT BUOY BOAT

Number	Completed	Remarks
40365-D thru 40368-D	1948–49	Built at CG Yard, Curtis Bay, MD; disposed of between 1966 & 1977

Cost   N/A

Hull
Displacement (lbs)   23,315 fl (1968)
Length   40'4"
Beam   12'6"
Draft   4'2" normal (1968)

Machinery
Main Engines   1 Gray Marine or General Motors diesel
BHP   225 or 165
Propellers   single

Performance
Max Sustained   10.4 kts, 254-mi radius (1968)

Logistics
Fuel Oil (95%)   300 gal
Complement   3 men (1968)

Design
The 40-foot buoy boat was built of wood and designed for operation in sheltered waters. It had a 5,000-lb cargo capacity.

CG-40366 on 15 Sep 49.

General-Purpose Craft

43-FOOT FAST COASTAL INTERCEPTORS

Number	Completed	Remarks
43501 thru 43505	Apr 87	Used primarily for LE; stationed at Miami Beach, Fort Lauderdale, & Islamorada

Cost   N/A

Hull
Displacement (lbs)	N/A
Length	43'6" oa
Beam	9'6" max
Draft	3'3" max

Machinery
Main Engines	2 Caterpillar diesels
BHP	750
Propellers	twin

Performance
Max Sustained	39 knots plus (1988)

Logistics
Diesel	340 gal
Complement	4 to 6 men (1988)

Electronics
Radar	navigation type

Design

The 43-foot FCI was designed and constructed by Tempest Marine for the CG. The craft is based upon a 25-degree V-bottom monohull, designed and developed to be a large offshore boat capable of operating in heavy seas at high speeds.

CG-43501 during 1987.

CG-41334.

41-FOOT UTILITY BOAT, LARGE

Number	Completed	Remarks
41300 thru 41448	Jul 73 thru Nov 78	Built at CG Yard, Curtis Bay, MD

Cost	$235,000 per unit (1979)
Hull	
Displacement (lbs)	28,500 (1980)
Length	40'8"
Beam	13'6" max
Draft	4'2" max (1980)
Machinery	
Main Engines	2 Cummins diesels
BHP	560
Propellers	twin
Performance	
Max Speed	26 kts (1980)
Cruising Speed	18 kts, 300-mi radius (1980)
Logistics	
Fuel Oil (95%)	480 gal
Complement	3 men (1980)
Electronics	
Radar	navigation type

Design

The 41-foot UTB was designed for SAR and PSS in moderate sea states. It can carry 4,000 pounds or 22 survivors. Three 42-foot boats were evaluated before this series went into production—42046 by the Coast Guard Yard; 42047 by Swiftships Inc., Morgan City, LA; and 40048 by Sewart Seacraft, Berwick, LA. The 41-foot UTB was designed to replace the 40-foot UTB.

The hull of the 41-footer is constructed of aluminum, and the superstructure is FRP. The boat is equipped with a 250-gal.-per-minute fire pump.

The 41-footer was designed by the Coast Guard, and all units were constructed at the Coast Guard Yard, Curtis Bay, MD.

40-FOOT UTILITY BOAT, LARGE

Number	Completed	Remarks
40369 thru 40699	8 Sep 50 thru 16 May 66	Most units built at CG Yard, Curtis Bay, MD; none in service

Cost	$62,000 (1951)
Hull	
Displacement (lbs)	21,500 fl (1951); 28,765 fl (1980)
Length	40' oa
Beam	11'2" max
Draft	3'2" max (1951)
Machinery	
Main Engines	2 diesels
BHP	380
Propellers	twin
Performance	
Max Speed	20.3 kts (1951)
Cruising Speed	15 kts, 190-mi radius (1951)
	18 kts, 450-mi radius (1980)
Logistics	
Fuel Oil (95%)	228 gal (1951); 370 gal (1980)
Complement	3 men (1951 & 1980)

Design

The 40-foot UTB was designed for SAR and PSS in moderate sea states. It can carry 2,000 pounds or 11 survivors. The boat was designed to replace the 38-foot picket boat and numerous non-standard craft that had come into the service before and during WWII.

The 40-footer was constructed of a variety of materials. The first 20 units were built of wood, and most subsequent ones had steel hulls and aluminum superstructures and decks. Three units were constructed of fiberglass and one of plywood for testing and comparison purposes. Due to the long production run, numerous variations existed.

The 40-footer was designed by the Coast Guard.

CG-40548 on 25 Apr 55 running trials.

CG-30545 ploughs through rough water in Lake Ponchartrain.

30-FOOT UTILITY BOAT, MEDIUM

Number	Completed	Remarks
CG-30490 etc.	1962	Majority of units were constructed in southern states and operated in sheltered waters of southern states

Cost	$46,000 (1968)
Hull	
Displacement (lbs)	13,500 (1980)
Length	30'
Beam	10'7" max
Draft	3' max (1980)
Machinery	
Main Engines	1 Cummins diesel
BHP	270 or 280
Propellers	single
Performance	
Max Sustained	25 kts, 175-mi radius
Logistics	
Fuel Oil (95%)	112 gal
Complement	3 men (1980)

Design

The 30-foot UTM was designed to provide a low-cost alternative to the 40-foot UTB for many missions. The boat is constructed of fiberglass reinforced plastic. The 30-footer can carry 15 survivors or 2,700 lbs of cargo. CG-30489 was modified and participated in the Miami to Nassau powerboat race during 1962; it finished 5th out of 59 starters. CG-30564 was fitted with hydrofoils for test purposes. A prime builder has been the Pearson Corporation, Bristol, RI.

32-FOOT PORTS AND WATERWAYS BOAT

Number	Completed	Remarks
32301 thru 32350	1976	Stationed throughout the U.S.

Cost	$102,000 (1978)
Hull	
Displacement (lbs)	19,000 fl (1990)
Length	33'4" oa
Beam	11'9" max
Draft	
Machinery	
Main Engines	2 Caterpillar diesels
BHP	406
Propellers	twin
Performance	
Max	20.4 kts (1980)
Max Sustained	16.5 kts, 190-mi radius (1980)
Logistics	
Fuel Oil (95%)	200 gal

Design

The Port and Waterways Act of 1972 assigned the Coast Guard the responsibility for safety in these waters. The 32-footer was designed to aid in the carrying out of the task. The boat is constructed of fiberglass. It is equipped with fire monitors and can carry 2,000 lbs of cargo.

CG-32305 tests its fire monitors in New York harbor.

31-FOOT PORT SECURITY BOAT

Number	Completed	Remarks
31001 thru 31028	series began 14 Mar 64	Stationed throughout the U.S.

Cost	$55,051 (1969)
Hull	
Displacement (lbs)	16,285
Length	30'5" oa
Beam	11'6" max
Draft	3'11" max (1980)
Machinery	
Main Engines	1 General Motors diesel
BHP	197
Propellers	twin
Performance	
Max	14 kts (1980)
Max Sustained	12.5 kts, 165-mi radius (1980)
Logistics	
Fuel Oil (95%)	110 gal
Complement	3 men (1980)

Design

The 31-foot PSB was designed to train Coast Guard personnel in boat-handling techniques. The boat is constructed of fiberglass and is equipped with a 250-gal.-per-minute fire pump. CG-31001 thru 31004 were built by Bertram Boat Works, Miami, FL. CG-31005 thru 31019 were constructed at the CG Yard, Curtis Bay, MD.

CG-31009 in Nov 69.

A 25-foot motor cargo boat on 27 Oct 65.

25-FOOT MOTOR CARGO BOAT

Number	Completed	Remarks
25300 thru 253298	1949–73, 1979	Assigned to large cutters

Cost	$24,929 (1968)
Hull	
Displacement (lbs)	8,594 (1968)
Length	25'8" oa
Beam	7'11" max (1980)
Draft	2'5" max (1980)
Machinery	
Main Engines	1 Detroit diesel
Propellers	single
Performance	
Max Sustained	12 kts, 85-mi radius (1980)
Logistics	
Fuel Oil (95%)	40 gal
Complement	3 men (1980)

Design

The 25-foot Motor Cargo Boat is designed as a ship's boat for large cutters. It is constructed of fiberglass and can carry 16 persons or 2,000 lbs of cargo.

30-FOOT UTILITY BOAT

Number	Completed	Remarks
30376 thru 30598	1954 thru 1983	Most units built at CG Yard, Curtis Bay, MD

Cost	$36,391 (steel, 1957)
	$45,950 (plastic, 1967)

Hull
Displacement (lbs)	10,464 fl (steel, 1957)
	13,100 fl (plastic, 1967)
Length	30′ oa
Beam	8′9″ max
Draft	2′9″ max (steel, 1957)
	3′6″ max (plastic, 1967)

Machinery
Main Engines	1 diesel
Propellers	single

Performance
Cruising	22 mph, 220-mi radius (steel, 1957); 28 mph, 126-mi radius (plastic, 1967)

Logistics
Complement	3 men (1957 & 1967)

Design

This design underwent numerous changes during its 30-year evolution. The boat was designed for PSS and SAR in sheltered waters. Mark I was constructed of steel, Mark II of plywood, and Mark III of plastic. The 30-footers have an 18-person capacity.

CG-30412 on 14 Jan 76.

SMALL CRAFT BUILT TO COAST GUARD SPECIFICATIONS DISPOSED OF SHORTLY AFTER WORLD WAR II*

Number	Type	In Service
63300–63301	Harbor/Motorboat Tug	1936–62
63000–63078	Air-Sea Rescue Boat	1944–48
60012F–60019F	Fire Barge	1943–48
52302D–52310D	Buoy Boat	1944–72
50300F–50313F	Fire Barge	1942–48
50017–50081	Harbor Patrol Boat	1943–48
40335F–40364F	Fireboat	1944–48
40301 D Series	Buoy Boat	1942–79
40300	Motor Lifeboat	1940–?
38301–38836	Cabin Picket Boat	1931–64
36300 T series	Motor Lifeboat	1929–?
36300 TR series	Motor Lifeboat	1931–?
36024F–36029F	Fireboat	1943–47
30137F–30139F	Fireboat	1942–49
30032F–30131F	Fireboat	1942–49

*See Scheina, *WWII Cutters,* for details.

Coast Guard Districts

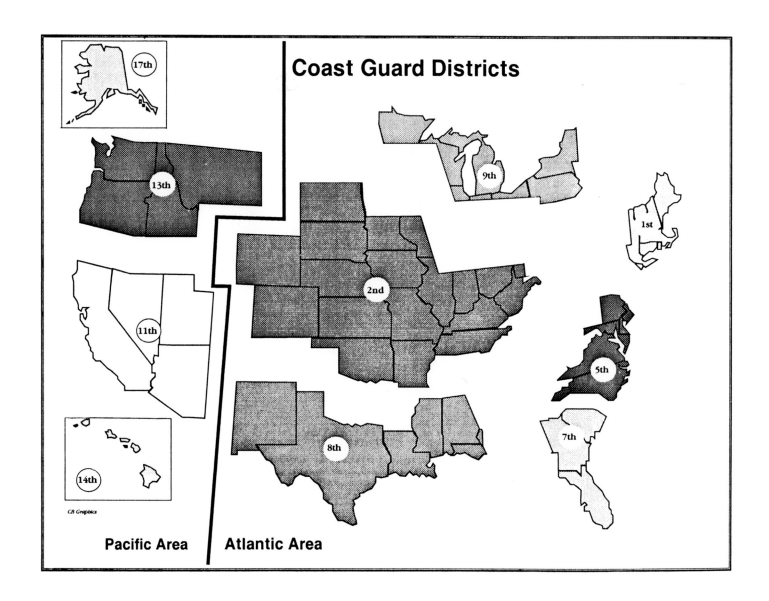

Coast Guard Districts

Pacific Area   Atlantic Area

Index

The number following each Coast Guard cutter is its hull number, thus allowing the user to distinguish among cutters of the same name. Lightships, with only two exceptions, did not have names; they were numbered. However, most individuals refer to the lightships not by their hull numbers, but instead, by the names of their stations. Within the index these station names are shown in quotation marks and not italics as are the names of all other ships and craft. Also, the addenda has been indexed; these entries are shown with an A.

Ships listed by length are indexed under the initial letter of their footage.

Addenda

Attu (W 1317)
16 Nov 89 recovered 200 pounds of cocaine floating in three ice chests off Puerto Rico.

Bear (W 901)
Mid-Sep 89 served as command-and-control platform for St. Croix relief operations following destruction of property and breakdown of civil order due to hurricane Hugo; 24 Nov 89 seized FV *Janeth* 150 mi S of Puerto Rico carrying 787 pounds of cocaine.

Cape Hatteras (W 95305)
22 Oct 89 helped seize former cruise ship *Prince George* because of a maritime lien against the vessel.

Chena (W 75407)
Fall 89–1990 stationed at Natchez, MS, and used for A/N.

Clover (W 292)
Oct 89 carried relief supplies to Santa Cruz, CA, following earthquake.

Cushing (W 1321)
2 Oct 89 seized Panamanian MV *Zedom Sea* approx. 450 mi S of Galveston, TX, carrying 5.5t of cocaine—the largest cocaine bust to that date.

Kanawha (W 75407)
Fall 89–1990 stationed at Pine Bluff, AR, and used for A/N.

Mallow (W 396)
6 Nov 89 helped bring flooding under control and towed ketch *Wizard* to Keehi, HI.

Manitou (W 1302)
21 Sep 89 damaged when a U.S. Navy tug snapped her mooring lines during hurricane Hugo and drifted down onto the cutter.

Mesquite (W 305)
5 Dec 89 grounded, badly holed, and abandoned three quarters of a mile off Keweenaw Point, Lake Superior, while removing A/N for the winter—of 53 on board, 4 suffered minor injuries.

Midgett (W 726)
18 Sep 89 seized South Korean FV *Gae Heog Ho* for illegal fishing in U.S. waters.

Morganthau (W 722)
1989 assisted with clean-up ops following oil spill caused by *Exxon Valdez* following its grounding on 24 Mar 89.

Nantucket (W 1316)
20 Sep 89 evacuated civilians from St. Croix during looting that occurred after the island was devastated by hurricane Hugo.

Naushon (W 1311)
5 Dec 89 grounded off SE Alaska causing moderate damage.

Nunivak (W 1306)
20 Sep 89 evacuated civilians from St. Croix during looting that occurred after the island was devastated by hurricane Hugo.

Point Harris (W 82376)
Late 1989–1990 stationed at Nawiliwili, HI, and used for LE and SAR; 6 Nov 89 helped bring flooding under control and towed ketch *Wizard* to Keehi, HI.

Point Spencer (W 82349)
9 Nov 89 seized FV *Margie T* in the Gulf of Mexico for taking undersized fish.

Polar Sea (W 11)
Winter 1988–89 deployed to Antarctic.

Polar Star (W 10)
Winter 1989–90 transited Northwest Passage from Greenland to Alaskan Arctic for second circumnavigation of North American continent within a year.

Sitkinak (W 1329)
Jul 89 helped seize Panamanian MV *Barlovento* in Gulf of Mexico carrying almost 2t of cocaine.

Shearwater (W 3)
Jul 89 helped seize Panamanian MV *Barlovento* in Gulf of Mexico carrying almost 2t of cocaine.

Storis (W 38)
14 Sep 89 seized South Korean FV *Kyang Yang Ho* for illegally fishing in U.S. waters.

Tahoma (W 908)
7 Nov 89 seized sailboat *Tsunami* 150 mi E of Ocean City, MD, carrying 1t of marijuana.

Vashon (W 1308)
20 Sep 89 evacuated civilians from St. Croix during looting that occurred after the island was devastated by hurricane Hugo.

In 1984 the Coast Guard evaluated and later leased the sea-based Aerostat as a means to improve surveillance throughout the Caribbean. The system consists of a ship (Mobile Aerostat Platform) fitted with a command-and-control center and a mooring for a 31-meter helium-filled balloon (Aerostat) fitted with a radar antenna.

By 1990 the Coast Guard was operating five systems throughout the Caribbean. Typically a ship remains on patrol for 27 days out of 30.

SEA-BASED AEROSTAT

Name	Number	Home Port	Disposition
Atlantic Sentry	SBA 1	Key West, FL	Apr 87—Active
Caribbean Sentry	SBA 2	Key West, FL	20 Dec 88—Active
Gulf Sentry	SBA 3	Miami, FL	30 Dec 88—Active
Pacific Sentry	SBA 4	Miami, FL	6 Mar 89—Active
Windward Sentry	SBA 5	Key West, FL	Nov 89—Active

Cost	N/A
Hull	
Displacement (lbs)	N/A
Length	192'
Beam	40' (SBA 1 and 5); 44' (SBA 2 thru 4)
Draft	15'
Machinery	
Main Engines	2 General Motors diesels
BHP	3,900
Propellers	twin
Performance	
Max. sustained	12.0 kts. (1989)
Cruising	10.0 kts., 7,000-mi radius (1989)
Logistics	
Fuel Oil (95%)	200,000 gals.
Complement	9 military, 10 civilians
Aerostat	
volume	56,000 cu ft
length	109'
diameter	37'

Sea-based Aerostat *Caribbean* Sentry.

The Naval Institute Press is the book-publishing arm of the U.S. Naval Institute, a private, nonprofit professional society for members of the sea services and civilians who share an interest in naval and maritime affairs. Established in 1873 at the U.S. Naval Academy in Annapolis, Maryland, where its offices remain today, the Naval Institute has more than 100,000 members worldwide.

Members of the Naval Institute receive the influential monthly naval magazine *Proceedings* and substantial discounts on fine nautical prints, ship and aircraft photos, and subscriptions to the Institute's recently inaugurated quarterly, *Naval History.* They also have access to the transcripts of the Institute's Oral History Program and may attend any of the Institute-sponsored seminars regularly offered around the country.

The book-publishing program, begun in 1898 with basic guides to naval practices, has broadened its scope in recent years to include books of more general interest. Now the Naval Institute Press publishes more than forty new titles each year, ranging from how-to books on boating and navigation to battle histories, biographies, ship guides, and novels. Institute members receive discounts on the Press's more than 300 books.

For a free catalog describing books currently available and for further information about U.S. Naval Institute membership, please write to:

Membership Department
U.S. Naval Institute
Annapolis, Maryland 21402

or call, toll-free, 800-233-USNI.

U.S. COAST GUARD CUTTERS AND CRAFT, 1946–1990

Designed by CR MacLellan

Composed by BG Composition
in Baskerville and Melior

Printed by Arcata Graphics, Inc./Halliday on
60-lb. Glatco Matte Smooth white
with matching white endsheets
and bound in Holliston Roxite B

Approximate locations of Ocean Stations
in the Atlantic Ocean